Geschichte und Gesellschaft

Zeitschrift für Historische Sozialwissenschaft

Sonderheft / Special Issue 26:
Moral Economies

Moral Economies

Herausgegeben von / Edited by

Ute Frevert

Vandenhoeck & Ruprecht

Bibliografische Information der Deutschen Nationalbibliothek:
Die Deutsche Nationalbibliothek verzeichnet diese Publikation in der
Deutschen Nationalbibliografie; detaillierte bibliografische Daten sind
im Internet über http://dnb.de abrufbar.

Umschlagabbildung: SchwabScantechnik, Göttingen

Satz: textformart, Göttingen | www.text-form-art.de
Druck und Bindung: ⊕ Hubert & Co. BuchPartner, Göttingen
Printed in the EU

Vandenhoeck & Ruprecht Verlage | www.vandenhoeck-ruprecht-verlage.com

ISSN 0944-2014
ISBN 978-3-525-36426-0

Table of Contents

Ute Frevert

Introduction

"This economy kills": these were the words of Pope Francis in his 2013 apostolic letter, which has been widely perceived as a general policy statement. The Pontifex Maximus found numerous supporters, among them the influential German Cardinal Reinhard Marx. In 2014 Marx passionately pleaded for a reconciliation of "markets and morals."[1] Others, especially conservatives and financial columnists, objected and criticized the papal letter as outright and offensively Marxist or even Leninist.[2]

Bernie Sanders, U. S. senator and president hopeful, was not among the critics. Instead, he boldly sided with Francis when he spoke at the Pontifical Academy of Social Sciences in 2016. Using barely veiled religious language he bemoaned that "our very soul as a nation has suffered" as the market economy treated workers as "disposable cogs of the financial system" and allowed "vast inequalities of power and wealth." He concluded his speech with an appeal to "bring the economy back under the dictates of morality and the common good."[3]

The notion of a "moral economy" has thus forcefully entered public discourse and been adopted by academics in many disciplines. Since the publication of Edward P. Thompson's seminal article on the "Moral Economy of the English Crowd" in 1971 many experts, above all in the fields of social anthropology and sociology, have used the concept for their own purposes. Some stayed close to its original meaning while others expanded the notion so as to encompass phenomena that were not directly related to economic activities and behavior.[4]

---

1 Reinhard Kardinal Marx, Ordnungspolitik als Versöhnung von Markt und Moral. Potenziale und Grenzen der Freiburger Idee aus der Sicht der katholischen Soziallehre, 17.1.2014, https://www.erzbistum-muenchen.de/cms-media/media-26636720.pdf.

2 Andrea Tornielli and Giacomo Galeazzi, This Economy Kills. Pope Francis on Capitalism and Social Justice, Collegeville, MN 2015, pp. vii f.

3 Bernie Sanders, The Urgency of a Moral Economy. Reflections on the 25th Anniversary of Centesimus Annus, https://berniesanders.com/urgency-moral-economy-reflections-anniversary-centesimus-annus.

4 It would fill many pages to cite all academic books and articles that have used the notion of moral economy since the 1970s. See, as a selection, James C. Scott, The Moral Economy of the Peasant. Rebellion and Subsistence in Southeast Asia, New Haven 1976; Evelyn S. Ruppert, The Moral Economy of Cities. Shaping Good Citizens, Toronto 2006; Stefan Svallfors, The Moral Economy of Class. Class and Attitudes in Comparative Perspective, Stanford 2006; Chris Hann, Moral(ity and) Economy. Work, Workfare, and Fairness in Provincial Hungary, in: European Journal of Sociology 59. 2018, pp. 225–254. Several journals have published special issues on moral economy: Journal of Global Ethics 11. 2015, no. 2; Anthropological Theory 16. 2016, no. 4. For a decidedly non-economic view on moral economy see Lorraine Daston,

For Thompson, moral economies belonged to a historical period that had not yet been tainted by capitalism. They came to the fore as soon as the new capitalist modes of production and trade clashed with traditional, paternalist modes of provision and fueled market riots during the eighteenth century. Morality, as the Marxist historian saw it, no longer played a role once capitalism became the dominant economic system.[5]

Without quoting him, Thompson echoed Karl Polanyi. In his 1944 book on "The Great Transformation," the left-leaning Austrian emigrant had criticized *laisser faire* capitalism for destroying formerly integrated societies, in which the exchange of goods and services was embedded in a larger social and moral framework. Those societies followed the principles of reciprocity, redistribution, and household production and used manufacture and trade to allow them to flourish. Capitalism, by contrast, as it developed from the Industrial Revolution onwards, broke the ties between social and economic relations, and established the self-regulating market as its central institution.[6]

What Thompson later called the "demoralizing of the theory of trade and consumption" found its equivalent in what Polanyi observed as the "demoralization of the people." Workers and entrepreneurs, poor and rich, allegedly lost their sense of honor and decency. While the poor were driven to the "veritable abyss of human degradation," the better-off middle classes removed "compassion [...] from the hearts, and a stoic determination to renounce human solidarity in the name of the greatest happiness of the greatest number gained the dignity of a secular religion."[7]

Both authors, Polanyi even more than Thompson, spoke in a highly moralizing tone. To them criticizing the new capitalist economy was tantamount to accusing it of a blatant lack of morality. Morality was translated into values like compassion, solidarity, decency, and an emotional commitment to the common or public good. Such values, in their view, had been prevailing in pre-capitalist social and economic systems. In Polanyi's opinion they would have to be reintroduced if capitalism and "industrial civilization" were to survive.[8]

The Moral Economy of Science, in: Osiris 10. 1995, pp. 2–24; Didier Fassin, Les économies morales revisitées, in: Annales HSS 64. 2009, pp. 1237–1266; id., Humanitarian Reason. A Moral History of the Present, Berkeley 2012, pp. 7 f. See also the 2018 Belknap Global Conversation at Princeton University, organized by Jeremy Adelman and Samuel Moyn, on the "idea of the moral economy" from the 18th century to the present, https://humanities.princeton.edu/2018/01/25/spring-2018-belknap-global-conversation-announced/.

5 Edward Palmer Thompson, The Moral Economy of the English Crowd in the Eighteenth Century, in: Past & Present 1971, no. 50, pp. 76–136, esp. p. 89.

6 Karl Polanyi, The Great Transformation. The Political and Economic Origins of Our Time [1944], 2nd ed., Boston 2001, esp. Part 2, I: "Satanic Mill," pp. 35–135.

7 Ibid., p. 41 and p. 107.

8 Karl Polanyi, Our Obsolete Market Mentality. Civilization Must Find a New Thought Pattern, in: Commentary 3. 1947, pp. 109–117, here p. 117. Polanyi sought to restore "the fullness of life to the person" instead of subjecting them to the "profit motive" only (pp. 115 f.).

Considered against this background, the notion of a moral economy carries a strong political subtext. However it can also be employed as a heuristic lamp post that sheds light on the complicated relationship between morality and capitalist market economies. This relationship is neither one-dimensional nor historically stable. Instead, we encounter a plurality of values shaping various economic systems at different times.

As recent debates have clarified, no economic system per se is value-free. Similarly, economics has been described as "a moral science" by some of its most important representatives.[9] As Kenneth Boulding pointed out fifty years ago, since science does not only investigate the world, but also "creates the world which it is investigating," moral propositions and value judgments are firmly entrenched in economic theory and practice.[10] They structure, give meaning and approval to or criticize economic behavior, and they can encourage collective action. Sometimes, moral issues are veiled and hidden and have to be unearthed by historical analysis. In other cases, they are openly pronounced and advertised, which makes the historian's work easier but not superfluous. What can be observed as a moralizing tendency still has to be examined in a broader context of countervailing currents and enabling forces.

Contexts and conflicts all figure prominently in the articles collected in this volume, which originated from a 2017 workshop at the Max Planck Institute for Human Development in Berlin. The workshop brought together senior and junior historians whose research focuses on the conjunction of economic and moral issues.[11] Most of them work on modern societies, sharing the assumption that these societies have seen not one but many moral economies. Moral arguments and morally induced behavior have by no means left the economic sphere untouched since the eighteenth century. Instead, they have played a crucial role in shaping the way in which citizens, as producers and consumers, as subjects and objects of charity, as debtors and creditors, as self-sufficient settlers and supporters of the DIY movement, have connected moral reasoning and economic concerns.

Setting the stage, the first article investigates the concept of moral economy as it has been defined and discussed across history. It traces its political usage and links it to the widespread critique of capitalism, which is as old as capitalism itself. Yet not only proponents but also defenders of the new mode of production

9 Kenneth E. Boulding, Economics as a Moral Science, in: The American Economic Review 59. 1969, pp. 1–12; Anthony B. Atkinson, Economics as a Moral Science, in: Economica 76. 2009, pp. 791–804.

10 Boulding, Economics, p. 3.

11 The juniors were mostly Ph.D. students enrolled in the graduate program at the International Max Planck Research School on "Moral Economies of Modern Societies." See https://www.mpib-berlin.mpg.de/en/research/research-schools/imprs-moral-economies. I thank Alexandra Esche, Jürgen Finger, Paul Franke, Natalie Lang, Sandra Maß, Brit Schlünz and Korinna Schönhärl—who, unfortunately, could not contribute to this volume—for their stimulating comments and suggestions.

used moral terms when they referred to the common good, to civilizational prog-ress, and individual wellbeing. Moral values also pervaded social organizations that sought to deal with the (unwanted) consequences of industrial capitalism and a free market economy. The contemporary quest to re-moralize the econ-omy thus fails to grasp the extent to which it has been firmly embedded in and surrounded by a web of morally responsible institutions and discourses since its very beginning.

Looking back at the early modern world, Laurence Fontaine distinguishes two economies that followed vastly different moral regimes: the aristocratic one, based on gift and charity, as opposed to the market economy, based on credit. While charity built on personal relationships and testified to aristocratic generosity and *bon plaisir*, credit was increasingly granted on the basis of economic performance and commitment to hard work. Both principles and practices engaged strong moral arguments as a means of self-justification. Drawing on rich source material from the eighteenth century, Fontaine shows how aristocratic practices like giving alms to beggars were increasingly put under pressure, but also were defended by rejecting bad habits of avarice attributed to capitalist merchants. In France, that crisis was resolved politically when the Revolution helped to install an economic system that heavily relied on the mechanisms of the capitalist market and its moral promise to promote liberty, equality, and universal happiness.

Moral conflicts over social and economic practices also occupy center stage in Mischa Suter's contribution. Analyzing politics of debt enforcement and debates on usury in Switzerland and Germany during the nineteenth and early twentieth centuries, he illustrates the way in which such conflicts were not simply coated in a moral language as a convenient communicative code, but were also informed by widely different views on what constituted "good" or "bad" behavior in eco-nomic matters and in society at large. Such views underwrote political campaigns against Jews, who were targeted as bearing responsibility for and benefitting from the allegedly immoral principles of industrial and financial capitalism.

Those principles were equally scrutinized—and rejected—by the German set-tlement movement that emerged in the 1890s and consisted of a colorful mix of land reformers, vegetarians, Zionists, and *voelkisch* actors. Anna Danilina's article sheds light on the many ways in which economic behavior was moralized in those "inner colonies," from preaching vegetarianism to doing gymnastics in order to prepare the body for useful and morally approvable work. Most settlements held on to thoroughly racialized notions of economic activity that they sought to implement in their own households and communities.

Households, as the primordial site of economic relations that were not restricted to narrowly conceived types of exchange and interaction, also featured in discourses on urban planning and the development of urban infrastructure. Investigating the case of New York City during the late nineteenth and early twen-tieth centuries, Björn Blaß finds that moral, economic, and political arguments for waste disposal and urban sanitation were closely linked. Middle-class women who were engaged in the municipal housekeeping movement deliberately drew on their own experience of household cleanliness when they set out to reform "the wasteful, pernicious and disgusting practice of dumping city refuse." Highly moralized concepts of purity—as opposed to disgust—were used to buttress women's claim to improve society by investing in private and public hygiene. As much as demands for municipal housekeeping legitimized women's participation in public administration and decision making, they also conveyed the image of the city as an *oikos*, in which moral, economic, and political processes were inextricably intertwined.

Similar linkages can be detected in public discourses on disabled veterans during and after the Great War. Taking the example of Cisleithanian Austria, Thomas Rohringer examines the role of work in reintegrating former soldiers into civilian life. He traces the conflicting visions of how reintegration should take place and carves out the moral dimensions attached to concepts of economic citizenship. He also discusses what was considered the moral obligation of the state to "pay back" the debt it owed those who served their country on the battlefields and returned visibly or invisibly impaired. The question as to which forms such compensation should take was thoroughly debated, with charity being relegated to private actors.

Reinhild Kreis's contribution returns to the moral economy of private households. In post-1945 West Germany, they were not only the site of crucial economic activities, but also acted as a moralizing force with regard to those activities. The decision to either buy ready-made goods and services or to produce them carried heavy moral baggage. As the analysis of the Do-It-Yourself movement shows, this was not only a question of economic scarcity or cost efficiency. Instead, DIY was increasingly marketed as a particular way of life that was deemed to be morally superior to the culture of buying and wasting resources. Adopted by left-wing counterculture movements of the 1970s and 1980s, it has now been adopted by extreme right-wingers who show their moral repugnance towards capitalist consumer society by producing most provisions themselves.

Till Großmann introduces East German economy and society around 1960 as two spheres of intense moral controversy. Linking the workplace with the family, campaigns on the formation of the "socialist man" (and, sometimes, woman) promulgated values and moral emotions that were thought of as instrumental in creating the GDR model of a socialist society based on the shared ownership of the means of production. How these campaigns resonated in people's experiences and attitudes, how they helped to transform gender roles and re-approached handed-down middle-class values is discussed through an analysis of letters that men and women wrote to the well-known physician and author Rudolf Neubert.

Concluding an intense intellectual exchange, the notion of moral economies has been found epistemologically useful and challenging for historical research. First, the notion itself has a history that can be traced back to the early modern period. It reflects both the importance of what was then known as the "moral sense" and the conflicting views on economic activities that went beyond the allegedly *doux commerce* and its civilizing impact. It therefore invites historians to analyze the changing meanings of "the moral" and "the economic" as well as their various connections and hybridity. However change and variety should not be restricted to their temporal dimension. Moral economies have been identified in manifold regions of the world, from Southeast Asian peasant societies to contemporary Turkey, China and Africa.[12]

Second, all existing research points towards the pivotal role of conflict in bringing moral arguments to the fore. On the one hand, conflicts over economic matters like wages or prices are often associated with moral claims. On the other hand, such claims are not only voiced by one particular group, as E. P. Thompson implied. Instead, moral justifications are provided by all the stakeholders. While one might feel tempted to dismiss these justifications as mere alibis or window dressing, they actually help to confirm and sustain morality as a general communicative code. They might relate to different moral orders, but they can also express diverging interpretations of the same moral reference system.

Third, studying moral economies through conflicts enables historians to examine how specific moral convictions and emotions are formed and shaped by education and experience. Education here refers to broader processes of formation that include school curricula as well as public media. Experience is meant to encompass social involvement in organizations and institutions that themselves work with and towards a certain moral repertoire. As social scientists and psychologists remind us, people are not born moral. They rather acquire moral emotions and perceptions during the course of their lives, in historically distinct ways that are dependent on factors like social class, gender, race, and religion.

Finally, engagement with moral economies as a topic of historical research allows historians to connect with contemporary conflicts and debates. This presents both opportunities and risks. The opportunities lay in the fact that historians can inform, maybe even enlighten their society on the presumed novelty and specificity of current matters viewed against the longer trajectories of moral-economic dispute and struggle. By considering the present in a historical perspective they can provide analytical clarity and distance. The risk involved is that historians might get enmeshed in their own experience as contemporaries, and fail to neatly distinguish between moral economies as prescriptive or analytical. Early on, colleagues have fallen into this trap. Criticism of their work might help future colleagues to avoid it.

12 Johanna Siméant, Three Bodies of Moral Economy. The Diffusion of a Concept, in: Journal of Global Ethics 11. 2015, pp. 163–175; Jean-Pierre Olivier de Sardan, A Moral Economy of Corruption in Africa?, in: Journal of Modern African Studies 37. 1999, pp. 25–52.

Ute Frevert

Moral Economies, Present and Past

Social Practices and Intellectual Controversies

Abstract: This article investigates the concept of moral economy, tracing its political usage in the widespread critique of capitalism across history. Yet not only proponents but also defenders of the new mode of production used moral terms when they referred to the common good, to civilizational progress, and individual wellbeing. Moral values also pervaded social organizations that sought to deal with the (unwanted) consequences of industrial capitalism and a free market economy. The contemporary quest to re-moralize the economy thus fails to grasp the extent to which, since its very beginning, it has been firmly embedded in and surrounded by a web of morally responsible institutions.

Current political discourse seems to be obsessed with morals. In political negotiation and decision-making processes as well as in public opinion, questions of morality loom large. Europe's recent refugee problem has been widely discussed in moralizing terms, and so have political approaches to the Greek sovereign debt crisis starting in 2010. Since 2013, the "Moral Monday" movement against social injustice has been spreading through the United States.[1] Protest groups of different political leanings increasingly engage moral language to express their concerns in "moral economy" frameworks.[2] During and after his presidential bid, U. S. Senator Bernie Sanders continuously called for a "moral economy" instead of a system that produces "stark inequality and injustice." He defined the new economy as "one that says, 'In the wealthiest country in the history of the world, all our people should be able to live with dignity and security.'"[3]

---

1 Cathy Lynn Grossmann, "Moral Monday" Expands to a Week of Social Justice Action across U.S., in: The Washington Post, 19.8.2014.

2 Susana Narotzky, Between Inequality and Injustice. Dignity as a Motive for Mobilization during the Crisis, in: History and Anthropology 27. 2016, pp. 74–92, using Spanish cases. How economic and moral struggles are intertwined and fuel right-wing populism has been marvelously studied by Arlie Russell Hochschild, Strangers in Their Own Land. Anger and Mourning on the American Right, New York 2016.

3 Anon., Bernie Sanders Calls for a "Moral Economy" at the Vatican, 15.4.2016, https://www.bbc.com/news/world-us-canada-36057229; Bryan Anderson, Bernie Sanders Pushes for a "Moral Economy" during the Duke University Visit, 19.4.2018, https://www.newsobserver.com/news/politics-government/article209386109.html.

Following the financial crisis of 2007–08, the behavior of major banks, in particular, has been under close scrutiny, with sharp criticism of excessive bonuses even for those who performed poorly. In her former position as France's finance minister, Christine Lagarde described the explosion in executive pay as "scandalous," and Jean-Claude Juncker, as President of the European Commission's Eurogroup of finance ministers, spoke of a "social scourge."[4] Using strong and morally charged language, politicians sought to prompt businesses to establish and maintain 'good' standards of corporate governance. At the same time it was feared that inappropriate levels of income would destroy public trust, as much as they strengthened the recipients' tendency to engage in risky and often unethical behavior.[5] Public trust also suffered when CEOs earned huge sums after making thousands of employees redundant. According to Peter Montagnon, director of investment affairs at the Association of British Insurers, this was "bad for the reputation of capitalism."[6]

Since Montagnon also served as Associate Director at the Institute of Business Ethics, he was well versed in the role of ethics in the public view and performance of capitalism. The ethical dimensions of doing business have been increasingly debated since the 1970s, within major corporations and the academia. The more economists like Milton Friedman, widely regarded as the "giant" in libertarian economics, preached the gospel of unfettered economic activity and free-market capitalism, the more entrepreneurs and CEOs seemed to be concerned with ethic codes and social responsibility. At first sight, this blatantly contradicted Friedman's advice. Asked if "*corporate executives*, provided they stay within the law, have responsibilities in their business activities other than to make as much money for their stockholders as possible," his answer was "no, they do not."[7] In his opinion, businesses were not supposed to have any social or moral responsibilities at all.

As long as they acted in their own self-interest however, Friedman did not "summon much indignation."[8] In fact, it turned out that businesses could indeed make good money by complying with social and moral expectations. Demonstrating their concern for fair production and trade, fighting pollution, eliminating discrimination, and subscribing to non-exploitative business ethics

4 Anon., Pay Attention, in: The Economist, 14.6.2008, pp. 81 f., here p. 81.
5 Nassim Nicholas Taleb, How Bank Bonuses Let Us All Down, in: The Financial Times, 25.2.2009, p. 13; Thomas Donaldson, Three Ethical Roots of the Economic Crisis, in: Journal of Business Ethics 106. 2012, pp. 5–8; Lynne M. Andersson and Thomas S. Bateman, Cynicism in the Workplace. Some Causes and Effects, in: Journal of Organizational Behavior 18. 1997, pp. 449–469; Horacio Ortiz, "Dans ses tendances, l'industrie financière ne se trompe pas, mais elle exagère toujours." Enjeux moraux dans les pratiques professionnelles de la finance, in: Didier Fassin and Jean-Sébastien Eideliman (eds.), Économies morales contemporaines, Paris 2012, pp. 53–72.
6 Anon., Pay Attention, p. 81.
7 Milton Friedman Responds, in: Business and Society Review 1. 1972, pp. 5–16, here p. 6.
8 Milton Friedman, The Social Responsibility of Business Is to Increase Its Profits, in: The New York Times Magazine, 13.9.1970, reprinted in Walther C. Zimmerli et al. (eds.), Corporate Ethics and Corporate Governance, Berlin 2007, pp. 173–178.

ultimately proved to be in a corporation's best interest. In contrast to Friedman's predictions—that such concerns and practices would harm the "foundation of a free society" and lead to "pure and unadulterated socialism"—they helped to stabilize capitalist modes of making profit and securing economic growth. They staged, one might say, capitalism as a moral economy and thus invested in its good reputation.

For academics other than economists, there is much to be learnt from such moral "window-dressing," as Friedman disdainfully called it. Over the last few years, sociologists, in particular, have become keenly interested in the moral order capitalism rests upon, as well as in the phenomenon of moralized markets.[9] They have pointed to the social and cultural embeddedness of markets that allows for strong moral claims to be made on both producer and consumer behavior.[10] They have studied the moral valuation of marketable as against non-marketable goods, like blood, organ or egg and sperm donations.[11] They have paid attention to concepts of fairness and justice and their moral underpinnings.[12] And they have analyzed the social organization of illegal markets and the extent to which moral issues defined what was deemed legal or illegal.[13]

Historians, by contrast, have rarely raised their voices in the debate.[14] This comes as a surprise for three reasons: first, the notion of moral economy is itself a historical one, forged during the eighteenth century. Second, it was reintroduced into historiography in the 1970s by Edward P. Thompson's promisingly attractive

---

9 Marion Fourcade, The Fly and the Cookie. Alignment and Unhingement in 21st-Century Capitalism, in: Socio-Economic Review 15. 2017, pp. 661–678; ead. and Kieran Healy, Moral Views of Market Society, in: Annual Review of Sociology 33. 2007, pp. 285–311; Nico Stehr et al. (eds.), The Moralization of Markets, New Brunswick 2006. As to earlier examples of moralized markets, see Viviana A. Rotman Zelizer, Morals and Markets. The Development of Life Insurance in the United States, New York 1979; ead., Pricing the Priceless Child. The Changing Social Value of Children, Princeton 1985.

10 Jens Beckert, Beyond the Market. The Social Foundations of Economic Efficiency, Princeton 2002; id., The Moral Embeddedness of Markets, in: Betsy Jane Clary et al. (eds.), Ethics and the Market. Insights from Social Economics, London 2006, pp. 11–25; id., The Ambivalent Role of Morality on Markets, in: Stehr, Moralization, pp. 109–128.

11 Kieran Healy, Last Best Gifts. Altruism and the Market for Human Blood and Organs, Chicago 2006; Rene Almeling, Sex Cells. The Medical Market for Eggs and Sperm, Berkeley 2011; Debra Satz, Why Some Things Should Not Be for Sale. The Moral Limits of Markets, New York 2010.

12 See, from the viewpoint of political philosophy, Michael J. Sandel, Justice. What's the Right Thing to Do?, London 2009; id., What Money Can't Buy. The Moral Limits of Markets, London 2013; id., Market Reasoning as Moral Reasoning. Why Economists Should Re-Engage with Political Philosophy, in: Journal of Economic Perspectives 27. 2013, no. 4, pp. 121–140.

13 Jens Beckert and Matías Dewey (eds.), The Architecture of Illegal Markets. Towards an Economic Sociology of Illegality in the Economy, Oxford 2017; Philippe Steiner and Marie Trespeuch (eds.), Marchés contestés. Quand le marché rencontre la morale, Toulouse 2014.

14 For a recent proposal to establish what they misleadingly refer to as "moral history" see Habbo Knoch and Benjamin Möckel, Moral History. Überlegungen zu einer Geschichte des Moralischen im "langen" 20. Jahrhundert, in: ZF 14. 2017, pp. 93–111, though with scant reference to economic matters.

interventions. Third, it has found strong reverberations in adjacent disciplines, especially in social anthropology, which has lent it a lasting intellectual presence.[15] Why then should historians remain aloof when the rest of society, as well as their colleagues in the social sciences and political philosophy, have embarked on a lively discussion of how markets and morals go together or not? What can they contribute to the discussion?

I. Moral Economies, Historically Defined

Morals, as suggested by the first edition of the "Encyclopaedia Britannica" (EB) in 1771, were thought to be permeating all sectors of society. Experiencing "reciprocal sympathy" in the family served as the first link "of the moral chain" that led to "agency, freedom, manhood." As much as men were "formed into families, drawn into particular communities, and all united, as by a common league, into one system or body, whose members feel and sympathize one with another," they were connected by a shared "moral sense" or conscience. Since individual feelings darted "into the hearts of others" and raised "correspondent feelings there," men were well prepared "for society and the delightful interchange of friendly sentiment and duties." These duties were primarily defined as filial, fraternal, spousal, and paternal obligations. Duties of friendship followed suit, and so did duties towards neighbors and, finally, strangers, among them commercial partners and competitors. The latter comprised issues like fair-dealing, sincerity in concluding contracts, and fidelity to secure such contracts.[16]

In short, human beings were conceived of as "moral agents" whose "moral sense" enabled them to distinguish clearly between "approveable, or blameable" actions. Defined as "perceptions or determinations," the moral sense functioned without explicit "reasoning" and was "antecedent to views of interest." It led "to a conduct beneficial to the public, and useful to the private system." It implied the "abhorrence of fraud and falsehood" and the "disapprobation of knavery, injustice, ingratitude, meanness of spirit, cowardice, cruelty and indecorum."

---

15 It has even reached out to fields other than economic exchange and interaction, as in Lorraine Daston's article on The Moral Economy of Science, in: Osiris 10. 1995, pp. 2–24, or Didier Fassin's work on humanitarianism and French immigration policies (Compassion and Repression. The Moral Economy of Immigration Policies in France, in: Cultural Anthropology 20. 2005, pp. 362–387; Humanitarian Reason. A Moral History of the Present, Berkeley 2012, pp. 7 ff.). Such extensions will remain beyond the scope of this article.
16 Moral Philosophy, or Morals, in: Encyclopaedia Britannica, 1st ed., vol. 3, Edinburgh 1771, pp. 270–309, here pp. 270–272, p. 274 and p. 291. The entry in the 7th edition of 1842 (vol. 15, pp. 456–489) remained almost identical. Authors and editors of the EB were committed to the ideas of the Scottish Enlightenment and frankly borrowed from other contemporary sources (Michael Levy et al., Encyclopaedia Britannica, https://www.britannica.com/topic/Encyclopaedia-Britannica-English-language-reference-work).

Positively, it meant a "sense of candor and veracity," of "fidelity, justice, gratitude, greatness of mind, fortitude, clemency, decorum." The latter were esteemed as virtues, that is, as a "conduct conformable to reason." Such conduct relied on an "order and oeconomy of powers and passions" that prompted human beings "to attract and pursue good, or to repel and avoid ill." The "moral good" thus lay "in the right conduct of the several senses and passions, or their just proportion and accommodation to their respective objects and relations."[17]

Should those objects and relations be situated in the sphere of commercial connections, individuals were morally obliged to refrain from fraud and dishonesty, instead displaying virtuous dispositions. A "moral economy" might therefore be defined as a system of economic interactions and transactions whose agents behaved in a morally acceptable way. Interestingly, however, this was not how contemporaries used the term. Theologians liked to talk about moral economy as reflecting the divine order of the universe. They frequently spoke about the "moral oeconomy of God" alluding to divine judgment over human immorality. Other authors kept closer to the EB's definition of moral sense and discovered a "moral oeconomy" in the harmony of the human will as being equally determined by passion and reason. When Immanuel Kant's "Die Religion innerhalb der Grenzen der bloßen Vernunft" of 1793/94 found an English edition four decades later, his phrase "Angemessenheit des Lebenswandels" was translated as "the moral economy of man."[18]

It was only in the 1830s that the term migrated into the economic sphere. By now the latter had visibly emerged as a separate realm of human agency. Older notions going back to Aristotle had stressed the embeddedness of economic activities that formed part of the *oikos* as an extended household. This was how many authors had used the word "economy," be it in the translation of the Kantian *Lebenswandel* (literally the way to conduct one's life) or in Francis Hutcheson's 1728 "oeconomy" of passions "which would constitute the most happy State of each Person, and promote the greatest Good in the whole." "Oeconomy" here meant to keep those passions in a "just ballance," which was exactly what the 1771 EB entry had in mind.[19] Starting in the later eighteenth century such broader

---

17 Ibid., p. 274, pp. 276 f., p. 279 and p. 283. As to the essential link between sensibility and moral sense, see Jessica Riskin, Science in the Age of Sensibility. The Sentimental Empiricists of the French Enlightenment, Chicago 2002, pp. 1 ff.

18 Norbert Götz, "Moral Economy." Its Conceptual History and Analytical Prospects, in: Journal of Global Ethics 11. 2015, pp. 147–162, here pp. 149 f.

19 Francis Hutcheson, An Essay on the Nature and Conduct of the Passions and Affections, with Illustrations on the Moral Sense, ed. Aaron Garrett, Indianapolis 2002, p. 47. Recent adoptions of the term, like those by Daston and Fassin, among others, seem to apply such broad notion of economy rather than buying into the more narrowly defined term. See Fassin's definition of moral economies as "la production, la répartition, la circulation et l'utilisation des sentiments moraux, des émotions et des valeurs, des normes et des obligations dans l'espace social" (Les économies morales revisitées, in: Annales HSS 64. 2009, pp. 1237–1266, here p. 1257). This is criticized by Chris Hann who insists on either using the proper notion of economy or dropping the term altogether: Moral(ity and) Economy. Work, Workfare, and Fairness in Provincial

notions of economy were succeeded by views that emphasized the independence and autonomy of economic behavior, and restricted its scope to the production and exchange of goods and services.[20] Only under these new conditions did it make sense to explicitly connect the moral and the economic sphere. In ancient thought, as Norbert Götz pointed out, this would have been redundant and tautological.[21] The modern concept of the economy, however, invited philosophers, economists, and others to think about its moral dimension.

In his 1835 study of the "Philosophy of Manufactures," Andrew Ure investigated the "moral economy of the factory system" alongside its scientific and commercial aspects. A few years later, an anonymous author wrote about the "political and moral economy of socialism" in Robert Owen's journal *New Moral World*. In his own newspaper *National Reformer*, the Chartist James Bronterre O'Brien distinguished the "political economy" of production and profit accumulation from the "moral economy" of reproduction. Charging "large capitalists" and the "division of labour" with creating "the inferior human being" tied to a "single and fixed occupation," Bronterre praised the "domestic virtues which were wont to dwell in the farmer's house when flax spinning, weaving and knitting were social and happy occupations."[22]

To Bronterre, as well as Friedrich Engels and Karl Marx, the modern factory system had unhinged the previous moral order. According to the Communist Manifesto of 1848 capitalism and its principal agent, the bourgeoisie, had

put an end to all feudal, patriarchal, idyllic relations. It has pitilessly torn asunder the motley feudal ties that bound man to his 'natural superiors', and has left remaining no other nexus between man and man than naked self-interest, than callous 'cash payment'. It has drowned the most heavenly ecstasies of religious fervour, of chivalrous enthusiasm, of philistine sentimentalism, in the icy water of egotistical calculation. It has resolved personal worth into exchange value, and in place of the numberless indefeasible chartered freedoms, has set up that single, unconscionable freedom—Free Trade [...] The bourgeoisie has torn away from the family its sentimental veil, and has reduced the family relation to a mere money relation.[23]

Hungary, in: European Journal of Sociology 59. 2018, pp. 225–254, here pp. 229 f. Similarly, Andrew Sayer, Approaching Moral Economy, in: Stehr, Moralization, pp. 77–97, defines "moral economy" as "the study of how economic activities of all kinds are influenced and structured by moral dispositions and norms, and how in turn those norms may be compromised, overridden or reinforced by economic pressures" (p. 78). See also Jaime Palomera and Theodora Vetta, Moral Economy. Rethinking a Radical Concept, in: Anthropological Theory 16. 2016, pp. 413–432, who claim to bring "capital accumulation" and class back into the term.

20 Johannes Burkhardt et al., Wirtschaft, in: Otto Brunner et al. (eds.), Geschichtliche Grundbegriffe, vol. 7, Stuttgart 1992, pp. 511–594.
21 Götz, "Moral Economy," p. 148.
22 Quoted in ibid., p. 151.
23 Karl Marx and Frederick Engels, Manifesto of the Communist Party, in: id., Collected Works, vol. 6: Marx and Engels: 1845–48, New York 1976, pp. 477–519, here pp. 486 f.

In his 1844/45 publication on "The Condition of the Working-Class in England" Engels also juxtaposed the preindustrial moral world to the world of industrial manufacturing. Before the introduction of machinery, he wrote, weavers led a "passably comfortable," "righteous and peaceful life in all piety and probity." They could determine their working hours, found recreation in the garden or field, took part in the games of their neighbors, and were physically strong and healthy. "They were 'respectable' people, good husbands and fathers, led moral lives because they had no temptation to be immoral." In their "unquestioning humility," they regarded the squire as their "natural superior" and "gave him all honour." Such "cosily romantic" existence was abruptly brought to an end by the industrial revolution. It rendered workers "machines pure and simple" and deprived them of "the last trace of independent activity."[24]

This work of destruction, however, ultimately served a beneficial purpose. The old regime, as Engels described it, might have felt cozy and romantic. But in fact, it was "not worthy of human beings" since it separated them from the "mighty movement which, beyond their horizon, was sweeping through mankind." This movement was about the emancipation of all human beings from any kind of exploitation, be it "feudal" or capitalist. It forced everyone to "think and demand a position worthy of men," thus complying with "the universal interests of mankind."[25] In a similar vein, in his 1858 "Outlines of the Critique of Political Economy" *(Grundrisse)*, Marx celebrated the "GREAT CIVILIZING INFLUENCE OF CAPITAL" (in capital letters). Under this influence, bourgeois society surpassed all previous stages of development. Moving "beyond the traditional satisfaction of existing needs and the reproduction of old ways of life confined within long-established and complacently accepted limits," capital was "destructive towards, and constantly revolutionises, all this." It tore down the "barriers which impede the development of the productive forces, the extension of the range of needs, the differentiation of production, and the exploitation and exchange of all natural and spiritual powers."[26] In the end, however, capitalism would itself be destroyed by its own contradictions, giving way to a communist society with an altogether different moral order and economy.

24 Frederick Engels, The Condition of the Working-Class in England, in: Karl Marx and id., Collected Works, vol. 4: Marx and Engels: 1844–45, New York 1975, pp. 295–596, here pp. 307–309.
25 Ibid., p. 309.
26 Karl Marx, Outlines of the Critique of Political Economy (Rough Draft of 1857–58), in: id. and Frederick Engels, Collected Works, vol. 28: Marx: 1857–61, New York 1986, pp. 49–537, here pp. 336 f. See Jürgen Kocka, Capitalism. A Short History, Princeton 2016, pp. 7–16, for a concise summary of Marx's understanding of capitalism, followed by equally helpful passages on Weber and Schumpeter.

II. Economic Theories and Moral Arguments

As we know, Marx failed miserably in his predictions. Still, he presented a critical analysis of capitalism that has proven to be immensely influential and in many ways still holds its ground. But why did he, in 1858, revoke his early moral critique of capitalism? Acknowledging a civilizing influence meant, in contemporary semantics, accepting its moral superiority. Every time the proponents of colonialism spoke of their country's civilizing mission, for instance, they alluded to the "improvement" or "betterment" of the colonized country whose "moral and material progress" would include the refinement of manners, emotions, and values.[27]

Marx and Engels clearly detested capitalism and yet applauded it as the necessary step towards communism and the final liberation of mankind from exploitation and alienation. Cloaking their critique in highly moralized language and denouncing the capitalist bourgeoisie's "naked self-interest" and "egotistical calculation" went along with celebrating pre-capitalist, or, as they put it, feudal social relations and exchange. Even though such "patriarchal" modes of interaction and communication had been no less exploitative and humiliating (which was disclosed at the end of the argument), they initially got extolled as "idyllic" and praised as expressing chivalry, enthusiasm, and sentiment, all positively connoted. This might just have been a Manichaean way to strengthen the argument about capitalism's evil and morally reprehensible cast. Still, it resonated with the vivid contemporary mood of mourning the world that was lost to capitalist development and progress.[28]

On the other hand, progress was appreciated and embraced even by its most fervent critics. Marx and Engels supported capitalism's tendency to universalize and expand globally, thus transcending narrow localism and regionalism. They acclaimed the liberation of human ingenuity and the explorative curiosity of the time. They even seemed to admire capital's resoluteness to eliminate "religious and political illusions," and stood by its principle of "naked, shameless, direct, brutal exploitation."[29] This positive evaluation might have been due to the hope that through its sheer and undisguised brutality capitalism would provoke resistance

---

27 Damien Tricoire, The Enlightenment and the Politics of Civilization. Self-Colonization, Catholicism, and Assimilationism in Eighteenth-Century France, in: id. (ed.), Enlightened Colonialism. Civilization Narratives and Imperial Politics in the Age of Reason, Cham 2017, pp. 25–45; Michael Mann, "Torchbearers Upon the Path of Progress." Britain's Ideology of a "Moral and Material Progress" in India. An Introductory Essay, in: Harald Fischer-Tiné and Michael Mann (eds.), Colonialism as Civilizing Mission. Cultural Ideology in British India, London 2004, pp. 1–26.

28 For conservatives' criticism of capitalist markets, see Jerry Z. Muller, The Mind and the Market. Capitalism in Western Thought, New York 2002, ch. 4: "Justus Möser. The Market as Destroyer of Culture," pp. 84–103, and ch. 5: "Edmund Burke. Commerce, Conservatism, and the Intellectuals," pp. 104–138.

29 Marx, Outlines, p. 336; Marx and Engels, Manifesto, p. 487.

and thus expedite its final downfall. But it also showed how greatly impressed the two German radicals were by the explosion of productivity and the promises this held for the future.

Such promises had first been given by Adam Smith, in his 1776 work on "The Wealth of Nations."[30] He had famously argued that the principles of self-interest and division of labor were spurring economic development, with free markets and free trade at its very core. At first sight, morals were conspicuously absent. According to one of his most frequently quoted lines, "it is not from the benevolence of the butcher, the brewer, or the baker that we expect our dinner, but from their regard to their own interest. We address ourselves, not to their humanity but to their self-love."[31] Still, in the long run, such self-love and self-interest would produce wealth, freedom, and justice for all. In some ways, this resonated with Bernard Mandeville's treatise on private vices engendering public benefits.[32] Yet while in the early eighteenth century Mandeville had condemned the vice of ruthless vanity and naked egoism, Smith deliberately refrained from moral criticism. Instead, he pointed to the ability of free markets to coordinate people's behavior in a way that everyone would gain in material and immaterial terms. Compared to the manifold restrictions of economic activity of former times, free markets were lauded as mechanisms that would ultimately bring about more freedom and happiness for all and even spur the advent of a civil society.[33] In this sense, they could be called moral.

Markets might also be thought of as moral in that they improved people's "conduct" and rendered it "beneficial to the public, and useful to the private system," as the EB had put it.[34] "Whenever commerce is introduced into any country, probity and punctuality always accompany it," Smith stated approvingly. "Of all the nations of Europe, the Dutch, the most commercial, are the most faithfull to their word."[35] This was Smith's version of the *doux commerce* argument that has often been traced back to Montesquieu's "Spirit of the Laws" from 1748: "Everywhere there is commerce, there are gentle mores," since commerce "polishes and softens barbarous mores, as we see every day."[36] But the argument is even older than that. In Samuel Ricard's 1704 "Traité Général du Commerce," which saw many editions and foreign translations, commerce was applauded for its civilizing impact:

It affects the feeling of men so strongly that it makes him who was proud and haughty suddenly turn supple, bending and serviceable. Through commerce, man learns to

30 Lisa Herzog, Inventing the Market. Smith, Hegel, and Political Theory, Oxford 2013; Emma Rothschild, Economic Sentiments. Adam Smith, Condorcet, and the Enlightenment, Cambridge, MA 2001.

31 Adam Smith, The Wealth of Nations, ed. Andrew Skinner, Harmondsworth 1973, p. 119.

32 Bernard Mandeville, The Fable of the Bees. Of Private Vices, Publick Benefits, with a Commentary Critical, Historical, and Explanatory, ed. Frederick Benjamin Kaye, Oxford 1924.

33 Pierre Rosanvallon, Le liberalisme économique. Histoire de l'idée de marché, Paris 1989.

34 Moral Philosophy, in: Encyclopaedia Britannica, p. 279.

35 Adam Smith, Lectures on Jurisprudence, eds. Ronald L. Meek et al., Oxford 1978, p. 538.

36 Montesquieu, The Spirit of the Laws, eds. Anne M. Cohler et al., Cambridge 1989, p. 338.

deliberate, to be honest, to acquire manners, to be prudent and reserved in both talk and action. Sensing the necessity to be wise and honest in order to succeed, he flees vice, or at least his demeanor exhibits decency and seriousness so as not to arouse any adverse judgement on the part of present and future acquaintances; he would not dare make a spectacle of himself for fear of damaging his credit standing.[37]

Through commerce, Ricard wrote, all other "moral and physical passions are superseded by interest which is its basis and mobilizing force."[38] This argument is also encountered in Albert Hirschman's 1977 book "The Passions and the Interests." To Hirschman, the concept of interest served to "oppose and bridle such other passions as ambition, lust for power, or sexual lust." It helped to make human behavior predictable and constant, in contrast to passions, which were deemed volatile, incalculable, and episodic. As soon as passions were moulded into interests, they could act as a "civilizing medium" instead of being socially disruptive and destructive.[39]

Four decades earlier than Hirschman, John Maynard Keynes, the most renowned economist of his time, had made a similar observation:

Dangerous human proclivities can be canalised into comparatively harmless channels by the existence of opportunities for money-making and private wealth, which, if they cannot be satisfied in this way, may find their outlet in cruelty, the reckless pursuit of personal power and authority, and other forms of self-aggrandisement.[40]

Here again, market activities were considered morally beneficial. They not only helped to coordinate people's economic pursuits, therefore proving to be "useful to the private system" with happiness as its ultimate goal. They also delivered public benefits as they protected the social body from the destructive forces of individual passions, transforming the latter into civilized, respectful conduct.

---

37 The translation is Albert Hirschman's (Rival Views of Market Society, in: id., Rival Views of Market Society and Other Recent Essays, Cambridge, MA 1992, pp. 105–141, here p. 108).

38 Samuel Ricard, Traité Général du Commerce, revised ed., vol. 2, Amsterdam 1781, p. 463 (my translation): Without commerce, "les hommes seroient encore dans la plus affreuse barbarie. Le Commerce les attache les uns aux autres par une utilité réciproque & fait taire chez eux toutes les autres passions morales & physiques pour faire place à l'intérêt qui en est la base & le mobile."

39 Albert O. Hirschman, The Passions and the Interests. Political Arguments for Capitalism before its Triumph, Princeton 1977, p. 41, passim. A more recent endorsement of this view is Deirdre McCloskey, The Bourgeois Virtues. Ethics for an Age of Commerce, Chicago 2006. See also her Bourgeois Dignity. Why Economics Can't Explain the Modern World, Chicago 2010, and Bourgeois Equality. How Ideas, Not Capital or Institutions, Enriched the World, Chicago 2016. As to other pro-market arguments, see Lisa Herzog, Markets, in: Edward N. Zalta (ed.), The Stanford Encyclopedia of Philosophy (Fall 2017 Edition), https://plato.stanford.edu/archives/fall2017/entries/markets/.

40 John Maynard Keynes, The General Theory of Employment, Interest and Money [1936], London 1960, p. 374.

The way in which the market operated, however, was determined by factors beyond morals. At least this was what classical economic theory postulated. According to John Stuart Mill's writings of 1844, this theory was exclusively concerned with man "as a being who desires to possess wealth, and who is capable of judging on the comparative efficacy of means for obtaining that end." Only through "entire abstraction of every other human passion or motive" could political economy successfully establish itself as an independent and autonomous field of academic research during the nineteenth and twentieth centuries.[41]

Of course, Mill was well aware that people did not always act in the way they were supposed to. As much as Smith in his earlier treatise on "The Theory of Moral Sentiments" knew about the power of sympathy in fostering social cooperation and communication, Mill cited "those laws of human nature" that called forth "the *affections*, the *conscience*, or feeling of duty, and the love of *approbation*" among human beings. No political economist, Mill claimed, "was ever so absurd as to suppose that mankind are really thus constituted," i. e. "determined, by the necessity of his nature, to prefer a greater portion of wealth to a smaller in all cases." Economic science, though, had to "necessarily proceed" in this mode of narrow determinism in order to reach proper conclusions in its own field. Needless to say that in other fields other "laws" pertained.[42]

To define the economic field as special, unique, independent, and separate from others served different ends. As much as it expressed the desire of academics to prove, establish, and monopolize their professional expertise, it accompanied and enhanced the process of functional differentiation that characterized the advent of modernity. Moreover, it co-produced the illusion that human activity could be neatly divided into different segments, with each segment obeying different "laws" and criteria. What Mill had called "*conscience*, or feeling of duty" was thus, in theory, excluded from the economic sphere and might instead find its place in religious charity or welfare work.

Yet not all economists shared this opinion. In the 1890s, Gustav Schmoller, head of the Younger Historical School of National Economics in Germany, underlined the degree to which the economy remained part of social life in general. According to Schmoller, every economic phenomenon, such as the increase in grain prices or wages, bore traces of people's "feelings, motives and actions" and was shaped by "morals and institutions." Historical knowledge was necessary in order to account for those institutions and moral attitudes. The assumption that a

41 John Stuart Mill, On the Definition of Political Economy; and on the Method of Investigation Proper to It, in: id., Essays on Some Unsettled Questions of Political Economy, London 1844, pp. 120–164, here p. 137. See, for Mill, Joseph Persky, The Ethology of Homo Economicus, in: Journal of Economic Perspectives 9. 1995, pp. 221–231. As a critique, see Samuel Bowles, The Moral Economy. Why Good Incentives Are No Substitute for Good Citizens, New Haven 2016, pp. 75 f.

42 Adam Smith, The Theory of Moral Sentiments [1759], Amherst 2000; Mill, Definition, p. 134 and pp. 137–139.

person was an individual exclusively governed by egotistical interests and selfish preferences was synonymous with misreading the complex frames of reference in which human motives and "drives" were formed and acted upon. Even when it came to acquisitive impulses (*Erwerbstrieb*) and the desire to get rich and richer, substantial differences could be identified within and among various nations, social milieus, and cultures.[43]

This view was strengthened by anthropological fieldwork conducted since the early twentieth century. In 1922, Bronislaw Malinowski published his widely influential ethnography of the Trobriand Islands in the Western Pacific. He had placed special emphasis on studying patterns of reciprocity and exchange in gifts, payments, and transactions that dominated culture and society. By no means were such transactions purely economic, in the modern sense of the word, in that they affected the satisfaction of a person's material wants. As Richard Thurnwald confirmed, gains or the desire to make profit were virtually absent in "primitive communities." In Margaret Mead's observation, men's and women's "ordinary economic affiliations" were neither separate nor independent from other parts of their lives. Instead, the give-and-take of goods and services was firmly embedded in a complex web of social relationships and conformed to shared norms of what was morally acceptable and unacceptable.[44]

Against this background of "primitive" as well as other pre-modern societies, the modern world looked strikingly different. At least this is how, in 1944, Karl Polanyi approached "The Great Transformation" that had allegedly taken place during the long nineteenth century and started with England's industrial revolution. The emergence of a liberal market economy, he argued, rendered it possible to perceive the economy as a distinct and autonomous sphere. By getting rid of its former social embeddedness, the economy could now be—and was—regarded as independent from other types of human relations. According to classical economic theory this amounted to a huge liberation and explosion of economic activities. However, as Polanyi pointed out, it also meant a sharp social and moral rupture. The market functioned as an "unfeeling mechanism" that threw many into poverty while it made a few others exorbitantly rich. In Polanyi's account, the industrial revolution figured as the "veritable abyss of human degradation,"

---

43 Gustav von Schmoller, Die Volkswirtschaft, die Volkswirtschaftslehre und ihre Methode [1893], Frankfurt 1949, p. 12, pp. 15 f., p. 31, p. 44 and p. 56. See Erik Grimmer-Solem, The Rise of Historical Economics and Social Reform in Germany 1864–1894, Oxford 2003, esp. ch. 4: "Empirical Knowledge and the Reform of Society, 1864–1872," pp. 127–168.

44 Bronislaw Malinowski, Argonauts of the Western Pacific. An Account of Native Enterprise and Adventure in the Archipelagoes of Melanesian New Guinea, London 1922, esp. ch. 6: "Launching of a Canoe and Ceremonial Visiting—Tribal Economics in the Trobriands," pp. 146–194; Richard Thurnwald, Economics in Primitive Communities, Berkeley 1932; Margaret Mead, The Arapesh of New Guinea, in: ead. (ed.), Cooperation and Competition among Primitive Peoples, New York 1937, pp. 20–50, here p. 31. Their work was later cited by Karl Polanyi (see below).

as an "avalanche of social dislocation" whose dangerous consequences were never really addressed and overcome.[45]

III. Moral Economies Reviewed: E. P. Thompson and beyond

Describing the market and its operations as "unfeeling," Polanyi made a strong moral statement. Lacking affections like sympathy, pity, or compassion—what Smith had formerly called "moral sentiments"—was tantamount to lacking morality. This reproach had already been brought up by Marx and Engels and other early critics of capitalist markets. It nearly always went hand in hand with the implicit or explicit praise of pre-capitalist conditions as being more moral, i. e. more acceptable in terms of the common good and individual happiness. This kind of moral-amoral juxtaposition never became obsolete. It lived on in orthodox Marxist historiography and its contention that the industrial revolution had raised the level of poverty and spurred large-scale pauperization.[46] It also reverberated in the work of Edward P. Thompson, a non-dogmatic Marxist historian who published his soon famous study on "The Making of the English Working Class" in 1963, to be followed, eight years later, by an influential article on "The Moral Economy of the English Crowd."[47]

Up to this very day, the article has instigated wide interest in the concept of moral economy, academic as well as political. In the 1970s and 80s, it was often read as a reminder of anti-capitalist protest during the early years of industrialization.[48] According to Thompson such protest was rooted in older beliefs about reciprocity and provision. Studying food riots in the eighteenth century, he rejected the dominant opinion of economic historians (informed by classical-neoclassical thought) that those riots were the logical outcome of unemployment and high food prices. Criticizing this interpretation for its "abbreviated view of economic

45 Karl Polanyi, The Great Transformation. The Political and Economic Origins of Our Time [1944], Boston 2001, pp. 41 f. and p. 87. See also id., Aristotle Discovers the Economy, in: id. et al. (eds.), Trade and Market in the Early Empires, Glencoe, IL 1957, pp. 64–94. For an intellectual history approach to Polanyi's work, see Tim Rogan, The Moral Economists. R. H. Tawney, Karl Polanyi, E. P. Thompson, and the Critique of Capitalism, Princeton 2017, ch. 2: "Karl Polanyi," pp. 51–91.

46 For an orthodox-dogmatic marxist view, see Jürgen Kuczynski, Die Geschichte der Lage der Arbeiter unter dem Kapitalismus, vol. 1: 1789–1849, Berlin 1961; vol. 2: 1849–1870, Berlin 1962.

47 Edward P. Thompson, The Making of the English Working Class, London 1963; id., The Moral Economy of the English Crowd in the Eighteenth Century, in: Past & Present 1971, no. 50, pp. 76–136. See Rogan, Moral Economists, ch. 4: "E. P. Thompson," pp. 133–183.

48 For a critique of Thompson's political bias see Chris Hann, Moral Economy, in: Keith Hart et al. (eds.), The Human Economy. A Citizen's Guide, Cambridge 2010, pp. 187–198; Manfred Gailus and Thomas Lindenberger, Zwanzig Jahre "moralische Ökonomie." Ein sozialhistorisches Konzept ist volljährig geworden, in: GG 20. 1994, pp. 469–477.

man," Thompson instead set out to explain rioters' behavior as "modified by custom, culture, and reason." They were informed, he wrote, "by the belief they were defending traditional rights or customs; and, in general, that they were supported by the wider consensus of the community." This consensus basically concerned what Thompson referred to as "moral economy": a device for determining "what were legitimate and what were illegitimate practices in marketing, milling, baking, etc."

The distinction between legitimate and illegitimate or, in the EB's 1771 wording, between approvable and blamable behavior depended on how people defined the "common weal." Thompson claimed that it comprised a set of "social norms and obligations" supported by "the paternalist tradition of the authorities." This tradition entailed the principle of direct and open markets bringing farmers and consumers together; those markets were to be officially controlled with weights and measures supervised. In the second half of the eighteenth century, however, markets increasingly abandoned regulations and direct encounters. The new liberal creed of free markets clashed with the old moral economy of provision and finally succeeded it. In Thompson's view the theory of trade and consumption was "disinfested of intrusive moral imperatives" and thoroughly demoralized.[49]

This is the familiar picture of moral imperatives guiding the "old" economy and the absence of moral obligations in the new capitalist economy based on the private ownership of capital and regulation-free markets. But is it correct? In his 1971 text, Thompson melancholically bid farewell to the old model that, as he saw it, found a last reflection in Robert Owen's cooperative movement. Twenty years later, though, when he revisited and reviewed his argument, he had second thoughts. First, he self-critically reconsidered his earlier critique of a free market economy as befitting the general political and ideological *zeitgeist* of the late 1960s and early 1970s. Second, he distanced himself from his former distinction between moral (traditional) and moral-free (modern) economies. As the economic historians Alfred William Coats and Elizabeth Fox-Genovese had pointed out, both were moral in their own self-image, and Thompson agreed.[50] Back in 1971, he had dismissed classical economics' concern for the public good as mere "intention" that he considered "a bad measure of ideological interest and of historical consequences." In 1991, he still emphasized the difference between theory and practice. Yet he also conceded that any market, be it a traditional or

49 Thompson, Moral Economy, pp. 78 f., p. 83, pp. 89 f. and p. 136.
50 Alfred William Coats, Contrary Moralities. Plebs, Paternalists and Political Economists, in: Past & Present 1972, no. 54, pp. 130–133, esp. p. 133; Elizabeth Fox-Genovese, The Many Faces of Moral Economy. A Contribution to a Debate, in: Past & Present 1973, no. 58, pp. 161–168, here p. 166. This view is supported by more recent research in social and cultural history. See, f. ex., Steve Poole, Scarcity and the Civic Tradition. Market Management in Bristol, 1709–1815, in: Adrian Randall and Andrew Charlesworth (eds.), Markets, Market Culture and Popular Protest in Eighteenth-Century Britain and Ireland, Liverpool 1996, pp. 91–114.

modern one, "cannot be isolated and abstracted from the network of political, social and legal relations in which it is situated."[51]

Overall, however, Thompson stood by his earlier argument that a moral economy could mainly be found operating in peasant and early industrial communities that regulated many economic relations "according to non-monetary norms. These exist as a tissue of customs and usages until they are threatened by monetary rationalisations and are made self-conscious *as* a 'moral economy'." And he sided with Charles Tilly's admonition that the term would lose its conceptual force if it merely meant "tradition, custom, or exchange outside the established market."[52]

But what is an "established market"? Conceptually, it is difficult to speak about one market only. Depending on the goods and services, one can distinguish different markets with different rules and mechanisms. Judged against the classical model some markets are highly imperfect in that they show great power asymmetry.[53] Some negotiate noncontroversial objects while others navigate in morally dubious waters. Although many states have tried to control markets and set legally binding rules, they have been unable to completely abolish so-called "toxic markets" or, straightforwardly, "illegal" markets.[54] "Black markets" have existed not only during war and post-war periods, but continue to flourish in many sectors of the modern economy, from the building industry to private households with their insatiable demand for nannies and other caretakers.[55]

Stressing the diversity of markets and how they operate helps to dismantle Thompson's inherently antagonistic notion of moral economy. Instead of perceiving it as "being in resistance to the economy of the 'free market'," it may be used as a torch to shed light on the hybridity of moral economies.[56] Any economic order, so the argument goes, had to come to terms with moral issues. Whenever people reflected on the good life or the common good, they laid claim to the organization of work and wealth, to the production and distribution of goods and services. In the modern period, such claims were pressed by a wide variety of economic agents, be they merchants, entrepreneurs, managers, peddlers, blue or white collar workers. But moral concerns were also voiced from without the

---

51 Thompson, Moral Economy, p. 89; id., The Moral Economy Reviewed, in: id., Customs in Common, London 1991, pp. 259–351, here p. 271, p. 277 and p. 286 (quote). As to the social and moral embeddedness of capitalist markets, see Mark Granovetter, Economic Action and Social Structure. The Problem of Embeddedness, in: American Journal of Sociology 91. 1985, pp. 481–510.

52 Thompson, Moral Economy Reviewed, p. 338 and p. 340.

53 Herzog, Markets.

54 See n. 11 and n. 13.

55 Malte Zierenberg, Berlin's Black Market 1939–1950, New York 2015.

56 Thompson, Moral Economy Reviewed, p. 340. As to the hybridity of moral economies, see Ute Tellmann, Verschulden. Die moralische Ökonomie der Schulden, in: ilinx 3. 2013, pp. 3–24, here pp. 5–9.

economic system, by religious women and men as well as by social reformers, philanthropists, protest movements, political parties, and activists.

Moreover, those concerns were not monopolized by radical opponents of free market capitalism. Its proponents and defenders, too, employed moral arguments in order to legitimize the new economy and prove its advantages over other types. From the beginning classical economic theory has emphasized the efficiency of free markets to provide goods and services and thus foster the "greatest happiness of the greatest number" of people. Jeremy Bentham claimed that the latter principle was the "foundation of morals." Anything that contributed to maximizing individual and social "utility," defined by John Stuart Mill as the amount of happiness and pleasure, could thus be called moral.[57] At the same time, utilitarian ethics were firmly based on the belief that such pleasures were only fully enjoyed in a state of liberty. Men's—and, for Mill, even women's—freedom to make their own choices and follow their personal preferences mattered greatly, and economic and political liberalism strove to put such freedom into action. Even neoclassical theorists of the Austrian school, like Ludwig von Mises and Friedrich August Hayek (and their American disciple Friedman), protected the "reasoning of liberalism," though "not neutral with regard to value judgments," from its critics. Liberalism as it endorsed private ownership of the means of production appeared to them "as the only policy that can lead to lasting well-being" for all humans. Furthermore, it guaranteed personal and political freedom that in turn depended on "freedom in economic affairs." The latter was best served, as Hayek put it in 1944, by the "impersonal and anonymous mechanism of the market."[58]

Understanding this mechanism and modelling its operations, therefore, came close to qualifying economics as a morally approvable science that genuinely and thoroughly benefited mankind. But economists tried to do even more. They also actively produced the reality that they thought to describe and predict, particularly with regard to the notion of *homo oeconomicus*. Under this leitmotif, anyone entering the market, as producer or consumer, capitalist or worker, was considered a wealth- or pleasure-maximizing agent. Consequently (though not automatically), men, more than women, learnt to play this role as perfectly as possible. As Keynes observed in 1937, they desperately wanted to "behave in a manner which saves our faces as rational, economic men."[59] Instead of being a

57 John Troyer (ed.), The Classical Utilitarians. Bentham and Mill, Indianapolis 2003; Bernard Williams, Morality. An Introduction to Ethics, ch. 10: "Utilitarianism," pp. 82–98, Cambridge 1993; Don A. Habibi, John Stuart Mill and the Ethic of Human Growth, Dordrecht 2001, ch. 3: "Mill's Moral Philosophy," pp. 62–116.

58 Ludwig von Mises, Epistemological Problems of Economics, Princeton 1960, p. 39; Friedrich August Hayek, The Road to Serfdom [1944], Chicago 1994, p. 16 and p. 29. On Hayek, see Muller, Mind and Market, ch. 13: "Friedrich Hayek. Untimely Liberal," pp. 347–387. See also Joseph A. Schumpeter, History of Economic Analysis, Oxford 1954, p. 44 and p. 394.

59 John Maynard Keynes, The General Theory of Employment, in: The Quarterly Journal of Economics 51. 1937, pp. 209–223, here p. 214.

mere methodological tool and "construct," as Joseph Schumpeter had suggested in 1908, *homo oeconomicus* was gradually transformed into a social concept that sought to inform people's self-perception, frame their moral preferences, and shape their habits and habitus.[60]

IV. Markets and Morals: Historical Venues

How this occurred deserves further scrutiny. Remarkably little research exists on the ways in which economists went about spreading their concepts and influencing the public. What made economic theory enter the hearts and minds of ordinary men and women, and to what extent did it shape their decisions and actions? Friedman's concerted efforts and media campaigns are, of course, well known. His "Free to Choose" 1980 TV series is available on YouTube, and his books have sold millions of copies.[61] In addition to media, education in family, schools, and church has helped to form children's moral views on economic issues like saving and spending, the relevance of work, or the distribution of wealth.[62]

Those views, however, were rarely consistent or one-dimensional. They depended on a complex set of factors, such as social class, gender, religion, or ethnic traditions. What was deemed offensive or blamable differed as much as what was held to be approvable or, at least, acceptable. Trying to conform to the ideal of *homo oeconomicus* and adjusting, somehow or other, to what Max Weber had famously called the "iron cage" of the economic order was by no means synonymous with abolishing "moral sentiments."[63] Indeed, such sentiments developed within and without that order in manifold ways.

60 Joseph A. Schumpeter, The Nature and Essence of Economic Theory [German original 1908], ed. Bruce A. McDaniel, New Brunswick 2010, p. 55.
61 Sören Brandes, "Free to choose." Die Popularisierung des Neoliberalismus in Milton Friedmans Fernsehserie (1980/90), in: ZF 12. 2015, pp. 526–533.
62 As to monetary education, see Sandra Maß, Kinderstube des Kapitalismus? Monetäre Erziehung im 18. und 19. Jahrhundert, Berlin 2018; ead., Children, Savings Banks and Politics. The Savings Movement in the Last Third of the Nineteenth Century, in: FUNCAS Social and Economic Studies 4. 2017, pp. 7–18; ead., Useful Knowledge. The Monetary Education of Children and the Moralization of Productivity in the Nineteenth Century, in: Peter-Paul Bänziger and Mischa Suter (eds.), Histories of Productivity. Genealogical Perspectives on the Body and Modern Economy, London 2017, pp. 74–91. As to work-related attitudes, see Daniela Saxer, Persönlichkeiten auf dem Prüfstand. Die Produktion von Arbeitssubjekten in der frühen Berufsberatung, in: Historische Anthropologie 19. 2011, pp. 354–371; Peter-Paul Bänziger, What Makes People Work. Producing Emotional Attachments to the Workplace in Post-World War II West-German Vocational Schools, in: Anne Schmidt and Christoph Conrad (eds.), Bodies and Affects in Market Societies, Tübingen 2016, pp. 41–57.
63 Max Weber, The Protestant Ethic and the Spirit of Capitalism, trans. Talcott Parsons, New York 1958, p. 181.

Most importantly, they colored the legal framings of modern capitalist markets. It has long been known and re-emphasized by new institutional economics, that those markets were not as free and self-organized as some economists claimed. Instead, they crucially depended on legally enshrined norms and sanctions that carried heavy moral baggage. When commercial codes were drafted during the nineteenth century moral considerations generally loomed large, as is evident, for instance, in bankruptcy laws. "In every bankruptcy," Napoleon I forthrightly stated, "there is evidence of offense." A person who was declared bankrupt should therefore "no longer be able to affect an air of triumph, or at least that he present himself in public with the abasement of a man who has suffered a great misfortune."[64] Although resonating with public and literary opinion, the Emperor's demands were not entirely met by the 1807 French Commercial Code. Still the Code dictated severe penalties for *banqueroute* that followed a debtor's gross mismanagement or fraud. Legal punishment went along with scrutinizing the debtor's character and moral comportment and usually resulted in his social death. In contrast, a *faillite* was thought to result from unfortunate economic circumstances and did not entail moral, legal, and social condemnation.[65]

Similarly debates on usury laws provided ample opportunity to negotiate moral convictions and claims. After many centuries of banning excessive interest rates, the nineteenth century finally abolished usury laws and interest limits. As the Austrian finance minister held in 1858, money "like every other commodity" became "subject to the law of competition of supply and demand according to its respective price." Nevertheless clauses that prohibited credit transactions remained in place to prevent exploitation of the borrowers' "inexperience or hardship." Especially in times of economic crisis, such transactions were closely monitored. In 1879, an influential Prussian squire and member of the conservative party sharply criticized the peasants' growing dependency on creditors, who, to him, represented "the powerful, egoistic domination of capital without moral foundations." In order to avoid domination and abolish exploitation, many political actors from various parties called for new usury laws that particularly targeted Jewish merchants and money-lenders. Starting in the 1880s, relevant laws were crafted and reintroduced in Germany and Austria as well as in some Swiss cantons.[66]

---

64 Erika Vause, "He Who Rushes to Riches Will Not Be Innocent." Commercial Values and Commercial Failure in Postrevolutionary France, in: French Historical Studies 35. 2012, pp. 321–349, here p. 325.

65 Ibid.; Robert Beachy, Bankruptcy and Social Death. The Influence of Credit-Based Commerce on Cultural and Political Values, in: Zeitsprünge 4. 2000, pp. 329–343.

66 Mischa Suter, Usury and the Problem of Exchange under Capitalism. A Late-Nineteenth-Century Debate on Economic Rationality, in: Social History 42. 2017, pp. 501–523; Martin H. Geyer, Defining the Common Good and Social Justice. Popular and Legal Concepts of "Wucher" in Germany from the 1860s to the 1920s, in: Willibald Steinmetz (ed.), Private Law and Social Inequality in the Industrial Age. Comparing Legal Cultures in Britain, France, Germany, and the United States, New York 2000, pp. 457–483.

Moral prejudice against "high finance" and its many Jewish representatives also played into the hands of those who demanded a stronger control of stock exchange trading. Driven by a passionate hatred against the rule of "capital" and its alleged lack of "moral foundations," opponents, mostly members of the Prussian land-owning class, waged a vicious war against financial trading operations during the late nineteenth century. Those operations, they claimed, undermined the social, moral, and economic well-being of large parts of the German population and therefore deserved far stricter control and regulation. In 1896, their claims and demands were met by a new law that put a cap on forward business and futures trading, among others. Moral considerations, including a distinct anti-Semitic bias, had permeated the legislative process and buttressed the stance of those who sought to defend their power in a rapidly changing world by all means.[67]

Moral issues were also at stake when life insurance emerged as a major business sector during the nineteenth century.[68] Insurance companies generally used heavy moral pressure in order to convince reluctant clients of the "necessity that exists for every head of family to make proper provision for the sustenance of those dear to him after his death." Life insurance was marketed as the duty of a good and responsible husband and father who, "with soul sanctified by the deed, wings his way up to the realms of the just." In 1868, the *United States Insurance Gazette* claimed that society was "fast tending to regard the man who leaves his family destitute, when a Life Insurance Policy can so cheaply be purchased, as foolish and criminal in his neglect." Women, as part of that society, thought otherwise, though. Destined to be the chief beneficiaries, they often opposed the "capitalization of affection" and refused "the blessings of life insurance." They considered it to be "blood money," a monetary bargain that turned their husbands' or fathers' sacred life into an "article of merchandise."[69]

Moral attitudes and conventions prevailed in other economic domains, too. Since laws could not always guarantee the abiding behavior of contractual partners, trust, as a morally sensitive emotion, was needed to make contracts happen and fulfilled. Trust often relied on a sense of proximity and affinity: sharing similar social, ethnic, or religious backgrounds, believing in similar values and sources of respectability clearly enabled exchange and cooperation. By contrast, perceived strangeness or moral doubt might effectively block and prevent further communication.[70]

---

67 Christof Biggeleben, Das "Bollwerk des Bürgertums." Die Berliner Kaufmannschaft 1870–1920, Munich 2006, pp. 234–307.

68 As to its beginnings in the early modern period, see Geoffrey Clark, Betting on Lives. The Culture of Life Insurance in England, 1695–1775, Manchester 1999; Robin Pearson, Moral Hazard and the Assessment of Insurance Risk in Eighteenth- and Early-Nineteenth-Century Britain, in: Business History Review 76. 2002, pp. 1–35.

69 Zelizer, Morals and Markets, quotes p. 43, pp. 45 f., p. 50 and p. 56.

70 Ute Frevert, The Moral Economy of Trust. Modern Trajectories, London 2014; ead., Trust as Work, in: Jürgen Kocka (ed.), Work in a Modern Society. The German Historical Experience in Comparative Perspective, Oxford 2010, pp. 93–108.

Even if notions of personal respectability *(Ehrbarkeit)* were no longer practiced as strictly and solemnly as in the early modern period, they still permeated, in one way or another, economic activities and relations.[71] In Anthony Giddens' terms "moral integration" proved to be a crucial condition of social integration and was ensured by practicing shared ideas and a "common moral ethos."[72] Those businessmen whose behavior violated the group ethos quickly found themselves excluded. Failing in one's business and declaring bankruptcy was a case in point. Although it did not automatically bar tradespeople from further receiving credit as respectable men, insolvency was often associated with moral misdemeanors and "bad habits."[73]

In the German-speaking countries no less than in France, merchants and businesspeople were generally suspected of lacking in morality. During the long nineteenth century, widely publicized scandals of fraud and speculative trading operations heightened distrust in broad sections of the population and raised concerns about business morals.[74] Financial traders and merchants, in particular,

71 For earlier economic relations of trust and honor, see Craig Muldrew, The Economy of Obligation. The Culture of Credit and Social Relations in Early Modern England, Houndmills 1998, who describes the early modern economy as a "system of cultural, as well as material, exchanges in which the central mediating factor was credit or trust" (p. 4); credit in turn was a mechanism of "circulating judgement about the value of other members of communities" (p. 2). See also id., Interpreting the Market. The Ethics of Credit and Community Relations in Early Modern England, in: Social History 18. 1993, pp. 163–183; John Smail, Credit, Risk, and Honor in Eighteenth-Century Commerce, in: Journal of British Studies 44. 2005, pp. 439–456. Laurence Fontaine, The Moral Economy. Poverty, Credit, and Trust in Early Modern Europe, Cambridge 2014, also focuses on credit and trust as constituting economic relations in pre-capitalist times. As to Jewish notions of *koved* (honor) in business, see Natalie Zemon Davis, Religion and Capitalism Once Again? Jewish Merchant Culture in the Seventeenth Century, in: Jeremy Adelman and Stephen Aron (eds.), Trading Cultures. The Worlds of Western Merchants, Turnhout 2001, pp. 59–86, here pp. 74f.
72 Anthony Giddens, Elites in the British Class Structure, in: Sociological Review 20. 1972, pp. 345–372, here p. 350. See Biggeleben, "Bollwerk," pp. 242 ff., for practices of moral integration and exclusion in Berlin's business community of the late 19th and early 20th centuries.
73 For continuous credit options, see Margot C. Finn, The Character of Credit. Personal Debt in English Culture, 1740–1914, Cambridge 2003, p. 305. For perceptions of moral failure, see Bernhard Kleeberg's introduction, in: id. (ed.), Schlechte Angewohnheiten. Eine Anthologie 1750–1900, Berlin 2012, pp. 9–66; Mischa Suter, Rechtstrieb. Schulden und Vollstreckung im liberalen Kapitalismus 1800–1900, Konstanz 2016, pp. 92–101 and pp. 173–220; id., *Falliment.* The Social Life of a Legal Category. Knowledge and Morals in Bankruptcy Proceedings (Basel, 1840s), in: Andreas Gestrich and Martin Stark (eds.), Debtors, Creditors, and Their Networks. Social Dimensions of Monetary Dependence from the Seventeenth to the Twentieth Century, London 2015, pp. 217–251. As to the gendering of business failure, see Toby L. Ditz, Shipwrecked; or Masculinity Imperiled. Mercantile Representations of Failure and the Gendered Self in Eighteenth-Century Philadelphia, in: Journal of American History 81. 1994, pp. 51–80.
74 Biggeleben, "Bollwerk," p. 217 and pp. 234 ff. As to the morally dubious figure of the speculator that rose to prominence during the 19th century, see Urs Stäheli, Spectacular Speculation. Thrills, the Economy, and Popular Discourse, Stanford 2013.

were criticized for allegedly succumbing to speculation as the "*mal du siècle*." This evil drove them to "rush to riches" rather than engage in "old commerce" fortune building across the generations. The "new commerce" of investing in modern stock companies and speculating in real estate raised serious doubts about its solidity, "honor" and social responsibility. Although litigants in bankruptcy cases used to stress their own honorable conduct against the allegedly self-centered actions of their opponents, public prosecutors and judges tended to cast a critical eye on such strategies of exoneration. At the same time, large parts of the public— legislators, journalists, pamphleteers, and businesspeople themselves—insisted on holding those in commerce to particularly high standards of morality. Since "public wealth, prosperity and the happiness of citizens are attached to the prosperity of commerce," the latter had to be meticulously monitored and disciplined. Engaging in fraudulent operations, risky investment, and excessive speculation would inevitably destroy public trust and thus harm the public good.[75]

Politics of debt and credit serve as good examples of the hybrid connections between economic behavior and morality. Banks generally granted credit only to those clients whom they considered solid, honest, and reliable. Apart from checking their credit history, they also collected information on family relations, character, and "moral" behavior.[76] Similar markers were investigated by the many credit and rating agencies that emerged in the 1840s and operated on behalf of merchants, companies, and retailers.[77] In England, so-called Guardian societies spread from London to other cities during the first half of the nineteenth century. In order to protect trade from swindlers and sharpers, they heavily relied on personal characteristics, from dress to sexual orientation, in determining their customers' creditworthiness. When local societies formed a national association in 1865, they defined its purpose as, first, "to give confidence to the manufacturer and merchant in the extension of sound, legitimate trading," second, "to furnish additional facilities for credit to the industrious, honest, and frugal [...] capitalist," and, third, "to prevent losses by bad debts through the reckless, insolvent, or dishonest."[78]

Favoring the former and excluding the latter was also on the agenda of the new type of cooperative banks or credit unions that emerged in Germany during the second half of the nineteenth century. Founded by Hermann Schulze from Delitzsch, Saxony, such unions formed a capital stock from which they granted

---

75 Vause, "He Who Rushes," pp. 342 ff.; ead., Disciplining the Market. Debt Imprisonment, Public Credit, and the Construction of Commercial Personhood in Revolutionary France, in: Law and History Review 32. 2014, pp. 647–682, here p. 680.

76 Rowena Olegario, A Culture of Credit. Embedding Trust and Transparency in American Business, Cambridge, MA 2006.

77 Hartmut Berghoff, Markterschließung und Risikomanagement. Die Rolle der Kreditauskunfteien und Rating-Agenturen im Industrialisierungs- und Globalisierungsprozess des 19. Jahrhunderts, in: VSWG 92. 2005, pp. 141–162.

78 Finn, Character of Credit, p. 299.

advances to members, mostly small businessmen and artisans in need of extra capital. In rural areas, the concept was launched by Friedrich Wilhelm Raiffeisen, who, in 1849, founded an association to help poor farmers buy cattle or machinery. Such cooperatives lent money only to members, but accepted capital contributions also from non-members. The general assembly decided on interest rates and functioned as controller.

Since the cooperatives were usually located in small towns or villages, members knew each other fairly well and could evaluate a borrower's economic standing. Moreover, they took his "moral" conduct into consideration, including his behavior as a husband and father, his religious bearings, and his after-work activities. At the same time, they considered their own operations as a profoundly moral intervention that would improve trust, honesty, and responsibility among members. To preach the gospel of solidarity, as Schulze-Delitzsch and Raiffeisen did, also meant to raise the self-confidence of the lower classes and turn them away from the "red ghost" of socialism. People would learn to trust in themselves as well as in others. They would experience the "joy of work and saving" and refrain from condemnable habits like consuming too much alcohol or engaging in "excessive," "reckless" and "slothful" behavior. They would, in short, become morally approvable individuals who cared for their own families and for the good of the community.[79]

As these cooperative banks spread through and beyond the German-speaking countries, they established themselves as powerful financial agents, both in economic and moral terms. Defying competition of various novel banking models, the two strands of credit unions merged in the early 1970s and comfortably survived the financial crisis of 2007–2008.[80] Even though the moral component of giving and receiving credit has been considerably diminished in recent years and decades, the principles of local embeddedness and participatory decision-making have contributed to the institutions' ongoing success.

How and why morals were cast off by the credit business is a question that needs further exploration. Evidently, there was great interest in the finance industry to expand credit options. Demoralizing debt became a robust and ultimately successful financial strategy during the second half of the twentieth

---

79 Hermann Schulze-Delitzsch, Vorschuß- und Creditvereine als Volksbanken. Praktische Anweisung zu deren Gründung und Einrichtung, Leipzig 1867⁴, p. 3, p. 6 and p. 224; Friedrich Wilhelm Raiffeisen, Die Darlehnskassen-Vereine als Mittel zur Abhilfe der Noth der ländlichen Bevölkerung, sowie auch der städtischen Handwerker und Arbeiter, Neuwied 1866, p. 1, p. 6, p. 11, p. 16, p. 18 and pp. 21 f. See also Timothy W. Guinnane, Cooperatives as Information Machines. German Rural Credit Cooperatives, 1883–1914, in: Journal of Economic History 61. 2001, pp. 366–389. A similar link between moral worth and economic advancement through saving was established by the early American thrifts: Heather A. Haveman and Hayagreeva Rao, Structuring a Theory of Moral Sentiments. Institutional and Organizational Coevolution in the Early Thrift Industry, in: American Journal of Sociology 102. 1997, pp. 1606–1651, here p. 1612.
80 Ute Frevert, Vertrauensfragen. Eine Obsession der Moderne, Munich 2013, pp. 112 f.

century. Accompanying the development of modern consumer societies, new debt and credit forms gradually changed the spending behavior of large parts of the population. When new installment sales methods spread from the United States to Europe from the 1920s onwards, they were initially sharply criticized as morally reprehensible and corrupting. Solid cash payment seemed to be the morally superior and financially sustainable means to buy goods and services. By contrast, it was thought that payment by installments seduced people into spending more than they could actually afford, thereby threatening to increase household indebtedness.[81]

Borrowing money had long since held various meanings and found different explanations. Motives played a major role in determining its moral standing. Using credit in order to finance extravagant desires that did not match one's own economic status was widely considered as morally unacceptable. By contrast, debts that arose from personal hardship could be forgiven. Investing borrowed money to start or expand one's business and thus increase the happiness of one's family was even more justified. Against this background, it did not come as a surprise that the "American" system of credit financing and the slogan "buy now, pay later" took long to win over German, French or Japanese consumers.[82]

Consumption, however, was not the only economic activity coming under close moral scrutiny. Production had in fact and by far preceded consumer behavior in attracting moral attention and concern. Right from the beginning of the industrial age, labor relations were a constant source of conflict. What counted as "fair wages" was as much contested as the notion of a "just price." Both shared a semantic field that referred to moral demands and general ideas of a common good.[83] Such demands loomed large in the political lexicon of the early labor movement, as Thompson and many other social historians have pointed out. Some were rooted in religious beliefs, some were associated with more secular concepts of human equality, and others reflected traditional notions of how people should live together and lead a good life. When workers and journeymen first organized to collectively bargain for higher wages, shorter hours, and healthier living and working conditions, they chose names which alluded to brotherhood and friendship as morally charged concepts. As brothers and friends, members

81 Jan Logemann, Introduction. Toward a Global History of Credit in Modern Consumer Societies, in: id. (ed.), The Development of Consumer Credit in Global Perspective. Business, Regulation, and Culture, New York 2012, pp. 1–20; id., Americanization through Credit? Consumer Credit in Germany, 1860s to 1960s, in: Business History Review 85. 2011, pp. 529–550,

82 See other articles in Logemann, Development, esp. those by Isabelle Gaillard and, resp., Sabine Effosse on postwar France, Andrew Gordon and, resp., Charles Yuji Horioka on Japan. See also Jan Logemann, Different Paths to Mass Consumption. Consumer Credit in the United States and West Germany during the 1950s and '60s, in: Journal of Social History 41. 2008, pp. 525–559.

83 Fabio Monsalve, Scholastic Just Price versus Current Market Price. Is It Merely a Matter of Labelling?, in: European Journal of the History of Economic Thought 21. 2014, pp. 4–20; Niklas Luhmann, Die Wirtschaft der Gesellschaft, Frankfurt 1988, pp. 23 f.

were connected not only by common interest and values, but also by mutual obligations and responsibilities.[84]

Solidarity as practiced by workers' associations, though, came with moral strings and ties. Particularly in self-help organizations, members had to subscribe to a code of honesty and decency that attempted to rule out free riding and fraud. Sickness funds, as they were set up by workers and unions, called on their members to control the recipients and ensure that they behaved appropriately. As a matter of fact, they did not accept people with ailments inflicted by bad moral conduct, such as drunkenness, "sexual excess" or fights.[85]

Turning against their employers, workers also used moralizing techniques to shame them into less exploitative politics. Embracing early-modern traditions of popular justice, they staged charivaris (or what was called "rough music" in England) and ridiculed ruthless and cruel-hearted businessmen in mock trials and processions. Such older repertoires of contention, as Charles Tilly called them, coexisted and interacted with modern types of organized protest, like strikes and rallies.[86] As late as the 1970s, factory protests in Italy often adopted carnivalesque forms when, for instance, a company's head of personnel was forced to march around the factory yard. A worker walking next to him held a placard with the manager's name and the word "THIEF." In 1971, protesters hung a rag-doll representing the director's face on the Autobianchi car factory gates and adorned it with a rabbit, the Italian symbol of cowardice. Five years later, workers at a major Italian steelwork factory broke into the manager's office and left a donkey as a jibe.[87] All these acts were meant to embarrass and shame the powerful so that they would eventually adhere to "good," i. e. morally approvable practice. As sociologist Donatella della Porta put it they expressed "a moral claim against immoral authorities," in this case corporate bosses and leading executives.[88]

As these—and many other—stories demonstrate moral claims were always relevant to economic relations. Max Weber's 1904 observation that "present-day capitalistic economy" imposed its norms and "rules of action" on all those

---

84 Thomas Welskopp, Das Banner der Brüderlichkeit. Die deutsche Sozialdemokratie vom Vormärz bis zum Sozialistengesetz, Bonn 2000; Wolfgang Schieder, Brüderlichkeit, in: Otto Brunner et al. (eds.), Geschichtliche Grundbegriffe, vol. 1, Stuttgart 1972, pp. 552–581.

85 Ute Frevert, Professional Medicine and the Working Classes in Imperial Germany, in: Journal of Contemporary History 20. 1985, pp. 637–658.

86 Ilaria Favretto, Introduction. Looking Backward to Move Foreward. Why Appreciating Tradition Can Improve Our Understanding of Modern Protest, in: ead. and Xabier Itçaina (eds.), Protest, Popular Culture and Tradition in Modern and Contemporary Western Europe, London 2017, pp. 1–20; Charles Tilly, The Contentious French, Cambridge, MA 1986, p. 46 and pp. 391 f., who argued that over time, new forms replaced older ones as the latter could no longer cope with the modern development of nation states and industry.

87 Ilaria Favretto, Rough Music and Factory Protest in Post-1945 Italy, in: Past & Present 2015, no. 228, pp. 207–247, here p. 209 and pp. 217 f.

88 Donatella della Porta, Afterwords. Old and New Repertoires of Contention, in: Favretto and Itçaina, Protest, pp. 249–260, here p. 259.

involved in market relations holds only half true.[89] On the one hand, the "rules of action" that Weber mentioned had not been established in a moral void. They were based, among others, on a highly moralized notion of work as an essential and respectable human activity.[90] Such notions, often religiously framed, were appropriated and translated into action in various ways. Women's work in the family and private household became moralized as an expression of altruistic love towards household members, with crucial consequences for women's formal employment.[91] Men's work, by contrast, was often cloaked in notions of masculine pride and competition that made workers outperform production targets even without being forced to.[92]

On the other hand, those targets and the imperatives they followed were continuously reformulated and morally contested, both within the economic field and without. Factory legislation started early and banned child labor after persistent moral campaigning. Workers' unions were finally accepted as counterparts of powerful entrepreneurs and given a say on shorter hours and fairer wages. Workers' rights to health, occupational accident, and unemployment benefits as well as pensions were gradually affirmed and institutionalized, with employers having to contribute their share. Such insurance and welfare schemes profoundly affected and readjusted the moral trajectories of capitalist labor relations. Largely, although not exclusively, responding to moral criticism of the kind Karl Marx had waged in the 1860s, they themselves worked, in the longer run, to provide citizens with a sense of what they could desire and legitimately expect in terms of a good and happy, i. e. moral life.[93]

---

89 Weber, Protestant Ethic, pp. 54 f.

90 Jürgen Kocka, Work as a Problem in European Society, in: id., Work in a Modern Society, pp. 1–15; Thomas Welskopp, The Vision(s) of Work in the Nineteenth-Century German Labour Movement, in: Kocka, Work in a Modern Society, pp. 55–71; Hann, Moral(ity and) Economy, pp. 232 ff.

91 See the polemical essay by Gisela Bock and Barbara Duden, Arbeit aus Liebe—Liebe als Arbeit. Zur Entstehung der Hausarbeit im Kapitalismus, in: Frauen und Wissenschaft, Berlin 1977, pp. 118–197; Kathleen Canning, Languages of Labor and Gender. Female Factory Work in Germany, 1850–1914, Ithaca 1996; Karin Hausen, Work in Gender, Gender in Work, in: Kocka, Work in a Modern Society, pp. 73–91.

92 Thomas Welskopp, Sons of Vulcan. Industrial Relations and Attitudes toward Work among German and American Iron- and Steelworkers in the Twentieth Century, in: Schmidt and Conrad, Bodies and Affects, pp. 23–39; Michael Burawoy, Manufacturing Consent. Changes in the Labor Process under Monopoly Capitalism, Chicago 1979 (as a sociological and ethnographic study on workers in an agricultural equipment plant near Chicago); Paul Willis, Masculinity and Factory Labor, in: Jeffrey C. Alexander and Steven Seidman (eds.), Culture and Society. Contemporary Debates, Cambridge 1990, pp. 183–195.

93 Marx described the "general law of capitalist accumulation" as establishing "an accumulation of misery, corresponding with accumulation of capital. Accumulation of wealth at one pole is, therefore, at the same time accumulation of misery, agony of toil, slavery, ignorance, brutality, mental [in the German original: moral] degradation, at the opposite pole" (Karl Marx and Frederick Engels, Collected Works, vol. 35: Karl Marx, Capital, vol. 1, New York 1996, p. 640).

V. Moral Economies Past and Present

Viewed against this background of current and former claims and related practices, the notion of moral economy presents itself as an epistemologically helpful tool to investigate the complex hybridity of economic and moral systems in modern as well as premodern societies. In historical perspective, it is striking that the notion has continued to galvanize political debates and controversies about capitalism since the nineteenth century. Rooted in early modern ideas of morals as the "art of being virtuous and happy," such promises cast their spell over generations to come. They resonated in the efforts put forth by proponents of capitalism who lauded the new economic system for its genuine proclivity for promoting people's liberty and well-being. At the same time, they informed the criticism of those who condemned the system for not delivering on its promises, instead plunging the working population, as Marx put it, into the dismal state of "moral degradation" and economic "misery."

The fact that controversy about capitalism and its moral components has continued over two centuries is both an asset and a burden for scientific analysis. On the one hand, it confirms the historical and actual relevance of moral economies beyond merely academic interest. On the other hand, it might taint this interest, obscuring changes in form and content. In order to avoid such intellectual pitfalls, it is necessary to bear in mind that moral issues pervade all types of economic systems. Regardless of the way in which economic activities are organized, they are bound to mesh with concepts of what society or social groups hold as morally approvable or blamable. Even capitalist markets have never been totally free and self-sufficient but depended on a web of legal frames, political support, social conventions, and moral attitudes. This was reflected, early on, in the term "political economy," which has proliferated since the eighteenth century and conceptually related processes of production and consumption to law, customs, and government.[94] Whenever practitioners and theoreticians of "economics" tried to liberate themselves from such relations they encountered strong social and academic resistance. Moral concerns and evaluations of economic behavior prevailed, in liberal societies as much as in totalitarian ones. Both fascism and communism openly and deliberately worked towards politicizing and moralizing economic activity. Liberal democracies also witnessed strong attempts to remind corporations of their responsibility to stakeholders and shareholders alike. Many liberal constitutions codified the principle that private property holds social

As to the normative consequences of welfare institutions and public policy, see Stefan Svallfors, The Moral Economy of Class. Class and Attitude in Comparative Perspective, Stanford 2006, esp. pp. 1 f., who, however, cripples the "feedback mechanism" between morals and policies by disregarding the moral origins and incentives of social policy.

94 Barry R. Weingast and Donald Wittman (eds.), The Oxford Handbook of Political Economy, Oxford 2008.

obligations, with legislation on matters from tenant law to worker participation following suit.[95]

Political economies thus have had a robust moral substance that informs the legal framework in which markets operate. Such substance might stem from religious teachings, but can also have secular sources. Since the nineteenth century, the egalitarian promise of civil societies has spurred quests for justice and fairness.[96] At the same time, older notions of brotherhood (and, sometimes, sisterhood) have influenced politics of solidarity within and beyond class lines. Vulnerability, bodily and emotionally defined, has become a major argument for protecting human beings, especially children, from economic exploitation. This is connected with what Hans Joas has called the increasing sacralization of human life. He finds the belief in a person's sacredness backed both by Judeo-Christian traditions and the French Enlightenment.[97]

Sacralization affected capitalist markets in many ways. Certain goods were deemed non-marketable, such as a person's life and freedom. Nobody was allowed to sell themselves into slavery—even though such markets did exist, albeit in secret and illegal ways. Notwithstanding that slavery was politically and legally abolished in the early nineteenth century, so-called white slavery, above all the sexual trafficking of young women and girls, persisted and even increased. States again took legal action and were pushed and supported to do so by public opinion and moral campaigns launched by women's organizations. In 1910, U.S. congress passed the White Slave Traffic Act prohibiting the transport of women across states for "immoral purposes" like prostitution and debauchery. Similar attempts to outlaw the market and stop trading "female flesh" were made by other countries.[98]

What exactly raises moral concerns and is deemed immoral underlies historical changes. Prostitution is a case in point, and so is the consumption of alcohol

---

95 In Germany, both the Weimar Constitution of 1919 and the Basic Law of 1949 stated that private property entails obligations towards the common weal. See Traugott Jähnichen, Vom Besitzindividualismus zur gemeinwohlorientierten Sozialpflichtigkeit—Der neuzeitliche Eigentumsbegriff in der Entwicklung des Privat- und Verfassungsrechts, in: Günter Brakelmann et al. (eds.), Auf dem Weg zum Grundgesetz. Beiträge zum Verfassungsverständnis des neuzeitlichen Protestantismus, Münster 1999, pp. 233–246. See also Gregory S. Alexander, Ownership and Obligations. The Human Flourishing Theory of Property, in: Hong Kong Law Journal 43. 2013, pp. 451–462, electronic copy available at http://ssrn.com/abstract=2348202.

96 On justice and fairness (and their many different interpretations), see Sandel, Justice, esp. ch. 4: "What Matters Is the Motive. Immanuel Kant," pp. 103–116.

97 Hans Joas, The Sacredness of the Person. A New Genealogy of Human Rights, Washington D.C. 2013.

98 Brian Donovan, White Slave Crusades. Race, Gender, and Anti-Vice Activism, 1887–1917, Urbana 2006; Marion A. Kaplan, The Jewish Feminist Movement in Germany. The Campaigns of the Jüdischer Frauenbund, 1904–1938, Westport 1979, ch. 4: "Prostitution, Morality Crusades, and Feminism," pp. 103–145; Irene Stratenwerth et al., Der Gelbe Schein. Mädchenhandel 1860–1930, Bremerhaven 2012. See, for a broader contemporary critique, Laurie Penny, Meat Market. Female Flesh under Capitalism, Winchester 2011.

or other drugs. In more recent times, the trade of organs and donor eggs and sperm has come under intense moral scrutiny, at least in some Western countries. Different societies hold different ideas about what they perceive as immoral and contemptible. How such perceptions are individually formed is progressively studied by psychologists and neuroscientists, even though philosophers are quick to remind them that "you can't learn about morality from brain scans."[99] As much as moral attitudes vary over time and follow different rationales, they continue to be shaped by social and cultural negotiation, some institutionalized, some not. NGOs, social movements, political parties, and ethics committees have successfully established themselves as collective moral agents. Criticism of environmental pollution and an ever-expanding carbon footprint increasingly draws on the moral obligation of individual consumers to reduce their personal share in carbon emissions by, among others, changing their travel and eating habits.

Such claims can be traced back to the 1970s and the newly popular notion of the individual responsibility to actively contribute to the world's well-being.[100] It went along with a highly moralized pressure towards critical self-inspection and was supported by what Ronald Inglehart famously diagnosed as a trend to embrace post-materialistic values.[101] These attitudes can be seen as fostering morally responsible agency defined by the philosopher Lisa Herzog as holding "one another accountable for what we do: we expect ourselves and others to be able to explain and justify our behavior. This is not a question of high-flying moral ideals, but of basic moral decency." The latter resided in the "minimal duty to avoid harming others when one can easily do so" as well as in the "duty to inform oneself about the risk of harming others and about possible alternatives."[102] Even if those duties needed institutional support and "epistemic infrastructure," the

---

99   See Thomas Nagel's 2013 review of Joshua Greene, Moral Tribes. Emotion, Reason, and the Gap between Us and Them, New York 2013: You Can't Learn about Morality from Brain Scans, https://newrepublic.com/article/115279/joshua-greenes-moral-tribes-reviewed-thomas-nagel. For a historically and sociologically informed view on morals, see Jesse J. Prinz, The Emotional Construction of Morals, Oxford 2007, esp. ch. 6: "The Genealogy of Morals," pp. 215–243; Jonathan Haidt, The Moral Emotions, in: Richard J. Davidson et al. (eds.), Handbook of Affective Sciences, Oxford 2003, pp. 852–870.

100 Stephen Milder, Thinking Globally, Acting (Trans-)Locally. Petra Kelly and the Transnational Roots of West German Green Politics, in: Central European History 43. 2010, pp. 301–326. Hans Jonas, The Imperative of Responsibility. In Search of an Ethics for the Technological Age, Chicago 1984, was widely influential for and within the German Green movement.

101 Ronald Inglehart, The Silent Revolution. Changing Values and Political Styles among Western Publics, Princeton 1977. See the contextual analysis by David Kuchenbuch, "Eine Welt." Globales Interdependenzbewusstsein und die Moralisierung des Alltags in den 1970er und 1980er Jahren, in: GG 38. 2012, pp. 158–184.

102 Lisa Herzog, The Epistemic Division of Labor in Markets. Hayek, Global Trade, and the Preconditions of Morally Responsible Agency (paper presented at the Berlin-Berkeley workshop on Moral Economies, 20.2.2018); see also her Reclaiming the System. Moral Responsibility, Divided Labour, and the Role of Organizations in Society, Oxford 2018, esp. ch. 2: "Moral Responsibility, Socially Embedded," pp. 23–45, and ch. 3: "Moral Norms in Social Contexts," pp. 46–59.

improvement of moral practices in economic matters also relied on the personal commitment of both consumers and producers.[103]

Yet these definitions of moral responsibility are by no means universally accepted. They bear the traces of a specific moral discourse as it developed in European and North American societies at a specific point in time. Even Europeans, however, do not always act as the discourse wants them to act. Corruption proliferates not only in African, Asian, or South and Central American countries, but also in Western Europe and the United States, although to a far lesser degree.[104] Here, respectable citizens engage in all kinds of morally dubious and unfair economic practices, from fare dodging and not paying TV license fees to requesting "cash in hand" in order to avoid taxes. Selling exam essays has become a million-pound business in Britain and other countries, thus knowingly inviting buyers to cheat and commit fraud.[105]

Critical voices have long since pointed out that such self-centered and profit-seeking behavior is an integral and necessary part of the modern market economy. The more this economy extends into other realms of everyday life and seeps through love relations, education, or spirituality, the more its principles and values abound and reign.[106] At the same time, selfish market behavior got historically restrained through moral notions of social responsibility, decency, fairness, justice, and solidarity. Over the last two hundred years, these notions have shifted in scope and intensity. Some economic activities, like lending and borrowing, have become thoroughly demoralized, with the help of skillfully launched media campaigns and highly attractive incentives. Others, like disregarding safety standards in production, trading "toxic" goods or evading taxes, have undergone a process of increased moralization. While this has only had a limited impact on changing consumer behavior and everyday crime, it has turned attention toward big businesses and corporate crime. Moralizing arguments have also touched upon the problem of opportunity structures that allowed illegal and unfair practices to flourish.

As a result of such moralization, business ethics emerged as a growing field of academic and practical knowledge. As mentioned earlier, moral standards of doing business had been negotiated since early modern times, with a marked increase

103 Ead., Who Should Prevent Sweatshops? Duties, Excuses, and the Division of Moral Labour in the Global Economy, in: Hans-Christoph Schmidt am Busch (ed.), Die Philosophie des Marktes. The Philosophy of the Market, Hamburg 2016, pp. 255–277.

104 Corruption Perceptions Index 2017, https://www.transparency.org/news/feature/corruption_perceptions_index_2017.

105 Susanne Karstedt and Stephen Farrall, The Moral Economy of Everyday Crime. Markets, Consumers and Citizens, in: British Journal of Criminology 46. 2006, pp. 1011–1036.

106 For capitalist markets' tendency to determine "the life of the body social," see Karl Polanyi, Our Obsolete Market Mentality. Civilization Must Find a New Thought Pattern, in: Commentary 3. 1947, pp. 109–117, as well as Eva Illouz, Consuming the Romantic Utopia. Love and the Cultural Contradictions of Capitalism, Berkeley 1997; ead., Cold Intimacies. The Making of Emotional Capitalism, Cambridge 2007.

around 1900.[107] Since the 1970s, business ethics has been firmly established as an academic discipline, with prestigious journals and a mass of influential publications.[108] This testifies and adds to the growing interest of corporations to publicly affirm their responsibility to clients and employees, but also to society as a whole. Codes of ethical conduct usually address issues like fairness and honesty, fraud and harassment, environmental protection and sustainability. Starting in the 1990s, many corporations have appointed ethics and compliance officers, often as a reaction to widely publicized scandals that caused public indignation and threatened to invite political-legal interventions. Their effectiveness, however, has been called into question. Faced with solid resistance from powerful CEOs such officers have had very little power to uphold and implement a company's code of conduct and push its "commitment to working ethically and with integrity," as the case of Volkswagen demonstrated in 2015.[109]

These failures not only provoked moral outrage but also drew attention to the complicity of various interest groups, from engineers and CEOs to shareholders and consumers. Seeking the moral high ground proved to be difficult in a society whose wealth depended, to a large extent, on the economic performance of the car industry. The fact that sales figures did not plummet after the "Dieselgate" scandal also plays into the hands of those who doubt that moral considerations have an impact on marketplace behavior.

Yet the jury is still out on moral economies. Discarding moral arguments as mere alibis or window dressing does not account for their ongoing presence and ubiquity. Seen in a historical perspective, those arguments have been exchanged between proponents and opponents of capitalism. They have been used to critically confront the existing, allegedly immoral or moral-free economy with the vision of a morally approvable economic system that embraces principles of fairness and justice, both locally and globally. At the same time they have insisted that even the capitalist economy in its various shapes adheres to moral norms upholding the well-being or, formerly, happiness of nations and citizens, potentially all around the globe. By invoking moral principles and standards, both sides helped to keep those principles alive. Enshrined in legal norms and social

---

107 See Biggeleben, "Bollwerk," pp. 256 ff. on the introduction of honor courts among merchants and traders; Gabriel Abend, The Moral Background. An Inquiry into the History of Business Ethics, Princeton 2014, on U. S. Chambers of Commerce and business schools founded since the 1880s. See, from a philosophical point of view, Jeffrey Moriarty, Business Ethics, in: Zalta, Stanford Encyclopedia of Philosophy, https://plato.stanford.edu/archives/fall2017/entries/ethics-business/.

108 The Journal of Business Ethics was founded in 1982, Business Ethics Quarterly in 1991. Books on Business Ethics abound and usually see multiple editions. They are mostly written by U. S. authors but translated into many languages, increasingly Asian. See, for example, Richard T. DeGeorge's "Business Ethics" from 2005 that is currently in its 7th edition and available, among others, in Chinese, Japanese, and Russian.

109 Anon., VW Risks New Pay Row as Compliance Chief Lands EUR 10m Payoff, https://www.theguardian.com/business/2017/jan/31/volkswagen-head-of-legal-affairs-christine-hohmann-dennhardt-10m-pay-off.

institutions, they continue to shape people's expectations, desires, and behavior. Unearthing their complexity and hybridity over time is a major task for historians who, along with social scientists in anthropology, sociology, and economics, aim to debunk the self-fabricated myth of capitalism's moral-free stance. This myth is not only sustained, to this very day, by libertarian economists. It also resonates in current critics' quest for a new, truly moral economy—which is arguably not so new after all.

Laurence Fontaine

Reconsidering the Moral Economy in France at the End of the Eighteenth Century[*]

Abstract: The article discusses the concept of moral economy coined by E. P. Thompson, which places moral excellence at the heart of the legitimation to govern, through the study of charity, which dominated the relation between privileged groups and the common people, legitimizing the power of the former. The article analyzes essays written in 1777 "on the means of eradicating mendicancy by making the beggars useful to the state without making them unhappy." The debates reflected in these essays allow us to inscribe E. P. Thompson's thesis in the greater intellectual and political context of religion, human rights, Enlightenment, and the aspiration of a part of the population to political equality.

E. P. Thompson's essay "The Moral Economy of the English Crowd in the Eighteenth Century" was a major influence on historians of revolts and of the working class, who generally agreed with him that the advent of capitalism spelled the end of a moral economy and that the latter would not have survived anywhere, but among the people who put it into practice in their revolts for centuries.[1] In this essay, the Marxist historian establishes the domination of the working-class avant-garde by attributing to the proletariat the moral virtue at the heart of the legitimation to govern, held by the leading classes of the Old Regime. With this recognition he gives the proletariat the right to illuminate and govern society. His analysis, which stresses the fundamental role moral issues play in legitimizing power, poses the question of whether attributing moral virtues to one particular group might be a major instrument for legitimizing its domination over other social groups.

After showing that in early modern age, moral excellence underlay the domination of the first two orders of the Old Regime society, I will focus my analysis on one virtue, charity, which was an imperative obligation for the first two orders and the major economic instrument in the fight against poverty. Certainly, in the Old Regime, the moral excellence of the leading groups touched on all domains of social life, whereas for E. P. Thompson, it confines itself to the economy—hardly a surprising choice, since in Marxist philosophy, the economy determines all other

---

[*] Translated from the French by Dr. Naomi Shulman.

[1] Edward Palmer Thompson, The Moral Economy of the English Crowd in the Eighteenth Century, in: Past & Present 1971, no. 50, pp. 76–136.

aspects of society. Choosing to analyze charity therefore allows for an introduction of the subject while also discussing a virtue that concerns the economy.

To understand the debates around this fundamental value of the society of orders, I will analyze an exceptional source, the essays written in 1777 for a contest by the Academy of Châlons-sur-Marne, concentrating on the way in which the authors intended to finance their projects.[2] This period is especially interesting, because the state was unable to conquer poverty and with it begging and vagrancy, which made the roads unsafe, mobilized rural areas, and attracted the uprooted to the cities, and because the country was also struggling with the new values of liberty and equality, which called into question the society of orders. The debates that are reflected in these essays thus allow us to inscribe E. P. Thompson's thesis in the greater intellectual and political context of religion, human rights, Enlightenment, and the aspiration of a part of the population to political equality.

These analyses may therefore help to clarify why a society that was constructed based on the place of individuals in the process of production needed to establish the social hierarchies that it intended to institute initially in the same way as societies that based them on birthright. Put another way, this essay asks whether the analyses in terms of morality are characteristic of societies founded on predefined hierarchies, be it by blood as in aristocratic society, the caste as in Indian society, or politics as in societies based on a sole party. If I do not add capitalism to this list, it is not because it is morally neutral, which it is not, but because, contrary to other political economies, wealth alone justifies social hierarchies, and the richest do not need to legitimize their domination with a collection of moral qualities that only they possess. Of course, capitalism—like all political economies—engenders particular moral behaviors and specific presentations of the self.[3]

I. Foundations of the Society of Orders

The king, the nobility, and the clergy received their power from God, and the priests formed the first order of society. Traditionally, there was a division between the first two orders: the state performed sovereign tasks (the defense of the territory, internal security, and justice), and all the orders of society had to contribute to this. The church did so with donations, the aristocrats with military service, and the commoners with taxes. The church handled societal questions: in addition to counting the souls from birth to death, it ensured education and the conduct of residents throughout the cycle of life. It organized social rituals and

2 On the role of contests in the Republic of Letters, see Jeremy L. Caradonna, Prendre part au siècle des Lumières. Le concours académique et la culture intellectuelle au XVIIIe siècle, in: Annales HSS 64. 2009, pp. 633–662.

3 Laurence Fontaine, The Moral Economy. Poverty, Credit, and Trust in Early Modern Europe [French original 2008], New York 2014, pp. 316 f.

administered the sacraments, including that of penitence, which followed confession. Thus, it handled health, education, and poverty. It was funded through donations and the legacies of the rich, the tithe on all products of the land, and regular collections for a number of different reasons.

In the Old Regime society, the supremacy of the first two orders was based on their moral excellence, which had to govern all aspects of their behavior. However, charity had a unique position: since the early Middle Ages, it had structured the feudal social order. During this era, a powerful mechanism of land-grabbing drove free men of humble origins to the poorest strata of society. In addition to what one calls the structural poor (the elderly, the sick, the infirm, the children, for they did not have—or no longer had—the strength to work), the texts condemned the construction of large properties, which impoverished numerous landowners, making them likely to need the aid of the powerful one day, in exchange for the sale of their real estate. In this way, the humble became coupled with the powerful, the *paupers* with the *potent*.[4] Hence, the church interfered in this couple by opposing both wealth—which leads to sin, according to the teachings of the scriptures—and poverty, given that material degradation was too often the prelude to moral degradation. Thus, the church promoted the construction of a durable relation between the rich and the poor: the former engaging in charity to be pardoned of their crimes and sins and the latter expressing their gratitude in their prayers and with their submission. To impose charity on the rich, the church developed a pedagogy of fear of the hereafter. It exerted pressure on the sovereigns to sensitize them to poverty, and it instituted tariffed penance, compelling the laity to assist the poor in concrete ways after their confession.[5] Consequently, charity was at the heart of secular power such as God instituted it: it allowed for the salvation of the rich and, with the gratitude of the poor who received it, legitimized the power of the donor.

For the nobility of the sixteenth and seventeenth centuries, *nobilitas est virtus*, and this adage was to be taken seriously. One cannot emphasize the obsessive nature of this adage enough, writes Arlette Jouanna, because "true nobility" was neither power nor property nor force of arms, but an internal quality, a human excellence that deserved to be placed at the forefront.[6] Don Luis' reply to his son Don Juan perfectly expresses this moral supremacy that legitimized the nobility:

Are you not ashamed, sir? Ashamed to still bear it? What have you ever done to earn the right to be called a gentleman? Did you think it was simply a matter of one's birth? Did it never occur to you it might concern the manner of one's life? No sir; rank is nothing, without at least decency. A man has no right to claim his family's privileges unless he

4 Régine Le Jan-Hennebicque, "Pauperes" et "potentes" dans l'Occident carolingien aux IXe et Xe siècles, in: Revue du Nord 50. 1968, no. 197, pp. 169–187.

5 Jean-Pierre Devroey, Puissants et miserable. Système social et monde paysan dans l'Europe des Francs, VIe–IXe siècles, Bruxelles 2006, pp. 317–351.

6 Arlette Jouanna, Le devoir de révolte. La noblesse française et la gestation de l'État moderne, 1559–1661, Paris 1989, p. 40.

shares its values! [...] I tell you, a man who lives as you do is no gentleman, sir; that distinction is a reward, not a right; that a good name counts for nothing, without a good life lived [...].[7]

In this speech, Don Luis explains to his depraved son that nobility is first and foremost a question of moral virtue. Don Luis associates it with friendship and credit, and his analysis recovers the definition of the word credit as it appears in the dictionaries of the period. Furetière's dictionary gives three meanings. The first is: "Faith, an esteem that one earns in public with one's virtue, probity, good will, and merit [...]." The second: "Credit also refers to the power, the authority, the riches that one acquires by means of the reputation that one has earned. That Minister has acquired great *credit* at the court where the mind of the Prince is concerned." And the third: "Credit is used more ordinarily in commerce to refer to that mutual loan comprised of money and merchandise, on the reputation of the probity and solvency of a trader [...]."[8] Thus, before referring to a mutual loan between traders, the word signified first moral excellence and then the political and financial power that was its reward.

In the eighteenth century, the moral foundations of the domination of the privileged orders and the supremacy of the French monarchy were called into question more and more,[9] and despite the general increase of the population's wealth, food crises had not disappeared, like the one called "the Flour War," which broke out in 1775 and resulted in riots and pillaging.

II. The Essay Contest of Châlons of 1777

It is in this context that two years later, in 1777, the newly created Academy of Châlons-sur-Marne[10] introduced a very topical subject for its first contest, since it asked for reflections "on the means of eradicating mendicancy by making the beggars useful to the state without making them unhappy." This project, initiated by Gaspard Louis Rouillé d'Orfeuil, the intendant of Champagne, reflected the progressive transformation of the academic contest since the second quarter of the eighteenth century into a space of critical exchanges and sometimes into the breeding grounds conducive to supplying the general controllers and the intendants with ideas, who, for lack of a sufficient number of experts in the state apparatus, appealed to civil society through the academies to sustain their action. In fact, the abbot Leclerc de Montlinot, who came in second in 1777 in Châlons

---

7 Molière, Don Juan, trans. Neil Bartlett, London 2004, p. 62 (act IV, scene 4).
8 Antoine Furetière, Dictionnaire universel, Rotterdam 1690, vol. 1, art. "Credit" (no pagination).
9 Jeffrey W. Merrick, The Desacralization of the French Monarchy in the Eighteenth Century, Baton-Rouge 1990.
10 Daniel Roche, La diffusion des lumières. Un exemple: l'Académie de Châlons-sur-Marne, in: Annales ESC 19. 1964, pp. 887–922.

and first in 1779 in the contest on mendicancy of the Agricultural Society of Soissons, was hired by the intendant of Soissons to reform the local depository before being appointed to the National Assembly's Committee of Mendicancy.[11]

The contest was enormously successful, since some 125 essays were submitted, the following prize competitions attracting at best a few dozen responses. Aristocrats, clerics, but also numerous members of the legal professions, doctors, intellectuals, and merchants put pen to paper, as well as a certain number of authors who preferred to remain anonymous. Of the 85 identified participants, some twenty were Parisians, 19 from Champagne, 16 from the Midi south of the Bordeaux-Marseille axis, and 12 from Northern and Central France. Texts also arrived from Bruges, Antwerp, Brussels, Courtrai, and the Hague, as well as Madrid, Trieste, and Saint Petersburg.

A few essays reflected on the realities of the life of the working classes, on the constant efforts that each person made in order to avoid poverty. They failed to recognize that once fallen into poverty, these men and women depended on vertical and horizontal forms of solidarity, which they managed to mobilize hoping to stay in their village.[12] Nevertheless, some essays, among them that of Monsieur de Saint Félix, expressed awareness that through no fault of their own, the poor became "the refuse of misfortune and the hospitals. Without parents, without support, without asylum, [they] no longer have any hope except for the commiseration of the public."[13] A former controller of the house of Madame la Dauphine went into detail: "let us suppose that the unfortunate person makes 15 sols per day over the course of the entire year, is there enough to buy food for him, his wife, and his children?" Not to mention the problem of bad weather and of holiday expenditures, "if he is indisposed, then an entire family is reduced to begging." The taxes were added to these budgets without any room for maneuver: "he pays all kinds of taxes, *tailles*, the *vingtième*, capitation, industry, relief, salt tax, fodder, winter quarters, militia, coast guards, tools, chores, military lodgings, barracks, harbormasters, release fees, six *deniers* for *livres* allocated to the collector of the *tailles*, fees on meat, tobacco, and on all beverages, occupations that involve preventing smuggling, which are a very onerous tax for the countryside." They and their wives and children often ended up as beggars (no. 43).

Yet similarly to a number of philosophers,[14] of those who entered the contest, almost none cared about the social mechanism at work in these paths, instead condemning individuals' moral depravity, which impelled them to liberate them-

11 Caradonna, Prendre part, pp. 639–644.

12 Jean-Pierre Gutton, La société et les pauvres en Europe (XVIe–XVIIIe siècles), Paris 1974; Michel Mollat, Les Pauvres au Moyen Age, Paris 1978; Fontaine, Moral Economy, ch. 1: "Poverty, Credit, and Social Networks," pp. 15–40.

13 Archives départmentales de la Marne, IJ38–41, no. 112. Hereafter, only the number of the essay will be given.

14 Laurence Fontaine, Pauvreté, in: Bronislaw Baczko et al. (eds.), Dictionnaire critique de l'utopie au temps des Lumières, Chêne-Bourg 2016, pp. 929–949.

selves from social ties. The financing of these projects, which oscillated between confinement and a return to the village under the supervision of a charitable agency, is therefore a good vantage point to take up the moral economy of poverty and the battle the contemporaries waged around it.

III. Preserving the Freedom of Charity

To finance their projects, the authors proposed multiple solutions ranging from charity to taxation. Yet charity and taxes were two radically opposed modes of financing, since charity was a donation made freely at the moment chosen by the donor and to the person or the intermediary of his choice, while taxes were a compulsory levy, deducted on dates fixed by the authorities and whose use was not observable. Thus, charity manifested itself in the gift, which was the economic relation *par excellence* of the aristocracy, the only one capable of demonstrating the virtue and the superiority of the donor.[15] Whatever the nature of the projects, charity remained the dominant mode of financing. Many recalled that it was the foundation of society and religion, because the ties that it created established the harmony of society: "the creator wanted man to aid his fellow man in order to test the faithfulness of the one in his distribution and the patience of the other in his need; he interweaves the rich and the poor, if one may put it that way, [...] so that in helping one another with mutual services, they can be sanctified, the ones through honest generosity, the others through humble appreciation" (nos. 18, 90). An oratorian put charity at the heart of the "social pact," in which "every individual has tacitly made a compromise with society approximately in these terms: if you will take me under your wing, I will contribute to your glory; I will collaborate in your happiness, provided that you also attend to mine: I will aid you with my strength and you will aid my weakness." Religion reinforced the social pact, tightening "those first ties that sociability and nature have formed between human beings, in commanding us to love our neighbor as we love ourselves" (no. 113). The imbrication of the social pact and of religion was thus complete: "it is proven that in the matter of religion, giving alms is at least as useful to the rich person who gives them as it is to the poor person who receives them" (nos. 88, 90, 89).

For certain authors, the bond of charity was so internalized that it prevented renouncing mendicancy, as the competition demanded it. One notary refused to eradicate mendicancy entirely, "which would be contrary to what the Gospel heralded" (no. 30). One could suggest improvements, but "be that as it may, mendicancy is not a crime. It has been subjected to tragic abuses; in abolishing these, I extract all that is odious in it! [and] nothing will remain except what we will require to exercise this Christian virtue" (no. 55). In the name of morality, the inhabitant of Beaune who wrote these words declared loud and clear that

---

15 Fontaine, Moral Economy, pp. 217–235 and pp. 253–258.

nothing had changed. He took issue as much with incarceration as with charity that was channeled into charity offices as a remedy to the shame of beggars forced to arouse the pity of potential donors. Beginning with the verses of Mark (16 v. 7) For ye have the poor with you always, and whensoever ye will ye may do them good, he added that all the pages of the Holy Scripture exhort us to give alms. He attacked the horrible rich people and the voluptuous who were behind these policies as well as the means of raising money: "the author of the journal of Bouillon reports that in Montauban, they had the idea to host dances, of which the profit would have to be given to the charity bureau." This scandalized him. Therefore, he proposed to revive the relation of charity and to anchor it in the knowledge of one another, forbidding the poor to beg outside of their parish, except if they had obtained a passport. And he concluded with the same verses from Mark (no. 120). Monsieur de Créquy, a descendant of an illustrious family of old nobility, who wrote anonymously, but whose name the contest papers give, took up the old tradition of the king and of the Grandees, which required a charitable gift for every favor granted. In this way, everything that any person undertook, family ceremonies as well as commercial transactions, had to be "consecrated by alms": he revived the old "denier for God" that sealed exchanges (no. 31).

IV. The Subversion of the Values of Charity

Yet having just stated the social harmony that charity offered, the authors began to lament, observing that bad behavior, on the part both of the beggars and of the benefactors, had destroyed it. The donors forgot that charity "must be given with patience, with kindness; [...] must be free of jealousy, pride, ambition, malice, irate slander, injustice." They had to refuse the secret satisfaction that resulted from the recipient's obligation "to acknowledge our superiority. Thus one gives less to satisfy the duties of charity than to make dependence felt..." What is more, the donors had to be wary of their antipathies, because "the real merit of charity consists in offering relief to one's neighbor for his own sake, without expecting anything in return" (nos. 18, 54). In this way, they took up the warnings of the theologians and the preachers again, who, drawing on the famous verses of the Sermon on the Mount, ceaselessly condemned the hypocrisy of using almsgiving for the purposes of personal glorification.[16] Worse than bad charity was the refusal to give of "cruel and barbarous men, who have multiplied inordinately, [and who] refuse their neighbor the necessary aid [...] from this, the race of beggars proliferates" (no. 108). In fact, the aristocracy was renewed by the entry of merchants in the seventeenth and eighteenth centuries, resulting in a modification of

---

16 Jean Starobinski, Don fastueux et don pervers. Commentaire historique d'une Rêverie de Rousseau, in: Annales ESC 41. 1986, pp. 7–26, here p. 11.

52   Laurence Fontaine

values and a decrease in generosity compared with earlier eras and with families of old nobility.[17]

The beggar was just as perverted: charity had made him lazy, and "the abundant gifts bequeathed to the poor are absorbed as pure waste by mendicancy, [...] [which], like the miser, wants more the more one gives" (nos. 92, 81, 113, 60). This continually encountered leitmotif led sometimes to debauchery and sometimes to avarice. The first prize went to the able-bodied beggars, who lived better than the working poor by "using alms for roguishness and debauchery" or by "accumulating them with sordid greed" (no. 114). He recalled the distinction between poverty and mendicancy, the former being a social phenomenon that could not be prevented, while the latter was a vice of the individual that had to be eradicated, because it disrupted the link between the poor and the rich: if "the beggars suffer from their own indigence," the rich suffer "from importunity, idleness, insolence, and sometimes from the roguishness of several beggars." Thus, this meant helping the poor so that the rich were not inconvenienced (no. 57) and the poor were not treated contemptuously in return. And shame paired easily with debauchery, because "the profession of the beggar has its charms." It was easy money, since "what one gathers effortlessly disappears quickly: what one gains with difficulty also spends itself." There were recurring descriptions of the lust of these gangs. An abbot from Champagne bemoaned that everything had been reduced to a cold selfishness and to the beggar who abused the commiseration of the compassionate citizen to the detriment of "the indigent who is only unhappy without being guilty" (no. 23).

A merchant exposed the consequences of subverting this relation, which had become a reciprocal hard-heartedness: "the wealthy person who too often does not indulge the importunity of the poor man, except to get rid of him with the help of the smallest coin, will nevertheless believe himself to be even with this beggar as a fellow man, a Christian, and a citizen, and the pauper, who in the depths of his being preserves the imprint of these august titles, not to read his duties there, but to return ceaselessly to the crushing realization of the affluence of the rich [...], will develop as a result a secret resentment in the depths of his soul, [...] an implacable hatred against an adversary whom he regards as the creator of all his misfortunes. [...] Thus, one must continually work to reunite the hearts divided between the rich and the poor." It was the task of religion and the wise monarch to do so (nos. 111, 122).

17 Guy Chaussinand-Nogaret, The French Nobility in the Eighteenth Century. From Feudalism to Enlightenment, trans. William Doyle, Cambridge 1985, pp. 34f.; Kathryn Norberg, Rich and Poor in Grenoble, 1600–1814, Berkeley 1985, p. 123 and p. 152.

V. Mediating the Personal Bond at the Heart of Charity

These analyses pushed the authors to undo the personal link that was central to charity in favor of intermediaries, who were charged with receiving the alms and putting them in a common repository. The first approach to breaking this link was repressive: to punish those who ask and those who give. The argument of repression relied on those countries—such as the Netherlands and the Swiss cantons—which had successfully prohibited alms because of their perverse effect of multiplying the number of beggars instead of reducing it, an effect that many authors condemned.[18] If the Swiss cantons had chosen to impose a modest fine on the donor, followed by prison in the case of recurrence, some people demanded a more exemplary severity, combining straightjacket, whip, prison, and arbitrary fines depending on the state and the quality of the donor (nos. 37, 56, 101). An oratorian of the Academy of Rouen wanted to spread the fine of two *Louis d'or* (gold coins), imposing it on those who gave alms and on those who received them. It would be divided between the informer or the one who made the arrests and the poor of the parish who did not beg. Likewise, monasteries that distributed food at their doors would also be fined: "instead of feeding unuseful mouths every day with the scraps from your refectory, reduce the surplus of your table: do the households in the families get leftovers?" He justified his severity with the fact that multiple royal rulings of the last 150 years had not been applied, among them the one of 5 March 1626, which forbade giving alms in public and housing vagrants under penalty of 200 *livres* of fines (no. 113).[19] As far as beggars were concerned, they would be marked with an M on the arm, wear the sign "beggar" on the forehead, and be taken to a house of corrections for one year for the first infraction. "The recurrence will be punished with the whip, the pillory, and exportation to the island of Corsica to be employed there to clear the lands for the profit of the state or the hospitals. These exported people will receive the same treatment and serve the same purpose in Corsica as our negroes bound to particular residences in America." The female beggars would suffer life-long imprisonment in *maisons de force*. For this purpose, the oratorian intended to use certain nunneries, where they would do chores in proportion to their sex and physical strength. But he added that one could grant liberty to the most industrious, "with the wise precaution of giving them, at the time of their release,

18 Jean Starobinski demonstrates how men of letters have dealt with this theme of the perverted gift from Antiquity to Antonin Artaud, and Albert O. Hirschman has shown its political recurrence in relation to social programs from the French Revolution to the twentieth century. Starobinski, Don fastueux et don pervers; Albert O. Hirschman, The Rhetoric of Reaction. Perversity, Futility, Jeopardy, Cambridge, MA 1991.

19 On royal politics, see Vincent Denis, Une histoire de l'identité. France, 1715–1815, Seyssel 2008; Marie-Claude Blanc-Chaléard et al., Police et migrants. France, 1667–1939, Rennes 2001; Daniel Roche (ed.), La ville promise. Mobilité and accueil à Paris, fin XVIIe–début XIXe siècle, Paris 2000.

the advance of primary materials, to enable them to make their living from now on with their work" (nos. 113, 112).

Responding to this policy, the abbot Montlinot argued that even if a fine had been instituted in some countries for those caught engaging in charity, the measure could not be executed: one would need too many spies and archers "to punish two culprits that the angels would not dare to judge" (no. 66).

The justification for breaking the personal bond of charity was to deny alms the quality of charity. The coins that wealthy people gave in front of their door were not alms, because they were nothing but a way of getting rid of the bothersome pauper: "more generosity is necessary to do good," an attitude that justified always giving the offerings to the same person, putting them in the collection boxes and no longer dispensing them at the doors of houses (no. 32). The example of Holland allowed distinguishing between charity and almsgiving, to praise the former and reject the latter: "In Holland, there are no beggars and not a single house of charity: if someone is in need, he receives help, but he is justly arrested if he is nothing but a vagabond and lazy. [...] I revolt against the manner of giving alms and not charity, which constitutes the essence of Evangelical morals" (nos. 66, 92).

With the distinction between alms and charity, which attacked the founding personal bonds of the society of orders, the religious injunction was replaced by political analysis. Citing Montesquieu, Mirabeau, de Forbonnais, and the *Journal of Verdun*, a nobleman spoke out against the project proposed by several good citizens to eradicate mendicancy by assisting the beggars' return to their country to work with a general distribution of alms to all the priests, who would administer them: this treatment would only have a temporary impact, and if it worked, one would achieve the opposite effect, since "far from obliterating mendicancy and idleness, the hospitals and the alms would never do anything but support, nourish, and accredit them" (no. 112). He concluded that above all, one had to force beggars to return to work. Voltaire was another reference, whom the master of arts and of the boarding school of Bayonne paraphrased in denouncing mendicancy as "a vermin that attaches itself to wealth."[20] The abbot Montlinot opposed the political to the religious: "If I had the mission of the Christian orator, I would content myself with crying, <u>Wealthy, give alms!</u> Without burdening myself with the manner in which the bread of the alms would be distributed—but this is not my task—it is from the political side alone that I must consider the question that occupies me by proving that alms, which do not recompense work, support mendicancy, harm poor households and make a lucrative profession of the most menial trade, the one most contrary to the common good." It is very hard to refuse the call of the pauper, because it is difficult to "reject this ever so natural sentiment, which we have in common with the animals and which the lack of particular words forces us to call compassion as well [...] In this way, we are guilty

20 No. 118, which cites Voltaire.

of wronging society when we give alms to the beggar who scoffs at our pity, and we are guilty of wronging humanity when we refuse the pauper the compassion that he may deserve."[21]

VI. Rationalizing Alms

Yet the two extremes of the spectrum of opinions, the stirring plea for freely chosen alms and the social bond that they created, which recalled the foundations of feudal society, and the differentiation between charity and alms, with the radical condemnation of the latter, were positions rarely adopted in the essays. For the most part, the essays favored freely chosen alms, once the personal bond between the one who gave and the one who received had been severed. There were three reasons for this: free alms were at the heart of the social contract; they were accepted by everyone, even if some gave little or not at all and others more; and these authors believed that all in all, the alms sufficed to support all the paupers in the hospital or in town, in winter, when there was no work—one simply had to administer them differently (nos. 88, 61, 15, 64, 114). The basis of doing so was to rationalize and centralize the alms and establish a "charity fund," a "common purse." One would deposit there all charitable deeds, the revenues from the various hospitals in town, recent and former foundations and donations, the profit from the traditions of alms given during family ceremonies, the alms from the chapters, and the product of collections that took place in the town with varying frequency. Some added to this the funds intended for the preachers, but also the returns of the *taille*, the royal and seigniorial fines, and a portion of the public collections for future members of a religious order (nos. 50, 114). Collections in churches, which "interrupt the Divine Office and disturb the attention of the congregation," would have to be abolished and money should be collected in inns to reach traveling strangers (nos. 101, 111 and 122, 91, 109, 23, 3). An abbot from Champagne reminds us that the persons most distinguished by their work, their riches, or their birth usually took this on and that these rich and charitable people gave away a tenth or perhaps a fifteenth of their income every year (no. 23). The scale of this fund was in accordance with the magnitude of the projects, which might be local, regional, or national.

But it was not only for the love of God that the essays proposed to leave it at charity. Rather, it was equally due to the hatred of the personal taxes, the *impôts*,[22] because these deductions, which rested on individual persons, went against the values of feudal society. Certain essays explicitly reminded us that taxes were

21 No. 66, which paraphrases Voltaire's article "Beggars [Gueux]" in his Dictionnaire philosophique, published in Geneva in 1764.

22 *Impôts* are those taxes that are levies on persons, and in principle, taxes are deductions on objects, unless it is a matter of personal taxes.

"always a revolting proposition" (nos. 55, 46), like the *taxes* when they rested on individuals, because they destroyed the freedom of giving, which was also a moral discipline, as the doctor who received the first prize emphasized: "the contribution to alms is freely chosen in our plan; thus, apart from granting those persons who give alms all the credit for charity, it is not odious like extortion or the fear that enslaves different peoples through taxes or personal contributions" (no. 114). The church had already subverted charity by overburdening people with collections, which were ultimately taxes, even if they were voluntary (nos. 108, 9). At most, as one merchant wrote, one could ask everyone to make a plan of what they had to give every year, like in Montluçon, where this practice prevailed, and where the intendant completed the takings with a sum that varied between 1000 and 600 *livres*, depending on the year (no. 111).

All the essays denounced taxes on the grounds that they ruined the peasants, that the state misappropriated them, and that the detested financiers and private traders, the *traitants*, raised them for their own profit. Some nevertheless admitted their embarrassment, like the former controller of the house of Madame la Dauphine, who regretted that the broad consensus of his contemporaries to refuse taxes would prevent applying the project of the royal tithe of the Marshall of Vauban,[23] "a system so wise and so little appreciated" that after formulating it, he abandoned it for the benefit of freely chosen, traditional charity (no. 43). Others also described a tax plan before giving it up (nos. 21, 96, 89).

So for want of acceptable alternatives to freely chosen charity, the authors worked to revive it. They counted on the eloquence of the hallowed speakers (nos. illegible, 114, 113, 75). They also remembered to flatter the vanity of the benefactors by "printing every year [...] the names of the subscribers and the amount of their subscriptions." Moreover, they proposed to have them preside over the administration according to their rank of benevolence and, in case of equality, according to their affluence or their dignity (unnumbered essay), and to reward the notables with honors, as a Benedictine monk described it: "In the towns, the notables will be decorated with a purple sash as long and broad as the red or blue sashes and worn in the same way but only on the jacket. For the notables of the countryside, there will be a special bench in every church of every parish, which will be reserved to them alone and placed by the nave near the choir. There, they will have all the honors of the holy water and incense after the Lord and the following rank in the processions" (no. 69).

Material dividends could be added to the honors conferred by payments in symbolic currency, since one had to offer privileges to attract people "properly," as an anonymous author put it (no. 72). But what would the rewards be and at what rate would they be granted? Another anonymous author proposed municipal places, the ability to exempt a son from the militia, or the family from housing

---

23 Vauban, Projet d'une dixme royale (1707), who proposed dividing the French into ten classes and subjecting them to a tax that started at a twentieth of the revenues and ended at a tenth.

soldiers or guardianship. In addition, the most charitable, such as the notables of the countryside, would be exempt from tax collection and *corvée* (nos. 95, 55). A third anonymous author, who suggested founding an order of knights of charity to control the police and take care of the poor, demanded that in exchange for their unpaid engagement, the Prince would lavish the order with the finest privileges of honor and nobility and even elevate it above the order of the knights of Malta (no. 108). Even the Pope had to contribute: he would grant indulgences to those giving two percent or one-fiftieth of their income to the hospitals, after the expenditures necessary to their state and condition. According to the amount given, the indulgences would be proportionate to one-tenth, -twentieth, -thirtieth, and -fortieth of their income, and bequests of land or of buildings to the hospital would be handled in the same way.

To guard against embezzlement, another great preoccupation, practically all the authors demanded that the alms be put into "cases," "chests," "moneyboxes closed with good padlocks, of which the keys will be in the hands of the principal tax collectors, the *receveurs*" (nos. 12, 53, 49, 65, 70, 60). The collectors would be numerous, well-chosen from among "the richest, the wisest, and the most pious that can be found." They would always go two by two, accompanied by the priest or a clergyman (nos. 53, 49, 10bis). The donations would be spelled out in a "register," a "white notebook" carried by those making the collection (nos. 12, 26, 56, 91, 10bis), and each notebook would be bound, the pages numbered, and all would be initialed by the president of the town council. As far as the king was concerned, he could become involved by promulgating an edict "that stipulates that those alms will not be used for anything but the care of his subjects in need of permanent and daily aid" (no. 10bis).

VII. Imposing Constraints on Freely Determined Alms

The first reason that legitimized curbing the liberty of the donor was moral fault: donors had become miserly. Yet avarice was one of the seven deadly sins. Therefore, it was in the name of the Lord that one punished the miserly by imposing "contributions and taxes which avaricious spirits and pitiless hearts have made necessary" (no. 23). The lords were first in line, because charity established their dominant status: if they no longer played their charitable role, it was legitimate to tax them (no. 110). Some excluded from this punishment the high nobility of princes and dukes and the aristocracy that had demonstrated its generosity and those who "prove themselves to be the fathers of the poor through their voluntary and abundant contributions" (no. 11).

The second reason was vanity. Like avarice, this vice denatured the disparity of wealth intended by God. It manifested itself in luxury and required punishment. Criticism of luxury came not only from the Enlightenment but also from the humanist ethos of Montaigne and from the spirit of devotion instilled by the

Counter-Reformation (nos. 50, 89).[24] An anonymous author demanded that the government impose a tax "on this class of privileged men," for whom wealth served only to support vanity, while "burdening the people with a new contribution [...] would increase the number of the needy" (no. 98).

The first step consisted in imposing a minimum on freely chosen alms, which preserved the freedom to give the surplus of one's choice, mitigated the punitive character of the constraint, and spared the pride of the wealthy and the aristocrats. Similarly, an anonymous author believed that charity was not enough, and that as a result, all the heads of family of the parish would have to pay a certain sum for one or more terms and the first in advance. The fathers of the poor would lead by example, beginning with the priest. A list of these amounts would be drawn up. Those who failed to appear or did not wish to contribute would be taxed in proportion to the capitation tax at the approximate rate of one or two *sols* per *livre* (according to the needs of the poor) if they paid the capitation tax on the site, except if they were privileged or of privileged rank, in which case they would be taxed proportionately to their established abilities. However, "in order to retain the right to give some hand-outs themselves, be it to the sick, the infirm, or the ashamed poor in particular, but never publicly, [those who are accustomed to giving] could make submissions, which in any case would not be under one or two *sols* per *livre* of the capitation tax" (no. 101). Indeed, it was a matter of punishing the miserly by connecting personal tax, the *impôt*, to the capitation tax, which affected everyone, and by forcing those who managed to evade the latter to pay based on their estimated wealth. They were nevertheless left with an exit if they themselves suggested a contribution, but this could not be less than the established tax. Others explained that the program of taxing the population was fundamentally devised as alms that were "freely chosen, since one could always give more than what is imposed" (no. 71; see also 10bis).

But the chosen vocabulary indicated the writers' embarrassment: they did not speak of tax, that is of an *impôt*, but of "forced contribution" (nos. 67, 70), of "voluntary contribution" (no. 91), of "obligatory donation" (no. 10bis), of "general subscription" (no. 88), of "voluntary dues" (no. 115), and if the unbearable word "tax" was used, it was referred to as "soft tax" (no. 96) or with an oxymoron: "charity tax" (no. 69). Others corrected every use of the word: "this tax, or rather this charity" (no. 54), or never even used the word tax, while the project expected everyone to contribute in proportion to their abilities (no. 6). Ultimately, the word *taxe* seemed a good substitute, an "alms tax" (no. 18) which transferred to individuals a contribution first reserved to objects and to travel.

---

24 Fénelon, Les aventures de Télémaque (1699) analyzed in Jean-Pierre Gross, Progressive Taxation and Social Justice in Eighteenth-Century France, in: Past & Present 1993, no. 140, pp. 79–126, here pp. 88–91; Anon., Luxe, in: Denis Diderot and Jean Le Rond d'Alembert, Encyclopédie, ou Dictionnaire raisonné des sciences, des arts et des métiers, 1751–1772, vol. 9, Paris 1765, pp. 763–771, analyzed in Keith M. Baker, Condorcet. Raison et politique [1975], Paris 1988, pp. 33 f.

Thus, an academician from Pau wished to impose a tax but preserve the spirit of charity, and he constantly hesitated on the manner of proceeding: he demanded that donations be inscribed in a register but added that the one in charge of doing so would give a final report to the assembly, because "all having to be done with the spirit of charity, the nuisances of an account and all that could inspire disgust in those serving as the administrators of public charity will be avoided." But since charity might not suffice, he suggested establishing "a tax on all the inhabitants of the parish, following the example of military practice of withholding four *deniers* per *livre* on the appointments and pensions of the officers and soldiers." He insisted that his proposal did not constitute a tax: "Do not be alarmed, fearful citizens, it is not a royal tax that I propose; it is not even a tax. It is a charity that you owe to your fellow citizens, which each bureau will determine according to the recognized need of the poor of the parish and of which you will be informed. Therefore, one need not fear that this charity will one day be shifted to benefit the state; because for one it would not be fixed and for another it could take place one year and not be imposed another" (no. 54). In addition to constraint, he sought to limit the intrusion of the administration into private affairs, another reason for refusing the tax, whose implementation was experienced as a violation of individual liberty, an inquisitorial and tyrannic act.[25]

These taxes, proposed by those who defended the values of charity, had several shared characteristics in addition to the liberty to give more and so to choose the final amount: they were modest, temporary, the sum was decided each year depending on need, and they were levied locally, to avoid any misappropriation of their function as well as the collection fees claimed by the despised farmers and private traders, the *traitants*. In order for these taxes to remain modest, they were considered a compliment to other sources of revenue, which allowed the amounts to be contained (no. 23; see also nos. 98, 55, 6). A vicar in Nevers proposed a charity tax in the form of a redeemable pension, commensurate with "affluence," which would be abolished after thirty years (no. 115).

VIII. The Paradigm Change of the Men of the Enlightenment: Taxes as a Sign of Equality

Like the supporters of the society of orders, Enlightenment men condemned the arbitrariness, multiplicity, and collection of the taxes of their times. Panckoucke, Diderot's editor, lamented that war and the dissipation of finances had caused taxes to explode "beyond the capacities of the taxpayers," that the taxes were "attached to those who outlined the plans and combinations," turning the private traders into the trustees of the state revenues, of which they received a part as a "price of their greed." They thus drew in all the money of the kingdom, which -

25 Gross, Progressive Taxation.

ceased "to circulate freely in all its parts and to follow the natural inclination of commerce." As a result, the towns most involved in trade and those with the most manufactories became those where poverty made itself felt the most" (no. 44).

These authors defended taxes in the name of equality among citizens, a parity that concerned not only status but that also had to strive to equalize wealth. The doyen of the brewers of Brussels legitimized "forced donations" through equality among men: "Since the poor are our brothers and therefore our equals: let the costs be equal, and let everyone be taxed in proportion to their capacity and income. One day, we will be relieved of this burden with reward." If not, the poor "will remain in the care of the public and profitless" (nos. 53, 121). Like the thinkers of the old order, they condemned luxury as manifesting the arrogance of the privileged, and they believed that only a redistribution of wealth could overcome this.[26] They also developed the argument that taxes cost less than all forms of charity, reversing the usual order that introduced taxes as a compliment to charity, because their modest tax would produce a lot, since everyone would pay it, and, if necessary, charity would be added (nos. 69, 7).

To establish cloth manufactories in the 32 administrative districts of the Kingdom, the anonymous author who offered this suggestion needed nothing but initial funding, since sales should suffice to allow the establishments to run. He spoke of establishing "an alms tax" in each district, on everyone including the gentlemen and the clergy, whom he had counted: "1,777,324 people occupied only with holding their hands up to the sky," while the others fight, work, and plough. He added that "these forms of charity thus given by tax will be much more profitable and worth infinitely more than bad soups and some liards which the members of the clergy distribute, or have distributed, at their doors" (no. 18).

Some noblemen felt that the tax on the privileged was only just, in the name of the long history of the expropriation of the peasants and because the work of the poor had helped the rich to acquire their wealth. The Sir of Renneville thus demanded a tax on "every person, whether clergy or layperson, nobleman or not nobleman, all military forces or regular or secular communities that have houses in the towns or properties in the aforementioned parishes, but excepting the hospitals where hospitality is currently practiced, the priests with a small share of the tithe (the *portion congrue*)," and inhabitants who were recognized as poor. He was inspired by the Parliament of Paris during the fatal winter of 1740 to 1741, when the excessively high price of bread had reduced the poor to dire conditions. The tax demanded would be fair for two reasons: because before their disablement, these paupers had worked for these men, and because the latter had also increased their fortune from the "successive decadence" of the peasants, as the Sir of Renneville explained in his description of the mechanism of the formation of great estates and large farms (no. 58).

26 Cf. John Shovlin, The Political Economy of Virtue. Luxury, Patriotism, and the Origins of the French Revolution, Ithaca 2006.

As in the case of the royal taxes, numerous authors (nos. 6, 115, 53, 121, 18, 58) envisaged proportional taxes, with each person paying a percentage of their riches. But this calculation method weighed more heavily on the working class than on the rich, a fact which some of them did not realize.[27] However, for those who were not afraid of the word, taxes (the *impôt*) had to be progressive and redistribute wealth effectively. The royal tithe of Vauban was based on a progression of the tax, like other unsuccessful attempts that were subsequently devised.[28] In his entry "impôt" in the Encyclopedia, Jaucourt defended it and argued for a geometric progression (two, four, eight, sixteen) on all the elements of the fortune of the rich.[29] This tax was supported by Condorcet during the Revolution, and the poor were exempt from it, because the tax would have reduced their resources to below the threshold of surviving with dignity.[30]

Nearly all the essays declared that the poor must not be made to pay, since this tax was designed above all to punish the miserly, and because charity was a bond that linked the privileged to the poorest. Apart from the noble master of arts of a boarding school (no. 118), who defended Vauban's proposition, the essays did not take the idea of geometric progression up again. The proportionality that resulted in giving greater sums commensurate to wealth was enough for them, and they added taxes on luxuries to punish vanity. A Norman vicar justified redistribution by giving the eminent property of the lands to the state. He assumed that all good government was obligated to try to "make all individuals more or less happy." He granted each person a portion of the property initially and added that it was the responsibility "of a prince attentive to the happiness of his subjects to reestablish order by warding off an inequality that is too great. The simplest, fairest, and most natural way is to force the rich to provide for the needs of their indigent brothers, because those who possess the state funds must and can support the charges of the state alone. I believe this maxim to be incontestable" (no. 62).

Nevertheless, utility was the first angle for legitimizing the adoption of a progressive tax on the rich and the privileged. The idea developed from the work of the beggars on the roads and streets. A priest articulated the principle that underlay this plan: To finance the public work on the streets and roads, resources would be provided by using "the capacities of those who will derive the greatest advantage from it" (nos. 57, 7). In his article on the progressive tax, Condorcet generalized the principle of utility in the financing of public expenditures in order to justify the tax. He took the example of the roads used to transport merchandise, which served everyone but which only the wealthy used for private travel, and he assumed that the richer one was, the more one indulged in such travel. The

27 Mireille Touzery, L'invention de l'impôt sur le revenu. La taille tarifée 1715–1789, Paris 1994, with a preface by Michel Antoine, pp. v–viii; Nicolas Delalande, Les batailles de l'impôt. Consentement et résistances de 1789 à nos jours, Paris 2011, pp. 26f.
28 Touzery, Invention de l'impôt.
29 Jaucourt, Impôt, in: Diderot and d'Alembert, Encyclopédie, vol. 8, 1765, pp. 601–604.
30 Condorcet, Sur l'impôt progressif, in: Journal d'Instruction Sociale, no. 1, 1.6.1793, pp. 11–24.

state was thus perfectly entitled to establish progressive tax brackets, and, being a mathematician, he calculated them.[31]

The most accomplished example of financing projects by utility was the one proposed by Dom Pierre Paul, a Benedictine cleric. He imagined a new economy, the economy of cleanliness, which would rest on the work of the poor, and whose financing would be based on the utility that the inhabitants of the area would derive from the cleaning of the streets and the cesspools. A charity tax that would be freely chosen, but for which each person would fix in advance the sum he would like to give per year, would serve to relieve the poor who could not work, "the very elderly, the crippled, and the sick." Thanks to the new economy, the tax would not be higher than the entirety of the alms (nos. 69, 96).

Three safeguards were supposed to avoid all misappropriation by the king and to reintroduce the fundamental values of charity despite all constraints: The demanded amount was decided according to need, the tax was temporary (nos. 66, 115), and taxation remained at the level of the community (nos. 54, 6, 115). This was also a way of short-circuiting private traders and other financiers. The ambiguity of the administration and of accounts was another element hindering the development of a fiscal administration, a prelude to the money being misappropriated for the profit of the state (no. 54). Another solution intended to prevent misappropriating taxes for other needs was to regard them as sacred, which was necessary in particular for the tax that would replace *corvée* (no. 78).

IX. Taxing Material Things and Persons to Punish and Transform the Country

The interest that both state policy and contest projects took in taxes on material things stemmed from the fact that they forced the privileged groups to pay without entering into the battle of personal taxes, the *impôts*. All the attempts of the Crown to circumvent privileges and generalize the direct tax, with the creation of the capitation tax in 1695, then the tax of the *dixième* in 1710 and of the *vingtième* in 1749, led to meager results, the clergy hiding behind the free donation, the aristocrats and the urban elite using all their negotiating power to escape it. The *taille* itself had become an essentially rural tax that affected only the localities too modest to free themselves from it. It was therefore unthinkable to subject privileged persons to it as well. Taxes on material things were also free from the arbitrariness of personal taxes, insofar as declarations on revenue were perceived as an attack on liberty and as an insupportable intrusion of the

31 François Hincker, L'idéologie économique à l'œuvre dans les débats et les décisions concernant la fiscalité pendant la Révolution, in: État, finances et économie pendant la Révolution française, Paris 1991, pp. 355–363, here p. 361.

state into the affairs of individuals.[32] The authors anchored their demands in the ancient traditions of charity, going back to the Jews, Greeks, and Easterners and evoking the memory of the Golden Age of Christianity to legitimize the demand that each individual should give a small portion of his surplus (nos. 24, 114). The choice of objects to be taxed was sometimes intended to be punitive, sometimes redistributive, sometimes painless, and sometimes useful for the development of the country.

Taxing luxuries, the manifest sign of inequalities blamed for poverty, made it possible to reach the privileged orders and the rich, who "are the owners of the substance of all other men." The master of art of Bayonne therefore proposed ten *Louis* per year on every coach, five *Louis* on the cabriolets, and one *Louis* in addition on every horse, excepting those used in agriculture, for doctors, and for surgeons (no. 27; see also nos. 48, 91, 59, 118). Jaucourt also considered this necessary, and he added "that it would be no less necessary for stopping the depopulation of the countryside than for finishing to allocate the taxes in the way that is most consistent with distributive justice."[33] In 1755, in *A Discourse on Political Economy*, Rousseau extolled taxes on inessential consumptions as beneficial to the state without constraining the rich, since they have the possibility of renouncing their objects of luxury so as not to pay the tax. He wrote, "In this case, the tax may be regarded as a sort of fine, the product of which compensates for the abuse it punishes."[34]

Entertainment and pleasure were also subject to taxation. Either they infringed morality, or happy people, such as those whom luck had favored, could not be anything but generous, and this concept could include a wide range of activities: "on all sorts of public spectacles, game academies, on the winnings from all lotteries, on certain individual rights or privileges, on the franchise from which the merchants benefit in all the markets of the kingdom" (no. 10bis; see also nos. 116, 16, 11, 118, 75, 113).

The gift to the poor was traditional for funerals and family celebrations and, as an anonymous author tells us, "for many years now, [a royal ordinance] has obligated every testator to give a donation to hospitals, hardly a tenth of the movable property of the succession" (no. 3). The idea of taxing successions was sometimes retained. It would be collected from everyone, including the clergy, and in proportion to the fortune of each individual (no. 24; see also nos. 46, 11).

Property taxes, which targeted the privileged groups, also supplemented charity (nos. 12, 70, 66). The example of foreign countries was always stressed, although property taxes were at the heart of physiocratic theory, according to which the

32 Touzery, Invention de l'impôt, pp. v–viii; Delalande, Batailles de l'impôt, pp. 26 f.
33 Jaucourt, Impôt.
34 Jean-Jacques Rousseau, A Discourse on Political Economy, in: id., The Social Contract and Discourses, trans. George Douglas Howard Cole, London 1913, pp. 249–287, here p. 287. In French in Nicolas Delalande, Gouverner les conduites par la fiscalité? Une brève histoire des débats sur le pouvoir incitatif de l'impôt (XVIIIe – XXIe siècle), in: Sophie Dubuisson-Quellier (ed.), Gouverner les conduits, Paris 2016, pp. 61–91, here p. 66.

land was the only source of wealth. It must be noted that these taxes were applied in England and in Flanders and that the Parliament of Paris had employed them during the famines of 1693, 1709, and 1740.[35] But above all, another advantage of this tax was that "callous and inhumane people" would participate in it as well (no. 70).

Drawing inspiration from the Flemish example and to finance his project to aid every pauper financially during the winter months when there was no work, (with four *sols* per day for a man, three for a woman, and two for a child), and to care for those who could not work, the abbot Montlinot suggested adding to the alms, which were anyway insufficient, a tax on land, property, the rent of houses in town, and, in certain places, on the consumption of wine, too. In his view, everything was subject to the tax: "who would dare to oppose privileges to the sacred tax that we must all pay in the name of God? It is in vain that one will object that alms must be secret and voluntary. Rich and perverted men, I do not ask you for anything but the crumbs that fall from your table, and what I demand is perhaps not even the twentieth part of what you owe to the poor, to religion, to the state, and to humanity" (no. 66). Condorcet also based his scheme on rental value to avoid arbitrary evaluations and the entry of the state into the private sphere of individuals.

Yet taxing common consumer goods that were more prevalent in all layers of society was a controversial proposition. Some demanded these taxes, because they saw that Flanders and Holland had applied them. Others condemned them, even if they were already being collected at the entrances of Paris for the benefit of the hospitals. For these authors believed that the concept itself was flawed, since these taxes subjugated the poor as well as the rich, even more so when they were applied to essential commodities (no. 70). Traditional taxes on circulated goods were taken up again, but only on imported merchandise, following in the example of England to help the development of manufactories (no. 3).[36] The taxes were also used to deal with the problem of depopulation, which troubled the contemporaries. Those targeted first were single people (nos. 24, 113, 114). One aristocrat also envisaged a tax on children without siblings starting from the age of 16 (no. 59).

---

35 Marjorie K. McIntosh, Poor Relief in Elizabethan English Communities. An Analysis of Collectors' Accounts, in: Economic History Review 67. 2014, pp. 331–357, here pp. 332–35 and p. 356; Steve Hindle, The State and Social Change in Early Modern England, c. 1550–1640, Houndmills 2000; Bert de Munck, Fiscalizing Solidarity (from below). Poor Relief in Antwerp Guilds. Between Community Building and Public Service, in: Manon van der Heijden et al. (eds.), Serving the Urban Community. The Rise of Public Facilities in the Low Countries, Amsterdam 2009, pp. 168–193.

36 For England, see Julian Hoppit, Britain's Political Economies. Parliament and Economic Life, 1660–1800, Cambridge 2017; John Styles, An Ambivalent State. State-promoted Manufacturing in the British Isles, 1550–1800, Paper for World Economic History Conference Kyoto, August 2015, Panel on Global Court and State Manufactures, c.1400–1800.

X. The Church's Failure

All sides of the political spectrum expressed hostility towards the church: It had failed in its mission and had misappropriated the money of the poor. The authors liked to recall the history of charity and of the primitive church, which reserved a quarter of the alms for the poor. They recounted the bishops' appropriation of this share of the poor despite the exhortations of some saints and prelates. They invoked the First Council of Orléans, which urged the bishops to rescue the poor, because "the higher one ranks, the more one must merit it. The great must surpass other men even more with their good deeds than with their dignities." The lawyer who made these remarks concluded with the words of St Ambrose:

'God is just: he wanted all men to have enough to subsist. If he gave you lands in abundance, it was so you could sanctify yourselves through alms. This grain that you keep is the bread of the indigent. These clothes that you withhold are those of the poor. This money that you accumulate is the price of captives' [...] Let us apply St Ambrose's speech (nos. 89, 66, 113).

Targeted first were the monks and the mendicant orders, whom the controller of the octroi treated—like the beggars—as "hornets" (no. 1). They "are rich only from the donations of the poor," which justified taking their surplus in addition to the tithe of the harvests and forbidding that they beg, the clergymen with annuities having to support those without (no. 118). The church thus had to return this fourth part, which belonged to the poor and could serve to establish houses to remove the idle poor (no. 97).

Since the riches of the church and the luxurious lifestyle of the high clergy and the monasteries contradicted the doctrine of the church, a fact that the gospels and the councils did not cease to recall, "all that exceeds what is necessary (or, if you will, what is convenient) for the ecclesiastics is the legitimate portion of the inheritance and the patrimony of the poor." Furthermore compared with the taxes that the family patriarchs paid on their properties, their work, and their industry, the clergy's participation was limited. Hence, "Reason, Equality, Religion unanimously demand that, since the secular state is unable to contribute to the development of the proposed establishments, the ecclesiastical order be required to defray the costs of their execution, or at least patiently tolerate that a small portion of the goods that it possesses be allocated to it" (nos. 28, 78, 45). An anonymous author went into detail and condemned the use of "funds intended for the blessed bread in most of the parishes [...] [which] would be more edifying if it was used instead to benefit the poor." He also criticized the sumptuousness of the churches, claiming that half of the products of the church wardenship would be more usefully employed in taking care of the poor, since "thousands of candles are burnt at mid-day in the churches, while a vast crowd of miserable people can hardly obtain a lamp to give light at night." Regarding the monks' habits: "Would it not be wise to suggest altering the habits of each monk, since their ample cloth is certainly able to clothe two men decently?" And if this was insufficient, the government had to impose a tax on the privileged (no. 98; see also nos. 46, 105, 27, 45, 111). A professor at the University of Caen believed that they could finance all the poor who could not work, and he included pregnant women, mothers with children under the age of two years, and indigent or abandoned children, who would be raised, educated, or put to work in the conservatories he had planned. If one were to object that "this would mean attacking the estates" and "taking the thurible in hand," the professor responded that nobody respected the estates more than he did: "But is it indeed true that the ecclesiastics own their possessions; I am not speaking of the grounds, but of the fruits, the yield of their profits? […] After removing what is necessary for the beneficiary's subsistence and dress, the rest belongs to the poor" (no. 78).

The demand to tax the church on its possessions, not with the *vingtième*, as some general controllers tried to do, but with the *dixième*, was quite popular. In order to establish new hospitals, the church too would not only have to give a tenth of its possessions and revenue but also to dispense with deducting the tithe on the uncultivated lands of the lords, lands that would be cultivated (nos. 110, 72, 24). An anonymous author wrote that if a member of the clergy who had six thousand *livres* gave a thousand *livres* for the beggars every year (and so others proportionally), it would not be a great sacrifice: "I think to the contrary that this would still only partially fulfill his duty to the church." The archbishops and the bishops would have to give double this amount, so at least a third of their revenues (no. 72). To finance the houses of repentance in Berry, a nobleman suggested that twenty abbeys or monasteries of men and as many of women should pay directly to the office of the house, 600 *livres* per year for the former and 400 *livres* for the latter (no. 59). More respectful of tradition, the first prize invited all bodies of the clergy to set the amount of the alms themselves (no. 114).

Condemning the fact that the foundations of charity had been transformed into ecclesiastical assets was accompanied by the demand to restore charity to its primary purpose (no. 98). The police lieutenant of Meaux wanted to add to this the silver of the sacristies or, failing that, the interest of the amount that it represented, if one wanted to preserve them, in addition to requiring religious institutions to give a tenth of their revenues (no. 24). The oratorian of Rouen demanded that a fund be set up for the poor in every parish, taken from the income of benefices, hospitals, and priories, and managed locally (no. 113).

The crisis of vocations with the decrease in the number of monks also paved the way to a wide-ranging use of the monasteries, which could be converted to confine the poor (nos. 64, 28, 97, 110, 35, 112).

But not all clergymen were in the same situation, and low-level clergymen were often considered separately (nos. 83, 82). Moreover the priests of the towns and villages were at the center of numerous projects to return beggars to their village (no. 24). The high clergy also had to help the priests, whose profits were not immense. As a law professor wrote, one could divide the bishops' vast possessions into four portions: one for the bishop, the second for the clergy, the third for the poor, and the fourth for repairs. Authors often added that the bishops would be delighted and that "in this case, we will not take the thurible in hand except to offer the living God an incense that will please him more than a pomp that he detests and that would put those of his ministers who engaged in it in contradiction with the law that they teach" (no. 78).

As for the personal taxes, the *impôts*, some hesitated and suggested a contingency plan in case their initial proposal attracted "the people's hostility" or was not accepted (nos. 73, 59, 45, 78). Did these hesitations stem from the fact that these authors had signed their names, or did they indicate genuine doubt?

XI. The Role of the State

On the grounds that they profited from public works imposed on the beggars and that these works freed them from the *corvée*, the communities contributed to financing the beggars. The state was also urged to cover the cost of the roads considered to be of public interest, either in full (no. 12) or with mixed financing, half from individuals' contributions and half from the state (no. 70). Nevertheless the contemporaries found the concept of assigning the relief of the poor to the state (and not only the obligation to give them work by constructing infrastructure works of public interest) harder to accept, since this relief was thought to rely on the social bond and morality and so, above all, on the church and the charity of the elites.

This explains why one school of thought wished to revive traditional forms of solidarity in addition to charity, requiring parents to pay and forcing every village and every state to take care of its own by means of relief funds (no. 113, 64, 103, 52, 57, 58, 118, 5, 3). A sergeant major even estimated that if put to work as a community with good administration, those beggars who were able-bodied could support those who were not and moreover could ease the lot of the shameful poor (no. 15).

The need for equalization between rich and poor districts was thought to be the main purpose of state intervention (nos. 70, 86, 5), since with the exception of equalization, the role of the state was perceived as an additional financial burden, raising concerns regarding a corrupt administration, whose members were growing rich from public service. To avoid this, the police lieutenant of the town of Meaux suggested creating a society of "patriots" connected to the government, which would be responsible for helping individuals by finding them an occupation in their province in line with their character and talents, for rewarding every man who introduced a new art or perfected an art known in his country, for providing a pension to every man who, after 40 years of diligent work and an irreproachable reputation, was no longer able to earn enough to live on for the rest of his life, and for compensating every inhabitant whom the laws had unjustly oppressed through unfortunate circumstances, particularly those whose fortune had been ruined by the demands and trials of powerful bodies such as the rich monasteries. The office, which would not be remunerated, would even cost one hundred *livres* of admission fee (no. 24).

Another anonymous author, probably a doctor, went beyond the predatory vision of the state, establishing the basis of national solidarity with his concept of hospitality, the premise of the social state. He proposed following the example of those foreign countries, such as England or Holland, that levied a general tax to look after the sick and the unemployed poor who had to care for a family, or Russia and Sweden, where the same tax served the subsistence of the poor widows, or the Protestant countries of Germany, where tithes served not the priests but the poor, who thus were not forced to beg. He noted that Paris was the only town in France where a "hospitality tax" existed. He therefore laid the "first foundation of a general and unchanging hospitality toll," since this solidarity was a right that, like security, was a state matter, and therefore, it was legitimate that everyone should finance it, man being "entitled to compassion from his fellow men [...] Yet hospitality, whether what is at stake is moral or political aid, is just as much a natural right as the tithe is a divine right for the worship of the Lord." This tribute would be paid willingly, because it would be modest, and every person would have the prospect of being aided in all cases of misfortune." At the same time, he suggested reducing the multiplicity and inconvenience of royal taxation and to that end dividing the revenues of men's work (in agriculture and industry) into three parts: one third for the King, the second for the farmers' food, and the third for the agricultural fees and the sowing of the soil. He insisted on the accuracy of this distribution, since if one thwarted the king, one would strip him of the faculties necessary for granting his subjects the justice, the protection, and above all the hospitality that depended on his majesty. In conclusion, this author contended that the noblemen had to pay for hospitality, because they enjoyed privileges and even pensions taken from the national body; the clergy could evade this even less, since the councils and canonical laws allocated one third of the revenues from their assets to the subsistence of the poor (no. 123).

Certain authors explicitly reversed the hierarchy established between the state and charity, like an anonymous author who wrote in Latin and asserted that the state did not have to supplement alms, as the great majority of his contemporaries believed, but on the contrary, that it was the role of the state and the towns to finance the houses of work and education that he envisioned (no. 104). Monsieur Sabbathier, who invoked Enlightenment ideas and more particularly Montesquieu, praised the Enlightenment, which abolished an infinite number of ridiculous and barbaric practices, such as trials by ordeal and interrogations, and drove religious fanaticism and superstition to extinction; he ended his essay with an ode to the pleasure of giving. In a footnote, he cited a passage from Montesquieu on the state's duties towards the poor: "The alms given to a naked man in the street do not fulfil the obligations of the state, which owes to every citizen a certain subsistence, a proper nourishment, convenient clothing, and a kind of life not incompatible with health."[37] In addition to regal functions, the state had to seize the social ministry of the church.

XII. Conclusion: Return to E. P. Thompson

Thus, charity was at the heart of the social bond: it simultaneously legitimized the power of the powerful, founded on generosity, and the obedience of the popular classes, born of gratitude. Nonetheless, the impossibility of eradicating poverty required questioning this fundamental bond.

To protect and absolve themselves from all moral fault the majority of the elites in their writings imputed the rupture of the social bond to the beggars, since the latter had chosen to break this tie in order to live in idleness and debauchery. In doing so, these authors re-legitimized the society of orders, since they themselves, the privileged, had not failed in their role. Moreover, they distinguished clearly between poverty, which was willed by God so the rich man might earn salvation and was therefore an integral part of society, and vagrancy, fruit of the vice of beggars, which destroyed society, since itinerant men and women had broken the personal bonds that linked them to the powerful.

Some nevertheless not only held the poor accountable, but also condemned the avarice of the privileged. They thus attempted to revivify the bond of charity by forcing the rich to be generous, going so far as to fix a minimum on the alms that they were required to give: The duty of the church was to remind the rich of their obligations with impassioned preaching, and the task of the state was to add rewards in the form of privileges and exemptions in order to encourage the fulfillment of these obligations. One once again had to link morality and power to stimulate the generosity of the rich and resolve a part of the social question, since the other part came from the vanity of the privileged, who through their luxurious lifestyle, disrupted the inequality of wealth as willed by God. This second moral fault thus legitimized their punishment through taxing the manifestations of their vanity.

Yet progressively, certain elites understood that moral economy was an impasse, and so they performed a double displacement, dissociating alms from charity and destroying the personal bond that linked the recipient with the donor by establishing charity bureaus in charge of receiving the alms. Subsequently, the wish to morally redress the privileged prompted these supporters of the Old Regime society to accept forms of taxation to punish the miserliness of the rich, taxes that they alone paid, since they replaced charity, which did not concern the poor.

37 Montesquieu, The Spirit of Laws. Complete Edition, trans. Thomas Nugent, New York 2011, vol. 2, p. 25 [book 23, chapter 29].

In opposition to these evolutions in the governance of aristocratic society, which aimed to purify it of its moral faults, there was the interpretation of the Enlightenment men. Their conception abandoned the moral economy, even if they condemned the arrogance of the privileged, because their social project was radically different, since they aspired to create a society where all men would have equal rights and where all would be required to work. The corollary of this equality of status claimed for all citizens was the equality before taxation. Hence taxes occupied a more prominent position than alms to raise the funds necessary to put the beggars to work, charity thus being a matter of the exclusively private sphere.

The church, which was the great organizer of coexistence, was in turn criticized from both sides. For the supporters of aristocratic society it had failed in its mission of poverty and misappropriated the donations destined for the poor for its own profit. On this account, it was legitimate to force the church to return the surplus that it had accumulated and to use the monasteries to house beggars and the infirm. Only the low clergy was spared criticism. For the partisans of the Enlightenment critical views regarding the illegitimate wealth of the church were coupled with the wish to diminish its power and its spiritual influence, with the most radical voices demanding the church be stripped of its traditional functions in order to transfer them to the state.

Ultimately, these struggles expressed two ways of analyzing society, which referred to two radically different concepts. The morality approach blamed malfunction on individuals and in doing so prohibited all political questioning, since problems such as begging or vagrancy stemmed from misbehavior, a fact that assigned policy the task of morally redressing individuals. This vision was at the heart of the great confinement of the poor. But in the eighteenth century, another mode of analyzing the social, which privileged political over moral analysis, became more prevalent and entered the field of public discussion. It abolished the primacy of the moral economy for the benefit of structural reforms: it was no longer a matter of morally reeducating classes of individuals but of reforming society, regardless of the social bonds of domination founded on the moral values specific to the privileged, which would have legitimized their domination over the entire social body. It established a society of free citizens with equal rights.

In addition to the battle taking place in the field of moral virtues to legitimize or delegitimize certain social groups, there was another struggle—less visible but no less real—which transcended them, because it concerned all of humanity. This was the source of human rights. The essays rarely used the vocabulary of rights, with the exception of a single word: *humanitas*, the right to life. After giving thanks to the one "who established the maxim that you shall not do to others what you would not want done to yourself," according to the Christian tradition, the governor of the viscounty of Besançon observed that it was useless to prohibit begging if one did not provide for the needs of the poor, "because the natural law of self-preservation, superior to all other law," would always prevail over the bans on begging (no. 67). And this right was transformed into the right to relief: "the right of the poor to be relieved simply because they are men" (no. 9). As a Parisian lawyer wrote, the destitute "have the right to demand" that poverty be rendered "at least bearable" for them, and "it is also humanity's duty and in the interest of the government to bring an end to it." That was why his project addressed both "the glory of the state and the rights of humanity" (no. 28; see also nos. 29, 96, 10bis, 8).

Indeed, this right emerged from the Middle Ages onwards, driven by the church and in response to crises related to the high cost of wheat. It was embodied in the concept of price: in addition to the "going price" fixed by the market, the church recognized the authorities' right to fix prices arbitrarily, when their level was such that it even threatened the life of the poor or when merchants distorted the rules of the market through fraud or the creation of monopolies. Prices thus fixed in an authoritarian manner in the name of the survival of humanity and called "the just price" concerned essential commodities: grains, bread, meat, wine, and beer.[38]

The same understanding of *humanitas* was still alive in the eighteenth century: the "Encyclopédie" entry "price," written by Jaucourt, placed the concept of "humanity" in the category of possessions that eluded the market. He contrasted "legitimate prices" with "going prices," the latter arising from "the shared estimation of individuals, accompanied by the consent of the contracting parties," and the former from the impossibility to put a price on "things absolutely necessary to life, of which there is an abundance, & of which someone else in great need cannot avail himself elsewhere; so therefore it would be inhumane to take advantage of his indigence to demand an excessive *price* of him for something that is essential to his needs."[39]

The concept of humanity was shared by the elites and by the popular classes, and neither hesitated to use the argument of survival to justify pillagings during food riots. Thus, during the "Flour War" of 1775, which was provoked by the high prices of wheat, the rioters, as well as the commissioners, focused on poverty: the former to justify their actions, and the latter to petition that the robbers be pardoned. So when Jacques Laborde was judged for breaking into a farm and taking there "on different evenings, six bushels of oats," he justified himself by saying "that it was extreme poverty which forced him to do it," because he was "utterly destitute and did not know where to get money to buy bread when he was unemployed." The commissioners took up his argument to propose that he be pardoned: "We believe that these thefts were caused by the extreme poverty of Laborde, who must feed a wife and children."[40] Moreover, the concept of *humanitas* was part of the legal education. In the first pages of his "Treatise on

---

38 Raymond de Roover, The Concept of the Just Price. Theory and Economic Policy, in: Journal of Economic History 18. 1958, pp. 418–434.

39 Laurence Fontaine, Le Marché. Histoire et usages d'une conquête sociale, Paris 2014, ch. 6: "Logiques et faiblesses du marché," pp. 241–287.

40 Déborah Cohen, La procédure de grâce au XVIIIe siècle. Restaurer un ordre ou reconnaître l'innocence?, in: Revue d'histoire moderne et contemporaine 57. 2007, no. 2, pp. 91–116, several examples pp. 107 f.

Criminal Justice in France," published in 1771, Daniel Jousse pointed out that the necessities of survival might excuse the violence of people suffering from hunger.[41] Hence, with the right to the protection of life, inscribed in the concept of *humanitas* and translated as "the just price," the humblest maintained the right to feed themselves from the property of the rich during times of famine. This right to the protection of life, which allows crimes against property, thus replaces E. P. Thompson's analysis of the moral economy of the working classes in the history of human rights.

List of the Essays Used
1 Viot, controller of octrois of Reims
3 Anonymous
5 Louis Gidoin of Estampes in the Gers
6 The Baron Dubois d'Escordal, former cavalry captain
7 Anonymous
8 Bertin of Valenciennes (North)
9 Anonymous
10 bis Monsieur Jean Frédéric Senger of Bordeaux, at the house of Imperial Consul Monsieur Bethman
11 Monsieur Grignon of Bayard, knight of the royal order associated with the Academy
12 Descombres, officer in the German infantry regiment of la Marque
15 Monsieur Depons, major of Montmédy in the Meuse
16 Johann Loth of Saint Petersburg
18 Anonymous
21 Monsieur Rozé, doctor of law, lawyer at the Parliament, at the cloister in rue des Bernardins, Paris
23 Abbot Blanchard, in Tourteron in the Ardennes near Rethel en Champagne, 2nd honorable mention
24 Monsieur Decan, [Decoin?], police lieutenant of the town of Meaux
26 E. Jauge of Ste Foy-sur-Dordogne, former road commissioner
27 Mme Eglain of Paris
28 Monsieur de la Toise Prioul, lawyer, hotel Notre-Dame, rue des Rosiers in the Marais in Paris
29 Rabigot de la Croix, royal musician, sergeant of the Royal Chapel in Versailles
30 Barthélémy Miger, former notary and lieutenant of the bailiwick of Milly en Gâtinais who lives in Paris
31 Monsieur de Créquy, from a family of very old nobility of the sword, 3rd honorable mention
32 Le Brun, surgeon, correspondant of the Royal Academy of Surgery in Vandoeuvre, Champagne
35 Deval priest from Ussel in the Limousin and regent at the collège of Ussel
37 Anonymous
43 Monsieur De Vareilles, former controller of the house of the deceased Madame la Dauphine in Bordeaux
44 Panckoucke the younger in Paris (one of the first great industrialists of the printing press, editor of the *Encyclopédie* and then the *Encyclopédie méthodique*)
45 Manget père, fiscal prosecutor of Ste Memmie les Châlons
46 de Châteauvieux, with Mr Beauregard at Sèvres, Saint Cloud
48 Abbot Criquillion at the School of Saint Paul, Journay in Flanders. Essay in Latin. The Academy awarded him honors.

41 Ibid., p. 108.

49 Beaucourt de Noortvelve, fiscal lawyer of the Grand Bureau et Droits de S. M. JR in Bruges
50 Guéniot, doctor of medicine, lawyer at the court, assessor of the mounted constabulary and director of the positions in Tonnerre, affiliated with the Academy of Auxerre. The Academy awarded him honors.
52 Chauchard, royal notary, Bussière les Nonains, Allier
53 Henri Joseph Van des Borcht, doyen of the Brewers of Bruxelles
54 Bourdier de Beauregard of the Academy of Letters and Sciences, Pau
55 Félix Til-Léo, Beaune
56 Anonymous
57 Le Tonnelier, clergyman, priest of the parish of Autrèche in Picardie, diocese of Soissons
58 Charles Gabriel de la Balme, squire, Sir of Renneville, cavalry captain and lieutenant of the mounted constabulary of the district of Paris at the residence of Senlis
59 Trumeau de Lierne, Issoudun in Berry
60 Anonymous
61 the Knight de Nas de Tourres, former marine officer in Marseille
62 Boillet, vicar priest of a parish near Rouen
64 Monsieur de Serre, president of the Court of Auditors, Aids and Finances of Montpellier
65 André Jacques Le Clerc (son), Rue Caquerel, Rouen.
66 Abbot Montlinot, Honorary Canon of Lille, 1st honorable mention
67 Monsieur Danxison, judge and governor of the viscounty of Besançon, former magistrate of the same town. The Academy awarded him honors.
69 Dom Pierre Paul, Benedictine abbot of the Congregation of Saint-Maur at the Abbey of St Germain des Prés, Paris
70 Monsieur Sabbathier
72 Th D.B
73 Monsieur de Burbure, officer of the mounted constabulary, independent associate of the Academy of Chalons, Sillé le Guillaume dans le Maine
75 Garnon, lawyer from Narbonne
78 Roussel de la Bérardière, honorary counselor of bailiwick and presidial chair of Caen and professor of French law at the University of Caen
81 Pillin, priest, Vauban en Mâconnais
82 Lejeune, geographer and practitioner of Soissons
83 A "simple citizen" who does not give his name
86 Monsieur de la Brousse, lawyer, mayor and First Consul of the town of Arancon in Languedoc
88 Siméon Pierre Torchet, canon of the Royal Church of St Etienne de Troyes, associate of the Academy of Châlons
89 François Hubert Aubert, knight of Saint-Jean de Latran, lawyer at the parliament of Nancy, vice-librarian, former lawyer at the Royal Council of Poland and before that minister to several German princes
90 Gaillard, de Moriques (?), diocese of Soisson
91 Monsieur the knight of Moineville, former cavalry captain, knight of St Louis, Paris. The Academy awarded him honors.
92 Abbot Vibat de la Coste, canon and grand vicar, Cahors in Quercy
95 Anonymous
96 M. N. G. L. of Guebwiller in Haute Alsace
97 Anonymous
98 Anonymous
101 Anonymous
103 de Monfraboeuf, former royal guard, pensioner of the King, The Hague
104 Anonymous in Latin

105 Dr L. Domnus Felix de Mores, who writes his essay in Latin
108 Anonymous, who writes his essay in Latin
109 Anonymous, who writes in French but also in German
110 Monsieur de Losé
111 and 122 Anonymous, former administrator of the Hospital of Vitry le François
112 Monsieur de Saint Félix, Paris. The Academy considered the essay "also worthy of special attention."
113 de Romans de Coppier, Oratorian of the Academy of Rouen, 4th honorable mention
114 Clouet of Verdun, squire, counselor, personal physician of the King, doctor at the military hospital and the charity hospitals of Verdun sur Meuse, 1st prize
115 Monsieur the Vicar of Dosne of the diocese of Nevers near Moulin en Bourbonnais. The Academy awarded him honors.
116 Monsieur de Gavre
118 Monsieur Larroque de Brienne, master of arts and of a boarding school, Bayonne
120 Anonymous
121 Anonymous
123 Anonymous, probably a doctor
Unnumbered, he is from Reims and his name is a secret
No. illegible

Mischa Suter

Moral Economy as a Site of Conflict*

Debates on Debt, Money, and Usury in the Nineteenth and Early Twentieth Century

Abstract: This essay is a theoretical reflection on the concept of "moral economy," drawing mainly on sources concerned with the practices of debt enforcement in nineteenth-century Switzerland. I take conflict as the point of departure for moral economy and I propose a way to integrate historical-epistemological dimensions into the analysis. I further argue that colliding temporalities represented the categorial focal point of these conflicts. The last section briefly discusses debates on "usury" and "profiteering" *(Wucher)* between the nineteenth century and the Weimar inflation period. Here, moral economy appears as one contentious node among several in conflicts over monetary relations of exchange.

In late autumn of 1830, a confluence of street protests and a shift within the elite put a liberal government in power in the Swiss Canton of Zurich. The turn was accompanied by a wave of petitions from the countryside.[1] Some of the *cahiers de doléances* from areas with a large cottage industry demanded a ban on mechanical looms. They appealed to "moral principles" and the "general will of the people," which, they argued, were more important than the government's then current practices of "state wisdom."[2] Even more widespread were demands that procedures of debt collection be reformed. One petition stated that experience teaches that "a poor man" might try "with all his effort and toil to pay his interest or current debts in order to retain his citizen's honor as his most precious possession,"

---

* Translated from the German by Adam Bresnahan.

1 This essay puts forward a new perspective based on some of the findings of a completed work (Mischa Suter, Rechtstrieb. Schulden und Vollstreckung im liberalen Kapitalismus 1800–1900, Constance 2016) and some preliminary thoughts on my current research on the medium of money in modernity.

  On the context of the petitions see Rolf Graber, Demokratie und Revolten. Die Entstehung der direkten Demokratie in der Schweiz, Zurich 2017, pp. 71–79; Barbara Weinmann, Eine andere Bürgergesellschaft. Klassischer Republikanismus und Kommunalismus im Kanton Zürich im späten 18. und 19. Jahrhundert, Göttingen 2002, pp. 204–267; Albert Tanner, "Alles für das Volk." Die liberalen Bewegungen 1830/31, in: Thomas Hildbrand and id. (eds.), Im Zeichen der Revolution. Der Weg zum schweizerischen Bundesstaat 1798–1848, Zurich 1997, pp. 51–74.

2 Staatsarchiv des Kantons Zürich [hereafter STAZH], K III 258.3a, Petitionen des Zürcher Volkes 1830/31, no. 1–75, no. 56, Oberhittnau, 5.1.1831.

but that the administrative costs associated with debt enforcement proceedings often doomed this effort to failure.[3] The petitions were thus motivated by the assumption that there existed a more fundamental form of politics than the politics of state: namely, those "moral principles" that stand in accord with the "general will of the people." These principles were seen as having a significant bearing on practices of debt and debt collection, which had become a nexus of issues related to civil rights and political equality due to the fact that in Switzerland, male debtors who went into bankruptcy lost most of their civil privileges. Economy and morality were thus entangled on a number of levels. On the one hand, the petitions referred to the social norms that caused bankrupt debtors to lose their honor and with it their rights, and on the other, they implied that "a poor man" who tried his best was deserving of a certain degree of protection.

Debts are profoundly relational phenomena that fuse moral judgments and economic calculation. This fact makes the history of debt fitting terrain for an actualization of the concept of "moral economy." I will make the case for this claim here by first analyzing sources related to the legal measures taken to enforce debts in nineteenth-century liberal Switzerland and, after that, by offering a brief analysis of the uses and meanings of the concept of "usury" in the late nineteenth and early twentieth century.

This exploration of the realities of debt and finance in early industrial pauperism is driven by an interest in contemporary processes of precarization.[4] Today, crises of debt and regimes of austerity weave together financial policy, street protest, and the politics of everyday survival, a fact well demonstrated by ethnographic studies of Greece.[5] In the contemporary world of global neoliberalism, a financialized economy of borrowing, pawning, and lending just to get by has come to determine the everyday lives of broad swathes of the population.[6]

---

3 Ibid., no. 40, Wetzikon, im Christmonat 1830, § 30.

4 On interesting comparisons between early industrialization and contemporary precarization see Timo Luks, Prekarität. Eine nützliche Kategorie der historischen Kapitalismusanalyse, in: AfS 56. 2016, pp. 51–80. From the perspective of literary history see Patrick Eiden-Offe, Die Poesie der Klasse. Romantischer Antikapitalismus und die Erfindung des Proletariats, Berlin 2017. On the epoch of pauperism in Switzerland see Erich Gruner, Die Arbeiter in der Schweiz im 19. Jahrhundert. Soziale Lage, Organisation, Verhältnis zu Arbeitgeber und Staat, Bern 1968, pp. 15–49; Rudolf Braun, Sozialer und kultureller Wandel in einem ländlichen Industriegebiet (Zürcher Oberland) unter Einwirkung des Maschinen- und Fabrikwesens im 19. und 20. Jahrhundert, Zurich 1965, esp. ch. 3: "Arbeits- und Lebensverhältnisse des Fabrikwesens als soziales Problem," pp. 109–184.

5 Daniel M. Knight, History, Time, and Economic Crisis in Central Greece, New York 2015; id. and Charles Stewart (eds.), Ethnographies of Austerity. Temporality, Crisis and Affect in Southern Europe, in: History and Anthropology 27. 2016, pp. 1–18; on the history of state debt see "Staatsverschuldung," GG 41. 2015, no. 3, ed. by Julia Laura Rischbieter and Hans-Peter Ullmann.

6 Clara Han, Life in Debt. Times of Care and Violence in Neoliberal Chile, Berkeley 2012; Hadas Weiss, Gift and Value in Jerusalem's Third Sector, in: American Anthropologist 113. 2011, pp. 594–605.

After the 2008–2009 financial crisis, new forms of "fringe finance" found fertile ground for expansion; in 2017, in the U.S., there existed more payday lenders than McDonald's restaurants; in 2015, the central debt collection agencies had put demerits in the files of about 9.3 percent of Germany's population.[7]

How can everyday practices of debt, indebtedness, and debt enforcement give us a better grasp on the concept of moral economy? This essay pursues two related arguments. First, it defines moral economy as an analytic concept centered on conflict. Second, it demarcates how conflicts within moral economy also had an epistemic dimension. Forging a connection between moral economy thus understood and practices of debt and indebtedness might become more intuitive if one considers sociologist Ute Tellmann's remark on Marcel Mauss' classic work: "with debts, we are always dealing with an irreducible impurity of economic categories and problematizations." One might thus inquire into the kinds of norms and standards certain historical actors were working with when they sought to measure, classify, and assess debts.

A "'metrology' of the evaluation of debts" can help to make clear the different ways in which moral and economic categories were bound together in practices of debt and indebtedness.[8] Beyond that, however, such a metrology can help us discern two further things. First, it underscores how grappling with debt was a conflict-ridden process for those involved. Second, it can shine light on the epistemological assumptions implicitly being negotiated in these conflicts, because different *conceptions* of economy, the good, and the socially acceptable were in play.

In short, viewing practices of debt and indebtedness as a moral economy is a heuristic approach that lays bare forms of social inequality and points of epistemic contention. This essay seeks to bring together empirical case studies and more general theoretical reflections. Most of the sources are derived from German-speaking Switzerland in the period from 1830 to 1870. In order to offer some material for contrast and comparison, the article briefly touches upon the various uses and meanings of the concepts of "usury" and "profiteering" *(Wucher)* in the German-speaking countries from the Panic of 1873 to the period of hyper-inflation in the Weimar Republic.

In the first part, I discuss debt enforcement procedures in nineteenth-century Switzerland with the aim of identifying some of the entanglements of economy and morality in practices of debt and indebtedness and of teasing out certain aspects of the concept of moral economy, such as communal norms, emotionally invested ideas of justice, and context-specific forms of legitimacy. In the second part, I analyze the ways in which classifying somebody as bankrupt wrought

---

7 Rob Aitken, Fringe Finance. Crossing and Contesting the Borders of Global Capital, London 2015; Stacy Cowley, Payday Lenders Face Tough New Restrictions by Consumer Agency, in: New York Times, 6.10.2017, p. B1 and p. B4; Silke Meyer, Das verschuldete Selbst. Narrativer Umgang mit Privatinsolvenz, Frankfurt 2017, p. 38.

8 Ute Tellmann, Verschulden. Die moralische Ökonomie der Schulden, in: ilinx 3. 2013, pp. 3–24, here p. 5 and p. 8; Marcel Mauss, The Gift. Forms and Functions of Exchange in Archaic Societies [1923/24], London 1954.

confusion in extant systems of personal, economic, and legal classification in the nineteenth century. The purpose of the analysis for this essay's theoretical project is to support my proposal that scholars study the historical-epistemological aspects of the everyday economy of debt and indebtedness. The third part makes the case for taking conflictuality as the starting point for the study of the moral economy of debt, arguing that the kernel of this conflictuality is to be found in the clash of heterogeneous temporalities. The fourth part assesses the concept of the moral economy of debt developed out of the first three parts: through a discussion of usury and profiteering in German-speaking countries, it inquires into the extent to which the concept of moral economy can help capture some, though certainly not all aspects of conflicts bound up with other practices of monetary exchange. The last part is then about the limits of the concept.

I. The Politics of Debt Enforcement
in Nineteenth-Century Switzerland

In 1800, Switzerland had just finished featuring as one front in a European war and revolutionary tumult had paved the way for an experiment in centralized state government. In the same year, Johannes Tobler, a theologian from Zurich, formulated a maxim that, in his mind, would have averted future revolutions and "healed" those that had already taken place. The maxim was: "'Forgive us our debts as we forgive our debtors.'" His reasoning was that "things would have turned out better than what the revolutions had (already) in their beginnings cost" if one had told "creditors through dignified teachers: Look, there is turmoil among the people, which threatens to cause great losses for your accounts: Accept the smaller loss; Reduce your interest rates (at least for a few years) by some percentage for your debtors and be doubly friendly with them."[9] Tobler thus mixed business-savvy calculations and the affective ties of the community into a single recommendation, stating that debt forgiveness would have "won hearts—could have bought them—which are certainly not so expensive and yet of inestimable value."[10]

The conciliatory theologian's thinking was clear: if the creditors let up a bit on their demands that debts be paid punctually with interest, then their debtors would fall in line and ultimately comply. It was a paternalistic strategy from those at the top forced on them by events going on down below.[11] Tobler's paternalism

---

9 Johannes Tobler, Gutartige Hierarchie. Armenbesorgung, und die schöne Friedensbitte, Zurich 1800, suppl., pp. 12 f.

10 Ibid., p. 13.

11 The relational conception of political legitimacy can be seen as a primary attribute of moral economy. See Johanna Siméant, The Three Bodies of Moral Economy. The Diffusion of a Concept, in: Journal of Global Ethics 11. 2015, pp. 163–175, here p. 165.

bears traces less of a pre-capitalist form of rationality and more of a relational conception of legitimacy; that such a conception of legitimacy seemed to have been washed away in the upheaval that put the *ancien régime* out of power was something that the author deeply bemoaned.

However, in the nineteenth century, the spaces and temporal rhythms of debt enforcement remained largely structured by localized procedures and policies. In 1805, a law was put into effect in the Canton of Zurich that sanctioned the so-called "Kirchenruf," which meant reading out in church the names of those involved in ongoing bankruptcy proceedings.[12] In the 1840s, newspapers took over this function, even in more remote parts of the canton. In the city of Lucerne, bankrupt debtors were shuffled out onto the market square while a trumpet announced their arrival up until 1848.[13] The aim was not just to shame them and deter others, but to make information public so that others would avoid doing business with the bankrupt person, whose assets were frozen and divided up among their creditors. Local administrators often sought to delay bankruptcy proceedings out of fear that insolvent debtors would place a heavy burden on the funds for poor relief. Thus, a circumscribed, dense set of local communal practices organized the ways in which people were included and excluded from social life through their practices of debt collection. Ultimately, the history of debt in Switzerland demonstrates that these traded local norms were conjoined with the newly developing procedures of the liberal state.

In the early industrial period, credit and lending practices constituted a tightly woven net of economic and social relations. Unfortunately, as of yet no quantitative analysis of credit networks in nineteenth-century Switzerland exists.[14] Nevertheless, it is indisputable that the founding of cantonal banks exerted a considerable influence: after all, up until then, farmers had complained less about unmanageable debts than they had about the scarcity of affordable credit.[15] To vertical ties and communal boundaries with their moralizing mechanisms were

---

12 Hochobrigkeitliche Verordnung vom 16ten Julii 1805, betreffend die Auffallsverhandlungen, Pfandbücher und Pfandversilberungen, in: Officielle Sammlung der von dem Großen Rathe des Cantons Zürich gegebenen Gesetze und gemachten Verordnungen, und der von dem Kleinen Rath emanierten allgemeinen Landes- und Polizey-Verordnungen, vol. 3, Zurich 1808, pp. 108–113, here pp. 109 f. As a literary source on fear of the "Kirchenruf" see Johann Jakob Reithard, Eine schweizerische Dorfgeschichte, in: id. (ed.), Neue Alpenrosen. Eine Gabe Schweizerischer Dichter, Zurich 1848, pp. 249–350.

13 Staatsarchiv Luzern, AKT 35/21 A.1, 15.6.1848, Dekret des Präsidenten und Grossen Rats für einstweilige Aufhebung der öffentlichen Ausstellung der Failliten.

14 See, however, Ulrich Pfister, Le petit crédit rural en Suisse aux XVIe-XVIIIe siècles, in: Annales HSS 49. 1994, pp. 1339–1357; id., Rural Land and Credit Markets, the Permanent Income Hypothesis, and Protoindustry. Evidence from Early Modern Zurich, in: Continuity and Change 22. 2007, pp. 489–518.

15 The Cantonal Bank of Zurich was established in 1870. Arthur Wolf, Ein Beitrag zur Erkenntnis der Verschuldung des bäuerlichen Grundbesitzes im Kanton Zürich. Grundbesitzverteilung und Bodenverschuldung der Gemeinde Waltalingen bei Stammheim, Zurich 1912.

added horizontal channels, which is to say that often, people were at once creditors and debtors.

Research on other parts of Europe, including a pioneering study on Westphalia, attests to the continuing dominance of personal credit as opposed to bank loans; it also attests to the coexistence of a wide array of different forms of credit in a very small area.[16]

This diversity was particularly shaped by the category of gender. In the nineteenth century, women played roles on all levels of the precarious loan–borrow–pawn economy. At the same time, they were restricted legal subjects who lived under gender guardianship. Just as well, the symbolic dimensions of debt were also gendered: when a man went bankrupt and as a consequence lost his civil privileges, masculine honor was translated into a matter of state politics.[17]

From an economic perspective, indebtedness did not necessarily mean loss of social status. But in the realm of social experience, debt was often connotated with dependency and powerlessness, a point not irrelevant for this essay's focus on the concept of moral economy. Johann Jakob Treichler, a Zurich publicist who in the 1840s held lectures on socialism, articulated a pointed insight in a widely received speech: the bankruptcies of artisans and craftsmen and the indebtedness of farmers were for him key factors in the generation of a Swiss proletariat. By proletariat, he understood not only a propertyless economic class whose members had "founded their existence on nothing" and shared the condition of being "slaves of capital," regardless of whether they were factory workers or artisans drowning in debt.[18] Treichler saw an even more indicative feature of the status of being

---

16 Anna Carolina Vogel, Credit, Trust, and Social Networks. Mortgage Credit in the Industrializing Town of Esslingen (Württemberg, Germany), in: Andreas Gestrich and Martin Stark (eds.), Debtors, Creditors, and Their Networks. Social Dimensions of Monetary Dependence from the Seventeenth to the Twentieth Century, London 2015, pp. 71–97; Johannes Bracht, Geldlose Zeiten und überfüllte Kassen. Sparen, Leihen und Vererben in der ländlichen Gesellschaft Westfalens (1830–1866), Stuttgart 2013; Martin Stark, Soziale Einbettung eines ländlichen Kreditmarktes im 19. Jahrhundert, Ph. D. Diss. Universität Trier 2012; Hakan Lindgren, The Modernization of Swedish Credit Markets, 1840–1905. Evidence from Probate Records, in: Journal of Economic History 62. 2002, pp. 810–832; Gilles Postel-Vinay, La terre et l'argent. L'agriculture et le crédit en France du XVIIIe au début du XXe siècle, Paris 1998.

17 Annamarie Ryter, Als Weibsbild bevogtet. Zum Alltag von Frauen im 19. Jahrhundert—Geschlechtsvormundschaft und Ehebeschränkungen im Kanton Basel-Landschaft, Liestal 1994; on the nexus between bankruptcy and male loss of honor see Toby L. Ditz, Shipwrecked; or Masculinity Imperiled. Mercantile Representations of Failure and the Gendered Self in Eighteenth-Century Philadelphia, in: Journal of American History 81. 1994, pp. 51–80; Scott A. Sandage, Born Losers. A History of Failure in America, Cambridge, MA 2005.

18 Johann Jakob Treichler, Gibt es in der Schweiz ein Proletariat? Aus einer Vorlesung über Sozialismus in der Schweiz, in: Das Westphälische Dampfboot 2. 1846, no. 1, pp. 113–122, here pp. 113–115. See also the 12.9.1845 issue of Treichler's newspaper Der Bote von Uster (for a time called the Needs and Help Paper, Noth- und Hülfsblatt) on usury by banks. Proletarization through debt was a recurring figure in German publications around 1848, see for instance K., Über Wucherei, in: Das Westphälische Dampfboot 1. 1845, no. 2, pp. 260–264; Fr. Schnake, Die gesellschaftlichen Zustände der civilisirten Welt: XIII. Die gegenwärtige Noth und der

proletarian in the loss of male voting rights suffered by bankrupts and recipients of poor relief. In essence, for Treichler, being proletarian meant being stripped of one's political rights as an autonomous man and of one's capacity to participate in state affairs.[19] Of course, Karl Marx had a different view on the subject. While he did think that indebtedness led to economic proletarization, he thought that the political consequences, as articulated in the "Eighteenth Brumaire," were contradictory. Marx saw in the indebted farmer an amorphous social being that had as of yet no place in the symbolic order of political life. Isolated and dispersed, farmers with debt seemed incapable of developing the kind of mass social coherence necessary to constitute a class. "They cannot represent themselves, they must be represented," Marx wrote of the small peasants. This mass of isolated, politically impotent non-subjects that made up a bulk of French society had, in Marx's eyes, made possible the dictatorial Caesarism of Napoleon III.[20]

Thus, the talk of proletarization through debt was not just a critique of economic poverty; it also made a scandal of exclusion from political life in the state. Since the liberal turn in many cantons around 1830, Switzerland had granted a particularly large swathe of men voting rights, especially in comparison with its European neighbors. It was precisely for this reason that disenfranchisement had such symbolic weight in Switzerland.[21] Even after the establishment of the federal state in 1848, almost twenty percent of adult men were barred from voting, one reason among others being bankruptcy. And when Switzerland's first federal bankruptcy law was passed in 1889, the so-called "honor demerits" associated with insolvency were such a contentious issue that deciding how to deal with it was ultimately left to the cantons.[22] The figure of social death joined personal experience and political non-representation in an emotionally-laden form. "A bankrupt in the Canton of Zurich is dead in all relations," he is "completely cut off from life," wrote a petitioner in a complaint filed as part of an 1868 protest

Wucher, in: Gesellschaftsspiegel. Organ zur Vertretung der besitzlosen Volksklassen und zur Beleuchtung der gesellschaftlichen Zustände der Gegenwart 2. 1846, pp. 73–79. See Eiden-Offe, Poesie der Klasse, pp. 122 f.

19 § 1 of the manifesto: Johann Jakob Treichler, Politische Grundsätze, Basel 1846, demanded that bankrupt people and recipients of poor aid be granted voting rights.

20 Karl Marx, The Eighteenth Brumaire of Louis Bonaparte, in: Robert C. Tucker (ed.), The Marx-Engels Reader, New York 1978, pp. 594–617, here p. 608.

21 Oliver Zimmer, A Contested Nation. History, Memory, and Nationalism in Switzerland, 1761–1891, Cambridge 2003, p. 122, esp. n. 13; Paul Nolte, Gemeindebürgertum und Liberalismus in Baden 1800–1850. Tradition, Radikalismus, Republik, Göttingen 1994, pp. 132 f.

22 Albert Tanner, Ein Staat nur für die Hablichen? Demokratie und politische Elite im frühen Bundesstaat, in: Brigitte Studer (ed.), Etappen des Bundesstaates. Staats- und Nationsbildung der Schweiz, 1848–1998, Zurich 1998, pp. 63–88; id., Arbeitsame Patrioten—wohlanständige Damen. Bürgertum und Bürgerlichkeit in der Schweiz 1830–1914, Zurich 1995, p. 569. In the Canton of Bern in particular, a conservative, Protestant movement fought for retaining strict rules. Staatsarchiv Kanton Bern, BB 3.1.540, Ehrenfolgengesetz 1893 ff. See also Theres Maurer, Ulrich Dürrenmatt, 1849–1908. Ein schweizerischer Oppositionspolitiker, Bern 1975, pp. 188–190.

movement that ultimately led to a revision of the constitution. The anonymous writer continued: "Not all bankrupts are negligent or slovenly. Most who go bankrupt have tortured themselves over the difficult experience."[23]

But the practical dimensions of the loss of rights that came with bankruptcy were even more significant than the incapacity to participate in the political life of the state. While the symbolic aspect of the loss of rights received the most attention in the sphere of state politics, official interrogations of individual bankrupts illustrate the fear and anxiety provoked by the threat of being stripped of a local residency permit or being deprived of power of disposition over a wife's property.[24]

Taken as a whole, the complex economics of debt was shot through with tensions on a number of fronts: in the vertical relations between powerful creditors and their debtors, in the support networks of families and communities as well as in their mechanisms of exclusion, in the world of participation in civil life, and in the protests over social death. State politics were transformed by the pressure of revolt and demands of economic equality, making debt into both a practical matter and a political bone of contention.[25]

The relational collectivities that the debt nexus engendered were founded on repeated interactions, which developed different complexes of expectations and obligations. These collectivities extended over diverse social sites without, however, converging into one single outlook; rather, divergent approaches coexisted.

This is to say that if it makes sense to speak of a moral economy of debts, this concept must be sharply distinguished from the holistic idea of an early modern mentality of a "socially embedded" economy.[26] This reservation is shared by historians working in the tradition of E. P. Thompson. In situating English riots within the broader context of the early modern politics of provision, scholars have shown that rioters sometimes used the language of the market, sometimes the rhetoric of "old rights."[27] In urban markets of the eighteenth century, people often

---

23 STAZH, M2 18.1., Eingaben Verfassungsrat 1868, Eingabe Nr. 94. After 1830, liberal jurists worked to invalidate the language of social death. See Friedrich Ludwig Keller, Ueber den Rechtszustand der Falliten, in: Monatschronik der zürcherischen Rechtspflege 1. 1833, pp. 113–121.
24 Suter, Rechtstrieb, pp. 200–211.
25 This confirms the findings of an important work of synthesis on the political history of nineteenth-century Switzerland. See Graber, Demokratie und Revolten.
26 It is beyond the limits of this essay to compare and contrast with the necessary thoroughness the concept of moral economy with Karl Polanyi's concept of the social embeddedness of economy. It suffices to note that moral economy, as a non-holistic concept, need not be reduced to an early modern mode of economy embedded in society. For a critique of a holistic conception of embeddedness see Laurence Fontaine, The Moral Economy. Poverty, Credit, and Trust in Early Modern Europe, New York 2014. On the distinction see Jaime Palomera and Theodora Vetta, Moral Economy. Rethinking a Radical Concept, in: Anthropological Theory 16. 2016, pp. 413–432; Karl Polanyi, The Great Transformation. The Political and Economic Origins of Our Times [1944], Boston 2001[2].
27 John Bohstedt, The Politics of Provisions. Food Riots, Moral Economy, and Market Transition in England, c. 1550–1850, Burlington, VT 2010.

worked as both merchants and purchasers, adapting their idiom to the situation.[28] The vicissitudes of price controls in France make clear that "taxation" was only partially motivated by subaltern claims for entitlement; rather, the regulation of the market by way of price controls was influenced by diverse motives.[29]

This necessitates a conception of moral economy that is at once specific and malleable.[30] Anthropologist Didier Fassin has sought to pluralize the concept. He uses it to denote the conflicts ("les enjeux et les conflits") between various systems of affects, values, norms, and duties.[31] In this sense, moral economies involve both a qualitative, evaluative component that can be condensed into the question "what is good," and a classificatory, normative component that can be condensed into the question "what is appropriate." Viewing historical phenomena through the lens of moral economy allows researchers to analyze customary routines and practices together with questions of context-specific views on what is good and just. This understanding of moral economy goes beyond the focus on subaltern classes and their views of things by making the concept applicable to all spheres of society. Moreover, the key object of analysis for this conception of moral economy is not shared group values, but the instable, contested aspects of political subjectivity.[32]

Fassin is interested in conducting critical research on morality and he reads the "economy" part of the concept as a metaphor for varying moral regimes. In contrast, my interpretation of the concept defines economy as a system that places subjects in particular positions and produces inequality among them, all the while functioning as the decisive factor in their material survival.[33] The urgency with which people have demanded the good and the just has been conditioned by situation-specific, historically shifting views on the right to subsistence, and the economy as a system has been the object of diverging interpretations. Thus, in order to expand the concept's heuristic value, it is important that the analysis of moral

---

28 Simona Cerutti, Processus et expérience. Individus, groupes et identités à Turin, au XVIIe siècle, in: Jacques Revel (ed.), Jeux d'échelles. La micro-analyse à l'expérience, Paris 1996, pp. 161–186 (includes a discussion of Renata Ago's research).

29 Dominique Margairaz, Philippe Minard, Marché des subsistances et économie morale: ce que "taxer" veut dire, in: Annales Historiques de la Révolution Française 2008, no. 352, pp. 53–99; Marcel Streng, Subsistenzpolitik im Übergang. Die kommunale Ordnung des Brot- und Fleischmarktes in Frankreich 1846–1914, Göttingen 2017. On subsistence protests as demands to entitlements see Louise A. Tilly, Entitlements and troubles de subsistances in Nineteenth-Century France, in: André Burguière (ed.), L'histoire grande ouverte. Hommage à Emmanuel Le Roy Ladurie, Paris 1997, pp. 199–213.

30 My turn of phrase is loosely inspired by Ute Tellmann, who treats the concept of "the economic" as at once specific and malleable. Ead., Life and Money. The Genealogy of the Liberal Economy and the Displacement of Politics, New York 2018.

31 Didier Fassin, Les économies morales revisitées, in: Annales HSS 64. 2009, pp. 1237–1266, here p. 1265.

32 Ibid., p. 1264. See also Palomera and Vetta, Moral Economy.

33 Though exclusively dealing with protests, see also Johanna Siméant, "Économie morale" et protestation—détours africains, in: Genèses 81. 2010, pp. 142–160.

economy bring into its purview historical forms of knowledge that stood counter
to the rising dominance of the discipline of political economy.[34] This perspective
makes it possible to recognize moral economies as expressions of social logics and
strategies of legitimation that constituted their own forms of rationality.[35]

II. Epistemological Perspectives:
Categorial Confusion in Practices of Debt Enforcement

But wherein lies the *logic* of a social logic? Interest in the standards historical
actors have drawn upon in their evaluations of debt has shifted researchers' focus
towards analyzing how orders of knowledge originate.[36] Demonstrating how
orders of knowledge are "made possible by certain normative regimes" is the aim
of historical epistemology,[37] which seeks to uncover "the conditions *under* which,
and the means *with* which, things are made into objects of knowledge. It focuses
thus on the process of generating scientific knowledge and the ways in which it is
initiated and maintained."[38] However, as far as economic practices are concerned,
orders of knowledge are not restricted to the field of science alone, but involve a
wide range of actors and places.[39]

A series of influential studies have elucidated the diversity of actors who took
part in the rise of fundamental categories of economic knowledge such as "value,"
"exploitation," "productivity," "reproduction," "risk," or, indeed, "insolvency."[40]

---

34 Political economy, of course, was also historically formed by conceptions of morality, as researchers were eager to point out immediately after the publication of Thompson's essay. See
Elizabeth Fox Genovese, The Many Faces of Moral Economy. A Contribution to a Debate, in:
Past & Present 1973, no. 58, pp. 161–168; for a further adaptation of the concept to the history
of science, see Lorraine Daston, The Moral Economy of Science, in: Osiris 10. 1995, pp. 2–24.

35 I follow Dieter Groh in understanding social logic as "a specific, reconstructable rationality
constituted out of an ensemble of practical norms and behavioral rules." The following seeks
to further explain the "rationality" part of this definition. Dieter Groh, Strategien, Zeit und
Ressourcen. Risikominimierung, Unterproduktivität und Mußepräferenz—die zentralen Kategorien von Subsistenzökonomien, in: id., Anthropologische Dimensionen der Geschichte,
Frankfurt 1992, pp. 54–113, here p. 60–61.

36 Tellmann, Verschulden, p. 8.

37 Omar W. Nasim, Was ist historische Epistemologie?, in: Nach Feierabend. Zürcher Jahrbuch
für Wissensgeschichte 9. 2013, pp. 123–144, here pp. 136 f.

38 Hans-Jörg Rheinberger, On Historicizing Epistemology. An Essay, trans. David Fernbach, Stanford, CA 2010, pp. 2 f.

39 Ann Laura Stoler, Along the Archival Grain. Epistemic Anxieties and Colonial Common Sense,
Princeton 2009, p. 42; Simone Lässig, The History of Knowledge and the Expansion of the
Historical Research Agenda, in: Bulletin of the German Historical Institute, Washington DC
59. 2016, pp. 29–58, here p. 38.

40 Mary Poovey, Genres of the Credit Economy. Mediating Value in Eighteenth- and Nineteenth-Century Britain, Chicago 2008; Étienne Balibar, Exploitation, in: Political Concepts.
A Critical Lexicon, http://www.politicalconcepts.org/balibar-exploitation; François Vatin, Le

Other historians have analyzed the acts of classification that transformed everyday actions into economic actions and the thought styles and normative expectations that informed these acts.[41] And yet others have studied the practical routines and the material surroundings that molded specific historical spheres of economic activity.[42] Lorraine Daston's project of a "moral economy of science" seeks to lay out the important role played by divergent values and emotions in the constitution of scientific knowledge. And the inverse holds as well: categories of knowledge are always involved in the formation of value judgments.

An example from our subject might help make this last point clearer. In the mid-nineteenth century, the administrators entrusted with bankruptcy proceedings in early industrial Basel followed a moral script. In their regular reports to the higher-ups, they identified a cause for every case. Common attributions included "unwillingness to work," "laziness," or a lack of economic prudence, alongside other factors like poor earnings and bad real estate purchases.[43] As these cases show, grids of comprehension emerged in the intertwining of (moral) judgments and (epistemological) verification. The administrators strove to realize what Daston and Peter Galison call "epistemic virtues" like precision and certainty while keeping in check their opposite: "epistemic anxieties"[44] or categorial uncertainty, anxieties that gave impulse to take new tacks in the search for knowledge.[45]

The administrators thus always found the cause of insolvency in the individual and his or her behavior, telling a story of mistakes and bad habits that might have been avoided and corrected by more proper self-comportment. Occupational misfortune in this narrative was always the result of a chain of effects that had the individual at its origin. Even during the 1848 food crisis, administrators refused to accept the social and economic conditions of the time as an exhaustive

travail. Économie et physique, 1780–1830, Paris 1993; Anson Rabinbach, The Human Motor. Energy, Fatigue, and the Origins of Modernity, Berkeley 1992; Dana Simmons, Vital Minimum. Need, Science, and Politics in Modern France, Chicago 2015; Jonathan Levy, Freaks of Fortune. The Emerging World of Capitalism and Risk in America, Cambridge, MA 2012.

41 Sandra Maß, Kinderstube des Kapitalismus? Monetäre Erziehung im 18. und 19. Jahrhundert, Munich 2017; Daniel Vickers, Errors Expected. The Culture of Credit in Rural New England, 1750–1800, in: Economic History Review 63. 2010, pp. 1032–1057; Alexandra Shepard, Accounting for Oneself. Worth, Status and the Social Order in Early Modern England, Oxford 2015.

42 Rebecca L. Spang, Stuff and Money in the Time of the French Revolution, Cambridge, MA 2015; Timothy Mitchell, Rule of Experts. Egypt, Techno-Politics, Modernity, Berkeley 2002; Jane I. Guyer, Marginal Gains. Monetary Transactions in Atlantic Africa, Chicago 2004.

43 A sample of 260 cases between 1841 and 1851 turned up the following explanations (often combined): 50 diagnoses of prodigiality, 50 of uselessness, 43 cases of occupational issues (lack of dexterity, lack of knowledge), 41 of laziness, 41 of bad real estate purchases, 32 of immoral changes in life, 30 of alcoholism, 23 of marital or familial issues, 14 of failed speculative investments. And that's just naming the more common diagnoses. See Staatsarchiv Basel-Stadt [hereafter STABS], Justiz J8, Collocationen der Stadt, 1840–1851.

44 Lorraine Daston and Peter Galison, Objectivity, New York 2007, p. 48, speak of "epistemological fears." On "epistemic anxieties" in the colonial context see Stoler, Along the Archival Grain.

45 Daston and Galison, Objectivity, p. 372 and p. 375.

explanation. Economic failure, in other words, was always a diagnosis of an individual condition, a point of strong overlap between the procedures of Basel's city administration and those of liberal philanthropy.[46]

But the bankruptcy officials' process of discovery faced hurdles at every step of the way. Bankrupt people failed to appear, dug up possessions at the last minute, gave evasive answers during hearings, and offered their own takes on how they ended up where they were. Officials acted on rumors and other unreliable information. One chief of police wrote to the government that the reports were "generally so shoddy that we almost always find ourselves in the dilemma of figuring out what exactly we should reproach the person for."[47] Only in the 1860s, when an overheated property market exponentially increased the number of bankruptcies, were the individual, narrative reports replaced by standardized forms.[48]

Bankruptcy proceedings constantly got swallowed up in quicksand. The formulaic catalog of moral slip-ups that administrators used to classify case histories was printed on the brittle paper of profound uncertainty. Fears of being duped, doubts about their own resources, confusion over the complex of an individual's economic and social relations, rights, claims and counterclaims that bankrupt people filed: all of this made for ongoing confusion on the ground.

Making a determination of bankrupt status was not the only area where the construction of an object of knowledge went hand-in-hand with epistemic anxiety. The seizure of property as collateral during debt enforcement proceedings, and in particular the jailing of debtors, was another.[49] Seizing property had a "tendency to animate objects and to objectify persons"; when somebody was sent into debt imprisonment, the person themself was transformed into collateral.[50] In nineteenth-century Europe, imprisonment for debts was less prominent in countries where the laws made it quite easy to seize a debtor's property (such as France and Switzerland) than in countries that had more stringent legal protections for property (England).[51] Some contemporaries saw the imprisonment of

46 On the philanthropy's focus on individual cases see Christian Topalov, Naissance du chômeur 1880–1910, Paris 1994, pp. 205–209.

47 STABS, Justiz J7, Einzelne Concurssachen 1853–1862, Polizeidirektor Bischoff an Kleinen Rat, 23.8.1855.

48 But here too, officials continued to insist on the significance of narrative reports and regularly supplemented the forms with notes. STABS, Justiz J8, Collocationen 1860–1880, C. F. Burckhardt für das Amtsgericht an den Kleinen Rat, 19.12.1867.

49 For a historical epistemology of asset collateral see Mischa Suter, Debt and Its Attachments. Collateral as an Object of Knowledge in Nineteenth-Century Liberalism, in: Comparative Studies in Society and History 59. 2017, pp. 715–742.

50 A foundational work for historical research on shifts between mobility and fixity caused by debts is Margot C. Finn, The Character of Credit. Personal Debt in English Culture, 1740–1914, Cambridge 2003, here p. 10.

51 Erika Vause, In the Red and in the Black. Debt, Dishonor, and the Law in France between Revolutions, Charlottesville 2018; Thomas M. Luckett, Credit and Commercial Society in France, 1740–1789, Ph. D. Diss. Princeton University 1992, p. 105; Christoph Bergfeld, Über die Aufhebung der Schuldhaft in Frankreich und in Deutschland, in: Jean-François Kervégan and

debtors as a barbaric practice that hindered civilizatory progress.[52] Nevertheless, aside from such shouts of injustice, the fact is that putting debtors in prison was a mundane, everyday practice that gradually came to be used exclusively against poor debtors, as Margot Finn has showed in a study of England.[53] And it seems that because it was increasingly only poor people put in lock-up for their inability to pay, debtors' prisons gradually fell out of journalists' sight: the practice was expanded, but received less and less public attention. This generally held for Switzerland as well, although the numbers of actual imprisonments were much lower than in England. In Switzerland, up until 1874, jailing insolvent debtors was a marginal practice that nevertheless posed a looming threat for indigent debtors, but was rarely seen as a scandal in the public eye.[54]

In a treatise written around 1840 that constitutes one of the few objections made against imprisonment for debts that argued with legal reasoning, the author complained that imprisonment caused disorder in formalized bankruptcy proceedings. He saw in them an internal contradiction: not only were people jailed when they were suspected of concealing assets *before* being determined legally bankrupt; they could also be imprisoned after completing court-ordained measures upon the request of a single creditor.[55] The trained jurist protested that rather than taking consideration of all the debtor's creditors through a well-organized haircut, jailing gave a single creditor exclusive rights to the debtor's assets, leaving the others out in the cold.

What was more, he argued, it was wholly illogical that creditors could exert such power even in cases where the court had determined that the debtor had zero assets. The result was the officially sanctioned exertion of "the most unjust private revenge" against the debtor that stuck him with "the dark fate of a fretful, fleeting outlaw's life."[56] Thus, "arbitrariness, caprice, passion" took the place of the methodic clearing of unpaid debts,[57] giving debtors incentive to "do dishonest deeds" and make secret deals.[58] In short, the author said that imprisonment for

Heinz Mohnhaupt (eds.), Wechselseitige Beeinflussungen und Rezeptionen von Recht und Philosophie in Deutschland und Frankreich, Frankfurt 2001, pp. 329–378.

52 Gustav Peebles, Washing Away the Sins of Debt. The Nineteenth-Century Eradication of the Debtors' Prison, in: Comparative Studies in Society and History 55. 2013, pp. 701–724.

53 Thus, in 1869, in England, jailing for large sums was abolished, while it was retained for small sums up into the twentieth century. See Finn, Character of Credit, pp. 151–155 and p. 186.

54 There are hardly any contemporaneous statistics on imprisonment for debt in Switzerland. The few available numbers for the Canton of Zurich in the 1860s tell us that the median of warrants which made imprisonment possible (though actual enforcement appears to have been much more infrequent) was 858 (the canton's population rose in the same decade from 255,265 to 284,047). Thus, the number of actual debtors put in jail was rather low. For an attempt to interpret these numbers see Suter, Rechtstrieb, p. 236 and pp. 244–246.

55 STAZH, P 37, [Conrad Melchior] Hirzel, Dissertation über das Wortzeichen (manuscript, undated, before 1842), part 1, here p. 13 and p. 18.

56 Ibid., part 2, p. 9; ibid., part 1, p. 23.

57 Ibid., part 2, p. 8.

58 Ibid., part 2, p. 10.

debts was a tool of revenge, not of justice. Rather than representing a rational way of dealing with things, it fostered passionate affects; rather than ensuring transparency, it encouraged backdoor maneuvers. The problem for the author was not the fundamental paradox of treating a human body as a thinglike asset, but rather the epistemic and moral obscuration of the relations between debtors, creditors, and the state.

Bankruptcy proceedings and imprisonment for debt in nineteenth-century Switzerland demonstrate the extent to which moral judgments and knowledge practices were interfused. The examples help illustrate how social logics came into being and offer insight into questions of the agency of historical actors. After all, well-known is the fact that the concept of moral economy was developed as an attempt to attribute subaltern groups with their own forms of rationality and thereby give them a voice.[59] But the ideas that came out of this venture often assumed a "theoretically simplistic concept of the subject."[60] The emphasis on agency homogenized the plurality of subaltern practices by painting them over with the abstract concept of autonomous individuality.[61]

Nearly thirty years ago, Joan Scott proposed a solution to this issue, suggesting that historians view experience not as an explanation, but rather as something that needs explaining, treating actors as "subjects whose agency is created through statuses and situations conferred on them."[62] Scott urged historians to give up the notion of experience as an irreducible horizon of historical truth and to make their project "not the reproduction and transmission of knowledge said to be arrived at through experience, but the analysis of the production of that knowledge itself." This effort, I believe, can be helped along by integrating practical epistemologies into historical research, which makes it possible to discern the interrelations between moral judgments on the one hand and calculative knowledge and evaluation on the other.[63]

59 Simona Cerutti, Who is below? E. P. Thompson, historien des sociétés modernes. Une relecture, in: Annales HSS 70. 2015, pp. 931–955.
60 Jakob Tanner, "Kultur" in den Wirtschaftswissenschaften und kulturwissenschaftliche Interpretationen ökonomischen Handelns, in: Friedrich Jaeger and Jörn Rüsen (eds.), Handbuch der Kulturwissenschaften, vol. 3: Themen und Tendenzen, Stuttgart 2004, pp. 195–224, here p. 214.
61 Walter Johnson, On Agency, in: Journal of Social History 37. 2003, pp. 113–124, here p. 117; Lynn M. Thomas, Historicising Agency, in: Gender & History 28. 2016, pp. 324–339.
62 Joan W. Scott, The Evidence of Experience, in: Critical Inquiry 17. 1991, pp. 773–797, here p. 793.
63 Ibid., p. 797.

III. The Future as a Lost Past and Colliding Temporalities

A more complex understanding of the subject, however, does not mean giving up the concept as such. We might recall here Thompson's pithy remark that through the "junction-concept" of experience, "structure is transmuted into process, and the subject re-enters history."[64] Thompson's formulation seeks to hone in on conflict-ridden moments in the process of the formation of a subject, moments that motivated historical actors' vocabulary of moral economy in the first place. To underscore this point with another example from practices of bankruptcy in early industrial Basel, consider the fact that, in hearings with the police, bankrupt people often countered the administrators' moralistic scripts of individual blame with alternative narratives. They depicted themselves as caring fathers and breadwinners who had tried very hard but had become, due to unfavorable circumstances outside their control, overburdened by debt. In doing so, they appealed to the normative concept of the home and its hierarchy of genders and generations.[65] They insisted that they were willing to do what it takes to ensure that they and their children could live a dignified life. On the other hand, however, some facing insolvency complained that being exposed to the market meant being exposed to a mechanism without memory, which is to say, a mechanism that refused to recognize the labor they had put into their endeavors. The insolvents themselves, however, remembered their travails from the past quite well and found that they justified a claim to at least some rewards.[66]

Conflicts between divergent logics did not necessarily have to be spectacular, and indeed often took place without much commotion. In their defenses, bankrupt Baselers made reference to norms and values that were certainly shared by the officials questioning them.

A focus on process teaches us to look not so much at the collision of otherwise static ideas as at the dynamic of the encounter itself. The notion that insolvent workers were fixated on an early modern mentality that resisted the rising logic of the market tells us little. Analyzing how different systems interacted in con-

---

64 Edward Palmer Thompson, The Poverty of Theory or an Orrery of Errors, London 1995, p. 229.

65 See David W. Sabean, Property, Production, and Family in Neckarhausen, 1700–1870, Cambridge 1990, ch. 3: "The Ideology of the House," pp. 88–123; Joachim Eibach and Inken Schmidt-Voges (eds.), Das Haus in der Geschichte Europas. Ein Handbuch, Berlin 2015. An important critique of Otto Brunner's fiction of an autarchic "whole house" can be found in Claudia Opitz, Neue Wege der Sozialgeschichte? Ein kritischer Blick auf Otto Brunners Konzept des "ganzen Hauses," in: GG 20. 1994, pp. 88–98; Valentin Groebner, Außer Haus. Otto Brunner und die alteuropäische "Ökonomik," in: GWU 46. 1995, no. 2, pp. 69–80.

66 For the 1840s see, for instance, STABS Justiz J7, Einzelne Concurssachen 1836–1845, Verhör mit Christoph Gysin, 8.5.1845; Verhör mit Rudolf Kübler, 17.2.1845; STABS Justiz J7, Einzelne Concurssachen 1846–1852, Verhör mit Friedrich Klingelfuß, 4.2.1846; Verhör mit Otto Landerer, 6.2.1846; Verhör mit Friedrich Otto, 6.2.1846; Verhör mit Georg Oppermann, 18.10.1847; Verhör mit Johann Jacob Reischacher-Hirt, 26.1.1848; Verhör mit Johann Jakob Schlueb, 11.4.1848; Verhör mit Johann Carl Peschel, 30.4.1849.

crete events, however, is where the juxtaposition of moral economy and political economy can be made fruitful. In his research on struggles for better wages during the 1848 revolutions in Europe, Ahlrich Meyer argued that, at a time when capitalist accumulation and valorization was undergoing a profound structural transformation, the subaltern classes' rhetorical appeals to "old rights" gained revolutionary force.[67]

One example of this antagonistic rhetoric can be found in the work of utopian communist Wilhelm Weitling. A tailor from Magdeburg, Weitling developed a theory of pauperism in which debt played a central role while he was living in exile in Switzerland from 1841 to 1843.[68] Borrowing and lending featured high on his list of suggestions for communists interested in practices of commoning among one another.[69] Thus, Weitling transformed the everyday experiences of the economy of makeshifts into a theory that did not distinguish between production and reproduction and that, in contrast to other early socialist ideas, did not ennoble work. He found in debts the subjective side of what he and his fellow communists called "the money system."[70]

Because he thought about money from the perspective of debt and indebtedness, Weitling conceived of it not as an instrument of exchange, but rather as a "generator and stabilizer of social inequality."[71] Debt, he wrote, was the reverse side of wealth; it took on its own dynamic by thrusting itself upon people as the concrete reality of the absence of money. In an article he published in *Die junge Generation* (The Young Generation), a newspaper he had founded, Weitling wrote that money was a system of social segregation that set up a literally metal gate between production and consumption, "work and enjoyment." He painted an image of poor people sitting before the gate, "hustling and bustling, and when they've gathered together a little pile, the gate opens up and the rich claw it in," while the poor were hardly capable of saving a few crumbs.[72] Another article with the title "Was ist Geld?" (What is money?) described the lack of money as a plastic

---

67 Ahlrich Meyer, Massenarmut und Existenzrecht, in: id., Die Logik der Revolten. Studien zur Sozialgeschichte, 1789–1848, Berlin 1999, pp. 93–256.

68 The state of knowledge on Weitling's biography is excellent thanks to Waltraud Seidel-Höppner's monumental study. See ead., Wilhelm Weitling (1808–1871). Eine politische Biografie, 2 vols., Frankfurt 2014. Still useful are Wolfgang Schieder, Anfänge der deutschen Arbeiterbewegung. Die Auslandsvereine im Jahrzehnt nach der Julirevolution von 1830, Stuttgart 1963; Marc Vuilleumier, Weitling, les communistes allemands et leurs adeptes en Suisse. Quelques documents (1843–1847), in: Revue européenne des sciences sociales 11. 1973, no. 29, pp. 37–100; Hans-Arthur Marsiske, "Wider die Umsonstfresser." Der Handwerkerkommunist Wilhelm Weitling, Hamburg 1986.

69 Wilhelm Weitling, Das Evangelium des armen Sünders [reprint of the second edition from 1845, first edition 1843], Hamburg 1971, pp. 129–131.

70 Die junge Generation July 1842, no. 7, herausgegeben und redigiert von einigen deutschen Arbeitern [reprint], Leipzig 1972, p. 127; Olwen Hufton, The Poor of Eighteenth-Century France, 1750–1789, Oxford 1974.

71 Eiden-Offe, Poesie der Klasse, p. 209.

72 Die junge Generation August 1842, no. 8, p. 134.

presence: "But what is *no* money?", the author asked.[73] "No money is a thing that fills all empty pockets and that everyone who has nothing in his hand can grasp with his fingers." From this, he drew the conclusion: "No money is a quiet beckoning of nature to accrue debts and a loud command to not repay them." From the lack of money Weitling deduced the imperative to make debts and not pay them back. In doing so, the author conducted an about-face that called into being an antagonistic principle, making the refusal to repay debts into an expression of a break with dominant social relations.

William Reddy once claimed that moral economy was the counterpart to the expansion of capitalism, because something like moral economy would always appear in those places where people refused to allow their lives—control over their own bodies, their routines, and their familial relations—to be translated into monetary values.[74] By no means must this story be told as one of loss or as a contradiction between the old duality of tradition versus modernity. Rather, moral economy indicates how the encounter of different temporalities itself engendered new dynamics.

The analysis of colliding temporalities is especially pertinent in postcolonial perspectives on history.[75] Dipesh Chakrabarty asks historians to write histories of "relationships that do not lend themselves to the reproduction of the logic of capital," but that nevertheless need not be pre-modern, pre-industrial, or pre-capitalist.[76] Early works by the Subaltern Studies Group of Indian historiography, too, took as their point of departure not tradition, but rather intersubjective spaces in which divergent logics came into conflict with one another, such as in colonial bureaucracy or medicine.[77] The claim is not that non-European economic practices were "moral" as opposed to the supposed straitjacket of colonial "political economy."[78] Rather, the point is that moral economy, on a categorial level, was always realized as a conflict between divergent temporalities.

To come back to Wilhelm Weitling: the romantic anti-capitalism touted by Weitling and other thinkers of 1848 engaged in a retroactive temporality, as Patrick Eiden-Offe has shown in a study on literary history. In other words, they

---

73 Die junge Generation April 1842, no. 4, p. 62 (emphasis mine). The author cannot be identified with certainty. Seidel-Höppner believes that, alongside Weitling, it may have been August Becker. Seidel-Höppner, Weitling, vol. 1, p. 214.

74 William M. Reddy, The Rise of Market Culture. The Textile Trade and French Society, 1750–1900, Cambridge 1984, p. 334.

75 Kalyan Sanyal, Rethinking Capitalist Development. Primitive Accumulation, Governmentality, and Post-colonial Capitalism, London 2007.

76 Dipesh Chakrabarty, Provincializing Europe. Postcolonial Thought and Historical Difference, Princeton 2008 [2000], p. 64. Among the nuances of Chakrabarty's argument that make it immune to accusations of telling a tale of loss is the fact that it is based on a discussion of Karl Marx' thoughts on the money form.

77 Veena Das, Subaltern as Perspective, in: Subaltern Studies 6. 1989, pp. 310–324, here p. 313.

78 Partha Chatterjee, Lineages of Political Society. Studies in Postcolonial Democracy, New York 2011; Ritu Birla, Stages of Capital. Law, Culture, and Market Governance in Late Colonial India, Durham, NC 2009.

portrayed their political aims as something that had been lost.[79] "In earlier times, nobody was denied a handful of fruit from the field of his neighbor in order to still the forceful pangs of hunger; today, gaunt, impoverished figures crawl our streets, and in the furrows in their cheeks one can read the Fourth Petition."[80] In these writings, the past serves not so much as an idyll, but as an imaginary contrast that makes it easier to shine light on the inacceptability of the present.

The uses of imaginary pasts for political projects in the modern era has taken all sorts of different guises, which have long been an object of historical research.[81] In this sense, Weitling's imagined past was nothing new. His rhetoric was unique in the sense that the recollection of the lost past was supposed to bring about a new future by ushering in a radical break with the present, communism as a utopia to be realized right here right now.[82] One key demand was that "all debt receipts, bonds, and bills of exchange" be annulled.[83] The forgiveness of debts would help facilitate the abolition of money as an instance of social subjugation.

Aside from the explicitly political discussion of debt from the likes of Weitling, too, different temporalities beat the rhythm of relations of debt and indebtedness in the nineteenth century. Bills of exchange combined enhanced circulation with strict enforcement at the moment payments fell due. Certain forms of paper secured by real property were, at least theoretically, valid "in eternity"; they were resold and changed hands, and only after 1853 could both the creditor and the debtor in the Canton of Zurich cancel them.[84] Thus, by the 1860s, commentators were remarking that new forms of bonds would compete with the existing securities, accelerate the rural debt economy, and render payments more exact.[85] Before a national law on debt enforcement was passed in 1889, representatives of the agricultural Canton of Fribourg remarked:

---

79 Eiden-Offe, Poesie der Klasse, p. 29 f.

80 Wilhelm Weitling, Garantien der Harmonie und Freiheit [1842], with an introduction and notes by Fr. Mehring, Berlin 1908, p. 52.

81 For a wholly different example, also from the nineteenth century, see Nolte, Gemeinde-bürgertum.

82 Ahlrich Meyer, Frühsozialismus. Theorien der sozialen Bewegung 1789–1848, Freiburg 1977, p. 209.

83 Weitling, Garantien, p. 238.

84 Gesetz über die Ablösung grundversicherter Forderungen überhaupt und über die Natur und Wiederauflösung der durch den Uebergang von Unterpfändern auf dritte Besitzer entstehenden Rechtsverhältnisse insbesondere, in: Officielle Sammlung der seit Annahme der Verfassung vom Jahre 1831 erlassenen Gesetze, Beschlüsse und Verordnungen des Eidgenössischen Standes Zürich, vol. 9, Zurich 1853, pp. 280–286; Martin Schaffner, Die demokratische Bewegung der 1860er Jahre. Beschreibung und Erklärung der Zürcher Volksbewegung von 1867, Basel 1982, pp. 91–97. On rural financial bonds see Markus Mattmüller, Agrargeschichte der Schweiz im Ancien Régime, vol. 2, Vorlesung im WS 1978/79 und SS 1979, Historisches Seminar Basel, Basel 1979 (manuscript, library of the department of history, Universität Basel), pp. 365–392.

85 Gottfried Farner, Der Schuldbriefverkehr und das zürcherische Notariatswesen unter der Initiative, Zurich 1869, p. 9.

Il ne faut pas perdre de vue qu'il y a solidarité (que l'on nous permette l'expression) entre les parties d'une industrie agricole, que surtout chaque chose y a son temps, que si l'on agit à contre-temps, on la compromet plus ou moins, ou même on la désorganise. Il n'en est pas de même dans le commerce et l'industrie manufacturière.[86]

A farmer had resources, but he could not immediately turn them into money, at least not all year around. Political debates on the rhythms of debt repayment tackled the issue of how to collectively agree upon how to shape individual relations of debt, especially considering that the expectations, obligations, and insecurities of those involved in them always influenced the strategies they took.[87] Legal regulation channeled the countless temporal frictions of individual debts and this in turn influenced the shape of capitalist temporalities.

Questions as to how to conceptualize the temporalities of capitalism have been met with a number of responses from scholars. William Sewell speaks of a dialectic of the restless activity of capitalism on the one hand and the monotonous, repetitive cycles of capital accumulation on the other.[88] From this system-oriented perspective, which does justice to the importance of abstraction in capitalism, repetition and difference give direction to the circulation and reproduction of capital. Nicos Poulantzas described the "segmentation and serialization" of time in the factory floor's division of labor. From this angle, time appears as an instrument of discipline: homogenous, but broken up into different units; geared towards a goal, the production of commodities, but without end.[89] Jens Beckert analyzes the fictive expectations, the projects for the future constructed by economic actors living in constant uncertainty.[90] For Beckert, capitalist activity is driven by imagined futures.

But in the end, little empirical research has been conducted on the concrete temporal regimes of nineteenth-century capitalism. Viewed from a bird's-eye perspective, the genealogy of debt enforcement in Switzerland reveals a gradual synchronization of received practices, without, however, homogenizing them: the stabilization of debt enforcement proceedings through the 1889 federal bankruptcy law combined asset seizure and bankruptcy proceedings in such a

---

86 Bundesarchiv Bern [nachfolgend BAR] E22 1000/134 2607*, Az. 6.7.4., Mittheilungen aus den Eingaben kantonaler Behörden zu dem Entwurfe eines Bundesgesezes [sic] über Schuldbetreibung und Konkurs, Bern 1874, pp. 22 f.

87 Foundational here are Pierre Bourdieu's elaborations on the role of intervals in the strategies of practical action: Pierre Bourdieu, Outline of a Theory of Practice, trans. Richard Nice, Cambridge 1977, pp. 6–15.

88 William H. Sewell, The Temporalities of Capitalism, in: Socio-Economic Review 6. 2008, pp. 517–537.

89 Nicos Poulantzas, State, Power, Socialism [1978], London 1980, p. 110.

90 Jens Beckert, Imagined Futures. Fictional Expectations and Capitalist Dynamics, Cambridge, MA 2016.
    Similar arguments, but with a stronger historical grounding, can be found in the contributions in Nadine Levratto and Alessandro Stanziani (eds.), Le capitalisme au futur antérieur. Crédit et spéculation en France (fin de XVIIIe–début XXe siècles), Brussels 2011.

way as to allow the coexistence of varying rhythms of repayment. The example of debt enforcement practices thus suggests that everyday economic relations in nineteenth-century Switzerland were permeated by divergent temporalities rather than a consistent orientation towards the future, which has been mostly only ever been observed at the commanding heights of entrepreneurial activity.[91] For instance, deadlines punctuated the temporality of debt repayment: after a deadline had passed, qualitatively new situations involving things like the seizure of furniture or demands that relatives help pay kicked in.[92]

This punctuated time was syncopated with other rhythms, such as debtors' efforts to maintain continuity in their everyday lives and earnings. The pressure of the past and looming deadlines in the future could place considerable strains on an individual's present. Conversely, remembering one's past efforts could give debtors—and creditors for that matter—the capacity to actively forge a sense of continuity. Both debtors and creditors made use of a variegated repertoire of temporal rhythms. Thus, the moral economy of debt is not about old versus new, nor about the defense of traditional practices against new, state-run procedures of debt enforcement. Rather, on a categorial level, the moral economy of debts is grounded in the experience of conflicting temporalities itself.

IV. Moral Economy and Monetary Exchange:
"Usury" and "Profiteering" between the Panic of 1873
and Weimar Hyperinflation

The concept of moral economy is flexible and adaptable, but it is not a catch-all term. Comparing the concept's applicability to a separate phenomenon might help better articulate its limits: thus, as a sort of concluding experiment, I would like to briefly discuss the historical usages of the term "usury" (Wucher) in German-speaking countries. Often, but not always associated with anti-Semitic demonization, debates on usury as a diagnosis of the symptoms and cause of a crisis brought together morality and economy in particularly garish fashion. At first glance, one might situate discourses on usury as an aspect of moral economy; but things are more complicated. In debates on usury, an emotionally charged rhetoric over the right to entitlements stood alongside—without, however, merg-

---

91 For example, people's capacity to shape their economic futures seems to diminish in precarious economic circumstances, a point observed for very different conditions by Meyer, Verschuldetes Selbst, p. 37 and p. 159 as well as by Pierre Bourdieu, Job Insecurity is Everywhere Now, in: id. (ed.), Acts of Resistance. Against the Tyranny of the Market, trans. Richard Nice, New York 1998, pp. 81–87, here p. 82, or, for the "unpredictable economy" of the pre-industrial poor, by Fontaine, Moral Economy, p. 25.

92 The concept of "punctuated time" is borrowed from Jane Guyer, Prophecy and the Near Future. Thoughts on Macroeconomic, Evangelical, and Punctuated Time, in: American Ethnologist 34. 2007, pp. 409–421.

ing with—politicians' and economic experts' views on how the liberal economy and different areas of policy were supposed to function.

As Martin Geyer's foundational research has shown, the concept of *Wucher* (usury) in German had an especially broad extension in comparison to the analogous concept in other European languages. It denoted not only profit from interest, but also price gouging and other economic distortions.[93] During the hunger crisis of 1848, usury functioned as a code word for describing the experience of having to pay too much for the bare necessities.[94] The concept's use runs parallel to periods of economic crisis: when subsistence protests cooled off after 1848, usury was thematized less and less. By the 1860s, usury laws that placed limits on interest rates for loans were abolished in all of the German-speaking nations.[95]

But after 1877, usury laws were put back on the books in the Habsburg Empire, the German Empire, and Switzerland, even if the general understanding of what usury meant had shifted. Usury was now defined as the exploitation of another person's distress, inexperience, or foolishness for one's own profit by strapping them with extraordinary conditions for credit. Debates on usury centered on a subject lacking in economic rationality who was allegedly in need of protection.[96] In inquiries that placed social-scientific expertise at the service of anti-Semitic agitation, the Verein für Socialpolitik (Association for social policy) localized the primary instrument of usury in intransparent local practices of exchange and calculation.[97] Modernizers in the association set as their goal the reformation

93 Martin H. Geyer, Defining the Common Good and Social Justice. Popular and Legal Concepts of "Wucher" in Germany from the 1860s to the 1920s, in: Willibald Steinmetz (ed.), Private Law and Social Inequality in the Industrial Age. Comparing Legal Cultures in Britain, France, Germany, and the United States, New York 2000, pp. 457–483, here pp. 457–459.

94 Manfred Gailus, Straße und Brot. Sozialer Protest in den deutschen Staaten unter besonderer Berücksichtigung Preußens, 1847–1849, Göttingen 1990; Carola Lipp and Wolfgang Kaschuba, Wasser und Brot. Politische Kultur im Alltag der Vormärz- und Revolutionsjahre, in: GG 10. 1984, pp. 320–351, here pp. 344–346.

95 Representative of the corresponding liberal position is Walter Munzinger, Die Wucherfrage. Referat gehalten in der Versammlung des schweizerischen Juristenvereins in Aarau, 5.10.1866 (separate printing for the Zeitschrift für schweizerisches Recht, vol. XV), Basel 1866.

96 For a more detailed elaboration of the following see Mischa Suter, Usury and the Problem of Exchange under Capitalism. A Late-Nineteenth-Century Debate on Economic Rationality, in: Social History 42. 2017, pp. 501–523; for more focus on the anti-liberal tendencies of the usury discourse see Martin H. Geyer, Die Sprache des Rechts, die Sprache des Antisemitismus. "Wucher" und soziale Ordnungsvorstellungen im Kaiserreich und der Weimarer Republik, in: Christof Dipper et al. (eds.), Europäische Sozialgeschichte. Festschrift für Wolfgang Schieder, Berlin 2000, pp. 413–429.

97 Der Wucher auf dem Lande. Berichte und Gutachten veröffentlicht vom Verein für Socialpolitik, Leipzig 1887; Verhandlungen der am 28. und 29. September 1888 in Frankfurt a. M. abgehaltenen Generalversammlung des Vereins für Socialpolitik über den ländlichen Wucher, die Mittel zu seiner Abhülfe, insbesondere die Organisation des bäuerlichen Kredits und über Einfluß des Detailhandels auf die Preise und etwaige Mittel gegen eine ungesunde Preisbildung, Leipzig 1889.

of practices of monetary exchange, a key aspect of which was the exclusion of intermediaries imagined as Jewish.

Thus, one strain of the discourse on usury involved how to educate and protect subjects deemed incapable of conducting their economic affairs in a rational manner. In another strain, usury functioned as a mobilizer for a new form of political anti-Semitism.[98] The Panic of 1873 and the series of crises that followed out of it gave fuel to the anti-Semitic, anti-modern rhetoric of "stock market usury."[99] However, as Catherine Davies describes in her study on the Financial Panic of 1873 as a phenomenon of globalization, the denunciation of a morally depraved financial sphere constituted only one among several explanations of the causes of the crisis. Liberal economists insisted that the gold standard be adopted to place constraints on what were perceived as the opaque, heterogenous practices of the financial sphere.[100] Simply subsuming these variegated negotiations of the place of finance in society under the rubric of moral economy is insufficient. Rather, debates on usury in the nineteenth century were a site where divergent interpretations of economic phenomena came into confrontation with one another.

In any case, the associations between anti-Semitism and the discourse of usury go further back than the late nineteenth century. As Manfred Gailus has shown, anti-Semitism charged the discourse of usury in subsistence protests since the Early Modern period.[101] Viewing the role of debts and usury in riots reveals the "ugly side of collective action," which is "difficult to integrate into the empathic, positive concept of protest touted by older research on protests."[102]

When a charivari against the Jewish community of Endingen (Canton of Aargau) paraded through the streets in 1861, anti-Semites took the occasion

---

98 David Peal, Anti-Semitism and Rural Transformation in Kurhessen. The Rise and Fall of the Böckel Movement, Ph. D. Diss. Columbia University 1985; Helmut Walser Smith, The Discourse of Usury. Relations Between Christians and Jews in the German Countryside, 1880–1914, in: Central European History 32. 1999, pp. 255–276; Olaf Blaschke, Antikapitalismus und Antisemitismus. Die Wirtschaftsmentalität der Katholiken im Wilhelminischen Deutschland, in: Johannes Heil and Bernd Wacker (eds.), Shylock? Zinsverbot und Geldverleih in jüdischer und christlicher Tradition, Munich 1997, pp. 113–146.

99 See, for example, C. v. Thüngen-Roßbach, Die Wucher- und Wechselfrage. Vortrag, Berlin 1879.

100 Hannah Catherine Davies, Transatlantic Speculations. Globalization and the Panics of 1873, New York 2018.

101 Manfred Gailus, Was macht eigentlich die historische Protestforschung? Rückblick, Resümee, Perspektiven, in: Mitteilungsblatt des Instituts für soziale Bewegungen 2005, no. 34, pp. 127–154, here p. 147. On the figure of the usurer in the period between 1750 and 1850 see id., Die Erfindung des "Korn-Juden." Zur Geschichte eines antijüdischen Feindbildes des 18. und frühen 19. Jahrhunderts, in: HZ 272. 2001, pp. 597–622; Robert Jütte, Das Bild vom "Kornjuden" als Antifigur zum frühneuzeitlichen Prinzip der "guten narung" und der "moral economy," in: Aschkenas 23. 2013, no. 1–2, pp. 27–52.

102 Gailus, Protestforschung, p. 139. Christhard Hoffmann et al. (eds.), Exclusionary Violence. Antisemitic Riots in Modern German History, Ann Arbor 2002.

to kick off a series of protests in the context of which anti-Jewish rhetoric came to infuse discussions on economics.[103] Jews were maligned as ruthless profiteers in sentences like: "Their remorseless usury is and remains the only tie that binds them to Christians" and "Today they are the masters, tomorrow they are bankrupt."[104] The political goals of the movement, however, had nothing to do with practices of debt and indebtedness.[105] Rather, the protests attacked the legal equality of Jews in Lengnau and Endingen (where about forty percent of the Jewish population of Switzerland were de facto compelled to reside),[106] which the federal and then cantonal governments had only granted them after considerable economic pressure from abroad.

While there is no necessary link between the political culture of anti-Semitism and the ways in which people made judgments about economic practices, the two could align in certain contexts: The material trigger of the uproar in Aargau was a new survey of the common forests, which would have seen Christian Endingers lose part of their timber to the newly established Jewish community. Another anti-Semitic outlash in 1883 in the city of St. Gallen targeted a well-known Jewish socialist and owner of a retail credit business. While older analyses have focused on the anti-socialist aspects of this riot, a new study considers the competition between shopkeepers (the majority of the perpetrators) and the hire-purchase businesses that were on the ascent in the 1880s.[107] At any rate, the politics of anti-Semitism were not restricted to a direct causal nexus between economic crisis and violence, and they reached beyond habitual notions of legitimation that were based on economic practices.[108]

However, while the discourse of usury changed over time, emotion-laden demands from below did not disappear. Martin Geyer writes that the First World War ushered in a turn.[109] When the war caused shortages of essential goods in

103 Alexandra Binnenkade, KontaktZonen. Jüdisch-christlicher Alltag in Lengnau, Cologne 2009, pp. 178–233; Aram Mattioli, Der "Mannli-Sturm" oder der Aargauer Emanzipationskonflikt 1861–1863, in: id. (ed.), Antisemitismus in der Schweiz 1848–1960, Zurich 1998, pp. 135–169.

104 Die Abberufung. Ein paar Worte der 19 "Mannli" des Döttinger Komite an ihre aargauischen "Mitmannli," n.p. 1862, p. 21; Zur Judenfrage. Ehrerbietige Vorstellung der christlichen Gemeinden Ober-Endingen und Lengnau an den Tit. Regierungsrath zu Handen des Tit. Großen Rathes des Kanons Aargau, n.p. n.d. [1861], p. 19.

105 On contacts between Jews and Christians in Aargau in which debts played an important role see Binnenkade, KontaktZonen, ch. 5: "Kredit, Medium der Kontaktzone," pp. 243–265, Jews had debts with Christians, Christians with other Christians, Jews with other Jews, and only sometimes did Christians have debts with Jews.

106 Mattioli, Mannli-Sturm, p. 135.

107 Matthias Ruoss, Fighting Creative Destruction. The Bamberger Riot and the Emergence of Hire Purchase in Switzerland around 1900, in: Journal of Social History (forthcoming).

108 Arno Herzig, Judenhaß und Antisemitismus bei den Unterschichten und in der frühen Arbeiterbewegung, in: Ludger Heid (ed.), Juden und deutsche Arbeiterbewegung bis 1933. Soziale Utopien und religiös-kulturelle Traditionen, Tübingen 1992, pp. 1–18. See also Smith, Discourse of Usury.

109 Geyer, Defining the Common Good, p. 460.

Germany, protests at the market against rising prices marked a return to suppos-
edly "early modern" forms of direct action. The Europe-wide food riots constitute a powerful example: suffering the vicissitudes of the war economy, protestors
decried *"Wucher,"* "profiteering," and "vie chère."[110] In Paris, consumers' protests
became a springboard for revolutionary demands of equality that appealed not
to tradition, but to an "alternative model of consumer citizenship."[111] Demands
for "fair prices" were addressed to representatives of the modern state. All of
this led to new forms of collectivity being expressed in new places. In Germany,
emergency laws on the rights to provisions for essential goods were written
in the language of suprapersonal categories. And during the second half of
the war, poor residents of the large cities protested for more equal distribution
of goods.[112]

After the war, too, usury featured prominently in political debates on welfare
provisions, and state institutions tasked with price control were expanded during
Weimar inflation.[113] The inflation turned relations between debtors and creditors
on their head, and at its apex, it caused money's functions to collapse. During this
period of epistemic and social crisis, in which various forms of both economic
and moral evaluation collided, usury blurred the distinction between the two in
the context of everyday economic relations. At the same time, the actions of the
völkisch movement introduced a new element of violence into the protests.[114]
Among the best-known examples of anti-Jewish violence were the pogroms in
the Bavarian town of Memmingen in 1921 and in Berlin's Scheunenviertel in
November 1923.[115] The Scheunenviertel Pogrom, in which at least hundreds—

110 For Great Britain see Christine Grandy, "Avarice" and "Evil Doers." Profiteers, Politicians, and
     Popular Fiction in the 1920s, in: Journal of British Studies 50. 2011, pp. 667–689.
111 Tyler Stovall, Paris and the Spirit of 1919. Consumer Struggles, Transnationalism and Revo-
     lution, Cambridge 2012, p. 13 (quote) and p. 184; id., Du vieux et du neuf. Economie morale
     et militantisme ouvrier dans les luttes contre la vie chère à Paris en 1919, in: Le mouvement
     social 1995, no. 170, pp. 85–113.
112 Belinda Davis, Home Fires Burning. Food, Politics, and Everyday Life in World War I Berlin,
     Chapel Hill, NC 2000, p. 160, p. 190.
113 Martin H. Geyer, Verkehrte Welt. Revolution, Inflation und Moderne: München 1914–1924,
     Göttingen 1998, ch. 5: "Die Desorganisation des Marktes: Konsumenten und Wucherfrage,"
     pp. 167–204; Carl Falck, Preisüberwachung nach Abbau der Zwangsbewirtschaftung, Berlin
     1920.
114 Davis, Home Fires Burning, p. 243; Martin H. Geyer, Teuerungsprotest und Teuerungsun-
     ruhen 1914–1923. Selbsthilfegesellschaft und Geldentwertung, in: Manfred Gailus und Hein-
     rich Volkmann (eds.), Der Kampf um das tägliche Brot. Nahrungsmangel, Versorgungspolitik
     und Protest 1770–1990, Opladen 1994, pp. 319–345.
115 Nevertheless, these were not the only two instances of violence. There were anti-Semitic
     attacks in Breslau, Karlsruhe, Erfurt, Nuremberg, Coburg, Bremen, Oldenburg, and other
     places. Trude Maurer, Ostjuden in Deutschland 1918–1933, Hamburg 1986, pp. 329–344,
     here p. 334; David C. Large, "Out with the Ostjuden." The Scheunenviertel Riots in Berlin,
     November 1923, in: Hoffmann et al., Exclusionary Violence, pp. 123–140, here p. 127; Gailus,
     Protestforschung, pp. 138 f. and p. 148; Michael Wildt, Hitler's Volksgemeinschaft and the
     Dynamics of Racial Exclusion. Violence against Jews in Provincial Germany, 1919–1939, New

and maybe even more—of Jewish persons were physically attacked, was a focal point of violence instigated by *völkisch* agitators. Yet it took place in a broader context of protests against rising prices that for their part had diverse aims and targets.[116]

Between the late nineteenth century and Weimar inflation, conceptions of usury ranged from street protest to policies ushered in by liberal modernizers and the nascent welfare state; they encompassed emotionally charged outcries and forms of demonization alongside measures to educate and improve economic subjects. Taken together, one cannot reduce these different conceptions into something that could be fit into an all-encompassing notion of moral economy. In contrast, an analysis of the heterogeneous ideas and practices denounced as usury shows that moral economy was one changing element among many in a series of struggles over the problem of monetary circulation in modern capitalism.[117]

V. Conclusion

In nineteenth-century Switzerland, debt and indebtedness had a political dimension. They were highly emotional topics precisely because of their association with male personal autonomy and male citizens' rights and privileges. In local-level social relations, the politics of debt enforcement were bound up with community norms and the interests of the local administrations tasked with carrying out the procedures. What makes debts a fitting object for the analysis of moral economy is the fact that scholars from Thompson to Didier Fassin have understood moral economies as sites where questions of legitimacy are negotiated.

The concept of a moral economy of debts proposed here, however, pinpoints something more specific than the general moralization of economic activities. It involves context-specific, conflicting social horizons and heterogeneous forms of legitimacy within the economy as a system of material survival. It seeks to shed

York 2012, pp. 54–56; Paul Hoser, Die Rosenbaumkrawalle von 1921 in Memmingen, in: Peter Fassl (ed.), Geschichte und Kultur der Juden in Schwaben, vol. 3: Zwischen Nähe, Distanz und Fremdheit, Augsburg 2007, pp. 95–109.

116 Molly Loberg, The Struggles for the Streets of Berlin. Politics, Consumption, and Urban Space, 1914–1945, Cambridge 2018, pp. 61 f.; Robert Scholz, Ein unruhiges Jahrzehnt. Lebensmittelunruhen, Massenstreiks und Arbeitslosenkrawalle in Berlin 1914–1923, in: Manfred Gailus (ed.), Pöbelexzesse und Volkstumulte in Berlin. Zur Sozialgeschichte der Straße, Berlin (FRG) 1984, pp. 79–124, pp. 109–118; Maurer, Ostjuden, pp. 329–344; Andrea Lefèvre, Lebensmittelunruhen in Berlin 1920–1923, in: Gailus and Volkmann, Kampf um das tägliche Brot, pp. 346–360; Wildt, Hitler's Volksgemeinschaft, pp. 53–58; Tobias Metzler, Tales of Three Cities. Urban Jewish Cultures in London, Berlin, and Paris (1880–1940), Wiesbaden 2014, pp. 198–205.

117 On the concept of asymmetries in monetary exchange see the extensive study in William M. Reddy, Money and Liberty in Modern Europe. A Critique of Historical Understanding, Cambridge 1987.

light on the divergent norms and standards that have informed judgments about debts and their significance, judgments which themselves were in turn evaluated in different ways. In this sense, moral economy can be studied from the perspective of a historical epistemology, a field that has uncovered the moral foundations of scientific knowledge by identifying the values and styles of argumentation shared by scientists in concrete historical situations.[118] In a related sense, this essay sought to elucidate how moral judgments were hypostatized into epistemic certainties, a phenomenon observable in the pains taken by Basel officials to declare a person bankrupt and in debates over the legally contradictory nature of debtors' prisons.

The moral economy of debts was not a mosaic of different thought styles, but a site of conflict in which different modes of judging the significance of debts came into contact with one another. These conflicts were realized as the confluence of heterogeneous temporalities, which were experienced by those involved as at once a continuous sequence and as staggered events. Analyzing the conflicts involved in the affect-laden "moral economy of the poor" promises to be a fruitful venture for historians because it can help uncover the elements of a type of rationality counterposed to political economy.[119] Developing a concept of moral economy from the vantage point of debt and indebtedness might help bridge the gap between epistemological critique and social critique.

In some cases, the medium of debt relations—money—was itself the object of political strife. Broadly speaking, the word usury pointed a finger at the problems of a precarious form of monetary circulation. The term usury dramatized monetary relations of dependency; but not every statement about usury fits well into the analytic framework of moral economy, because it is by no means true that a rationality diverging from political economy came to the fore in every single case. In contexts where usury signified the fusion of money making and exploitation, it paved the way "for the most predictable forms of reactionary ideology," including that of the middle-man as "the origin of oppression."[120] Locating exploitation in circulation stood behind the anti-Semitic construction of the Jew as usurer.

Exchange, consumption, and circulation are, however, not only the sites that gave occasion to riots, but are also spheres of contention crucial for the provision of basic needs and the reproduction of society. In today's financialized capitalism, the proliferation of multifarious, often contradictory forms of exchange is on the rise. Not people's relation to the means of production alone, but also their relation to the means of exchange and payment has played a significant role in shaping

---

118 Daston, Moral Economy; Daston and Galison, Objectivity.
119 Edward Palmer Thompson, The Moral Economy of the English Crowd in the Eighteenth Century, in: Past & Present 1971, no. 50, pp. 76–136, here p. 79.
120 Max Horkheimer and Theodor W. Adorno, Dialectic of Enlightenment. Philosophical Fragments [1944/1969], trans. Edmund Jephcott, Stanford, CA 2002, pp. 142 f.; Peter Stallybrass, Marx's Coat, in: Patricia Spyer (ed.), Border Fetishisms. Material Objects in Unstable Spaces, New York 1998, pp. 183–207, quote pp. 199 f.

social relations in historical capitalism.[121] Placing emphasis on the capacities of actors, the non-holistic perspective on conflicting social logics provided by the concept of moral economy might help us better understand these relations.

121 This is emphasized by Spang, Stuff and Money, esp. pp. 273 f., and Jeffrey Sklansky, Labor, Money, and the Financial Turn in the History of Capitalism, in: Labor. Studies in Working-Class History of the Americas 11. 2014, pp. 23–46.

Anna Danilina

Die moralische Ökonomie der »inneren Kolonie«

Genossenschaft, Reform und Rasse
in der deutschen Siedlungsbewegung (1893–1926)

Abstract: "Inner colonies" of the German settlement movement were spaces thriving on contestation. The conceptual grid of moral economies invites us to think through the divergent positions as a field of relations between land reformers, vegetarians, Zionists, and *völkisch* actors. Deliberations about what constituted a just economy established relational concepts of land, nutrition, community, and the body. They moralized economy, marketed ethics, and economized the (racial) self. This article rethinks the continuities between inner colonies, garden cities, cooperative, Zionist, life-reform, and *völkisch* settlements, placing them in discourses about colonialism, commodification, and exclusion.

Nachdem Theodor Fritsch den »Antisemiten-Katechismus« (1887) veröffentlicht, die Antisemitische Deutschsoziale Partei (1889) mitbegründet, »Die Stadt der Zukunft« (1896) publiziert, die Deutsche Mittelstandsvereinigung (1898) und den Hammer-Verlag (1902) gegründet und die Deutsche Erneuerungs-Gemeinde (1904) ins Leben gerufen hatte, machte er es sich 1909 mit der Siedlung Heimland zur Aufgabe, Kartoffeln zu ernten. Die Prämisse, Bodenbewirtschaftung und Gemeinschaftsmoral seien untrennbar verbunden, teilten völkische Protagonisten mit prominenten Akteuren unterschiedlicher Lager im Kaiserreich und in der Weimarer Republik. Der völkisch-antisemitische Agitator Fritsch, der Soziologe und Zionist Franz Oppenheimer, der Freiwirtschaftler und Ökonom Silvio Gesell, der völkische Ernährungsreformer Gustav Simons und der Bodenreformer Adolf Damaschke fanden hier einen gemeinsamen Nenner. Ihre Konzeptionen »gerechter« (und »artgerechter«) Arbeits-, Wirtschafts- und Siedlungsformen in der Genossenschaft griffen einerseits auf geteilte Vorstellungen von Moral, Gemeinschaft und deren Grenzen zurück. Doch wurden Ökonomie- und Moralvorstellungen in den Auseinandersetzungen, im Zusammenleben und -arbeiten auch neu ausgehandelt und geprägt. Die gemeinsame Sprache sowie Praktiken einer moralischen Ökonomie und Gemeinschaft waren weniger Voraussetzung als vielmehr Ertrag eines konfliktbehafteten und doch geteilten Experimentierfeldes.

Freilich kann die Zusammenarbeit derart unterschiedlicher Protagonisten durch den Verweis auf eine gemeinsam empfundene Krise der Moderne begriffen werden. Sozioökonomische Veränderungen der Industrialisierung, Landflucht und Verstädterung in Deutschland führten, so viele historiografische Studien

zur Siedlungsbewegung, zu einem Konsens der Großstadtfeindlichkeit und ro-
mantisierter Vorstellungen der Rückkehr zur Natur.[1] Insbesondere die völkische
Siedlungsreform gilt zwar in der jüngeren Literatur nicht länger als durchweg
anti-modern, doch verbleibt die Analyse meist dualistischen Begriffspaaren von
modern und anti-modern sowie einem nationalen Interpretationsrahmen ver-
haftet. Dadurch wird eine Reihe von Fragen verstellt und, zumindest implizit, der
Gedanke eines deutschen Sonderwegs nahegelegt. Wurde die These vom deutschen Sonderweg auch mittlerweile vielseitiger Kritik unterzogen, hat sie sich
doch tief in die Begriffe eingeschrieben, mit denen wir historische Akteure be-
zeichnen und ihr Handeln deuten. Sie unterteilt Bewegungen in politisch gegen-
sätzliche Lager, deren Protagonisten sich jedoch keineswegs im Widerspruch
sahen. Vor dem Hintergrund des Nationalsozialismus wurden ferner Begriffe
und Perspektiven der Geschichtswissenschaft neu ausgerichtet. Dies veränderte
nach 1945 die Betrachtung des Zionismus – und verstellte den Blick auf den Zusammenhang von völkischer und zionistischer Siedlungsbewegung. Auch in der
Literatur zu lebensreformerischen Siedlungen und Gartenstädten werden völkische Protagonisten meist als getrennte Gruppe und oft als im reformerischen
Spektrum unerwünschte Parallelerscheinung behandelt. Wird auch nicht explizit
eine Sonderwegsperspektive angelegt, so erscheinen völkische Positionen innerhalb der Historiografie doch stets in einer, wenn auch gebrochenen, Kontinuität
zum Nationalsozialismus.[2] Freilich soll hier weder der Erklärungsgehalt perso-
neller, symbolischer und ideologischer Kontinuitäten in Abrede gestellt werden
noch sollen Unterscheidungen nivelliert werden. Doch entsteht durch diese Betrachtung eine Perspektive, die bestimmte Zusammenhänge ex post als relevant
ansieht, während andere aus dem Blick geraten. Dies betrifft in erster Linie den
transnationalen und kolonialen Kontext der Siedlung.

Völkische, lebensreformerische, viele der kommunistischen und anarcho-
syndikalistischen Siedlungen wurden ebenso wie Gartenstädte als »innere Kolonien« begriffen. Dieser Zusammenhang wird im Kontext der Maßnahmen der
inneren Kolonisation im Osten Deutschlands und in Polen verständlich. Protagonisten und Akteure der inneren Kolonisation wiederum sahen sich explizit in
einer Kontinuität mit dem deutschen Kolonialismus und Imperialismus einerseits, mit »innerer Kolonisation« in Amerika und Russland andererseits. Diesem
breiten Kolonialbegriff blieben stets rassische Kategorien und Unterscheidungen
inhärent. Zwar wurde der Rassebegriff nicht in der gesamten Siedlungsbewegung
als so zentral propagiert wie von ihren völkischen Vertretern. Doch wurde er in
Diskurs und Praxis innerer Kolonisation stets mitgetragen und prägte Kategorien
von Klasse, Subjekt und Gemeinschaft, Territorium und Kultur. Völkische Positionen waren somit weder der Ursprung noch der alleinige Ort des Rassedenkens.

---

1 Ulrich Linse (Hg.), Zurück, o Mensch, zur Mutter Erde. Landkommunen in Deutschland
  1890–1933, München 1983, S. 7 f.
2 Uwe Puschner u. Ulrich Großmann (Hg.), Völkisch und national. Zur Aktualität alter Denk-
  muster im 21. Jahrhundert, Darmstadt 2009.

Rasse war integrales Moment der moralischen Ökonomie innerer Kolonisation und eine Kontinuität zwischen Kolonie, Siedlung, Gartenstadt und »Lebensraum im Osten«.

Der Begriff der moralischen Ökonomie kann hier eine neue Perspektive auf die Siedlungsbewegung offerieren, die drei Analyseebenen miteinander verschränkt: Erstens fasst sie ein gemeinsames moralisches und ökonomisches Experimentierfeld völkischer, lebensreformerischer und zionistischer Akteure. Sie alle vertraten das bodenreformerische Konzept der Genossenschaftssiedlung als eine moralisch begründete Wirtschaftseinheit. Diese stand zum einen im Gegensatz zu Kapitalismus und industrieller Großstadt. Zum anderen wurde sie in einer kolonialen Genealogie als kulturell höherwertige (und arteigene) Wirtschaftsform begründet. Fragen von Bodenbesitz und Bodenbewirtschaftung wurden so moralisiert und an Kategorien von Volk und Raum geknüpft.[3] Boden wurde in der Siedlung aus dem Warenkreislauf ausgenommen und zu einem mit dem Volk verwachsenen Organismus. Ziel war hingegen die Erzeugung gesundheitlich, ethisch oder hygienisch aufgewerteter Waren der eigenen Produktion und Konsumption. Somit wurde zweitens Ökonomie moralisiert und Moral ökonomisiert. Durch die Moralisierung von Ökonomie im engeren Sinne (als Wirtschaft) wurde eine moralische Ökonomie im weiteren Sinne (als gemeinschaftlich geteiltes System von Werten und Normen) geschaffen.[4] Drittens beinhaltet die moralische Ökonomie der Siedlung nicht nur die Produktion von Gütern und Waren und der ihr zugrunde gelegten Moral, sondern – im Sinne einer politischen Ökonomie – eine an spezifische Produktions-, Arbeits- und Vergesellschaftungsprozesse gebundene Genese von Subjekt und Gemeinschaft. Sofern Moral stets an Affekt, und Gefühl an Körperlichkeit gebunden sind, wird die moralische Ökonomie der Gemeinschaft im Einzelnen internalisiert. Die Grenze von Raum und Gemeinschaft schreibt sich als »innere Grenze« dem Subjekt ein – sowohl in dessen

---

3 Den Begriff der moralischen Ökonomie wendet James Scott, ausgehend von E. P. Thompson, auf subalterne Bauerngemeinschaften in Südostasien an. *Moral economy* verweist dabei auf das moralisch verstandene Wirtschaften der Subsistenzethik und Reziprozität ebenso wie auf das System der Werte und Normen, die mit bestimmten Arbeitsformen verbunden sind und moralische Ansprüche einer subalternen Gruppe an Ressourcen (beispielsweise Land) generieren. Die innere Kolonie kann in doppeltem Sinne als *moral economy* im Sinne Scotts gelten: als moralisch begründete Wirtschaftseinheit, die sich um den Anspruch auf und Umgang mit Boden formiert, zum einen, und als durch Abgrenzung entstehendes System von Werten und Normen der Gemeinschaft zum anderen. James C. Scott, The Moral Economy of the Peasant. Rebellion and Subsistence in Southeast Asia, New Haven 1976; Elisabeth Emma Ferry, Not Ours Alone. Partimony, Value, and Collectivity in Contemporary Mexico, New York 2005.

4 Lorraine Daston versteht *moral economy* nicht in wirtschaftlichen Begriffen, sondern als System von emotional verankerten Werten und Normen, die in einem geregelten Verhältnis zueinander stehen. Vgl. Lorraine Daston, The Moral Economy of Science, in: Osiris 10. 1995, S. 2–24. Insofern ist die moralische Ökonomie der Siedlung als Wertezusammenhang der Gemeinschaft zu denken, der zugleich als Wertevorstellungen und Gefühle der einzelnen Subjekte internalisiert und von ihnen reproduziert wird.

Vorstellungen, Empfinden als auch im Körper und auf dessen Oberfläche.[5] Im Diskurs um Kolonisation, Volkshygiene und -gesundheit, Erziehung und Körperkultur waren darin entstehende Konzeptionen und Praktiken von Individuum und Kollektiv explizit oder implizit rassisch codiert.

I. Bodenreform, Kolonialismus und Innenkolonisation

Die Bodenreformbewegung verhandelte im Kaiserreich die soziale Frage als Problem der Kommodifizierung von und Spekulation mit Boden. Ihre Protagonisten – aus dem völkischen, lebensreformerischen, liberalen, sozialistischen und zionistischen Lager gleichermaßen – positionierten sich gegen die Veräußerung von Boden als Ware. Anschließend an den US-amerikanischen Ökonomen Henry George zielten die deutschen Verfechter der Landreform auf die Kollektivierung des Bodens – zumeist in der Kommune oder Genossenschaft.

Die deutsche Bodenreform- und Freilandbewegung bezog sich vornehmlich auf die Schriften des jüdisch-österreichischen Nationalökonomen Theodor Hertzka, des antisemitischen Nationalökonomen Eugen Dühring und des national-sozialen Boden- und Lebensreformers Adolf Damaschke. Hertzkas einflussreicher Roman »Freiland – Ein soziales Zukunftsbild« entwarf seine Freilandutopie als Kolonisation im heutigen Kenia. Diese stand im Kontext zionistischer Diskussionen um ein geeignetes »Neuland« und übte auf Theodor Herzls politischen Zionismus Einfluss aus.[6] Herzls Altneuland in Palästina und Hertzkas Freiland in Ostafrika markierten die prominentesten Gegenpositionen ihrer Zeit.[7] Sah Herzl in Eugen Dühring vor allem den Mitbegründer des Rassenantisemitismus,[8] baute Hertzkas Freilandtheorie zum Teil auf Dührings »Cursus der National- und Socialökonomie« auf.[9] Zugleich gab es unter den Völkischen zahlreiche Befürworter des Zionismus. Der völkische Lebensreformer und FKK-Gründervater Heinrich Pudor verstand den Zionismus als »einzige Lösung der Judenfrage«.[10] Jedoch waren auch Gegenpositionen im völkischen Spektrum verbreitet, die einen jüdischen Nationalstaat als Teil der jüdischen Weltverschwörung fürchteten und,

5 Ann Laura Stoler, Interior Frontiers. Diagnostic and Dispositif, in: Political Concepts. A Critical Lexicon, issue 4, https://www.politicalconcepts.org/interior-frontiers-ann-laura-stoler/.

6 Stefan Vogt, Subalterne Positionierungen. Der deutsche Zionismus im Feld des Nationalismus in Deutschland 1890–1933, Göttingen 2016, S. 258.

7 Ulrich E. Bach, Tropics of Vienna. Colonial Utopias of the Habsburg Empire, New York 2016, S. 68–83.

8 Shlomo Avineri, Herzl's Road to Zionism, in: American Jewish Year Book 98. 1998, S. 3–15.

9 Eugen Dühring, Cursus der National- und Socialökonomie, Leipzig 1876; Franz Oppenheimer, Freiland in Deutschland, Berlin 1895; Theodor Broczyner, Die sozialistischen Systeme von Hertzka und Oppenheimer in ihrer Abhängigkeit von Eugen Dühring, Königsberg 1922.

10 Heinrich Pudor, Wie kriegen wir sie hinaus? Deutsche Nutzanwendungen, Leipzig 1913, S. 17 f., zit. n. Vogt, Subalterne Positionierungen, S. 361.

so beispielsweise die Haltung Dührings selbst, Juden ihrem Wesen nach als der nationalstaatlichen Organisation nicht fähig erachteten. Dühring band den Freiland- an den (arischen) Rassegedanken und eine normative Gemeinschaftsvorstellung – unter Ausschluss der Juden.[11] Als radikaler und einflussreicher Vertreter des frühen Rassenantisemitismus projektierte er bereits im späten 19. Jahrhundert Ausgrenzung, Deportation und Internierung der Juden. Zur gleichen Zeit forderte Paul de Lagarde die Deportation der jüdischen Bevölkerung Deutschlands nach Madagaskar – was im Nationalsozialismus als »Madagaskar-Plan« bekannt wurde.[12] Bereits 1900 schrieb Dühring von der »Vernichtung des Judenvolkes«.[13] Somit bilden die völkische Unterstützung des Zionismus als Ausgrenzung der Juden, Projektionen der Deportation und schließlich Ghettoisierung Kontinuitäten in einem Diskurs.

Für die deutsche Bodenreformbewegung und ihre Siedlungskonzepte waren zionistische Utopien ebenfalls ein wichtiger Bezugspunkt. Der in völkischen Kreisen aktive Adolf Damaschke hatte die Versammlungen Hertzkas 1893 in Berlin besucht. Dessen Pläne und (erfolglose) Expedition 1894 nach Britisch-Ostafrika fanden in einer breiteren Diskussion um deutsche Siedlungskolonien im In- und Ausland weit über jüdische Kreise hinaus Resonanz. Auch Damaschke sprach Hertzka nicht als Juden, sondern als Deutschen an. Er suchte, Hertzka und seine Anhänger von der »Innenkolonisation« zu überzeugen. »Ich trat Hertzka mit aller Entschiedenheit entgegen: Als Deutsche wäre es unsere Pflicht, in unserem Vaterlande die Kulturentwicklung nach dem Ziele sozialer Gerechtigkeit zu beeinflussen«.[14] Auch lebensreformerische und völkische Siedlungsideen entstanden in dezidierter Auseinandersetzung mit zionistischen Vorstellungen. Statt dem staatlichen Kolonialismus oder auch der Siedlungskolonisation in Palästina, Afrika oder Südamerika wollten die Bodenreformer ihr Ziel durch »innere Kolonien« verwirklichen.[15]

Damaschke, Gründer des Bundes Deutscher Bodenreformer und Genossenschaftsvorsitzender der Siedlung Eden, begriff die soziale Frage in Kategorien von Verteilungsgerechtigkeit, Bodenreform und Grundrente.[16] Die Bodenreform

---

11 Werner Bergmann, Art. Dühring, Eugen Karl (auch Carl), in: Wolfgang Benz (Hg.), Handbuch des Antisemitismus. Judenfeindschaft in Geschichte und Gegenwart, Bd. 2/1, Berlin 2009, S. 188–191, hier S. 189; Karlheinz Weissmann, The Epoch of National Socialism, in: Journal of Libertarian Studies 12. 1996, S. 257–294, hier S. 261.

12 Sebastian Conrad, »Eingeborenenpolitik« in Kolonie und Metropole. »Erziehung zur Arbeit« in Ostafrika und Ostwestfalen, in: ders. u. Jürgen Osterhammel (Hg.), Das Kaiserreich transnational. Deutschland in der Welt 1871–1914, Göttingen 2006, S. 107–128; Hans Jansen, Der Madagaskar-Plan. Die beabsichtigte Deportation der europäischen Juden nach Madagaskar, München 1997.

13 Bergmann, Dühring, S. 191.

14 Adolf Damaschke, Aus meinem Leben, Leipzig 1924, S. 288 f.

15 Auszug aus der Satzung der Deutschen Gartenstadt-Gesellschaft in Hans Kampffmeyer, Die Gartenstadtbewegung [1909], Leipzig 1913, S. 27.

16 Adolf Damaschke, Die Bodenreform. Grundsätzliches und Geschichtliches zur Erkenntnis und Überwindung der sozialen Not, Jena 1917, S. 59.

galt ihm als dritter Weg zwischen einem »undeutschen« Kapitalismus und Indi-
vidualismus und einem als internationalistisch und proletarisch verfemten Kommunismus.[17] Lohn und Zins sollten individuelles oder genossenschaftliches
Eigentum bleiben, während die Grundrente sozialisiert werden sollte.[18] Ver-
schuldbarkeit, Verpfändbarkeit und Bodenspekulation hätten zur Verarmung des
Bauernstandes und zur massenhaften Zwangsversteigerung landwirtschaftlicher
Güter geführt. Das wiederum sei der Grund für Landflucht, rasantes Wachstum
der Stadtbevölkerung und Wohnungsmangel, der erneut Anreiz zur Spekulation
biete. Hygienische Missstände in überfüllten Wohnungen sowie die »sittlichen
Gefahren« der Prostitution und des Alkoholismus folgten daraus.[19] Insofern war
für Damaschke die Bodenreform als moralische Ökonomie zentrales Moment
volksgesundheitlicher und hygienischer Überlegungen, und er selbst war in der
Naturheil- und Volksgesundheitsbewegung aktiv.[20]

Positiv bezog sich Damaschkes Bodenreform auf die Allmende des Mittelalters
und die badisch-sächsische Markgenossenschaft, deren Gemeinbesitz die »beste
Volksversicherung« in Hinblick auf die Erhaltung des »Deutschtumes« bilde.[21]
»Im Gegensatz zum unbeschränkten Privateigentum« war Boden in der Allmende Gemeindeeigentum einer zugleich »politische[n] Ortsbürger- und einer
vermögensrechtliche[n] Wirtschafts-Gemeinde«. Da das Konzept der Allmende
tief im deutschen Volk verwurzelt sei, habe es sich im »kulturell stärkeren« Westen und Südwesten Deutschlands erhalten können, nicht jedoch in den östlichen
Gebieten. »Eine ausreichende Allmende verhindert die Entstehung eines besitzlosen Landarbeitertums und macht Erscheinungen unmöglich, wie sie heut in
der Leutenot und der slawischen Wanderarbeiterflut beklagt werden müssen.« So
könnten eine »gesunde« Gemeinschaft und die Verbundenheit ihrer Glieder mit
der »Heimat« entstehen. Das »Moralische« der genossenschaftlichen Siedlung
war für Damaschke also zugleich das »Deutsche« in wirtschaftlich und kulturell
begründeter Abgrenzung und territorialer Verbundenheit.

Die erste moderne Verwirklichung der Bodenreform sah Damaschke jedoch nicht auf deutschem Boden, sondern in der »Musterkolonie« Kiautschou,
wo die Verwaltung des Marineministeriums ihre Grundsätze als Grundrente
in die Praxis umsetzte.[22] So verband er koloniale Wissensbestände mit moralisch aufgeladenen Gemeinschaftsvorstellungen in der Verknüpfung von Land,
wirtschaftlicher Organisation und nationaler Bevölkerung. Das politische Kon-

---

17 Uwe Schneider, Nacktkultur im Kaiserreich, in: Uwe Puschner u. a. (Hg.), Handbuch zur »Völkischen Bewegung« 1871–1918, München 1999, S. 411–435, hier S. 419.
18 Damaschke, Bodenreform, S. 62.
19 Ebd., S. 70–77.
20 Vgl. Judith Baumgartner, Ernährungsreform. Antwort auf Industrialisierung und Ernährungs-
   wandel, Frankfurt 1992, S. 30.
21 Dieses Zitat und die folgenden aus Damaschke, Bodenreform, S. 203, S. 200 f., S. 203, S. 213 u.
   S. 205.
22 Ders., Kamerun oder Kiautschou? Eine Entscheidung über die Zukunft der deutschen Kolonialpolitik, Berlin o. J. [ca. 1900].

zept des Lebensraums, das Friedrich Ratzel seit den 1890er Jahren prägte, hatte
bereits das Überleben eines Volkes an Kolonisation und Migration (im weiteren Sinne) geknüpft.[23] Kolonisationsbestrebungen in Übersee, in Europa und im
deutschen Inland waren Teil und Erweiterung dieses Diskurses. Den nationalen
Staat begriff Ratzel als Organismus, der sich aus den Eigenschaften des Volkes
und des Bodens zusammensetze.[24] Die Furcht vor der Vereinnahmung deutschen Bodens durch »slawische Menschenmassen«, wie sie auch Damaschke ar-
tikulierte, hatte in dieser Vorstellung der Verbindung zwischen Volk und Boden
ihren Ort. »Weil wir deutsche Menschen auf deutscher Erde brauchen, darum
brauchen wir eine Innenkolonisation großer Art.«[25] Territoriale Grenzen hingen
in dieser Vorstellung von der ethnisch-rassischen Identität der Bevölkerung und
des Bodens selbst ab. »Boden« war weder Ware noch einfach nur Ressource oder
Territorium – er wurde zu einem lebendigen Teil des Volkskörpers.[26]

Der konservative Agrarpolitiker Max Sering, Mitbegründer der Gesellschaft
zur Förderung der Inneren Kolonisation (1912) und Leiter des Deutschen For-
schungsinstituts für Agrar- und Siedlungswesen (1921), war der prominenteste
Vertreter innerer Siedlungsprojekte vor allem in den östlichen Gebieten Deutschlands.[27] In Bismarcks imperialer Politik war die vermeintlich existentielle Bedrohung Preußens durch den polnischen Nationalismus von Anbeginn zentrales
Thema. In den 1880er Jahren war besonders der preußische Osten von der Krise
der Getreidepreise und der daraus resultierenden Migration von Bauern in den
Westen Deutschlands und nach Nordamerika betroffen. Aufgrund des Arbeits-
kräftemangels wurden zunehmend Arbeiter aus Russisch-Polen angeworben, was
im Kontext der preußischen Assimilations- und Germanisierungspolitik in Polen
und darin geschürter Ressentiments als Bedrohung wahrgenommen wurde. Um
der befürchteten »Polonisierung« entgegenzuwirken, wurden sowohl Vorschriften
zur Verminderung der Zuwanderung und zur Ausweisung als auch Maßnahmen
zur Ansiedlung von Deutschen und zum Aufkauf polnischer Güter ergriffen.[28]
1882 wurde Max Sering vom Preußischen Landesökonomiekollegium und dem
Preußischen Landwirtschaftsministerium mit einer Forschungsreise nach Nord-

23 Woodruff D. Smith, Friedrich Ratzel and the Origins of Lebensraum, in: German Studies
   Review 3. 1980, S. 51–68; am deutlichsten ausformuliert in Friedrich Ratzel, Der Lebensraum.
   Eine biogeographische Studie, Tübingen 1901.
24 Ders., Der Staat und sein Boden. Geographisch betrachtet, Leipzig 1896, S. 19; vgl. Claudia
   Bruns, Die Grenzen des »Volkskörpers«. Interrelationen zwischen »Rasse«, Raum und Geschlecht in NS-Geopolitik und Kunst, in: Feministische Studien 33. 2015, S. 177–196, hier
   S. 180.
25 Damaschke, Bodenreform, S. 213 u. S. 215.
26 Weiterführend zur organischen Konzeption von Boden, Raum und »Rasse« vgl. Bruns, Grenzen
   des »Volkskörpers«; dies. (Hg.), »Rasse« und Raum. Topologien zwischen Kolonial-, Geo- und
   Biopolitik. Geschichte, Kunst, Erinnerung, Wiesbaden 2017.
27 Max Sering, Die innere Kolonisation im östlichen Deutschland, Leipzig 1893.
28 Sebastian Conrad, Globalisierung und Nation im Deutschen Kaiserreich, München 2006,
   S. 126 f.; Robert L. Nelson, From Manitoba to the Memel. Max Sering, Inner Colonization and
   the German East, in: Social History 35. 2010, S. 439–457, hier S. 442 u. S. 444.

amerika beauftragt, um zu untersuchen, was die Deutschen von der Kolonisation
des »leeren Landes« im Westen, an der amerikanisch-kanadischen Grenze, lernen
konnten.[29] Serings Antwort war die innere Kolonisation Preußisch-Polens, die
sich am nordamerikanischen Modell des Siedlungskolonialismus orientierte.[30]
So waren der Wilde Westen und Karl May nicht erst eine Faszination Adolf
Hitlers.[31] Vielmehr waren sie bereits für die Innenkolonisation Preußens der primäre Referenzpunkt und, nach der Radikalisierung im Ersten Weltkrieg, für den
kolonialen Grenzkampf in Polen.[32] Durch die Ansiedlung von Kleinbauern hoffte
Sering, sowohl die territorialen Grenzen Deutschlands zu festigen beziehungsweise auszuweiten als auch den Boden selbst zu germanisieren und in eine orga-
nische Einheit mit der deutschen Bevölkerung zu bringen. Ab den 1890er Jahren
betrieben der Ostmarken-Verein unter dem völkischen Philipp Stauff sowie der
Deutsche Frauenverein für die Ostmarken Siedlungsprojekte im Osten, um der
befürchteten »Verslawung« des »Deutschtums« entgegenzuwirken.[33] Zugleich
sollten Siedlung und Landwirtschaft der als gefährdet wahrgenommenen moralischen und körperlichen Konstitution der deutschen Bauern zugutekommen.
Zwar müssen die Kolonisation in Übersee und die Innenkolonisation im Osten
in zahlreichen Spezifika und ihren jeweiligen Kontexten unterschieden werden.
Als Kultur- und Zivilisierungsmissionen überlagerten sie sich jedoch im zeitgenössischen Diskurs und machen koloniale Ordnungen innerhalb Europas
sichtbar.[34]

Nicht nur in ideenhistorischer Hinsicht, sondern auch in der Kontinuität
des Zusammenhangs von Arbeit und sittlicher Erziehung der als bedroht – und
somit für die Gemeinschaft als bedrohlich – angesehenen Bevölkerungsgruppen
verschränkten sich koloniale Strategien mit der Behandlung der sozialen Frage
in Deutschland. Bereits 1849 hatte sich in Berlin der Verein für Colonisierung
im Inlande gegründet. Vorstandsmitglied und Schriftführer Otto Kraetz war
zuvor in der Gesellschaft für deutsche Auswanderung nach Nikaragua engagiert,
suchte nun mit dem Verein jedoch, die Auswanderung der arbeitslosen und ver-
armten deutschen Bevölkerung in die Amerikas und die Kolonien durch ihre
Übersiedlung und Beschäftigung in Ackerbau- und Arbeitskolonien in Preußen

---

29 Ders., The Archive for Inner Colonization, the German East, and World War I, in: ders. (Hg.),
    Germans, Poland, and Colonial Expansion to the East. 1850 through the Present, New York
    2009, S. 65–93, hier S. 66.
30 Nelson, From Manitoba to the Memel, S. 440; Sering, Innere Kolonisation.
31 Jürgen Osterhammel, Die Verwandlung der Welt. Eine Geschichte des 19. Jahrhunderts, Mün-
    chen 2009, S. 532.
32 Imanuel Geiss, Der polnische Grenzstreifen 1914–1918. Ein Beitrag zur deutschen Kriegsziel-
    politik im Ersten Weltkrieg, Lübeck 1960.
33 Uwe Puschner, Die völkische Bewegung im wilhelminischen Kaiserreich. Sprache, Rasse, Re-
    ligion, Darmstadt 2001, S. 112 f.; Ute Planert, Kulturkritik und Geschlechterverhältnis. Zur
    Krise der Geschlechterordnung zwischen Jahrhundertwende und »Drittem Reich«, in: Wolf-
    gang Hardtwig (Hg.), Ordnungen in der Krise. Zur politischen Kulturgeschichte Deutschlands
    1900–1933, München 2007, S. 191–214, hier S. 197.
34 Conrad, Globalisierung und Nation, S. 141.

zu stoppen.[35] Wies das Königliche Polizeipräsidium Kraetz' Gesuch 1849 noch als »unvollkommen durchdachte[s] und ausgearbeitete[s] Projekt« ab – nicht zuletzt, da die Vorstandsmitglieder selbst zum Teil mittellosen Schichten angehörten und man einigen von ihnen durch Hintergrundrecherchen Rechtsverstöße nachwies – wurden Arbeiterkolonien nach der Revolution zum Mittel sozialer Fürsorge.[36] Arbeiterkolonien im Kaiserreich – die im späten 19. Jahrhundert zunehmend das Problem der »Arbeitsscheu«, Obdachlosigkeit und Wanderarmut durch innere Mission und Erziehung zu Arbeit bekämpften – und Arbeiterkolonien in Deutsch-Ostafrika standen nicht nur begrifflich und rhetorisch, sondern auch durch den Transfer von Praktiken und Akteuren in einem konstitutiven Wechselverhältnis. So hatte sich Friedrich von Bodelschwingh sowohl in der Gründung von Arbeiterkolonien in Deutschland, die soziale Institutionen nach dem Prinzip »Arbeit statt Almosen« bildeten, als auch in Deutsch-Ostafrika engagiert.[37] In der Zeitschrift *Archiv für innere Kolonisation* (im Folgenden *AfiK*), seit 1908 Organ des Vereins für ländliche Wohlfahrts- und Heimatpflege und ab 1912 der Gesellschaft zur Förderung der Inneren Kolonisation, wurde 1911 die »Soziale Kolonisation« diskutiert. Unter direktem Bezug auf die Arbeiterkolonien Bodelschwinghs macht der Autor den Vorschlag, die Arbeitslosen in inneren Kolonien zu beschäftigen und so zu Arbeit und Gemeinschaftlichkeit zu erziehen, statt durch Almosen sowohl die Volkswirtschaft als auch das ethische Gefühl der Empfänger zu schädigen.[38] Über den Bezug zur Kolonie wird die Überlagerung von Klasse und Rassekategorien deutlich: Wie eine Zivilisierung der einheimischen Bevölkerung in den deutschen Kolonien in Afrika möglich sei, so könnten Arbeit und Leben in inneren Kolonien den Zweck erfüllen, »nieder gestellte« Bevölkerungsgruppen ethisch-moralisch, in Charakter und Körper, zu erziehen.

Die Mitbegründer der Gesellschaft zur Förderung der Inneren Kolonisation – Max Sering, der Regierungspräsident Brandenburgs Friedrich von Schwerin und der Alldeutsche Alfred Hugenberg – teilten einen weiten Begriff des Kolonialen. Kolonisation bedeutete die planmäßige Ansiedlung auf »leeren Landstrichen« – in Sachsen, Posen, Ungarn, Russland, Argentinien oder Kamerun.[39] In kolonialer Rhetorik galt als »leerer Raum«, was nicht durch europäische Siedler und Bewirtschaftung »kulturalisiert« war. Dennoch wurde der Begriff der

---

35 Geheimes Staatsarchiv Preußischer Kulturbesitz, Rep. 77, Tit. 1128, Nr. 32, Programm des Collonisations-Vereins für das Inland, 1.3.1849, S. 2.

36 Ebd., Stellungnahme des Polizeipräsidiums, 24.3.1849, S. 42–47, hier S. 45.

37 Conrad, »Eingeborenenpolitik«, S. 113; weiterführend zum Einfluss von Erziehungsmaßnahmen in europäischen Kolonien auf innereuropäische Konstitution und Kategorien von Klasse, Geschlecht und Rasse siehe Ann Laura Stoler, Carnal Knowledge and Imperial Power. Race and the Intimate in Colonial Rule, Berkeley 2002, S. 64.

38 Hans Ostwald, Soziale Kolonisation, in: Archiv für innere Kolonisation 3. 1911, S. 161–174, hier S. 161 f.

39 Nelson, Archive for Inner Colonization, S. 70. Alle benannten Orte der Kolonisation finden sich beispielsweise in den Ausgaben des *AfiK* 1911 und 1912.

Kolonie weder beliebig noch allein im Sinne einer Grenzexpansion verwendet. Die zeitgenössischen Akteure setzten vielmehr den Siedlungskolonialismus im Osten Deutschlands in direkten Bezug zu den deutschen Kolonien in Afrika, zur bodenreformerischen Genossenschaftssiedlung, zur Gartenstadt wie auch zur zionistischen Siedlung in Palästina.[40] Die definitorische Frage danach, was die Kolonie ist und was nicht, verstellt dabei den Blick auf die Morphologie, Relationen und Richtungsänderungen, die die Kolonie nicht als gesetzte Siedlung oder Herrschaftsform, sondern als Aushandlung und Antizipation einer Zukunft entwerfen.[41] Gerade in ihrer imaginierten Instabilität und Bedrohung sowie ihrer tatsächlichen Variation schafft und festigt sie die Grenzziehungen, Parameter und Kategorien des Innen und Außen, des Selbst und des Anderen. Erst von den Ambivalenzen und Fluchtpunkten der Kolonie her lässt sich verstehen, welche Subjekte sie bildete und und durch welche Unterscheidungen diese regiert wurden.[42]

Kolonial-rassistische Zuschreibungen und Unterscheidungen der Bevölkerung wurden in der inneren Kolonisation ebenso übernommen wie daraus legitimierte Zivilisierungsmaßnahmen und Kulturmissionen. Das *AfiK* widmete 1912 die »Kolonialnummer« der Zeitschrift dem Verhältnis der »Besiedlung im Inlande und in den Kolonien«. Da für die »afrikanische Siedlung [...] höher stehendes Material, energische, unternehmende und wagemutige Leute mit wenigstens 20.000 bis 30.000 Mark Vermögen in Betracht kommen«, während die Bauern im Osten weit weniger vermögend, als Arbeiter gar mittellos sein konnten, stünden die Kolonien in Afrika nicht im Wettbewerb mit den Kolonien im Osten.[43] Beide hätten so ihre Berechtigung und könnten in volkswirtschaftlicher, agrarischer und kulturmissionarischer Hinsicht voneinander lernen. Die Beitragenden zur »Kolonialnummer« berichteten über volkswirtschaftliche Betrachtungen, Siedlungsfähigkeit und -praxis in den Kolonien, die »Akklimatisierung des Europäers in den Tropenländern« sowie einzelne Siedlungen, Verfahren und Siedlungsfähigkeit in Deutsch-Ostafrika. Ein wesentlicher Grund, die Innenkolonisation

---

40 So enthalten die Ausgaben 1911 und 1925 des *AfiK* vermehrt Artikel zu Bodenreform und Gartenstadt, in der Ausgabe 1926 drei Artikel zur jüdischen Kolonisation in Palästina; Jürgen Brandt, Die jüdische Kolonisation in Palästina, in: Archiv für innere Kolonisation 18. 1926, S. 188–197.

41 Ann Laura Stoler, Colony, in: Political Concepts. A Critical Lexicon, issue 1, http://www.politicalconcepts.org/issue1/colony/.

42 1903 wurde vom Ostmarken-Verein mit Unterstützung des Alldeutschen Verbandes die Zentralstelle zur Beschaffung deutscher Ansiedler und Feldarbeiter gegründet und ab 1905 vom preußischen Landwirtschaftsministerium unterstützt. »Die Strategie der Zentralstelle, die zunehmend zur offiziellen Haltung der preußischen Regierung wurde, basierte auf einer Politik der Unterscheidung in Zeiten der Fluktuation. In- und Ausland, Deutsche und Polen, Eigenes und Fremdes sollten klar und möglichst dauerhaft voneinander geschieden werden; Paßzwang, Karenzzeit und Verstärkung der Grenzposten waren die Instrumente dafür. ›Deutsche Arbeit‹, ›deutscher Boden‹ und Germanisierung sollten in einer nicht immer übersichtlichen Situation Deutsche machen – und Polen.« Conrad, Globalisierung und Nation, S. 136.

43 Besiedlung im Inlande und in den Kolonien. Ein Vorwort zur Kolonialnummer, in: Archiv für innere Kolonisation 4. 1912, S. 145–147, hier S. 146.

als wichtiger einzustufen, sei, dass in den afrikanischen Kolonien die »schwarze[n] [Arbeitskräfte] nicht für höhere Produktionsarten geschult werden können«.[44] Sering bestand dabei stets darauf, dass in Deutschland der US-amerikanische Fehler vermieden werden solle, die einheimische Bevölkerung gänzlich vom Land zu verdrängen und in Reservaten sich selbst zu überlassen. Vielmehr sei nach kanadischem Beispiel die niedergestellte polnische Bevölkerung zu Arbeit und moderner Landwirtschaft zu erziehen.[45]

Im Sinne von Jürgen Osterhammels Definition von Siedlungskolonialismus sah man es als »Recht und Pflicht, den von minderwertigen Völkern oder gar minderwertigen Rassen unzureichend genutzten Boden in Kultur zu nehmen.«[46] Als die Königlich Preußische Ansiedlungskommission bei ihrer Politik in Posen und Preußen im Wettbewerb um den Aufkauf von Gütern gegen polnische Bieter unterlag, verschärfte sich die anti-polnische Politik und mit ihr die Maßnahmen zur Germanisierung der Bevölkerung. So wurde bereits 1898 an Schulen der Polnischunterricht mit dem Ziel einer Sprachkulturalisierung der Region durch Deutschunterricht ersetzt.[47] Auch Ludendorffs Kulturprogramm im Ersten Weltkrieg zeigte, wie der deutsche Einfluss auf polnischem Boden gerade durch Bildung und Erziehung der heterogenen einheimischen Bevölkerung verstetigt und der Herrschaftsanspruch legitimiert wurde.[48] Zugleich wurden Staatlichkeit und der Volkskörper der Nation durch die Kategorisierung, Hierarchisierung und Charakterisierung der regierten Bevölkerungsgruppen innerhalb der Siedlungsökonomie (re)produziert.[49] Die innere Kolonie war also als ökonomische Institution konzipiert, die durch Arbeit und deutsche Kultur zu Moral erzog, damit gleichzeitig rassisch codierte Kategorisierungen der Siedler und Arbeiter vornahm und daran nationales Deutschsein band. Durch die Germanisierung der Bevölkerung werde zugleich der bewirtschaftete Boden selbst germanisiert, was die politischen Grenzen quasi organisch ausweiten und festigen sollte.

Im Zeichen kolonialer Herrschaft war der Schritt von Kulturmission und Zivilisierung zur zunehmenden Rhetorik von Ausbeutung, Ausgrenzung und Vernichtung nicht weit. Nach dem Ersten Weltkrieg geschah eine rhetorische und politische Neujustierung: ging es der inneren Kolonisation zuvor darum, »leeren Raum« innerhalb Deutschlands zu besiedeln, dominierten ab 1918 Stimmen, die einen Mangel an Raum propagierten – und mit ihm Bestrebungen nach Kolonisation östlich der deutschen Grenze. Gebietsverluste hatten die reale geopolitische

---

44 Paul Rohrbach, Siedlungsbestrebungen in unseren afrikanischen Kolonien, in: Archiv für innere Kolonisation 3. 1911, S. 71–86, hier S. 78.

45 Nelson, From Manitoba to the Memel, S. 447.

46 Osterhammel, Verwandlung der Welt, S. 531 u. S. 535.

47 William W. Hagen, Germans, Poles, and Jews. The Nationality Conflict in the Prussian East, 1772–1914, Ph. D. Diss. University of Chicago 1971, S. 36 u. S. 38.

48 Vejas Gabriel Liulevicius, Kriegsland im Osten. Eroberung, Kolonisierung und Militärherrschaft im Ersten Weltkrieg, Hamburg 2018, S. 143–188.

49 James C. Scott, Seeing Like a State. How Certain Schemes to Improve the Human Condition Have Failed, New Haven 1998, S. 183.

Lage verändert, dies verstärkte und wandelte die Politik von Kolonisation und Germanisierung in den nun polnischen und durch den Korridor abgetrennten deutschen Gebieten. War zuvor die nichtdeutsche Bevölkerung und Arbeitskraft in östlichen Kolonien innerhalb und außerhalb der deutschen Grenze Gegenstand von Kulturalisierung und Germanisierung, so zeichnete sich nach 1918 mit verstärkt biologistisch-rassistischen Begründungen ein Diskurs von Vertreibung und bald Vernichtung ab.[50] So wurde die aggressive und rassisch motivierte Siedlungspolitik der Artamanen, eines 1924 gegründeten völkischen Bundes der deutschen Jugendbewegung, seit ihrer Gründung im *AfiK* als Teil der eigenen Bestrebungen rezipiert.[51]

Innerhalb der völkischen Bewegung schrieb Walther Darré die Konzeptionen der inneren Kolonisation von der Weimarer Republik in den Nationalsozialismus fort.[52] Damaschkes Bodenreform und Serings Kolonisation tat Darré jedoch als geringfügig ab und strebte größere Maßstäbe an. Über seine Ausbildung an der Kolonialschule Witzenhausen hatte auch Darré einen klaren Bezug zur deutschen Kolonialpolitik. In seinen Schriften zu Bauerntum, Blut und Boden re-interpretierte er bestehende Begriffe von Grenzziehung, Rasse und Land.[53] 1938 schließlich geriet Darré in Konflikt mit Heinrich Himmler, der selbst zentraler Akteur der Artamanenbewegung gewesen war, wurde von Hitler abgesetzt und durch eine technokratische Führungselite der SS unter der Leitung Himmlers ersetzt.[54]

II. Innere Kolonisation, Zionismus und Gartenstadtbewegung

Das *AfiK* akzentuierte nicht nur den Zusammenhang von »äußerer« und »innerer« Kolonisation. Regelmäßig erschienen auch Artikel zur Gartenstadtbewegung und Bodenreform. Im *AfiK* wurde rege diskutiert, welche wirtschaftliche Form für die Siedlungen der inneren Kolonisation im Osten die beste Organisationsform biete. Favorisiert wurde die genossenschaftliche Kleinsiedlung im An-

50 Nelson, Archive for Inner Colonization, S. 77 u. S. 81 f.

51 Beispielsweise wurden besprochen Georg Wilhelm Schiele, Naumburger Briefe, Heft 8. Artamanenheft (Freiwilliger Arbeitsdienst), in: Archiv für innere Kolonisation 17. 1925, S. 274–275; Wilhelm Kotzde, Die Burg im Osten, in: Archiv für innere Kolonisation 18. 1926, S. 228.

52 Kristin Kopp, Germany's Wild East. Constructing Poland as Colonial Space, Ann Arbor 2012; Nelson, Germans, Poland, and Colonial Expansion; David Blackbourn, The Conquest of Nature. Water, Landscape, and the Making of Modern Germany, New York 2006.

53 Richard Walther Darré, Innere Kolonisation [1926], in: ders., Erkenntnisse und Werden. Aufsätze aus der Zeit der Machtergreifung, Goslar 1940, S. 18–23; ders., Das Bauerntum als Lebensquell der nordischen Rasse, München 1929; ders., Neuadel aus Blut und Boden, München 1930; vgl. auch Bruns, Grenzen des »Volkskörpers«.

54 Mark Mazower, Hitler's Empire. How the Nazis Ruled Europe, New York 2008, S. 219 u. S. 285; Hansjörg Gutberger, Raumentwicklung, Bevölkerung und soziale Integration. Forschung für Raumplanung und Raumordnungspolitik 1930–1960, Wiesbaden 2017, S. 35.

schluss an die Bodenreform.[55] Als Damaschkes Bodenreform schließlich 1919 den Grundstein für das Reichssiedlungsgesetz des Artikels 155 der Weimarer Reichsverfassung legte, standen zwei Bodenreformentwürfe in Konkurrenz: jener von Max Sering und der von dessen ehemaligem Schüler Franz Oppenheimer.[56]

Obwohl Oppenheimer mit Damaschke nicht nur ideologische Motive, sondern auch eine »jahrzehntelange gute Kameradschaft« verband, warf er ihm vor, »die von Henry George eingeleitete große Menschheitssache zu einer bürgerlichen Steuerangelegenheit verniedlicht« zu haben. Oppenheimers Variante der Bodenreform sah eine radikalere »Beseitigung des Klassenmonopols am Boden« vor. Der konservative Agrarpolitiker Sering hatte jedoch Oppenheimers grundlegende Sozialisierung des Bodens schon zu Universitätszeiten abgelehnt – und wusste 1919 deren Realisierung in der Rechtsprechung durch den Einbezug von Kommissionsmitgliedern der »extremsten deutschnationalen Richtung« zu verhindern.[57]

Oppenheimer ging es um die Aufhebung der »Bodensperre« (des Privatbesitzes an Land), im äußersten Fall durch Revolution und gewaltsame Enteignung. Der zu favorisierende, friedliche Weg führte jedoch über ein sich ausbreitendes Netz genossenschaftlicher Siedlungen:

Wenn der erste Versuch ergab, daß [...] die landwirtschaftliche Produktivgenossenschaft, wie ich sie plante, sich der privaten Gutswirtschaft als überlegen erwies, dann durfte damit gerechnet werden, daß auch sie sich schnell ausdehnen, ein Privatgut nach dem andern durch ehrlichen Kauf erwerben und so allmählich, ohne Verletzung erworbener Rechte, im vollen Frieden, das deutsche Land in die Hände des deutschen Volkes zurückbringen würden.

An einer Reihe solcher Modellsiedlungen hatte Oppenheimer sich praktisch beteiligt: der Siedlung Eden bei Oranienburg (1893), Wenigenlupnitz bei Eisenach (1905), der Siedlung Merchawja in Palästina (1911) und der Siedlung Bärenklau bei Velten (1920). Oppenheimer war einer der entschiedensten Verfechter sozialpolitischer Ziele innerhalb der inneren Kolonisation, ob in Deutschland, wie in Wenigenlupnitz oder Velten, oder in Palästina. Sein System der schrittweisen Gründung und Vernetzung von Produktivgenossenschaften, um das »deutsche Land in die Hände des deutschen Volkes zurückzubringen«, hatte sich in Deutschland nicht verwirklicht. Die Siedlungsgenossenschaft wurde jedoch ab dem Zionisten-Kongress 1903, wo Oppenheimer in die Forschungskommission gewählt wurde, zur offiziellen Siedlungspolitik zionistischer Organisationen in Palästina.[58] Nach dem Neunten Zionisten-Kongress in Hamburg 1909 wurde

---

55 Walter Haidenhain, Gründung und Leitung einer Kleinsiedlungsgenossenschaft, in: Archiv für innere Kolonisation 2. 1910, S. 1–28.

56 Gutberger, Raumentwicklung, S. 32.

57 Diese Zitate und das folgende aus Franz Oppenheimer, Erlebtes, Erstrebtes, Erreichtes. Lebenserinnerungen, Düsseldorf 1964, S. 154 f., S. 242 u. S. 158.

58 Vogt, Subalterne Positionierungen, S. 183 f.

Oppenheimer damit beauftragt, die Siedlungsgenossenschaft in Palästina zu realisieren – und 1911 gründete er Merchawja als Modell.[59]

Oppenheimers gleichzeitiges Engagement für Bodenreform, lebensreformerische Genossenschaftssiedlungen in Deutschland, für die Nordau-Gartenstadt und Genossenschaftssiedlungen in Palästina oder Peru und seiner Tätigkeit als Vorstandsmitglied des Komitees für den Osten (zu Beginn noch »Oppenheimer-Komitee«, dann »Deutsches Komitee zur Befreiung der russischen Juden«) werden in ihrer Relation und gemeinsamen Stoßrichtung über den Link der inneren Kolonisation verständlich.[60] Nicht nur für Oppenheimer, sondern für den deutschen Zionismus hatte die innere Kolonisation Vorbildcharakter.[61] Umgekehrt berichtete das *AfiK* über die Kolonisation in Palästina als Teil ihrer Bestrebungen.

Als Voraussetzung und zentrales Moment des *social engineering* galt Oppenheimer die wirtschaftliche Organisation und Produktion innerhalb der Genossenschaft. »Alles Volkstum beruht auf der Verwurzelung einer Menschenmasse mit dem Boden, auf dem sie ruht, und diese Verwurzelung schafft nur die Landwirtschaft.«[62] Die »eigentliche Aufgabe der inneren Kolonisation« sah er darin, »den Landarbeiter im Lande zu verwurzeln«.[63] Ausgehend von der wirtschaftlichen Grundlage – die bereits eine moralische Gemeinschaft durch Gleichheit, Verteilungsgerechtigkeit, organischen Zusammenhalt von Mensch und Land sowie nicht entfremdete Arbeit formte – konnte innerhalb der Siedlungen ein weiterführendes Kultur- und Bildungsprogramm ansetzen. Freilich bleibt die moralische Ökonomie der Gleichheit und Gerechtigkeit eine, die erstens ihre Moral als Bedingung der Zugehörigkeit formuliert, sich zweitens als autarke moralische Ökonomie von einem unmoralischen Außen abgrenzt und drittens sowohl nach innen als auch nach außen bestimmte Bevölkerungsgruppen adressiert, kategorisiert und hierarchisiert.

Die primäre Zielgruppe der Agrarproduktivgenossenschaft waren die »Ostjuden« – sowohl als verfolgte und bedrohte Gruppe als auch durch ihre landwirtschaftlichen Kenntnisse und erhaltenen kulturellen Eigenschaften. Die angenommene körperliche, kulturelle und geistige Konstitution des Ostjudentums bildete somit einerseits die Voraussetzung, Siedler der Agrargenossenschaft zu sein. Andererseits war diese durch Rasse, Klasse und Kultur codierte ostjüdische Eigentümlichkeit das »Problem«, dem die Siedlungskolonie abhelfen sollte.

Im medizinisch-eugenischen Diskurs, der an Max Nordaus »Entartung«, Körperpraxis und Regeneration des »Muskeljuden« anschloss, bildeten Ostjuden

---

59 Dekel Peretz, Franz Oppenheimer. A Pioneer of Diasporic Zionism, in: Ulrike Brunotte u. a. (Hg.), Internal Outsiders – Imagined Orientals? Antisemitism, Colonialism and Modern Constructions of Jewish Identity, Würzburg 2017, S. 187–200, hier S. 192.

60 Zosa Szajkowski, The Komitee für den Osten and Zionism, in: Herzl Year Book 7. 1971, S. 199–240, hier S. 206.

61 Vogt, Subalterne Positionierungen, S. 180.

62 Franz Oppenheimer, Genossenschaftliche Siedlung in Palästina, Köln 1910, S. 5.

63 Ders., Erlebtes, S. 173.

die Abgrenzungsfolie zum Westjudentum.[64] Für Nordau selbst waren jedoch weder West- noch Ostjuden »degeneriert«, sondern vielmehr in ihrer Rasseneigentümlichkeit durch Unterdrückung und Verfolgung beschädigt. Diese Entwicklung ließe sich aber durch Umwelt und Lebenspraxis rückgängig machen. Auch Oppenheimer war im Anschluss an Nordau von der »Plastizität der Rasse« überzeugt und glaubte, durch sozioökonomische Umweltbedingungen – in erster Linie Ökonomie, Produktions- und Arbeitsbedingungen – die körperliche, geistige und seelische jüdische Konstitution beeinflussen zu können.[65] So schrieb er der bäuerlichen Landwirtschaft auf genossenschaftlicher Grundlage regenerative Wirkungen für das Ostjudentum zu, die weiteren Bildungsmaßnahmen vorausgehen müsse und sich positiv auf Physis, Charakter und Gemeinschaftsgefühl auswirke.[66] Grenzte sich Oppenheimers liberaler Sozialismus auch von zeitgenössischen marxistischen Strömungen ab, so war das Primat marxistischer Ökonomie, dass Subjektkonstitution und Gemeinschaftsbildung auf wirtschaftlicher Praxis aufbauten, Grundbaustein seiner Konzeption.

Annahmen über Natur, Charakteristika und Notstand der ostjüdischen Bevölkerung gingen dabei in die Wohltätigkeitsarbeit in Osteuropa ein. In der Arbeit des Komitees für den Osten, das 1914 von Oppenheimer, Max Bodenheimer und Adolf Friedemann gegründet wurde, können drei zentrale Aufgaben unterschieden werden: Erstens das Bestreben, der deutschen Regierung und Öffentlichkeit zu zeigen, dass die Juden im Osten Europas als natürliche Verbündete für die Festigung der politischen und kulturellen Hegemonie Deutschlands von großem Nutzen seien.[67] »Das ›Komitee für den Osten‹ verdankt seine Entstehung der Ueberzeugung, daß bei den kriegerischen Verwicklungen die Interessen der jüdischen Bevölkerung des Ostens, speziell in Russisch-Polen, mit denen unseres deutschen Vaterlandes identisch sind.«[68] Insofern positionierte das Komitee sein Programm der sozialen Fürsorge und der finanziellen und kulturellen Unterstützung jüdischer Ansiedlungen im Osten als Teil der inneren Kolonisation. Zweitens war es Ziel des Komitees, die amerikanische jüdische Öffentlichkeit davon zu überzeugen, dass die Darstellung Deutschlands als Herd des politischen Antisemitismus verfehlt war und sich der Sieg der Zentralmächte und der Einfluss des Deutschen Reiches positiv auf die Lage der Ostjuden aus-

---

64 Max Nordau, Entartung, Berlin 1892; Todd Samuel Presner, »Clear Heads, Solid Stomachs, and Hard Muscles«. Max Nordau and the Aesthetics of Jewish Regeneration, in: Modernism/Modernity 10. 2003, S. 269–296, hier S. 270.

65 Franz Oppenheimer, Die rassentheoretische Geschichtsphilosophie, in: Deutsche Gesellschaft für Soziologie (Hg.), Verhandlungen des 2. Deutschen Soziologentages vom 20. bis 22. Oktober 1912 in Berlin. Reden und Vorträge, Frankfurt 1969, S. 98–139, hier S. 120, http://nbn-resolving.de/urn:nbn:de:0168-ssoar-187970.

66 Peretz, Oppenheimer, S. 196.

67 Vogt, Subalterne Positionierungen, S. 222.

68 Archive of the Center for Jewish History [im Folgenden ACJH], Komitee für den Osten 1914–1918, reel 2, M. I. Bodenheimer, Bericht über die im Auftrage des ›Komitees für den Osten‹ im Mai-Juni 1915 unternommene Reise nach Russisch-Polen, S. 3.

wirken würden. »In mühevoller Arbeit ist es unserem Vertreter gelungen, eine Aenderung der Stimmung unter den jüdischen Massen zugunsten Deutschlands herbeizuführen.«[69] Schließlich galt es, die jüdische Bevölkerung Osteuropas in ihren ethnischen Eigenarten, ihrer Kultur und sozialen Situation zu erfassen, und ihre Notlage durch Armenfürsorge und kulturelle Erziehung zu lindern. Zwar wurden auch deutscher Geschichts- und Sprachunterricht an den Schulen und andere Angebote kultureller Erziehung gefördert, doch wurde stets betont, dass »die Juden des Ostens nach Sprache und Kultur eine besondere Gemeinschaft darstellen«. Daher sollte sowohl eine »Polonisierung« als auch eine »zwangsweise Germanisierung« vermieden werden.[70] Das Komitee für den Osten stand damit im Kontext einer Reihe von Hilfsorganisationen, die sich der sittlichen und hygienischen Erziehung osteuropäischer Juden annahmen – wie beispielsweise der OSE (Obschtschestwo Sdrawoochranenija Jewrejew – Gesellschaft für den Schutz der Gesundheit der jüdischen Bevölkerung). Deren Programm sollte den Missständen der jüdischen Bevölkerung in Russland und Osteuropa durch Maßnahmen körperlich-sittlicher Erneuerung durch »Luft, Sonne und Licht« abhelfen.[71] Naturverbundenheit und das Verständnis von Luft, Sonne und Licht als Mittel sozialer und körperlicher Hygiene decken sich dabei vielfach mit der deutschen Reform- und Siedlungsbewegung und mit dem völkischen Spektrum rassischer Regeneration.

Der Reformgedanke ging, stärker als bei den wirtschaftlich fokussierten Agrargenossenschaften, in die Konzeption von Gartenstädten ein. Diese verbanden Industrie- und Agrarwirtschaft, Stadt und Land. Innerhalb zionistischer Vorstellungen konnte die Gartenstadt eine Bevölkerung aus unterschiedlichen Kulturen und Regionen und mit unterschiedlichem Entwicklungsstand fassen. Zwar sollte auch die Gartenstadt auf genossenschaftlicher Grundlage aufbauen und jedem Bewohner die Nähe zur Natur sowie ein gesundes, regeneratives Leben ermöglichen. Doch ihre idealen Bewohner waren nicht nur die landwirtschaftlich sozialisierten Ostjuden. Die Gartenstadt war in unterschiedliche Bezirke unterteilt, in denen Menschen je nach Berufsstand, Vermögen und Herkunft leben konnten.

Die Gartenstadtbewegung wird heute als Beginn urbaner Stadtplanung verstanden und in der jüngeren Forschung in einem transnationalen und auch kolonialen Diskurs- und Praxisfeld verortet.[72] Ihr Ausgangspunkt wird meist in der 1898 in England erschienenen Schrift »To-Morrow: A Peaceful Path to Real Reform« Ebenezer Howards gesehen. Ziel war es, eine »Synthese von Stadt und

---

69 Ebd.
70 ACJH, Komitee für den Osten 1914–1918, reel 2, Franz Oppenheimer, Aus dem Brief an Dr. Nathan, S. 1.
71 Nadav Davidovitch u. Rakefet Zalashik, »Air, Sun, Water«. Ideology and Activities of OZE (Society for the Preservation of the Health of the Jewish Population) during the Interwar Period, in: Dynamis 28. 2008, S. 127–149.
72 Liora Bigon u. Yossi Katz (Hg.), Garden Cities and Colonial Planning. Transnationality and Urban Ideas in Africa and Palestine, Manchester 2014.

Land« herzustellen,[73] und so auf modernem Wege den gesundheitlichen, hygienischen und sittlichen Lastern der Großstadt abzusagen, ohne industriellen Fortschritt gegen Bauernromantik einzutauschen.

Zwei Jahre vor Howards Schrift erschien »Die Stadt der Zukunft« des völkischen Agitators Theodor Fritsch. Als Genossenschaften sollten Howards und Fritschs Gartenstädte der Bodenspekulation vorbeugen und so die ökonomische Grundlage für die Bildung einer moralischen Gemeinschaft und Entwicklung des Einzelnen schaffen. Die Städte sollten kreisförmig angelegt und mit Parks und Gärten durchwachsen sein, wobei einzelne Bereiche für unterschiedliche Zwecke – monumentale Gebäude im Zentrum, unterschiedlich große Wohn- und Gartenparzellen für verschiedene Gesellschaftsschichten im Mittelring, Kleingärten und schließlich Industrie und Felder im äußeren Ring – eingeteilt wurden. Wie in der Siedlungsgenossenschaft war das Ziel, einen mit der Gemeinschaft organisch verwachsenen Raum physischer und moralischer Regeneration zu schaffen. Auf völkischer Seite sollte die »Stadt der Zukunft« und die in ihr entstehende »Neue Gemeinde« eine »Pflanzschule deutschen Lebens« sein: »eine freie ungetrübte Entfaltung deutschen Wesens in Geist, Sitte und Geschmack […], in Summa: deutsche Lebenskunst und kunstgestaltetes Leben – *eine deutsche Kultur*«.[74] Basierend auf Fritschs Rassenideologie sollte eine Auslese des Zuzugs stattfinden,[75] um »alle unliebsamen Elemente fern zu halten. Körperliche und moralische Gesundheit wären vor allem zu fordern.«[76]

Ob Howard Fritschs Schrift rezipiert hatte, lässt sich nicht nachweisen. Doch ist die in der Literatur häufig gemachte Unterscheidung von Howards »humanistischem« und »progressivem« Entwurf und Fritschs »radikal rassistischer« und proto-faschistischer Schrift insofern verfehlt,[77] als dass sie zentrale Motive und Annahmen über den Zusammenhang von Mensch, Natur, Gemeinschaft und urbaner Segregation teilten. Beide blieben Bezugspunkte der Gartenstadtbewegung.

Laut ihrer Satzung verstand sich die Deutsche Gartenstadt-Gesellschaft dezidiert als Projekt der »Innenkolonisation«.[78] Zwar sollten deutsche Gartenstädte nicht nur im Osten des Landes entstehen, doch warb Hans Kampffmeyer, Generalsekretär der Gartenstadt Karlsruhe, in seiner 1909 erschienenen Schrift »Die Gartenstadtbewegung« für die Gartenstadt als Mittel der preußischen

---

73 Klaus Bergmann, Agrarromantik und Großstadtfeindschaft, Meisenheim 1970, S. 135, zit. n. Puschner, Völkische Bewegung im Kaiserreich, S. 157.

74 Theodor Fritsch, Die neue Gemeinde [Begleit-Schreiben zu der Schrift »Die Stadt der Zukunft«], Leipzig 1897, S. 7 (Hervorhebung im Original).

75 Puschner, Völkische Bewegung im Kaiserreich, S. 162.

76 Fritsch, Die neue Gemeinde, S. 6.

77 Dirk Schubert, Theodor Fritsch and the German (völkische) Version of the Garden City. The Garden City Invented Two Years before Ebenezer Howard, in: Planning Perspectives 19. 2004, S. 3–35, hier S. 3.

78 Auszug aus der Satzung in Kampffmeyer, Gartenstadtbewegung, S. 27.

Ansiedlungspolitik im Osten.[79] Die Kleinsiedlungsgenossenschaft biete für die »Zurückdrängung des Polentums« und die Ziele deutscher Volkswirtschaft keine ausreichend stabile Infrastruktur. Für die Germanisierung des Landes sei die Ansiedlung von Industrie und Landwirtschaft in Gartenstädten vonnöten.

Zur Zeit des Ersten Weltkrieges hatten sich Gartenstadtgesellschaften in elf meist europäischen Ländern sowie die International Garden Cities Association etabliert. Und auch für das zionistische Spektrum bot die Gartenstadt zunehmend die Möglichkeit einer stabileren Verwurzelung in Palästina als die Kleinsiedlungsgenossenschaft. So wurde zu Max Nordaus siebzigstem Geburtstag eine Gartenstadt für Palästina geplant. Die betreffende Festschrift beschrieb die Gartenstadt als Mittel der notwendigen »körperlichen Regeneration«, auf deren bodenökonomischer Grundlage ein neues Volkstum entstehen sollte:

> Vor allem ist die Bodenfrage zu lösen. Soweit als irgend angängig, muß der Boden Eigentum der Gesamtheit sein nach dem Satze der Bibel: ‚Mein ist das Land‘. Und unsere Städte sollen sich nicht aus russigen Mietshäusern zusammensetzen, sondern aus Eigenhäuschen, in Gärten gelegen und überragt von grünen Bäumen. So wird ein Geschlecht heranwachsen, stark und gesund, friedlich, doch selbstsicher, bescheiden und seines Wertes bewußt als der Nachfahren des ältesten lebenden Kulturvolkes der Erde.[80]

Neben diesem Beitrag Adolf Friedemanns, eines Mitbegründers des Komitees für den Osten, beinhaltete die Festschrift auch den Aufsatz »Gartenstadt« Franz Oppenheimers. Dieser führt in erster Linie die genossenschaftliche Organisation der aus Geldern des Nationalfonds geplanten Gartenstadt aus. An die ökonomischen Genossenschaftsstrukturen knüpften sich sozialpolitische und -hygienische Fragen. Bereits in seiner Einleitung zur Schrift »Die Gartenstadt Staaken« hatte Oppenheimer die Gartenstadt als Ort für »leibliche und sittliche Gesundheit« beschrieben. »Die deutsche Rassekraft ist ernstlich bedroht [...] Und das Unerläßliche ist eine Volkskur in Luft und Sonne!« Deutsche Gartenstädte sollten »Stätten deutscher Schönheit, deutscher Kraft, deutscher Sitte, deutscher Liebe zum Vaterland, zur Heimat« werden. Statt »Vermögenswirtschaft« werde dort »Menschenwirtschaft« getrieben.[81]

In der Nordau-Gartenstadt müssten die Erbzins- und Erbbauverträge an Verbote gebunden sein, »Irre oder Prostituierte zu beherbergen, alkoholische Getränke feilzuhalten, Schlafgänger und Aftermieter [...] aufzunehmen«. Durch letztere Regelung sei dem Zuzug »gesundheitlich geschwächter mitteloser Elemente« bereits vorgebeugt. So werde es, auch aufgrund der hygienischen Einrichtung und Architektur der Gartenstadt, kaum eine »Kranken- und Armen-

79 Ebd., S. 100 f.
80 Adolf Friedemann, Max Nordau, in: Hauptbüro des Jüdischen Nationalfonds (Hg.), Eine Gartenstadt für Palästina. Zum 70. Geburtstag von Max Nordau, Berlin 1920, S. 9–20, hier S. 18–20.
81 Franz Oppenheimer, Einleitung, in: Die Gartenstadt Staaken, Berlin 1918, S. 3–8, hier S. 5 f., S. 8 und S. 7.

last« geben. Ferner könnten »unerwünschte Elemente« dadurch ferngehalten werden, dass jeder Siedler erst als Mitglied der Genossenschaft akzeptiert werden müsse, bevor er Bürger werden könne. Die Mitgliedschaft könne ferner bei Rechtsvergehen oder einer Dreiviertel-Mehrheit der Stimmen der Genossen entzogen werden. Schließlich solle es neben dem Organ der Genossenschaft jenes der politischen Gemeinde geben. Letzterer seien die Mittel der Genossenschaft zur Verfügung gestellt, um davon »die Sicherheits- und Sitten-, die Markt- und Feuerpolizei, nicht nur Erziehung und Unterricht einschließlich des hier mit großen Mitteln gepflegten Spiels und Sports, nicht nur die öffentliche Hygiene [...], sondern auch und vor allem das eigentliche Kulturleben ihrer Bürgerschaft« zu gewährleisten, in dem »Kunst und Wissenschaft« eine zentrale Rolle spielten.[82] Insofern waren in Oppenheimers alternativem »Vorbild für die von Klassen- und Rassengegensätzen zerfetzte blutende Welt« arme und kranke Gesellschaftsmitglieder nicht vorgesehen und rassische Regeneration – mit Blick auf sein dynamisches Rasseverständnis – strukturell als Bedingung angelegt. Die Errichtung von Siedlungsgenossenschaften und Gartenstädten sollte jedoch einem weiteren Übel vorbeugen: der Assimilation der jüdischen Bevölkerung an die arabisch-palästinensische. Denn den Zweck des Zionismus in Palästina sah Oppenheimer primär darin, die von Antisemitismus und Verfolgung bedrohten Juden aus Osteuropa anzusiedeln. Im Ostjudentum sei »nach Abstammung, Religion, Kulturzustand und eigener Empfindung« noch eine jüdische Nation lebendig geblieben, die es »zu erhalten und durch Ansiedlung im eigenen Lande wieder zum Volk zu vollenden« galt – ohne sie dabei der Assimilierung mit den Arabern oder Türken auszuliefern.[83] Das Genossenschaftsmodell stellte dafür die optimale Struktur dar, sie brauchte sich nicht in eine bestehende ökonomische, politische und weltanschauliche Ordnung einzugliedern. Vielmehr konnte sie sich als eine von der umgebenden Bevölkerung relativ autarke Einheit etablieren und über ein Netz von Siedlungen schrittweise das Land besiedeln – wie Oppenheimer es zuvor bereits für die Innenkolonisation in Deutschland antizipiert hatte. Gerade deshalb blieben die Ostjuden für Oppenheimers zionistische Vision zentral: sie hatten sich noch nicht in Russisch-Polen assimiliert und so ihre ethnischen und kulturellen Eigenheiten, ihr »Volksbewußtsein«, beibehalten, auf denen ein autonomes landwirtschaftliches und kulturelles Gemeindeleben in den Siedlungen in Palästina aufbauen konnte.[84] Oppenheimers Ressentiment gegen Assimilation richtete sich auch gegen jene Juden, die der europäischen Assimilationspolitik nachgaben und selbst den kulturellen Code des Antisemitismus adaptierten, um sich so als Arier zu inszenieren.[85] Ihm ging es aber nicht darum, mit den Ariern zu bre-

---

82 Ders., Gartenstadt, in: Hauptbüro des Jüdischen Nationalfonds, Eine Gartenstadt für Palästina, S. 24–37, hier S. 28, S. 34 f. u. S. 37.

83 Ders., Ländliche Kolonisation in Palästina, in: Die Welt 1909, Nr. 42, 14.10.1909, S. 913–918, hier S. 914; Peretz, Oppenheimer, S. 192.

84 Franz Oppenheimer, Stammesbewußtsein und Volksbewußtsein, in: Die Welt 1910, Nr. 7, 18.2.1910, S. 139–143, hier S. 139; Peretz, Oppenheimer, S. 193.

85 Ebd.

chen, wie sein Engagement im Pro-Palästina Komitee, gelegentlich auch in der
Selbstbezeichnung Deutsch-Arisches Komitee zur Foerderung der juedischen
Palaestinabesiedelung, zeigt. Vielmehr sah er eine Gleichrangigkeit von Semiten
und Ariern. Oppenheimers Furcht und Kritik galten der Assimilation der Juden.
Gleichzeitig wollte er die arabische Bevölkerung Palästinas durch seine Pläne in
den jüdischen Volkskörper integrieren und assimilieren – im Gegensatz zu viele
Zionisten seiner Zeit jedoch nicht ausschließen.[86]

Zu der Gründung der Nordau-Gartenstadt ist es in Palästina nicht gekommen.
Hingegen wurde die Gartenstadtidee maßgebend für die Gartenvorstadt Ahusat
Bajit bei Jaffa, das sich später zu Tel-Aviv entwickeln sollte. Ahusat Bajit ent-
stand als Gartenvorstadt nach dem Vorbild kolonialer und mittelständischer Vor-
städte. Mit separierten Wohnvierteln für die europäische und die einheimische
Bevölkerung sah es eine Segregation nach Klasse und Ethnie beziehungsweise
Rasse vor. Die Gartenstadtidee und die infrastrukturelle Planung von Ahusat
Bajit lieferten Leitprinzipien für folgende urbane jüdische Siedlungen und die
Stadtplanung in Palästina im 20. Jahrhundert.[87]

III. Körperkultur, Vegetarismus und Rassebildung in Deutschland: Von Hellerau über Eden nach Heimland

Franz Oppenheimer, auf den die Implementierung der Gartenstadtidee in Palästina wesentlich zurückgeht, gehörte auch zu den ersten Vorstandsmitgliedern
der 1902 in Berlin gegründeten Deutschen Gartenstadt-Gesellschaft (DGG). Die
DGG vereinte kommunistische, anarchistische, lebensreformerische, zionistische
und völkische Akteure. Deren Zusammenarbeit wird in der 1909 gegründeten,
bekanntesten deutschen Gartenstadt Hellerau deutlich. 1912 besuchte Ebenezer
Howard die Gartenstadt Hellerau und lobte, sie sei nicht schlicht Imitation engli-
scher Gartenstädte, sondern Ausdruck des Wesens der deutschen Siedler.[88] Hellerau war als pädagogisches Zentrum für Kunst, Handwerk und gesundes Leben
sowie Modellsiedlung einer neuen ländlich-urbanen Form konzipiert. Sie war ein
Experimentierfeld für ganzheitliche Formen der Erziehung. Nicht »verschultes
Wissen«, sondern Moralempfinden, Körper- und Gefühlswissen standen im Zentrum ihrer experimentellen Bildung. Der Unterricht in Hellerau sollte »die har-
monische Entwicklung sämtlicher Anlagen« und »die soziale und menschliche
Gleichwertung von Kopf- und Handarbeit« verwirklichen.[89] Die international

86 Ebd.
87 Miki Zaidman u. Ruth Kark, Garden Cities and Suburbs in Palestine. The Case of Tel Aviv, in:
   Bigon u. Katz, Garden Cities, S. 167–189, hier S. 167 f.
88 Ebenezer Howard über Hellerau, in: Gartenstadt. Mitteilungen der deutschen Gartenstadt-
   gesellschaft 6. 1912, Nr. 10, S. 176.
89 Stadtarchiv Dresden, Bestand 8.13, Sig. 516/01, Schulverein Hellerau, Allgemeine Richtlinien,
   1.12.1919, S. 1.

bekannte Bildungsanstalt für rhythmische Gymnastik des Reformpädagogen Émile Jaques-Dalcroze in Hellerau zielte darauf, durch Rhythmik-, Musik- und Körperbildung den Schülern nicht Wissen, sondern Empfinden beizubringen. Wie der Raum der Gartenstadt selbst auf Mensch und Gemeinschaft wirken und sie durch Wahrnehmung und Bewegung verändern sollte, so wurde auf Grundlage der Kulturphilosophie Nietzsches für Dalcrozes Rhythmikschule ein Festspielhaus in Form eines griechisch-antiken Tempels errichtet, dessen Raum sich mit der Rhythmik des Körpers verbinden sollte.[90] Ganzheitliche Erziehung und Körperkultur waren im Kaiserreich und in der Weimarer Republik weit verbreitet. Allein die Zahl der Rhythmikschulen betrug in der Weimarer Republik mehrere hundert, die Zahl der Gymnastiktreibenden kann auf 400.000 Personen geschätzt werden.[91] Durch sie sollte ein »neuer Mensch« entstehen – der mehr oder minder explizit rassisch und deutsch verstanden wurde.

Fritz Winther publizierte 1914 die Übersichtsstudie »Körperbildung als Kunst und Pflicht«, die bis 1923 in fünf Auflagen erschien. Winther referiert (und idealisiert) die »rücksichtslosen Mittel der griechischen Rassenhygiene« und stellt die Aufgabe der Körperkultur heraus, eine »Einheit von Charakter und Körperbildung« zu schaffen und »Schönheit zum sittlichen Wert zu erheben«. Die rhythmische Gymnastik sollte die Gebiete »Rassenhygiene und Erziehungswesen« gleichermaßen durchdringen. Auf dem »gemeinsamen Boden« beider baue »sich Ethik, soziale Tätigkeit, Unterricht, Pflege gesunder Kunst und Schönheit auf«.[92] Hans Suréns »Deutsche Gymnastik« wurde in den 1920er Jahren in der Nacktkultur- und Körperkulturbewegung das prominenteste Gymnastiksystem – und wirkte weit darüber hinaus in die deutsche Öffentlichkeit. Suréns Werk »Der Mensch und die Sonne« (1924) hatte sich in der Freikörperkultur besser als jedes andere Werk verkauft und wurde 1936 in der Neufassung »Mensch und Sonne. Arisch-olympischer Geist« in die NS-Bibliografie des »wertvollen Schriftguts« aufgenommen.[93] Suréns Gymnastik war auf das deutsche Volk zugeschnitten: »Dem deutschen Volke nur deutsche Ausbildung!«[94] Eine solche Erziehung finde Winther zufolge am besten in der Gartenstadt oder Siedlung statt: »Führer, wie Volk brauchen für die Körperpflege einen richtigen Boden (in des Wortes eigentlicher Bedeutung). Der beste Boden für all diese Spielarten und Verwandte, des Triebs zur Gesundheit, zu körperlich-geistiger Bildung und sozialem Wirken ist eine Siedelung, welche die Vorteile von Stadt und Land vereinigt.«[95]

---

90 Thomas Nitschke, Die Gartenstadt Hellerau als pädagogische Provinz, Dresden 2003, S. 94 u. S. 96.

91 Bernd Wedemeyer-Kolwe, »Der neue Mensch«. Körperkultur im Kaiserreich und in der Weimarer Republik, Würzburg 2004.

92 Fritz Winther, Körperbildung als Kunst und Pflicht, München 1920⁴, S. 6 u. S. 79.

93 Maren Möhring, Marmorleiber. Körperbildung in der deutschen Nacktkultur (1890–1930), Köln 2004, S. 66 f.

94 Hans Surén, Deutsche Gymnastik, Oldenburg 1925, S. 53, zit. n. Möhring, Marmorleiber, S. 68.

95 Winther, Körperbildung, S. 81.

Teil des völkischen Flügels in Hellerau war Bruno Tanzmann, Mitbegründer der Artamanenbewegung, der mit seiner Volkshochschul- und Bauernhochschulbewegung in Hellerau ansässig war. In der Literatur wird der Einfluss Tanzmanns sowie der Völkischen Ernst Krauss und Emil Strauß, Personen aus dem Umfeld des Alldeutschen Verbands und des Werdandibundes, des völkischen Deutschnationalen Handlungsgehilfenvereins, völkischer Verlage und schließlich der Artamanenbewegung meist als zur Lebensreform parallele und unerwünschte Erscheinung dargestellt.[96] Doch waren die Lehrinhalte und Grundlagen beispielsweise von Tanzmanns Volkshochschule und deren »geistigem Germanentum« lebensreformerischen Geistes und verstanden sich als deren integrierter Teil. So sollte Rasse nicht nur in Wissen und Landarbeit, sondern auch in »Körperbildung, Gesang und Volkslied« zum Leben erweckt und gereinigt werden.

In Deutschland existierten vor dem Ersten Weltkrieg fünfzehn Gartenvorstädte.[97] Unter den Gründern der Deutschen Gartenstadtgesellschaft waren neben Franz Oppenheimer auch der völkisch-sozialistische Gustav Landauer, in ihrem Vorstand waren unter anderen der Sexualwissenschaftler und Vordenker der Eugenik Magnus Hirschfeld und der völkisch-lebensreformerische Künstler Fidus (Hugo Reinhold Höppener). Zu den Mitgliedern der DGG gehörten völkische Denker wie Theodor Fritsch, Bruno Tanzmann und Gustav Simons. Simons, völkischer Lebens- und Ernährungsreformer und Siedler der Obstbaukolonie Eden, bezieht sich in seiner 1912 erschienenen Schrift »Die Deutsche Gartenstadt« wesentlich auf zwei frühe Pioniersiedlungen der Gartenstadt: Hellerau und Eden.

»Der interessanteste Vorläufer der [deutschen] Gartenstadtbewegung ist die Obstbaukolonie Eden bei Oranienburg«, schreibt auch Hans Kampffmeyer 1913.[98] Die vegetarische Obstbau-Kolonie Eden war eine der ersten »Versuchsstationen« lebensreformerischer Siedlungen mit völkischen Tendenzen, und sie existierte bis heute. Franz Oppenheimer schrieb in der Gründungsphase die Statuten. Voraussetzung für die Ansiedlung waren die vegetarische Lebensweise und der Verzicht auf Alkohol und Tabak. Insofern war Eden als Reformsiedlung der gesundheitlichen, hygienischen und moralischen Regeneration verpflichtet – wie ab der Jahrhundertwende im Kaiserreich und in der Weimarer Republik Hunderte »weltanschaulich motivierte[r] Siedlungen«.[99]

Kolonialdiskurs und wirtschaftliche Not bewirkten ein »Auswanderungsfieber in Berlin«. Teile der lebensreformerischen, vegetarischen und völkischen Kreise entschieden sich zur Ansiedlung in Südamerika.[100] »Erst die nach und nach eingetretene Ernüchterung der Vegetarier infolge der Pleiten aller bisherigen tropischen

---

96 Nitschke, Geschichte der Gartenstadt Hellerau, S. 77 f., S. 100 u. S. 111.
97 Teresa Marie Harris, The German Garden City Movement. Architecture, Politics and Urban Transformation, 1902–1931, Ph. D. Diss. Columbia University 2012, S. 6.
98 Kampffmeyer, Gartenstadtbewegung, S. 25.
99 Linse, Zurück, o Mensch, zur Mutter Erde, S. 8.
100 Ders., Von »Nueva Germania« nach »Eden«, in: Bauwelt 83. 1992, Nr. 43, S. 2453 f., hier S. 2454.

Siedelungen ließen [...] den Entschluß zu einer gemeinsamen Siedelung auf rein vegetarischer Grundlage im heimischen nördlichen Klima« entstehen.[101] Zwar waren die Edener aus »volkswirtschaftlicher Ueberzeugung Kolonialfreunde«, sie selbst wollten jedoch zunächst alle Kräfte daransetzen, »durch planmäßige Innenkolonisation dem Volksganzen zu dienen«.[102] Zentral für die Auseinandersetzung zwischen innerer oder äußerer Kolonisation war die »Rassenfrage«, die Menschen unterschiedlicher »Arten« auch ein bestimmtes Habitat, eine spezielle Umwelt und Kultur zudachte. Die Migration auf »artfremden« Boden galt daher vielen als Auslöser degenerativer Entwicklung.

Trotz anfänglicher Schwierigkeiten blühte die Kolonie Eden schon in den ersten Jahren auf. 1897 wurden Druckerei und Buchbinderei sowie eine Schule eröffnet, 1899 das Gasthaus und Erholungsheim, bald darauf die Lehrstätte Siedelgart sowie ein Kinder- und Waisenhaus. Neben Obsterzeugnissen wie Säften und Marmeladen, die bereits im Kaiserreich »Weltruf« erlangten, wurden zahlreiche Reformprodukte hergestellt und verkauft.[103] Das »Pflanzenfleisch« und die Pflanzenmargarine, die als Prototypen der späteren vegetarischen Produkte gelten können, wurden von ansässigen Siedlern entwickelt und im eigenen Konsum- und Kolonial-Laden ebenso feilgeboten wie auf den Märkten außerhalb der Siedlung. War der Vegetarismus schon seit Beginn des 19. Jahrhunderts in Deutschland verbreitet, erst in Eden wurde er vermarktet. Als Waren wurden Obst und Gemüse nun durch die Ideale des Vegetarismus und der Volksgesundheit moralisch aufgewertet. Dazu gehörte ein entsprechendes Branding und Marketing mit dem Edener Wappen und einer Symbolik von Gesundheit und Familie. Man schaltete Anzeigen in diversen, teils vor Ort gedruckten Reformblättern: den *Edener Mitteilungen*, der *Vegetarischen Warte, Ethischen Rundschau* sowie in den völkischen Periodika *Neues Leben* und *Hammer*. Mit den Produkten wurden zugleich ein bestimmter Lebensstil und eine ethische Weltanschauung verbunden und vermarktet. Im Übergang von der Theorie zur Praxis begriff sich Eden als Aufklärungs- und Erziehungsanstalt. Die Moralisierung von Ökonomie und Ökonomisierung bestimmter Moral und Lebensethik nach außen und die Produktion neuer Gemeinschaft und Subjektivität nach innen waren also zwei Seiten einer Medaille.

Genossenschaftlicher Verbund und Besitz, schwere landwirtschaftliche Arbeit im Freien, die Produktion bestimmter Waren und vegetarische Ernährung waren nach ethisch-sittlichen, hygienischen und gesundheitlichen Grundsätzen konzipiert. Die Gemeinschaftsbildung setzte jedoch auch beim Einzelnen an, um vom Individuum aus Gesellschaft zu reformieren: »Die Gesellschaftsreform lässt

---

101 Gustav Simons, Die Deutsche Gartenstadt. Ihr Wesen und ihre heutigen Typen, Wittenberg 1912, S. 16 f.

102 Otto Jackisch, Unsere Stellung zur Kolonialfrage, in: Edener Mitteilungen 2. 1907, Nr. 1, S. 4.

103 Günther Stolzenberg, Weltwunder Vegetarismus. Lebensschutz, Ernährung, München o. J. [ca. 1982], S. 52; Baumgartner, Ernährungsreform, S. 198.

sich nur auf der Basis der Einzel-, der Selbstreform durchführen.«[104] Auch in völkischen Kreisen setzte die Ausbildung des deutschen und »arisch-germanischen Wesens« am Individuum an. Sie sollte »im Inneren [...] beginnen, eine Gedanken- und Willens-Welt« aufbauen,[105] »denn das Rasse-Wesen ist in letzter Linie auch eine Frucht der Erziehung«.[106] Rasse wurde dynamisch verstanden, sie schloss Moral, Gefühl und Verhalten ein – und konnte durch »artgerechte« Lebenspraxis, Körperkultur und emotionale Erziehung positiv beeinflusst werden.[107] In der Gartenstadt hingen der »planmäßige äußere Aufbau«, die Wirtschafts-, Besitz- und Produktionsverhältnisse und »allerlei innere Reformen des neuen Gemeinwesens« und des Einzelnen unmittelbar zusammen.[108] Fabrikarbeit sei »›rasseschädigend‹, weil sie ungesund sei und ›zur Unselbstständigkeit‹ führe. Dem völkischen ›Rassensinne‹ und der urgermanischen Tradition entsprächen vielmehr genossenschaftlich organisierte Siedlungen«.[109]

Neben spezifischen Arbeitsweisen waren bildende Kunst und Theater, Musik und Feste zentral für die Formung neuer Gemeinschaft und Subjekte. Weiterhin galten besonders Vegetarismus, germanische oder protestantische Religiosität sowie bestimmte Formen der Gymnastik und Körperpflege als »arteigen« und förderlich für die als geschädigt verstandene Rassenkonstitution. Mit der Vermarktung des Vegetarismus und einer bestimmten Lebensweise ging so die Vermarktung und Vermittlung des Menschenbildes einher, auf dem der Vegetarismus fußte: einer als körperlich, seelisch und moralisch verstandenen rassischen Subjektivität.

Physiologisch ging man davon aus, dass eiweißhaltige Nahrung schädlich sei und der Mensch Fleisch nicht verdauen könne. Daher führe Fleischnahrung zu »Krankheit, Zerrüttung, körperlicher und geistiger Natur«:[110]

Und mit der Lösung der Brot- resp. Ernährungsfrage verschwinden naturgemäss eine Menge widriger Erscheinungen, an denen die heutige Zeit leider krankt: die Prostitution in allen ihren Erscheinungen und Formen, die zunehmende Verrohung und Demoralisation, der aufreibende Kampf ums Dasein [...].[111]

Ökonomisch seien Anbau und Produktion von fleischloser Nahrung ertragreicher. Sittlich ziehe das ungezügelte Fleischessen, im Gegensatz zum bewusst-

104 Anon., Lebensreformen, in: Vegetarische Warte 35. 1902, Nr. 8, 23.4.1902, S. 173–175, hier S. 173.
105 Theodor Fritsch, Grundzüge der künftigen Religion, in: Hammer 2. 1903, Nr. 25, S. 305–308, hier S. 308.
106 Ders., Rasse oder Erziehung? Eine Antwort an den Herausgeber der Sachsenschau, in: Hammer 3. 1904, Nr. 35, S. 391–395, hier S. 391.
107 Dazu weiterführend Anna Danilina, Shaping Aryan Race. Affect and Embodiment in the Voelkisch Movement (1900–1935), in: Body Politics 5. 2017, S. 71–112.
108 Simons, Gartenstadt, S. 3.
109 Puschner, Völkische Bewegung im Kaiserreich, S. 156.
110 Anon., Lebensreformen, S.173.
111 H. Lemke, Geschlechtskrankheiten und Vegetarismus, in: Vegetarische Warte 54. 1921, Nr. 10, 14.5.1921, S. 76.

asketischen Vegetarismus, andere Laster wie den Genuss von Alkohol und Tabak nach sich. Aber auch sexuelles Begehren, dessen Regulierung im Zentrum der Diskussion um Prostitution sowie »Rassereinheit« stand, sollte durch die vegetarische Lebensweise auf die Reproduktion gelenkt werden. So war Vegetarismus eine Form der Selbstsorge, die zur hygienischen Gesundheit des deutschen Volkskörpers beitragen sollte.[112] Ethisch verderbe der »Tiermord« den Charakter und das »Gemüt« des Einzelnen.[113] Auch Gefühle, hieß es, seien an Ernährung gekoppelt und durch »Reinigung« des Körpers zu kultivieren. So sei »die auf reinen Substanzen aufgebaute Ernährung die beste Gewähr dafür, dass sich das Gemüt von allen Schlacken und Gebresten – wie Hass, Neid, Unlauterkeit, Schwermut« befreie.[114] Vegetarismus wurde als Erziehung von Körper und Gefühl betrachtet – und als Gesundheits- und Glücksversprechen vermarktet.

Schließlich galt Vegetarismus als »Grundstein der Religion« in doppeltem Sinn: einerseits in ethischer Hinsicht und im Hinblick auf das religiöse Gefühl, andererseits in der historisch-mythischen Genealogie des Vegetarismus als Philosophie und Ernährung der Germanen und Arier. Gegen den Vorwurf, der Vegetarismus sei zu international ausgerichtet, führte man die deutsche Vorgeschichtsforschung, Orientalistik und Sprachwissenschaft ins Feld:[115] Eine indogermanische Sprach- und arisch-germanische Abstammungsgemeinschaft begründeten die Adaption »arteigener« Praktiken, Religion und Ernährung aus dem indischen Raum.[116]

Um den Wirkungs- und Siedlerkreis Edens zu vergrößern, wurde 1903 jedoch das vegetarische Gebot in der Satzung geändert. Denn so sehr breite vegetarische Kreise Eden unterstützten, nur wenige Genossenschaftsmitglieder wollten in der Siedlung leben. Überdies hatte sich gezeigt, dass die rigiden Vorgaben nicht selten zu Streit und kleinlichen Schnüffeleien führten, wer das »vegetarische Reinheitsgebot« durch heimlichen Fleischkonsum gebrochen hatte.[117] Um den Zuzug zu fördern, war die vegetarische Lebensweise nicht länger Pflicht, wurde jedoch weiterhin empfohlen. Anbau und Produktion blieben der vegetarischen Nahrung verpflichtet, das Alkohol- und Tabakverbot bestand fort.[118] Ethisch wurde die Satzungsänderung mit dem missionarischen Ziel legitimiert, gerade durch das Zusammenleben unter vegetarischen Idealen auch Nichtvegetarier zu bekehren.

112 Ebd., S. 76 f.
113 Anon., Lebensreformen, S. 173.
114 Carl Zimmer, Ethik und Vegetarismus, in: Vegetarische Warte 35. 1902, Nr. 17, 8.9.1902, S. 402 f., hier S. 403.
115 Otto Wenzel-Ekkehard, Ist der Vegetarismus undeutsch?, in: Vegetarische Warte 35. 1902, Nr. 18, 23.9.1902, S. 421–424, hier S. 422.
116 Zur Herstellung von Gefühl und Körperlichkeit durch »artgerechte« Praktiken siehe Danilina, Shaping Aryan Race; zu ›arteigener Religion‹ siehe Stefanie von Schnurbein, Die Suche nach einer »arteigenen« Religion in ›germanisch-‹ und ›deutschgläubigen‹ Gruppen, in: Puschner, Handbuch, S. 172–185; dies. u. Justus H. Ulbricht (Hg.), Völkische Religion und Krisen der Moderne. Entwürfe »arteigener« Glaubenssysteme seit der Jahrhundertwende, Würzburg 2001.
117 Michael Winteroll, Das Paradies im Sande, in: Bauwelt 83. 1992, Nr. 43, S. 2456–2461, hier S. 2456.
118 Stolzenberg, Weltwunder Vegetarismus, S. 52.

Als Mitglied des Deutschen Bundes für Regeneration verschrieb sich der
Edener Gustav Simons der »rassische[n], körperlich-gesundheitliche[n] (konsti-
tutionellen), sittliche[n], geistige[n] und seelische[n] Erneuerung des deutschen
Menschen auf germanischer Grundlage«.[119] Zu diesem Ziel trug neben der Ernährungsreform eine spezifische »Leibesökonomie« des Einzelnen bei.[120] Sie
zielte einerseits auf den individuellen Leib, andererseits auf die Volksgesundheit.[121] Züchterische Ziele positiver Eugenik, wie sie Willibald Hentschel in der
Siedlungsutopie Mittgart, Richard Ungewitter in den Siedlungen des Treubundes
für aufsteigendes Leben, Paul Bombe in Wodanshöhe, Paul Zimmermann in
Klingberg und die Siedlungen des Bundes der Lichtfreunde anstrebten, wies
Simons jedoch zurück.[122]

Nach dem Ersten Weltkrieg wurden völkische Tendenzen in Eden nochmals
dominanter. So stellte die Gilde der älteren Wandervögel auf dem ersten Frei-
landsiedlungstag eine Auslese der Siedler nach Kriterien »deutschen Ariertums«
zur Diskussion.[123] Die Lehrstätte für Landwirtschaft Siedelgart diente völkisch
orientierten Siedlern wie Heinrich Tegtmeyer vom Bund für rassische Siedlungen
und Ernst Hunkel, dem Gründer der völkischen Siedlung Donnershag bei Sontra,
als Ausbildungsstätte.[124] Auch die Broschüre für Deutschvölkische Erbpacht-Sied-
lungen wurde von Richard Bloeck in Eden herausgegeben. Es wundert insofern
nicht, dass Eden auch zum Vorbild für streng rassisch-völkische und züchterisch
motivierte Siedlungen wurde. Ernst Hunkel hatte von Eden aus den Jungborn-
Verlag wie auch die Herausgabe der Zeitschrift *Neues Leben. Monatsschrift für
deutsche Wiedergeburt* und die Presseabteilung des in der inneren Kolonisation Preußens aktiven Deutschen Ostmarken-Vereins geleitet und war zudem
der Generalsekretär der Deutsch-Asiatischen Gesellschaft. 1919 schritt er zur
»Landnahme« in Sontra, wo er die rassisch-züchterische Siedlung Donnershag
gründete. Hunkels Frau Margart verlegte die Deutsche Schwesternschaft nach
Sontra, die sich der »Aufzucht rassisch wertvoller Kinder im Geiste deutscher

---

119 Die Loge des aufsteigenden Lebens, in: Richard Ungewitter (Hg.), Deutschlands Wiedergeburt
    durch Blut und Eisen, Stuttgart 1919, S. 467.
120 Gustav Simons, Unsere Volksgesundheit, die gefährdete von heute, die gehobene in Zukunft,
    Oranienburg-Eden 1915, S. 19.
121 Ders., Volkswirtschaft und Volksgesundheit, in: I. Kongress für Biologische Hygiene. Vor-
    arbeiten und Verhandlungen – Hamburg 1912, 12.–14. Oktober, Hamburg 1913, S. 343–358.
122 Willibald Hentschel, Mittgart. Ein Weg zur Erneuerung der germanischen Rasse, Leipzig 1904;
    Christoph Knüppel, Im Lichtkleid auf märkischem Sand. Die völkische Siedlung Wodanshöhe
    bei Groß Bademeusel, in: Forster Jahrbuch für Geschichte und Heimatkunde 7. 2011, S. 73–
    97; Ulrich Linse, Völkisch-rassische Siedlungen der Lebensreform, in: Puschner, Handbuch,
    S. 397–410.
123 Edener Mitteilungen 1916, Nr. 11, S. 49–56.
124 Sebastian Friedrich, Die Erneuerung von Mensch, Gesellschaft und Rasse? Völkisches Be-
    wusstsein in der lebensreformerischen Siedlung Eden bei Berlin von 1893 bis 1933, Stattzei-
    tung für Südbaden, Ausgabe 71, 2008; http://www.stattweb.de/baseportal/ArchivDetail&db=
    Archiv&Id=948.

Volks- und Lebenserneuerung« verschrieben hatte.[125] Und namentlich Theodor Fritsch orientierte sich bei der Gründung der völkischen Siedlung Heimland am Edener Vorbild.

Nach der ersten Vollversammlung der Siedlungsgenossenschaft Heimland 1908 in Berlin unternahmen die Anwesenden unter Leitung Fritschs einen Ausflug nach Eden. Die »Edener Freunde« hatten Fritsch versprochen, ihm bei der Gründung Heimlands »mit Rat und Tat« zur Seite zu stehen. Fritsch wollte sich »die Erfahrungen von Eden und anderen Kolonisationsversuchen zu nutze machen«.[126] Auch ihm ging es darum, in seiner »Reformgemeinde eine neue, dem deutschen Wesenzuträgliche Lebensform« zu gestalten – auf Grundlage »artgerechter« Bodenkultur.[127]

Wir fordern sonach die Unverschuldbarkeit und Unverkäuflichkeit des Grund und Bodens, wie sie im alten sächsischen Recht bestand. Da wir ferner in der Bodenkultur nicht nur die Quelle der unentbehrlichsten Lebensgüter, sondern auch die Grundlage der arischen Lebensordnung und Sittlichkeit erkennen, hegen wir eine innige Anteilnahme an dem Gedeihen der Ackerwirtschaft und des Bauernstandes.[128]

Fritsch missfiel jedoch an Eden die mangelhafte rassische Auslese der Siedler sowie die einseitige Betonung des Vegetarismus und Genossenschaftswesens. Er war zwar selbst Vegetarier, hielt jedoch vegetarische Lebensweise allein nicht für ausreichend.[129] Fritschs Programm bezeichnete sein enger Freund Willibald Hentschel, Siedlungsbewegter und Mitglied der Erneuerungs-Gemeinde sowie des Hammerbundes, als »vernünftige Rassen-Ökonomie«.[130] Da die Heimland-Siedler und Siedlerinnen sich aus der Leserschaft von Fritschs Zeitschrift *Hammer* rekrutierten, hofften die Gründer auf eine gemeinsame Weltanschauung in Fragen von Religion, Erziehung, Politik, Rasse und ganzheitlicher Erneuerung.[131] Die Satzung der Siedlungs-Gesellschaft begrenzte deren Mitglieder entsprechend auf Siedler »deutschen Stammes«, die nicht mit »erblichen oder ansteckenden Krankheiten behaftet« seien, keine Menschen, die jüdischer Abstammung oder »jüdischer Beziehungen nur irgend verdächtig« waren.[132]

---

125 Ernst Hunkel, zit. n. Linse, Zurück, o Mensch, zur Mutter Erde, S. 189.

126 Gedruckter Bericht von Theodor Fritsch, 14.10.1908, in: Christoph Knüppel (Hg.), Dokumente zur Geschichte der völkischen Siedlung Heimland bei Rheinsberg, Herford 2002, S. 32 f.

127 Anon., Erneuerungs-Gedanken, in: Hammer 7. 1908, Nr. 153, S. 641–646, hier S. 644.

128 Theodor Fritsch u. Willibald Hentschel, Grundzüge der Erneuerungs-Gemeinde, Leipzig 1908, in: Knüppel, Dokumente, S. 10 f.

129 Erster Brief, Rundschreiben von Theodor Fritsch, Januar 1896, in: Knüppel, Dokumente, S. 3–6, hier S. 5.

130 Willibald Hentschel, Rassen-Ökonomie, in: Hammer 5. 1906, Nr. 91, S. 190–196, hier S. 195.

131 Weka (Walter Kramer), Ist eine genossenschaftliche Landbau-Siedelung lebensfähig?, in: Hammer 7. 1908, Nr. 148, S. 508–510.

132 Satzung der Siedelungs-Gesellschaft »Heimland«. Eingetragene Genossenschaft mit beschränkter Haftpflicht, Leipzig 1908/09, in: Knüppel, Dokumente, S. 36–42, hier S. 37.

Die Wirtschaftsweise der Siedlung legte »das größte Gewicht auf die Erhaltung der rassischen Kraft«; zugleich sollte die genossenschaftliche Bodengemeinschaft die Grenzen der Gemeinschaft festlegen, um »innere und äußere Feinde« fernzuhalten.[133] Dabei wurde Fritsch nicht müde zu betonen, dass Heimland keine Zufluchtsstätte für Schiffbrüchige, Arme und Kranke sei, sondern sich als »Pflegestätte für Gesunde« verstehe.[134]

»Wir wissen, daß alle arischen Völker zugrunde gingen, die sich von der Mutter Erde loslösten und Grund und Boden zur käuflichen Ware erniedrigten«, schrieben Theodor Fritsch und Willibald Hentschel in den »Grundzügen der Erneuerungs-Gemeinde«. Hentschel war bereits 1904 einen Schritt weitergegangen, indem er mit seiner Siedlungsutopie Mittgart und der darauf fußenden real-existierenden Siedlung Niegard (1922) primär züchterische Ziele verfolgte. In Mittgart, Niegard und Heimland ging es dem Programm nach nicht um die Vermarktung einer Reformethik wie den Vegetarismus oder die Herstellung entsprechender Produkte. Ziel war vielmehr der neue, rassisch bestimmte Mensch. In den zukunftsgerichteten, präskriptiven Texten wurde dabei auch der Rasse-gedanke selbst »vermarktet«. Rasse wurde in züchterischer Logik wortwörtlich zu einem Produkt der moralischen Siedlungsökonomie.

IV. Fazit

»Imperial formations are polities of dislocation, processes of dispersion, appropriation, and displacement.«[135] Die inneren Kolonien in Preußen, die Gartenstadt, lebensreformerische Siedlungsgenossenschaften und völkische Rassesiedlungen waren »imperiale Formationen« – ineinander übergehende Formen des Kolonialen. Ihre Entstehung kann nur im wechselseitigen Bezug aufeinander und vor dem Hintergrund eines transnationalen und kolonialen Raums verstanden werden. Die innere Kolonie, als die ihnen gemeinsame Form, kann als Projekt einer spezifisch moralischen Ökonomie verstanden werden. Dabei eröffnet der Begriff der moralischen Ökonomie mehrere miteinander verschränkte Analyse-ebenen. Zum einen bezeichnet die moralische Ökonomie das gemeinsame Feld unterschiedlicher Positionen in der inneren Kolonisation. Sie ermöglicht eine relationale Perspektive. Das bedeutet, dass die Akteure und Bewegungen, die im Diskurs- und Praxisfeld der moralischen Ökonomie operierten, nicht parallel nebeneinander bestanden oder vergleichend verstanden werden können. Ein Erklärungsgehalt liegt nicht nur in der Unterscheidung von Kolonisten, Boden-

---

133 Fritsch u. Hentschel, Grundzüge der Erneuerungs-Gemeinde, S. 10 f.
134 Mitteilungen der Erneuerungs-Gemeinde Nr. 5, 24.8.1909, in: Knüppel, Dokumente, S. 59–61, hier S. 60.
135 Ann Laura Stoler u. Carole McGranahan, Introduction. Refiguring Imperial Terrains, in: Ann Laura Stoler u. a. (Hg.), Imperial Formations, Oxford 2007, S. 3–44, hier S. 8.

reformern, Gartenstädtern, Lebensreformern, Zionisten und Völkischen, sondern gerade in ihrer Bezugnahme und der Übertragung von Diskursen, Praktiken, Moral- und Gemeinschaftsverständnissen.

Ferner war die bodenreformerische Genossenschaft eine moralische Ökonomie als relativ autarke Wirtschaftsgemeinschaft, die nach außen und innen normative Unterscheidungen vornahm. Mit ihrem kolonialen Bezug auf Kiautschou bildete sie die Grundlage, auf der das Verhältnis von Volk, Boden und Moral verhandelt wurde. Die innere Kolonie in Ostpreußen führte dieses Verhältnis fort und brachte durch ihren Bezug zum Kolonialismus in Übersee kolonial-rassistische Unterscheidungen mit sich. Diese bestimmten, welche Gemeinschaft im Raum der Siedlung mit Zivilisation, Kultur und Fortschritt assoziiert wurde – und welche Subjekte von ihr beherrscht oder ausgegrenzt wurden. Nach kolonialem Vorbild wurde der Anspruch auf Boden moralisch mit kultureller – und rassischer – Überlegenheit legitimiert. Im Osten Deutschlands wurde der missionarische Impetus der Germanisierung der Bevölkerung auch in die Wohlfahrtspraxis hineingetragen. Wohlfahrt wurde moralisch legitimiert, wirkte normativ und generierte diskursiv die Unterscheidungen und Hierarchien, auf die ihre Praxis sich richtete. Die Hilfe für die »notleidende«, deutsche oder ostjüdische, Bevölkerung wurde zu einem Teil des politischen Programms innerer Kolonisation. Die Unterscheidung nach Rasse schrieb sich in die Unterscheidung nach Klasse und Kultur ein. Innere Kolonien wurden zu Orten der Rettung und Reinigung – vor hygienischen und gesundheitlichen Missständen und Degeneration. Doch wendete sich hier auch die Erziehung des rassisch Anderen zur rassischen Regeneration des Selbst. Die innere Kolonie wurde im lebensreformerischen Spektrum zum Ort der eigenen Disziplinierung und rassischen Regeneration. Die Gartenstadt und Siedlungsgenossenschaft operierten mit dieser Konzeption gesundheitlicher und moralischer Rettung und mit dem Ausschluss »schädigender Elemente«. Die innere Kolonie war auf eine autarke moralische Ökonomie bedacht, die zugleich klare Grenzen von innen und außen gewährte und produzierte sowie die Subjekte innerhalb der Siedlung moralisch, geistig und körperlich regenerierte.

Als moralische Ökonomie sollte die Genossenschaft ferner der kapitalistischen Spekulation entgegenwirken. Sie sollte eine gute, gesunde, gemeinschaftsfördernde Form von Arbeitszusammenhang, Produktion und Konsumption ermöglichen. Gleichzeitig sollte sie den Menschen an den Boden binden, nicht durch Zwang, sondern als Formung einer organischen Einheit von Volk und Land, von Mensch und Raum. In der Politik im Osten Deutschlands entstand eine spezifische Verbindung von Boden, Volk und Wirtschaft. Diese wurde in der Kolonisations- und Regenerationspraxis des Zionismus, der Lebensreform und der völkischen Siedlung übernommen. Auf Grundlage der wirtschaftlichen Praxis sollten der neue Mensch und die neue Gemeinschaft entstehen. Produkt dieser Ökonomie waren also Moral und Mensch selbst. In der völkischen Siedlung war ihr Produkt das Rassesubjekt, das durch artgerechten Raum, Ernährung, Arbeit oder auch Zucht geformt werden sollte. Die innere Kolonie war also eine moralisierte Ökonomie und eine Ökonomisierung von Moral und Subjekt. Darin brachte sie koloniale Wissens- und Praxisbestände in die Formierung von Subjekten, in die Vorstellungen guter und gerechter Wirtschafts- und Gemeinschaftszusammenhänge sowie in das Verhältnis von Boden und Volk ein.

Björn Blaß

Frauensache

Städtisches Haushalten als moralische Ökonomie in New York
(1880–1917)

Abstract: The article investigates the municipal housekeeping movement of the Progressive Era and its impact on the waste regime of New York as a form of moral economy that combined political activism, moral imperatives and economic concerns. It focuses on the achievements and contributions of female activists who took a keen interest in urban sanitation as a key to improving society. Individually and collectively, women surveilled both every-day practices of disposal as well as the services provided by the Department of Street Cleaning. To legitimize their actions, female reformers embraced gender-specific notions of household cleanliness while at the same time widening their sphere of influence.

Verschwenderisch, schädlich und widerwärtig – so lautete das Urteil der 1884 gegründeten Ladies' Health Protective Association (LHPA) über die Entsorgungspraktiken der New Yorker Stadtreinigung. Das Department of Street Cleaning (DSC), 1881 in Folge bürgerlichen Reformdrucks etabliert, stand von Beginn an in der öffentlichen Kritik: zu hoch die Ausgaben, zu gering der betriebene Aufwand seiner Mitarbeiter und zu abstoßend das äußere Bild, das die wachsende Stadt ihren Bewohnern bot.[1] Die hygienischen Verhältnisse, die die LHPA und andere Reformerinnen der *Progressive Era* vorfanden, galten als Sinnbild einer Transformation, die *America's first city* im Zuge von Industrialisierung, Urbanisierung und Zuwanderung durchlebte.

Im Laufe des 19. Jahrhunderts hatte sich New York zusehends von einer durch Handel geprägten Hafenstadt hin zu einer Industriemetropole entwickelt.[2] Die Nachfrage nach günstiger Arbeitskraft kreierte einen bis zum Ersten Weltkrieg andauernden Sog auf die transatlantischen Migrationsbewegungen. Während bis

---

1 Ladies' Health Protective Association (Hg.), Report of the Ladies' Health Protective Association of the City of New York, New York 1888, S. 15.

2 Mike Wallace, Greater Gotham. A History of New York City from 1898 to 1919, New York 2017, S. 305–338; Sven Beckert, The Monied Metropolis. New York City and the Consolidation of the American Bourgeoisie, 1850–1896, Cambridge, MA 2001, S. 46 f. Auch während der Industrialisierung blieb New York der wichtigste Warenumschlagsplatz der Vereinigten Staaten. Zur Jahrhundertwende erreichten und verließen noch rund 50 % der Im- und Exporte das Land über den Hafen. Vgl. Frederick M. Binder u. David M. Reimers, All the Nations under Heaven. An Ethnic and Racial History of New York City, New York 1995, S. 93 f.

zur Mitte des 19. Jahrhunderts vor allem irische und deutsche Einwanderer über-
wogen, waren es an der langen Wende zum 20. Jahrhundert vor allem Süd- und
Osteuropäer, die das Bild der »poor and huddled masses«[3] bestimmten. Die Be-
völkerungen New Yorks – und des zunächst eigenständigen Brooklyns – wuchsen
von 1,9 Millionen im Jahr 1880 auf 4,8 Millionen im Jahr 1910. Der US-Zensus
desselben Jahres erfasste 41 Prozent der Einwohnerschaft New Yorks als »foreign-
born«.[4] Beide Städte dehnten sich ebenfalls räumlich aus und wuchsen mit der
Eröffnung der Brücken über den East River (Brooklyn Bridge 1883, Williamsburg
Bridge 1903 und Manhattan Bridge 1909) auch ineinander. Mit der »Konsolidierung« Manhattans, Brooklyns, Queens, der Bronx und Staten Islands zu *Greater
New York* im Jahr 1898 sollte den bereits bestehenden Verflechtungen nun auch
administrativ Rechnung getragen werden.[5]

Die Folgen des rapiden Bevölkerungswachstums überforderten Politik und
Verwaltung. Vor allem arme Neuankömmlinge siedelten sich in den auf maximalen Profit ausgerichteten *tenements* von Manhattans Lower East Side an.[6] Die
extreme Bevölkerungsdichte – 1890 über 180.000 Menschen pro Quadratkilometer – wirkte sich hier am dramatischsten auf die hygienischen Bedingungen
aus.[7] Ein Mangel an Licht, Luft und Sauberkeit bestimmte das Straßenbild und
rief bürgerliche Reformerinnen und Reformer auf den Plan, die sowohl in den äußeren Lebensumständen als auch den Neuankömmlingen selbst zu regulierende
Gefahren für die Gesellschaft erblickten.[8]

In diesem Kontext nahm der Umgang mit Müll und Schmutz eine besondere
Stellung ein. Aus Sicht prominenter Stadt- und Sozialreformerinnen wie Jane
Addams, Florence Kelley oder Lillian Wald prägte vor allem der Zustand der phy-
sischen Umgebung den moralischen Anstand ihrer Mitglieder. Ein gesundes und

---

3 Die Wendung stammt aus dem Sonett »The New Collossus« (1883) von Emma Lazarus, das 1903
   als Plakette am Sockel der Freiheitsstatue angebracht wurde. Vgl. Max Cavitch, Emma Lazarus
   and the Golem of Liberty, in: American Literary History 18. 2006, S. 1–28.
4 Ira Rosenwaike, Population History of New York City, Syracuse 1972, S. 93.
5 »New York« steht in der Untersuchung für den Raum, den die Stadt in ihren heutigen Ausdehnun-
   gen umfasst. Wenngleich stadtgeschichtlich anachronistisch ergibt das Zusammendenken New
   Yorks und Brooklyns als Einheit *vor* 1898 als umweltgeschichtlicher Entsorgungsraum durchaus
   Sinn, wie das Beispiel Barren Islands verdeutlicht. Vgl. Benjamin Miller, Fat of the Land. Garbage
   in New York. The Last Two Hundred Years, New York 2000, Kap. 2: »Grease«, S. 45–92. Zum
   langwierigen und konflikthaften Konsolidierungsprozess selbst vgl. Edwin G. Burrows u. Mike
   Wallace, Gotham. A History of New York City to 1898, Oxford 2000², Kap. 69: »Imperial City«,
   S. 1219–1236. Zur Planung und Durchführung der Konsolidierung vgl. Barry J. Kaplan, Andrew
   H. Green and the Creation of a Planning Rationale. The Formation of Greater New York City,
   1865–1890, in: Urbanism Past & Present 8. 1979, S. 32–41; John A. Krout, Framing the Charter,
   in: Allan Nevins u. ders. (Hg.), The Greater City. New York, 1898–1948, New York 1948, S. 41–61.
6 Norman I. Fainstein, Transformationen im industriellen New York. Politik, Gesellschaft und
   Ökonomie 1880–1973, in: Hartmut Häußermann u. Walter Siebel (Hg.), New York. Strukturen
   einer Metropole, Frankfurt 1993, S. 27–50, hier S. 28.
7 Department of the Interior, Vital Statistics of New York City and Brooklyn. Covering a Period
   of Six Years Ending May 31, 1890, Washington, D. C. 1894, S. 101.
8 Richard Hofstadter, The Age of Reform. From Bryan to F. D. R., New York 1955, S. 11 u. S. 181–183.

hygienisches Umfeld galt als unabdingbare Voraussetzung für eine gesunde und stabile Gesellschaft. Daher galt es, besonders in den von Armut und Migration geprägten Stadtvierteln solche äußerlichen Bedingungen zu garantieren, die sich positiv auf die charakterliche Formierung Einzelner und letztlich der gesamten Stadtgemeinschaft auswirkten.[9]

Die Auseinandersetzungen über die Unzulänglichkeiten existierender Infrastrukturen und angewandter Reinigungspraktiken in New York selbst werden dort konkret nachvollziehbar, wo sich bürgerliche Reformerinnen und Reformer und städtische Administration mit Fragen effektiver Müllentsorgung und Straßenreinigung befassten. Aktivistinnen und Frauenorganisationen wie die LHPA und die Woman's Municipal League (WML) übernahmen innerhalb dieses Diskurses führende Rollen. Als Teil der Reformbewegung der *Progressive Era* prägten sie wirkungsvolle Strategien der Aufklärung und Intervention, die sie in der Forderung nach *municipal housekeeping* zusammenfassten.[10]

Der vorliegende Beitrag zeigt auf, wie unter diesem Schlagwort zeitgenössische Vorstellungen von häuslicher Sauberkeit, moralischer Erziehung und wirtschaftlicher Haushaltung im Ringen um ein effizientes und effektives Ordnungssystem für New York mobilisiert wurden.[11] Anders als frühfeministische Ansätze, wie sie Charlotte Perkins Gilman und Emma Goldman vertraten, stellten die hier untersuchten Reformerinnen geschlechterspezifische Zuschreibungen des »Kultes der Domestizität« nicht grundsätzlich infrage.[12] Das erklärte Ziel war nicht eine konsequente Veränderung im Verhältnis zwischen Männern und Frauen oder die Neuverhandlung häuslicher Arbeit. Stattdessen beförderten sie das viktorianische Ideal des *angel in the house*, worin sich Tugenden von Fürsorge und Sauberkeit mit Aufgaben der Erziehung und Kontrolle verbanden.[13]

---

9 Daniel E. Burnstein, Next to Godliness. Confronting Dirt and Despair in Progressive Era New York City, Urbana, IL 2006, S. 2. Zu den transatlantischen Verflechtungen der Reformbewegung vgl. Daniel T. Rodgers, Atlantic Crossings. Social Politics in a Progressive Age, Cambridge, MA 1998, Kap. 5: »Civic Ambitions«, S. 160–208.

10 Vgl. Richard S. Skolnik, The Crystallization of Reform in New York City, 1890–1917, Diss. Yale University 1964; Suellen M. Hoy, »Municipal Housekeeping«. The Role of Women in Improving Urban Sanitation Practices, 1880–1917, in: Martin V. Melosi (Hg.), Pollution and Reform in American Cities, 1870–1930, Austin 1980, S. 173–198.

11 Vgl. auch Burnstein, Next to Godliness, S. 23 f.

12 Zu Charlotte Perkins Gilman vgl. Falguni A. Sheth u. Robert E. Prasch, Charlotte Perkins Gilman. Reassessing Her Significance for Feminism and Social Economics, in: Review of Social Economy 54. 1996, S. 323–335. Zu Emma Goldman vgl. Oz Frankel, Whatever Happened to »Red Emma«? Emma Goldman, from Alien Rebel to American Icon, in: Journal of American History 83. 1996, S. 903–942; Clare Hemmings, Sexual Freedom and the Promise of Revolution. Emma Goldman's Passion, in: Feminist Review 2014, H. 106, S. 43–59. Zur Formation des »cult of domesticity« vgl. Mary P. Ryan, Cradle of the Middle Class. The Family in Oneida County, New York, 1790–1865, Cambridge 1981.

13 Zum Mythos des *angel in the house* vgl. Elizabeth Langland, Nobody's Angels. Domestic Ideology and Middle-Class Women in the Victorian Novel, in: PMLA 107. 1992, S. 290–304; Mildred Jeanne Peterson, No Angels in the House. The Victorian Myth and the Paget Women, in: American Historical Review 89. 1984, S. 677–708.

In ihrer Intervention zur Geschichte der Frauen während der *Progressive Era*
monierte die Historikerin Elisabeth Perry, dass Reformerinnen – nach langer
historiografischer Abwesenheit – auf die »Domestizierung der Politik« und den
Begriff »städtischer Haushälterinnen« reduziert wurden, die keine weiterreichenden gesellschaftlichen Veränderungen anstrebten. Diese Lesart würde starre Ge-
schlechterdichotomien reproduzieren.[14] Durch ihr sozialpolitisches Engagement
weiteten bürgerliche Reformerinnen aber ihre eigene Einflusssphäre über die
Grenzen des Privaten hinaus aus und beeinflussten die öffentliche Debatte maß-
geblich. Diese Ausweitung legitimierten die Aktivistinnen einerseits mit ihrer tra-
dierten, alltäglichen Haushaltsexpertise. Andererseits lag ihrem Aktivismus ein
holistisches Verständnis der Stadt als *oikos* zu Grunde, in dem moralische Werte
mit wirtschaftlichen und politischen Abläufen untrennbar verknüpft waren.[15]
    Diese Verbindungen legen eine Untersuchung der Reformbestrebungen und
ihrer Umsetzung als moralischer Ökonomie nahe. Verstanden als Ökonomisierung der Moral verweist der Ansatz metaphorisch auf Produktion, Mobilisierung
und Austausch von Normen und Wertvorstellungen.[16] Demgegenüber steht die
Moralisierung des Ökonomischen als Beeinflussung wirtschaftlicher Abläufe
durch normativ geprägte, soziopolitische Aushandlungen.[17] Jedoch gilt es, diese
Interpretationen des Konzepts nicht gegeneinander auszuspielen. Beide Ansätze
müssen in der Debatte um *municipal housekeeping* vielmehr als zwei Seiten derselben Medaille betrachtet werden. Moralisierung und Ökonomisierung waren
hierin Vorgänge, die sich auf vier ineinandergreifende Bereiche erstreckten: die
Planbarkeit und Gestaltung der urbanen Umwelt; die Möglichkeit politischer
Partizipation; der wirtschaftliche Umgang mit städtischen Finanzen; die Ein-
übung und Kontrolle hygienischer Ordnungsmuster. Jeder dieser Bereiche war
von moralischen Argumentationslinien durchzogen, die in einem übergeordne-
ten Reformziel zusammenliefen: der Steigerung des Gemeinwohls.[18] Derart ge-

14 Paula Baker, The Domestication of Politics. Women and American Political Society, 1780–1920,
    in: American Historical Review 89. 1984, S. 620–647; Elisabeth Perry, Men Are from the Gilded
    Age, Women Are from the Progressive Era, in: Journal of the Gilded Age and Progressive Era
    1. 2002, S. 25–48. Dabei hatte Mary Ryan in einer späteren Arbeit bereits aufgezeigt, dass das
    Verhältnis zwischen affirmativen Geschlechterbildern und politischer Öffentlichkeit ambiva-
    lenter war, als sie es selbst in »Cradle of the Middle Class« erfasst hatte. Vgl. Mary P. Ryan,
    Women in Public. Between Banners and Ballots, 1825–1880, Baltimore 1990.
15 Dieses Vorgehen ist dem von Sonya Michel und Seth Koven beschriebenen Maternalismus
    innerhalb der Entstehung wohlfahrtsstaatlicher Strukturen an der Wende zum 20. Jahrhundert
    anschließbar. Vgl. Seth Koven u. Sonya Michel, Womanly Duties. Maternalist Politics and the
    Origins of Welfare States in France, Germany, Great Britain, and the United States, 1880–1920,
    in: American Historical Review 95. 1990, S. 1076–1108. Neuer dazu Marian van der Klein u. a.
    (Hg.), Maternalism Reconsidered. Motherhood, Welfare and Social Policy in the Twentieth
    Century, New York 2012.
16 Vgl. Didier Fassin, Les économies morales revisitées, in: Annales HSS 64. 2009, S. 1237–1266.
17 Vgl. Edward Palmer Thompson, The Moral Economy of the English Crowd in the Eighteenth
    Century, in: Past & Present 1971, H. 50, S. 76–136.
18 Habbo Knoch u. Benjamin Möckel, Moral History. Überlegungen zu einer Geschichte des
    Moralischen im »langen« 20. Jahrhundert, in: ZF 14. 2017, S. 93–111.

lagert kann der Beitrag eine gesellschaftsgeschichtliche Erweiterung zur urbanen Umweltgeschichte liefern, in der die Frauenbewegung eine führende Rolle einnahm.[19] Um ihre Ziele zu erreichen, setzten bürgerliche Aktivistinnen auf einen pragmatisch-kooperativen Reformismus, der ihnen eine Form politischer Partizipation in einer Zeit ermöglichte, die ihnen Stimme und Teilhabe am politischen Prozess weitestgehend versagte.[20]

Zum Verständnis dieser Form des Aktivismus zeichnet der Artikel die Genese und Wirkung der *municipal-housekeeping*-Bewegung in New York zwischen 1880 und 1917 chronologisch nach. Diese entwickelte sich innerhalb vielfältiger Reformbestrebungen der *Progressive Era*, deren Vertreterinnen und Vertreter die »politische Maschine« der Stadtverwaltung als wirtschaftlich ineffektiv, politisch manipulativ und moralisch korrupt darstellten und attackierten.[21] Als eine der ersten Organisationen ihrer Art nahm die LHPA hierbei eine Vorreiterrolle ein. Der Verein kritisierte die Leistungen der Stadtreinigung und drängte auf Verbesserungen (I.). In einer kurzen Phase zwischen 1895 und 1897 setzte der neue Commissioner, George E. Waring Jr., etliche Reformen innerhalb des Departments durch und erkannte zudem die Bedeutung des weiblichen Engagements an. Sichtbare Resultate und eine neue Form von Öffentlichkeitsarbeit machten Waring zu einem Fixstern der Reformbewegung, der bis ins frühe 20. Jahrhundert ausstrahlte (II.). Auf nationaler Ebene erhob die Aktivistin Caroline Bartlett Crane *municipal housekeeping* zur Parole des Ordnungsdiskurses und verknüpfte diesen mit der sozialen Frage. Damit ermutigte sie die amerikanischen Hausfrauen, sich weiterhin vor Ort für die Verbesserung der Stadthygiene einzusetzen (III.). New Yorks WML griff diese Forderung auf und bemühte sich sowohl um Aufklärung über Müll und Sauberkeit in der Bevölkerung als auch um ein kooperatives Verhältnis zum DSC (IV.). Letztlich geht der Artikel auf die Umstrukturierungspläne Flora Spiegelbergs ein, die anhand technisch-rationaler Lösungen Effizienz und Effektivität in der Stadtreinigung zu steigern suchte (V.), ehe die Ergebnisse abschließend bewertet werden (VI.).

Die Folgen der rapiden und unregulierten industriellen Entwicklung New Yorks wurden bereits in der zweiten Hälfte des 19. Jahrhunderts im Stadtbild allgegenwärtig. Verschmutzung, sanitäre Missstände, eine hohe Umwelt- und Schadstoffbelastung sowie das Auftreten endemischer und epidemischer Krankheiten riefen eine vielstimmige und vielseitige Reformbewegung auf den Plan, die Fragen der (städtischen) Umwelt bereits vor der *Progressive Era* zum Politikum machte.[22]

---

19 Vgl. Martin V. Melosi, The Urban Environment, in: Peter Clark (Hg.), The Oxford Handbook of Cities in World History, Oxford 2013, S. 700–719; Christoph Bernhardt (Hg.), Environmental Problems in European Cities in the 19th and 20th Century, Münster 2001.

20 Martin V. Melosi, Garbage in the Cities. Refuse, Reform, and the Environment, Pittsburgh 2005, S. 93–99; Susan Strasser, Waste and Want. A Social History of Trash, New York 1999, S. 121. Das Frauenwahlrecht wurde in den Vereinigten Staaten erst 1920 eingeführt.

21 Hofstadter, Age of Reform, S. 16 f.

22 Vgl. David Rosner (Hg.), Hives of Sickness. Public Health and Epidemics in New York City, New Brunswick, NJ 1995.

Dazu zählte vor allem die bereits seit längerem etablierte und einflussreiche New York Academy of Medicine und die 1863 gegründete Citizens' Association, auf deren Betreiben hin der Gouverneur des Bundesstaats New York 1866 die Gründung des Metropolitan Board of Health veranlasst hatte.[23] Derlei Sorgen fielen zusammen mit einer weiterreichenden Kritik an Eigeninteressen und organisatorischen Missständen innerhalb der städtischen Verwaltung, die politisch progressive Reformgruppen monierten.[24]

Die Reformbewegung rekrutierte sich überwiegend aus einem bürgerlichen Milieu, das sich oft in themenspezifischen Organisationen und ehrenamtlichen Vereinen zusammenschloss und gegen die vorherrschenden politischen Entscheidungs- und Verwaltungsprozesse positionierte. Diese waren in New York – auf bundesstaatlicher, besonders aber auf städtischer Ebene – vom System der *political machine* geprägt, das sich aus Sicht seiner zeitgenössischen Kritiker durch fiskalische Intransparenz, Patronageverhältnisse und Korruption auszeichnete.[25]

Während der *Progressive Era* galten Müll und Schmutz in New York nicht nur als ästhetisches Ärgernis, sondern als omnipräsente Marker der wirtschaftlichen und der sozialen Frage, die eng an die hygienischen Bedingungen des urbanen Raums geknüpft waren und politischer Veränderungen bedurften. Die Anwendung wissenschaftlich-objektiver Methodik in Form von statistischen Untersuchungen führte bereits ab der Mitte des 19. Jahrhunderts im Bereich der öffentlichen Gesundheit zu einem verstärkten Interesse an den Lebens-, Wohn- und Arbeitsbedingungen von Stadtbewohnern. Im Fokus standen dabei die Entstehungsbedingungen von Epidemien, welche immer weniger als Strafe Gottes und zunehmend als Belastung der lokalen und nationalen Ökonomie betrachtet wurden. Elend und Erkrankungen wurden nicht mehr allein individuellem Fehlverhalten zugeschrieben, die moralische Komponente verschwand aber aus der städtischen Reformbewegung nicht komplett. Vielmehr wurde sie erweitert um ein wohltätiges Fürsorgeparadigma, das gesundheitspolitische und infrastrukturelle Reformprojekte prägte. Besonders Frauenvereine werteten den weitgehend unhygienischen Zustand New Yorks als Symptom und Ursache einer fehlgeleiteten Politik.

---

23 Vgl. John Duffy, A History of Public Health in New York City, 1866–1966, New York 1974, Kap. 1: »The Metropolitan Board of Health«, S. 1–31.

24 Die Organisationen hatten eine große Bandbreite und reichten von allgemeinen hin zu spezialisierten Interessengruppen. Während Vereinigungen wie der City Club, der City Reform Club, die Citizens' Union, der Social Reform Club, der East Side Civic Club oder die Woman's Municipal League eine Vielzahl von Reformthemen bearbeiteten, konzentrierten sich andere Vereine auf Einzelthemen wie Sport, Bildung, Kriminalität oder Steuerreform. Vgl. Richard Skolnik, Civic Group Progressivism in New York City, in: New York History 51. 1970, S. 410–439, hier S. 423. Bezeichnend ist auch, dass sich Aktivistinnen in unterschiedlichen Vereinen zur gleichen Zeit beteiligten oder gar, wie im Fall der Grande Dame der Sozialreformer, Josephine Shaw Lowell, mehrere Organisationen gründeten.

25 Burnstein, Next to Godliness, S. 32 f.

I. Die Ladies' Health Protective Association und
ihre Kritik an der dysfunktionalen Stadt

Als erste New Yorker Organisation ihrer Art arbeitete die 1884 gegründete LHPA auf die Verbesserung der hygienischen Zustände in der Stadt hin. Ihr Hauptanliegen war die Säuberung der Straßen, da diese »eine vitale Beziehung zu jedem Einwohner und zu jedem Besucher« herstellten.[26] Aus Sicht des Vereins bestand eine direkte Verbindung zwischen öffentlicher Gesundheit und Sauberkeit der Verkehrswege, die nur teilweise geteert oder gepflastert waren.[27] In ihrem Selbstverständnis »aggressiv«, untersuchte die LHPA auf eigene Kosten Praktiken und Techniken in anderen Städten, sowohl innerhalb als auch außerhalb der Vereinigten Staaten. In einem neunseitigen Bericht an New Yorks Bürgermeister, Abram S. Hewitt, monierte der Verein den Zustand der Straßen und verband darin zugleich moralische Vorstellungen von äußerer und innerer Ordnung:

Must we, your Honor, continue as housekeepers to submit to this increased trouble and expense, to these intense annoyances and disgusts, that result from the perpetual presence of dirt outside of our houses that we cannot control? Even if dirt were not the unsanitary and dangerous thing we know that it *is*, its unsightliness and repulsiveness are so great, that no other reason than the superior beauty of cleanliness should be required to make the citizens of New York, through their vested authorities, quite willing to appropriate whatever sum may be necessary, in order to give to themselves and to their wives and daughters, that outside neatness, cleanliness and freshness, which are the natural complement and completion of inside order and daintiness, which are to the feminine taste and perception, simply indispensable not only to comfort but also to self-respect.[28]

Die Beseitigung gesundheitsgefährdender Materialien und Betriebe war das erklärte Ziel des Vereins.[29] Besonders die in den 1880er Jahren populärer werdende Müllverbrennung und ihre Verheißung restloser Vernichtung von Abfall und potenzieller Krankheitserreger faszinierten die Aktivistinnen.[30] Während

26 LHPA, Report, 1888, S. 1. Alle Übersetzungen durch den Autor. Blockzitate und vollständige Sätze wurden nicht übersetzt.

27 Laut dem ersten Bericht des Department of Street Cleaning umfasste das New Yorker Straßennetz – zu dieser Zeit bestehend aus Manhattan und der Bronx – 575 Meilen. »Thirty-one percent were dirt and required no regular sweeping, 12 percent were macadamized (surfaces of broken stone) and cleaned by the Department of Public Works and Parks. The remaining streets were trapblocks (36 percent), granite blocks (19.5 percent), cobblestone (1 percent), asphalt (.3 percent) or wood and russ (.2 percent).« Steven H. Corey, King Garbage. A History of Solid Waste Management in New York City, 1881–1970, Diss. New York University 1994, S. 4.

28 Ebd. (Hervorhebung im Original); LHPA, Report, 1888, S. 12.

29 Anon., Against Fat-Rendering Factories. Ladies' Health Protective Association Also Speaks about Garbage, in: New York Times, 3.10.1894, S. 4.

30 Anon., To Try Cremating Garbage. A Scheme of the Ladies' Health Protective Association, in: New York Times, 12.12.1888, S. 8. Erste Verbrennungsversuche wurden bereits 1877 durch die Manhattan Cremator Company durchgeführt, ehe 1885 die erste Verbrennungsanlage auf Governor's Island folgte. Eine umfangreiche Verbrennung von Abfallstoffen erfolgte jedoch erst

der Frühphase der bakteriologischen Revolution wurde eine Kombination von Faktoren für das Auftreten von Krankheiten verantwortlich gemacht: Öffentliche Verschmutzung, hohe Bevölkerungsdichte und übelkeitserregende Gerüche wurden gemäß zeitgenössischem medizinischem Wissen mit einer in Hausmüll und Straßenkehricht lauernden Ansteckungsgefahr verbunden.[31] Praktizierende Ärzte, deren Ausbildung noch stark von miasmatischen Theorien geprägt war, erklärten das Auftreten von Epidemien wie der Cholera mithilfe von Hybridmodellen halb als Miasma, halb als Bakterium.[32] Die LHPA kooperierte eng mit der New York Academy of Medicine, deren Mitglieder sie regelmäßig zu Vorträgen einlud und deren Räumlichkeiten sie für ihre zweiwöchentlichen Treffen nutzte.[33] Durch diesen Austausch integrierten die Aktivistinnen den damals aktuellen Kenntnisstand in ihre gesundheitspolitische Argumentation. Auch wenn der Verein die Zusammenarbeit mit dem Department of Street Cleaning suchte, sprachen seine Mitglieder vor diesem Hintergrund die städtischen Missstände ungeschminkt und drastisch an:

The Association has received and investigated complaints of nuisances in the streets in various parts of the city, but in the present order of affairs their power ends with a protest. They are forced to admit that the streets of New York were never in a worse condition than at the beginning of this new year, 1888. This association does not mean to slacken its efforts, but trembles for the health of the city if no improvement appears when the hot season comes with the danger of imported cholera upon us.[34]

Die Strategie der Aktivistinnen zielte dabei auf vier Aspekte: Gesundheit, Arbeit, Ästhetik und Ökonomie. In ihrem Schreiben an Hewitt monierte die LHPA das Müll- und Verschmutzungsproblem als eine direkte Bedrohung für die öffentliche Gesundheit und das Gemeinwohl:

Modern science has fully exposed the imminent dangers that beset health and life in a malodorous and dust-covered town. Foul smells, such as in mysterious variety assail the sense even on Broadway in the summer, indicate the presence of decaying matter, and the dust with which our streets, our houses, and too often our faces are filled, is crowded with living organic germs, which need only a weakened human frame to make their victorious attack upon its tissues and eat it into death.[35]

---

mit der Öffnung der Sortier- und Verbrennungsanlage an der 18th Street am Tag der Konsolidierung am 1.1.1898. Vgl. Corey, King Garbage, S. 84 u. S. 99–103.

31 Duffy, History of Public Health, S. 91.

32 Burnstein, Next to Godliness, S. 12. Zur zeitgleich in Deutschland stattfindenden Debatte vgl. Anne I. Hardy, *Ärzte, Ingenieure und städtische Gesundheit. Medizinische Theorien in der Hygienebewegung des 19. Jahrhunderts*, Frankfurt 2005, S. 209–214; Richard Evans, Tod in Hamburg. Stadt, Gesellschaft und Politik in den Cholera-Jahren 1830–1910, Reinbek bei Hamburg 1990, S. 418–475.

33 Rosaline C. Wren u. a. (Hg.), Club Women of New York, New York 1904, S. 69.

34 LHPA, Report, 1888, S. 1.

35 Memorial of the New York Ladies' Health Protective Association, to the Hon. Abram S. Hewitt, Mayor of New York, on the Subject of Street Cleaning, 25.3.1887, in: LHPA, Report 1888, S. 11.

Als Hauptursache für diese Gefahr identifizierte der Verein die unregelmäßige und unzuverlässige Abholung des Hausmülls durch das bis dato sechs Jahre operierende DSC. Dies entwerte die im privaten Haushalt geleistete Arbeit vieler Frauen, die täglich die Müll- und Aschetonnen auf den Bürgersteig stellten, wo sie von Lumpensammlern und Nachbarsjungen durchwühlt oder umgestoßen wurden. Die offenen, nicht abgeholten Tonnen ebenso wie der faul und behäbig agierende Müllmann gehörten zum Bildrepertoire, das die Dysfunktionalität des städtischen Verwaltungsapparats und seiner Mitarbeiter markieren sollte.[36] In dieser Schilderung schwangen durchaus fremdenfeindliche Vorurteile gegenüber den Arbeitern des DSC mit. Das Department rekrutierte seine Müllwerker und Straßenfeger überwiegend aus den Reihen ungelernter Einwanderer.[37] Aus Sicht des bürgerlichen Establishments erfolgte die Anstellung in Diensten der Stadt nicht anhand von Leistungen, sondern als Teil politischer Patronageverhältnisse der politischen Maschine.[38]

Auf ästhetischer Ebene verdeutlichte die geschilderte Szene eine Ausweitung der häuslichen Sphäre in den öffentlichen Raum hinein. Die Stadt wurde als bewohnter Raum wahrgenommen und denselben Regeln von Ordnung und Sauberkeit unterworfen. Zwar stellte die LHPA eine geschlechtercodierte, viktorianische Trennung von öffentlicher und privat-häuslicher Sphäre nicht explizit infrage, forderte aber die Anerkennung der geleisteten Hausarbeit ein und versuchte diese aus der Unsichtbarkeit der eigenen vier Wände zu befreien und somit als stadtökonomischen Faktor geltend zu machen.[39]

Die wirtschaftlichen Überlegungen der LHPA bezogen sich auf eine Art Preis-Leistungsverhältnis. Unter Berufung auf den Ökonomen Richard T. Ely setzte der Bericht an den Bürgermeister Müllaufkommen und Ausgaben des DSC in Beziehung und verglich sie mit den Berliner Werten. Die Autorinnen betonten, dass die Pro-Kopf-Kosten für die Stadtreinigung in Berlin zwischen 50 und 60 Prozent niedriger lägen als in New York, bei angeblich besseren Resultaten. Dies ließe sich einerseits mit dem höheren amerikanischen Lebensstandard und einem gesteigerten Konsumverhalten erklären: mehr Obst, Konserven und Papierverpackungen sorgten für ein zwei- bis dreimal höheres Abfallaufkommen. Andererseits lege die Gegenüberstellung eine mangelnde Arbeitsmoral der DSC-Mitarbeiter nahe. Die LHPA forderte ein angemessenes Budget für das Department, das sich in seiner Verwendung aber an »den sorgsamen und ökonomischen Deutschen« orientieren sollte.[40]

Nicht nur die Kosten, sondern auch die in Berlin angewandten Methoden bei der Straßenreinigung wollten bedacht werden. Der Verein schlug daher eine Umstrukturierung der Arbeitsabläufe vor, die eine Neuaufteilung der Reinigungs-

36 Anon., The Refuse of the City, in: New York Times, 20.8.1874, S. 4.
37 Wallace, Greater Gotham, S. 673.
38 Hofstadter, Age of Reform, S. 181.
39 LHPA, Report, 1888, S. 10.
40 Ebd.

bezirke und die Einstellung von Bereichsaufsehern umfasste. In zwei Punkten sollte der neue Plan das Berliner Modell modifizieren. Erstens wollte die LHPA Straßenfeger und Müllmänner nicht pro Tag, sondern nach erbrachter Leistung bezahlen. Zweitens wollte der Verein nicht nur Männer, sondern auch Frauen zu Bezirksaufseherinnen ernennen: Ab acht Uhr morgens sollten intelligente, resolute Frauen die Straßen inspizieren und die Arbeit der Straßenfeger und Hausmeister kontrollieren.[41]

Die Inspektorinnen sollten Aufseherin und Erzieherin zugleich sein. Der von ihnen zu kontrollierende Grad der Sauberkeit bemaß sich wiederum an nahezu idealtypischen Vorstellungen einer abfallfreien, häuslichen Reinlichkeit, die sich auch in dem Lösungsansatz zur Entsorgungsfrage niederschlugen. Hier plädierte der Verein für den Bau von Müllverbrennungsanlagen, die er, nach englischem Vorbild, in den 1880er Jahren als einzige Option zur hygienischen und restlosen Vernichtung von Abfällen anpries, dabei allerdings Fragen des Geruchs, des Standorts oder der Rauchentwicklung ausklammerte.

II. »Naturgewachsen aus der Gewohnheit guten Haushaltens«: George E. Waring und die Rolle der bürgerlichen Frau

Auch wenn Stadtverwaltung und DSC den Vorschlag von Bezirksaufseherinnen nicht in die Tat umsetzten, konnte die Reformbewegung in New York Mitte der 1890er Jahre erste Erfolge erzielen. Als Teil einer Reformregierung unter der Führung von Bürgermeister William L. Strong wurde Colonel George E. Waring an die Spitze des DSC berufen.[42]

Der flamboyante Ingenieur, der sich gern mit seinem im US-amerikanischen Bürgerkrieg erworbenen Rang anreden ließ, verstand es, unter hohem finanziellem und personellem Aufwand die als uneffektiv geltende New Yorker Stadtreinigung einem radikalen Umbau zu unterziehen. Der gebürtige New Yorker war unter Frederick Law Olmsted an der Konstruktion des Central Parks beteiligt und daher auch mit der soziopolitischen Landschaft der Stadt vertraut.[43]

Waring bemühte sich, das negative Bild des »schäbigen« Müllmanns aufzubessern, auf das bereits die LHPA aufmerksam gemacht hatte. Zudem teilte er die Überzeugung vieler Reformerinnen, dass vorherrschende Geschlechterrollen Frauen besonders befähigten, zur urbanen Ordnung beizutragen. Diese Einstellung sicherte ihm die Rückendeckung des progressiven Bürgertums, insbesondere

---

41 Ebd., S. 17.
42 Zeitgleich wurde Theodore Roosevelt, der die Führungsposition beim DSC wegen ihrer geringeren Prestigeträchtigkeit ausgeschlagen hatte, Leiter der Polizeibehörde. Vgl. Miller, Fat of the Land, S. 69.
43 Vgl. Matthew Gandy, Concrete and Clay. Reworking Nature in New York City, Cambridge, MA 2002, S. 77–144.

der Frauenvereine.[44] Die Reinigung der Stadt benötige, so Waring, eine »systema-
tisierte Aufmerksamkeit für Details«, die sich für ihn »naturgewachsen aus der
Gewohnheit guten Haushaltens« ergebe.[45] Allerdings setzte ein gesellschaftliches
Engagement ein hohes Maß an verfügbarer freier Zeit voraus, was die Beteiligung
von Frauen aus Arbeiterfamilien erschwerte.[46]

Während seiner Amtszeit zwischen 1894 und 1896 führte Waring tiefgreifende
Reformen durch. Die Mitarbeiter des DSC befreiten vor allem in der Lower East
Side ganze Straßenzüge von teils kniehohem Abfall und Schmutz.[47] Waring ließ
die Straßenfeger von Hand arbeiten und verzichtete auf damals ineffektive Kehr-
maschinen. »It was Colonel Waring's broom that first let light into the slum. That
which had come to be considered an impossible task he did by the simple formula,
of ›putting a man instead of a voter behind every broom‹«, lobte sein Zeitgenosse,
der Journalist und Sozialreformer Jacob A. Riis.[48]

Riis spielte damit auf den weit verbreiteten Klientelismus an, den Waring innerhalb des DSC zeitweilig zurückdrängte. Die städtische Personalpolitik war
stark durch Patronageverhältnisse geprägt. Anstellungen bei der Stadtreinigung
und anderen städtischen Behörden winkten als Belohnungen für politische Ge-
fälligkeiten gegenüber der Tammany Hall, einer Seilschaft der lokalen Demo-
kraten, die als Synonym für Amtsmissbrauch, Korruption und die intransparente
Verwendung des städtischen Budgets stand.[49]

Beim Umbau des DSC verließ sich Waring nicht nur auf seine fachliche Expertise als Ingenieur, sondern auch auf seine militärische Vergangenheit und sein
Talent für Öffentlichkeitsarbeit. Nach Ende des Bürgerkrieges hatte er mehrere
Artikel in Fachjournalen und populären Magazinen publiziert und war somit
schon vor seiner Berufung in New York bekannt.[50] Vor dem Amtsantritt sicherte
er sich von Bürgermeister Strong alle Vollmachten, um seine Vision einer sauberen Stadt umzusetzen. Neben den unmittelbar sichtbaren Ergebnissen im Stadt-

---

44 William Gleason, »The Most Radical View of the Whole Subject«. George E. Waring Jr., Domestic Waste, and Women's Rights, in: Stephanie Foote u. Elizabeth Mazzolini (Hg.), Histories of the
   Dustheap. Waste, Material Cultures, Social Justice, Cambridge, MA 2012, S. 49–71, hier S. 66;
   Anon., Commend Waring's Work. Annual Meeting of the Ladies' Health Protective Association,
   in: New York Times, 2.12.1896, S. 9.
45 George E. Waring, Village Improvement Associations, in: Scribner's Monthly 14. 1877, S. 97–
   107, hier S. 98.
46 Ebd.
47 Der Journalist und Sozialreformer Jacob Riis dokumentierte die Zustände vor und nach Waring
   in seinen Fotografien. Vgl. Jacob A. Riis, The Battle with the Slum [1902], Montclair 1969,
   S. 272 f.
48 Ebd., S. 268 f.
49 Einen besonders schweren Fall in Bezug auf Stadtreinigung und Müllbeseitigung beschreibt
   Benjamin Miller. So waren an der privat gegründeten Müllverwertungsanstalt auf Barren Island
   mehrere Beamte als stille Teilhaber beteiligt und für die Vergabe des städtischen Entsorgungs-
   vertrages durch ihre Behörden direkt mitverantwortlich. Miller, Fat of the Land, S. 36–44 u.
   S. 73–90; Burnstein, Next to Godliness, S. 33.
50 Melosi, Garbage in the Cities, S. 42–65.

bild wertete Waring die »Truppen« der Stadtreinigung auf und baute sie nach militärischem Vorbild um. Dazu gehörte neben einer einheitlichen Schulung in Reinigungstechniken und der Disziplinierung der Mitarbeiter vor allem die Einführung einheitlicher, strahlendweißer Uniformen, die bis in die 1920er Jahre die Mitarbeiter von Straßenreinigung und Müllabfuhr kennzeichneten und ihnen die Spitznamen *White Wings, White Angels* oder gar *White Army* eintrugen.[51] Die neue Ausrüstung ließ das Department zu einem deutlich sichtbaren Teil des Stadtbildes werden, machte aber seine Mitarbeiter damit auch leichter kontrollierbar.[52] Diese negative Form der Disziplinierung glich Waring durch Selbstverwaltungsgremien aus, die bei Konflikten zwischen Mitarbeitern, Vorgesetzten und Administration regulierend eingriffen. Das sollte den Einfluss der Gewerkschaften innerhalb des DSC untergraben. Begleitet wurden diese Schritte von einer Nulltoleranzpolitik gegenüber streikendem Personal.[53]

Warings Popularität erklärte sich aus zwei Maßnahmen, die in bürgerlichen Kreisen der Stadt großen Anklang fanden. Erstens versuchte er in seinen »Truppen« ein moralisches Bewusstsein für zivilgesellschaftliche Verantwortung zu wecken. Dazu trug, neben den weißen Uniformen, die erstmalig 1896 abgehaltene Parade des DSC entlang der Fifth Avenue nebst anschließendem Festakt entscheidend bei. In seinem Grußwort appellierte Waring an den Berufsstolz der Mitarbeiter und führte ihnen vor Augen, wie viel Respekt und Anerkennung sie schon jetzt in der Bevölkerung genossen. Während vor seiner Amtszeit die Straßenreinigung lediglich als ein »Job« von »Männern am Besen« ausgeübt wurde, die kaum mehr als ein »schlechter Witz« waren, blickten Arbeiter und New Yorker mit Stolz auf die Männer in Weiß:

The Department of Street Cleaning is now a prime favorite with all the people. They care more about it than they do about any other department in the city, and they talk more about it. […] Now […] the expression 'White Wings' has passed as a common phrase and almost as a pet-name into the speech of the people of New York. No one has fault to find with the men, and everybody has something to say in their favor.[54]

Im Rahmen der Feierlichkeiten defilierten Straßenfeger, Müllkutscher und Kehrichtwagen durch Manhattan, außerdem wurden Mitarbeiter für besondere Verdienste öffentlich geehrt. Diese Tradition führte in späteren Jahren die WML fort. Zum Ausdruck ihrer anhaltenden Anerkennung hießen die Auszeichnungen Waring-Medaillen.

51 Zu Männlichkeitsidealen und der Militarisierung des DSC unter Waring vgl. Kevin P. Murphy, Political Manhood. Red Bloods, Mollycoddles, and the Politics of Progressive Era Reform, New York 2010, S. 71–73 u. S. 91–102.
52 Anon., Col. Waring on the Streets. He Tells How He Happened to Choose White for the Sweepers' Uniforms, in: New York Times, 20.2.1898, S. 16; Anon., Reform in Street Cleaning, in: New York Times, 11.10.1896, S. A1–2.
53 James B. Lane, Jacob A. Riis and the American City, Port Washington, NY 1974, S. 115 f.
54 Street Cleaning Department, Official Handbook of the Employees of the Department of Street Cleaning of the City of New York, New York 1897, S. 2.

Die zweite Maßnahme war das Bemühen um eine engere Kooperation zwischen Department und Bevölkerung. Da es sich bei Müll und Straßenschmutz um wiederkehrende Probleme handelte, war und ist die Stadtreinigung auf die Mitwirkung der Anwohnerschaft angewiesen. Sein besonderes Augenmerk richtete Waring in der Einwanderungsmetropole New York daher auf die Kinder. In Zusammenarbeit mit Wohltätigkeitsorganisationen rief er sogenannte Juvenile Citizens' Leagues ins Leben, in denen Kinder und Jugendliche zwischen neun und fünfzehn Jahren – insbesondere Jungen – als Aushilfsstraßenfeger in ihrer unmittelbaren Nachbarschaft nach dem Rechten sehen sollten. Vor allem aber erhoffte sich der Commissioner, dass besonders Kinder Werte von Ordnung und Sauberkeit in die eigenen Familien tragen und damit helfen würden, »ihre armen Eltern zu einer größeren Wertschätzung von Staatsbürgerlichkeit« zu erziehen.[55] Besonders »die ignorante, fremde, in den East Side Bezirken zusammengepferchte Bevölkerung« müsste erst zu »patriotischer« Ordnung erzogen werden, forderte ein DSC-Aufseher in einem von Waring herausgegebenen Band.[56] Warings eigene Haltung zu Migranten und ethnischen Minderheiten war ambivalent. Neben der verstärkten Einstellung afroamerikanischer Straßenfeger und Müllkutscher – auch um den Einfluss der Patronageverhältnisse Tammany Halls gegenüber italienischen Arbeitern zurückzudrängen – schätzte er die schwere und effiziente Arbeit, die italienische Migranten an den Sortierstellen und auf den Müllkähnen leisteten: »It does not make the slightest difference to me, whether a man is green, blue, black, or, white. [...] What I wish is good men, and that is all I care for.«[57]

Waring gelang es in seiner kurzen Amtszeit, ein positives Bild der Stadtreinigung zu kreieren. Ein Bewunderer erhob ihn gar zum »Apostel der Sauberkeit« und seine Amtsnachfolger mussten sich an seinen Verdiensten messen lassen.[58] 1901, drei Jahre nach Warings plötzlichem Tod, erinnerte Robert Underwood Johnson, Mitherausgeber des *Century Magazine*, wehmütig an dessen Leistungen:

II. He stormed the fetid street / Where Death with rapid feet / Strode fierce and glaring. / Shall we forget, alone, / When every grateful stone / Remembers Waring? // III. He, to your service true; / He. In his love of you / Himself not sparing; / Guardian of rich and poor; / Whom gold could not allure / Our Soldier, Waring! // [...] VI. Shall we be less than they / Who make the poor their prey, / No least one sparing? / They praise him, though they fill / Each tainted purse; they still / Remember Waring.[59]

55 Anon., Col. Waring in Brooklyn. Lectures on Disposal of Garbage and Municipal Cleaning, in: New York Times, 14.2.1896, S. 7.

56 David Willard, The Juvenile Street-Cleaning Leagues, in: George E. Waring (Hg.), Street-Cleaning and the Disposal of a City's Wastes. Methods and Results and the Effect upon Public Health, Public Morals, and Municipal Prosperity, New York 1898, S. 177–186, hier S. 177.

57 Anon., Has a Colored Foreman. Street Cleaning Department Employs Him on a Section, in: New York Times, 4.4.1895, S. 9. Vgl. auch George E. Waring, The Disposal of a City's Waste, in: The North American Review 161. 1895, S. 49–56.

58 Albert Shaw, Life of Col. Geo. E. Waring, Jr., the Greatest Apostle of Cleanliness, New York 1899.

59 Robert Underwood Johnson, Remember Waring!, in: New York Times, 23.10.1901, S. 8.

Der Text lässt sich zugleich als Appell zur Fortführung der stadtreformerischen
Tätigkeiten lesen.

III. Caroline Bartlett Crane, *municipal housekeeping* und die Antwort auf die soziale Frage

Mit der Umsetzung konkreter hygienischer Projekte und Praktiken kam das
Schlagwort vom *municipal housekeeping* in Gebrauch und Umlauf. Unter seinem
Banner nahmen die an der Wende zum 20. Jahrhundert in US-amerikanischen
Großstädten entstehenden Organisationen am reformorientierten Diskurs um
die Verbesserung und Gestaltung der städtischen Umwelt teil.[60]

Dabei machten sich deutliche Unterschiede zwischen den Geschlechtern be-
merkbar. Während männliche Reformer auf eine geschäfts- und kostenorientierte
Privatisierung der Stadtreinigung setzten, bevorzugten Frauenverbände eine Zentralisierung öffentlicher Dienstleistungen. Dabei griffen die hier engagierten
Frauen, deren aktiver Kern sich überwiegend aus der oberen Mittelschicht rekrutierte, immer wieder auf die Erfahrungen aus ihrer unmittelbaren Lebensumwelt – das private Heim – zurück.[61] Es war daher auch nicht verwunderlich,
dass die Probleme *für* und nicht *mit* den Arbeiterinnen und Arbeitern in den
Städten gelöst werden sollten.[62]

Darin lag allerdings ein Dilemma. Wirtschaftlich schwache Haushalte in New
Yorks *tenement*-Bezirken waren auf den sparsamen Umgang mit Ressourcen wie
Kleidung, Nahrung oder Haushaltsgegenständen angewiesen. Eigentlich eine Tu-
gend, gerieten Sparsamkeit und die damit einhergehenden Alltagstätigkeiten in
den beengten Wohnverhältnissen aus bürgerlicher Sicht zu unhygienischen und
somit gefährlichen Praktiken. Zwar begrüßten Sozialreformerinnen das Sam-
meln von Lumpen, die Wiederverwendung von Metallen oder die Nutzung von
Speiseresten, vertrauten darin aber nicht der sozialen Unterschicht.[63] Gegen eine
zentralisierte Sammlung und Verwertung von Abfällen nach industriellen Prin-
zipien unter der Kontrolle der Stadtverwaltung sprach aus ihrer Sicht hingegen
wenig.

---

60 Etwa zu den Beispielen Kalamazoo und Philadelphia vgl. Hoy, Municipal Housekeeping; Me-
    lanie S. Gustafson, »Good City Government is Good House-keeping«. Women and Municipal
    Reform, in: Pennsylvania Legacies 11. 2011, H. 2, S. 12–17.
61 Maureen A. Flanagan, Gender and Urban Political Reform. The City Club and the Woman's City
    Club of Chicago in the Progressive Era, in: American Historical Review 95. 1990, S. 1032–1050,
    hier S. 1046; Martin V. Melosi, The Sanitary City. Environmental Services in Urban Ame-
    rica from Colonial Times to the Present, Pittsburgh 2008, S. 118–120; Hoy, Municipal House-
    keeping, S. 173.
62 Burnstein, Next to Godliness, S. 9–11.
63 Carl A. Zimring, Dirty Work. How Hygiene and Xenophobia Marginalized the American Waste
    Trades, 1870–1930, in: Environmental History 9. 2004, S. 80–101.

Welche Praxis man positiv oder negativ bewertete, hing letztlich vom Klassenstandpunkt und den damit verbundenen materiellen Realitäten ab.[64] Diese aber waren, nach Überzeugung der Sozialreformer, nicht statisch, sondern dynamisch. Man konnte seinen sozialen Status durch eine Verbesserung der unmittelbaren Lebensumwelt – mehr Raum, mehr Licht, mehr Luft und vor allem mehr Sauberkeit – heben.[65] Die sozialen Unterschichten galt es zur Einhaltung bestimmte Standards zu erziehen; erst dann konnten sie als vollwertige Mitglieder der Gesellschaft angesehen werden.[66] Oder als Staatsbürger, denn viele der Immigranten waren mit den sich etablierenden Praktiken der Entsorgung nicht vertraut. Donna Gabaccia beschreibt in ihrer Studie zu sizilianischen Einwanderinnen und Einwanderern in der Elizabeth Street die divergierenden Ordnungsvorstellungen. Während italienische Hausfrauen die Wohnungen selbst penibel rein hielten, sah die Lage in den Fluren und Höfen anders aus: »[…] [W]omen took no responsibility for garbage, the ›mountains of uneaten food,‹ once it was swept or thrown outside the house itself: Tenement house inspectors complained unceasingly of garbage and junk in the rear yards, air shafts, cellars and spaces between the buildings.«[67]

Ein vergleichbarer erzieherischer Impetus bestimmte auch die ökonomische Ebene des Reformdiskurses, in deren Zentrum die Sorge um die Verschwendung öffentlicher Gelder stand. Besonders aktiv und sichtbar war dabei die Sozialreformerin Caroline Bartlett Crane. 1858 in Wisconsin geboren, arbeitete sie nach ihrem Studium am Carthage College als Lehrerin und Journalistin, bevor sie 1889 zur ersten unitarischen Pfarrerin in Kalamazoo, Michigan, ordiniert wurde. Ihr Interesse für die soziale Frage ließ Crane kurz nach der Jahrhundertwende zu einer führenden Expertin für öffentliches Gesundheitswesen und urbane Hygiene in den Vereinigten Staaten werden. Sie analysierte die Methoden und das System der New Yorker Stadtreinigung und überprüfte dessen Übertragbarkeit auf andere und kleinere Städte. Darüber hinaus verfasste sie eigene, sozialwissenschaftlich fundierte Studien zu den Hygienebedingungen in 62 Städten und 14 Bundesstaaten, publizierte und stellte ihre Erkenntnisse auf mehreren Kongressen zur Diskussion.[68]

---

64 Strasser, Waste and Want, S. 12–14.
65 Suellen Hoy, Chasing Dirt. The American Pursuit of Cleanliness, New York 1995, Kap. 3: »City Cleansing«, S. 59–86.
66 Burnstein, Next to Godliness, S. 5.
67 Donna R. Gabaccia, From Sicily to Elizabeth Street. Housing and Social Change among Italian Immigrants, 1880–1930, Albany 1984, S. 93. Vgl. auch Robert W. De Forest u. Lawrence Veiller (Hg.), The Tenement House Problem. Including the Report of the New York State Tenement House Commission of 1900, 2 Bde, New York 1903.
68 Linda Rynbrandt, Caroline Bartlett Crane and Municipalsanitation [sic]. Applied Sociology in the Progressive Era, in: Sociological Practice 6. 2004, S. 84–94, hier S. 85f.; dies., The »Ladies of the Club« and Caroline Bartlett Crane. Affiliation and Alienation in Progressive Social Reform, in: Gender and Society 11. 1997, S. 200–214, hier S. 200f. Suellen M. Hoy schreibt, dass sich Cranes Ursprungsinteresse aus einem selbst empfundenen Mangel an »hausfraulichen Qualitäten« ergab, in dessen Folge sie sich diese in Haushaltungskursen anzueignen suchte. Vgl. Hoy, Municipal Housekeeping, S. 181–188.

Der Schlüssel zu einer erfolgreichen Sozialreform war für die Aktivistin die richtige Verwendung öffentlicher Mittel. Auf einem nationalen Stadtplanungskongress in Baltimore äußerte Crane 1911 ihre Sorge:

It is certainly true that the present situation in most cities lends itself to partisan politics and to the exploitation of private interests, rather than to the work of justly governing the cities and promoting the welfare of the people. [...] The budget is of as much importance in public housekeeping as in private housekeeping. When you really know where and how the public money goes, you usually find that there is money to go wherever it is necessary that it should.[69]

Um die allgemeine Wohlfahrt zu verbessern und die hohen Mortalitätsraten zu senken, empfahl sie die Einführung und Beaufsichtigung hygienischer Mindeststandards:

Public housekeeping and public hygiene are in their essence one. The death rate in cities is lowered, [...] by clean streets and alleys and proper garbage disposal and pure water and the abatement of smoke, and the furnishing of pure milk and foods to the people. [...] Now, if there is any sense in trying to get people to come to us, to make a big city, there is certainly as much sense in keeping alive and efficient the people we have already got.[70]

Crane umriss in ihrem Plädoyer den gesamtgesellschaftlichen Nexus von Hygiene und (nationalen) wirtschaftlichen Kapazitäten. Luft-, Trinkwasser- und Lebensmittelqualität zu gewährleisten, hieß zugleich, die Verantwortung für die nachfolgende Generation ernst zu nehmen. Diese große Aufgabe übersetzte sich in zahllose kleine Alltagshandlungen:

These problems which affect such momentous interests are really such commonplace things. They resolve themselves into matters of civic housekeeping, and that resolves itself into matters of common cleanliness, which is certainly an uncommon achievement in American cities.

Den Konferenzteilnehmerinnen und -teilnehmern gab sie dementsprechend auf den Weg: »[H]elp make the laws and create the physical conditions and the moral atmosphere in which your children shall live.«[71] Der Aufruf Caroline Bartlett Cranes zum *municipal housekeeping* verband den moralischen Imperativ, für saubere Städte zu sorgen, mit der ökonomischen Prämisse der Wohlstandsmehrung. Cranes Konzept des »Wohlstands« ließ sich nicht beziffern, drückte sich aber in der Gesundheit und Leistungsfähigkeit der (arbeitenden) Bevölkerung aus, die in den Städten die ökonomischen Zentren belebten.

---

69 Caroline Bartlett Crane, Municipal Housekeeping. Reprinted from Proceedings of Baltimore City-Wide congress, March 8, 9, 10, 1911, [Baltimore] 1911, S. 209 f.
70 Dieses und das folgende Zitat, ebd., S. 209 f.
71 Ebd., S. 225.

IV. Zwischen Aufklärung und Kooperation:
Die Woman's Municipal League und das Department of Street Cleaning

Während Reformerinnen wie Caroline Bartlett Crane auf nationaler Ebene für das Ziel einer gesunden und sauberen Stadt warben, versuchten lokale Initiativen, wie die WML, konkrete Verbesserungen der Lebensumstände herbeizuführen. Dafür nutzten sie unterschiedliche Methoden, darunter vor allem die Vermittlung von Wissen und erzieherische Überwachung.

1897 von der Autorin und Sozialreformerin Josephine Shaw Lowell gegründet, sollte die Organisation als Informationsstelle für Frauen fungieren und deren Interesse für lokale Politik stärken. Bis zu 1.200 Mitglieder zählte die WML in New York, die mit Jahresbeiträgen zwischen 1 und 100 U. S.-Dollar die gesellschaftliche Arbeit des Vereins unterstützten.[72] Lowell war wie viele ihrer Zeitgenossinnen überzeugt, dass Frauen auch ohne Wahlrecht politisch und gesellschaftlich aktiv werden könnten und sollten.[73] Nominell offen für alle Bevölkerungsschichten, bildete die WML intern demokratische Strukturen aus und agierte nach außen hin über politische Gräben hinweg. Der Verein fuhr nur in wenigen Fällen einen konfrontativen oder offen parteilichen Kurs.[74]

Als Maßstab für eine gute Regierung und Verwaltung erachtete die WML den optischen und hygienischen Zustand der Stadt. Sie richtete ein Straßenkomitee ein, das sich eingehend mit der Arbeit des DSC, mit Techniken und Methoden der Stadtreinigung und mit der Information und Aufklärung der breiten Bevölkerung befasste. Dieses Komitee stand jahrelang unter der Leitung von Ida S. Cohen und lieferte beharrlich Verbesserungsvorschläge an das Department, wie etwa die nächtliche Abfuhr der Abfälle.[75] Auch wenn diese nur schleppend übernommen wurden, bemühte sich die WML um enge Beziehungen zu den städtischen Behörden und baute ein weitverzweigtes Netzwerk von Experten, Reformern und Lokalpolitikern auf.[76]

---

72 Woman's Municipal League of the City of New York, Year Book, New York 1911, S. 79–92.

73 Lloyd C. Taylor, Josephine Shaw Lowell and American Philanthropy, in: New York History 44. 1963, S. 336–364, hier S. 361. Zur Biografie und dem weiteren philanthropischen Engagement Lowells vgl. Joan Waugh, »Give This Man Work!« Josephine Shaw Lowell, the Charity Organization Society of the City of New York, and the Depression of 1893, in: Social Science History 25. 2001, S. 217–246; Marvin E. Gettleman, Charity and Social Classes in the United States, 1874–1900, I, in: American Journal of Economics and Sociology 22. 1963, S. 313–329. Vgl. auch Maureen A. Flanagan, America Reformed. Progressives and Progressivisms, 1890s–1920s, New York 2006; Ryan, Women in Public.

74 Mary Ringwood Hewitt, Annual Report of the President, in: WML, Year Book, S. 3–9, hier S. 3.

75 Cohen war zudem die Ehefrau des angesehenen Anwalts Julius Henry Cohen, der sich ebenfalls mit der Kontrolle des DSC befasste. 1906 war er Mitglied eines breit angelegten Untersuchungsausschusses, der die Geschäftspraktiken und Finanzen des DSC kritisch durchleuchtete. New-York Historical Society [im Folgenden N-YHS], F128 TD819.A25, Box 1, Special Comm. Of the Board of Aldermen, Report on the Administration of the DSC of the City of New York, 1906.

76 In ihrem Jahresbericht an den Vorstand berichtete Cohen über die lobenswerte Zusammenarbeit mit DSC-Commissioner Edwards sowie mit dem Stadtteilpräsidenten von Manhattan

Zu ihren Kernaufgaben zählte die WML die Erziehung von Kindern und Jugendlichen zu mündigen, stolzen und vor allem ordnungsliebenden Bürgerinnen und Bürgern. Gemäß zeitgenössischen pädagogischen Lehrsätzen galt es die moralische Charakterentwicklung von Jungen und Mädchen gegen schädliche Einflüsse der Großstadt zu wappnen. In den Augen vieler Sozialreformer prosperierten Alkoholkonsum, Glücksspiel und Prostitution dort, wo physische und soziale Umgebungen unstrukturiert und unkontrolliert blieben. Aus Sicht der WML galt dies besonders für migrantisch geprägte Bezirke. In einem Bericht über die Aktivitäten des DSC listete eine Aktivistin der WML »unclean nationalities« als eines der Haupthindernisse für die Arbeit des Departments in Greenwich Village.[77] Saubere Straßen und hygienische Praktiken stärkten hingegen die Selbstachtung und führten zu Wertschätzung des eigenen Haushalts, der städtischen Umwelt und des gesellschaftlichen Zusammenhalts.[78]

Um dieses Ziel zu erreichen, führte die Organisation die von George E. Waring gegründeten Juvenile Citizens' Leagues fort, die von seinen Amtsnachfolgern wenig beachtet wurden. Neben praktischen Anleitungen zur Reinhaltung der Stadt bemühte sich die WML darum, jungen Menschen den größeren Zusammenhang ihres Handelns anhand von Fakten darzulegen. Die Broschüre »What We Should All Know About Our Streets« klärte über den Müll in der Stadt, seine regelkonforme Entsorgung und die Arbeit der New Yorker Stadtreinigung auf.[79] Diese Form gesellschaftlicher Informationspolitik diente laut Cohen dazu, ein rücksichtsvolles Miteinander einzuüben und künftig zu praktizieren. Neben einer Geschichte des DSC enthielt der Band eine Liste der wichtigsten Verordnungen und einen Frage-Antwort-Teil, um die Entsorgung auf Haushaltebene leicht verständlich anzuleiten. Gleichzeitig warb Cohen um Respekt für die schwer arbeitenden Müllmänner, die tagtäglich auf ihren Touren Abfalltonnen von über 50 Kilogramm stemmen mussten.[80]

Obwohl sich der Band durch Faktenreichtum auszeichnete, war Cohen bewusst, dass blanke Zahlen allein bei ihren Leserinnen und Lesern nicht verfangen würden. Zur Verdeutlichung ihrer Botschaft verwendete die WML daher eine klare Bildsprache. Gleich am Anfang des Bandes führte Cohen die imposante Figur eines »modernen Straßenkolosses« ein: einen breitbeinigen, weiß gekleideten und behelmten, entschlossen blickenden Straßenfeger. Unter seinen Füßen verlief die Strecke von New York nach Kansas City. Diese Entfernung entsprach umgerechnet, so die Erläuterung in der oberen linken Bildecke, den von der New

---

und späteren Vorsitzenden des gesamtstädtischen Straßenausschusses, George McAneny. Ida S. Cohen, Annual Report of the Committee on Streets, in: WML, Year Book, S. 45–50, hier S. 45.

77 Eleanor M. Whaley, Report of Street Investigation for »Waring« Medals, in: Woman's Municipal League Bulletin 8/9. 1909, S. 5–7, hier S. 5.

78 Burnstein, Next to Godliness, S. 91–93.

79 Ida S. Cohen, What We Should All Know about Our Streets. Prepared for the Use of Our Young Citizens in the City Schools, New York 1916.

80 Ebd., S. 20 u. S. 24–26.

Yorker Stadtreinigung gesäuberten Flächen von über 23 Quadratkilometer.[81] Grafik, Statistiken und Vergleichswerte entlehnte Cohen dem aktuellen Bericht des DSC, das unter seinem neuen Commissioner, John T. Fetherston, die Kooperation mit zivilgesellschaftlichen Initiativen zu vertiefen suchte.[82] Gerade junge Leserinnen und Leser sollten sich von solchen anschaulichen Beispielen angesprochen fühlen und ein Interesse an städtischer Hygiene und Reinlichkeit entwickeln.

Immer wieder kam die Broschüre auf die Frage der Verwendung städtischer Mittel zurück. Das jährliche Budget der Stadtreinigung, das 1913 über 7,5 Millionen U.S.-Dollar betrug, könnte, so das Argument, verringert werden, wenn die New Yorker ihr alltägliches Wegwerfverhalten änderten. Um dies zu verdeutlichen, erklärte Cohen den Leserinnen und Lesern das damals gültige und hochtechnisierte Entsorgungsverfahren. Der in den Haushalten nach Asche, Abfall und Papier getrennte Müll wurde von den Pferdekarren des DSC an eine der 22 Sammeldeponien entlang der Wasserwege des Hudson und East River verbracht.[83] Dort angelangt, ließen Vertragsunternehmen die Müllladungen nach wiederverwertbaren Materialien durchsuchen: Zinndosen, Milchflaschen und Lumpen wurden eingesammelt und dem Produktionskreislauf wieder zugeführt.[84] Die Unternehmen bezahlten die Stadt für dieses Privileg. Die Weiterverarbeitung und Vermarktung der Hausabfälle auf Barren Island unternahm die privatwirtschaftliche New York Sanitary Utilization Company. Auch sie zahlte Konzessionen an die Stadt und trug somit zu den Einnahmen des DSC bei.

Diese idealisierende Darstellung des Reinigungs- und Entsorgungsprozesses verschwieg jedoch einige unbequeme Aspekte. Das Durchsuchen und Beladen der Müllkähne übernahmen überwiegend italienische Einwanderinnen und Einwanderer, die durch persönliche Netzwerke ins Land gelangt waren. Die hohen Einwanderungskosten mussten sie bei einem *padrone* begleichen. Der Journalist Jacob Riis hat die Lebensumstände von Einwandererfamilien fotografisch dokumentiert. Diejenigen, die im Müllgewerbe arbeiteten, lebten oftmals direkt an und unterhalb der wassernahen Müllkippen.[85]

Zudem verzichtete Cohen auf eine Beschreibung der Lebens- und Arbeitsverhältnisse auf Barren Island. Denn die aus dem Protorecycling gewonnenen Fette und Öle stammten nicht nur aus Küchenabfällen, sondern vor allem von

---

81 Ebd., S. 2.

82 John T. Fetherston, Annual Report of the Department of Street Cleaning, New York 1914, S. 6 f.

83 1900 zählte das DSC 1.068 Pferde und Müllkarren in seinen Diensten. Percy E. Nagle, Annual Report of the Department of Street Cleaning, New York 1900, S. 17. Die Motorisierung des Departments während der 1910er Jahre erfolgte schleppend. So weist der Jahresbericht von 1915 erstmals Traktoren und Lastwagen im Besitz des DSC aus. John T. Fetherston, Annual Report of the Department of Street Cleaning, New York 1915, S. 22.

84 Carl A. Zimring, Cash for Your Trash. Scrap Recycling in America, New Brunswick, NY 2005.

85 Jacob A. Riis, An Italian Home under a Dump, ca. 1890, Bildnegativ, Museum of the City of New York, http://collections.mcny.org/Collection/An%20Italian%20Home%20under%20a%20Dump.-2F3XC58WOU17.html.

in der Stadt verendeten Tieren, allen voran von Pferden und Hunden.[86] Die ge-
kochten und gefilterten Fette aus den Knochen der Kadaver wurden teilweise
nach Europa zur Parfumfabrikation verkauft und stellten ein lukratives Geschäft
sowohl für die Stadt als auch für die privaten Betreiber der Müllanlage dar. Allerdings konnte das kleine Eiland vor der Südostspitze Brooklyns die Abfallmenge
nicht allein verarbeiten. So wurde fast der gesamte Haushaltsmüll zwischen
1896 und 1917 in den städtischen Müllverbrennungsanlagen weitestgehend ver-
nichtet oder in den prototypischen Recyclinganlagen umgewandelt. Das Rest-
material wurde zu Klinkern verarbeitet und zum Bau oder zur Landauffüllung
verwendet.[87]

    DSC und WML waren sich darin einig, dass der Imperativ eines individuell
zurechenbaren Sauberkeitsverhaltens nicht nur moralisch grundiert war, sondern auch konkrete ökonomische Folgen zeitigte. Die WML stellte damit für
das DSC eine wichtige Verbündete dar. Anders als die LHPA forderte die WML
nicht nur Verbesserungen, sondern verstand sich als Förderin des Departments.
Angetrieben von der Überzeugung einer wechselseitigen Verantwortung, sah
sich die WML auch den Mitarbeitern der Stadtreinigung gegenüber moralisch
verpflichtet. Während diese tagtäglich gegen die Müll- und Schmutzmassen an-
kämpften, engagierte sich der Verein langfristig für eine faire Bezahlung der
DSC-Mitarbeiter, die Einrichtung einer entsprechenden sozialen Vorsorge, ad-
äquate Pensionsansprüche und eine Witwenrente.[88] Er verstand sich als ebenso
kooperatives wie korrigierendes Element innerhalb der weiteren städtischen Gemeinschaft. Die Maßnahmen der Fürsorge wurden durch Methoden der Überwachung und Disziplinierung ergänzt.

    In lokale Kapitel unterteilt, begann die Inspektion der städtischen Umwelt
für die Mitglieder der WML direkt vor der Haustür. Die aus Berlin stammende
Louise Morgenstern, langjährige Sekretärin von Ida S. Cohen, dokumentierte
über Jahre systematisch für das Straßenkomitee sämtliche Ärgernisse in der
Upper West Side.[89] Zusammen mit zehn weiteren Aktivistinnen ihrer Ortsgruppe
listete sie über 900 Beobachtungen auf: zugemüllte Baubrachen, nicht abgeholte
Aschetonnen bis hin zu verdrehten Straßenschildern. Morgenstern war auch verantwortlich für ein aufwändiges Informationsprogramm, das Ladenbesitzer und
Streifenpolizisten einbezog, um Anwohner der Riverside-Nachbarschaft über
korrekte Entsorgungsmethoden aufzuklären.[90] Ihre Tätigkeit wollte Morgenstern
eindeutig als Arbeit und wichtigen Beitrag für das Gemeinwohl verstanden wissen, wie sie in ihrem Abschlussbericht betonte:

---

86 Miller, Fat of the Land, S. 85.
87 Corey, King Garbage, S. 102 f.; Cohen, What We Should All Know, S. 8.
88 Ebd., S. 47; Katherine S. Day, Street Commission Endorses Pension Bill, in: Woman's Municipal
    League Bulletin 8/9. 1910, S. 8.
89 N-YHS, Woman's Municipal League records, 1909–1928, Ordner 2, Committee on Streets,
    Riverside Drive, 1910–1911.
90 Burnstein, Next to Godliness, S. 136 f.

The mere statement that all the thirteen avenues within the Branch were traversed four to six times while getting the data alone on street signs, mail boxes and house numbers, does not give any real idea of the true nature and extent of the work. The many hours devoted to careful watching and noting of defects, to the observation of street violations and in many instances to the sending of regular reports on these subjects, the number of these can never be estimated.[91]

Neben der Inspektion vor Ort beobachtete die WML auch die Arbeit des DSC. 1907 führte der Verein eine Postkarten-Kampagne durch, um die regelmäßige Säuberung der Straßen und die Abholung von Asche und Hausmüll zu kontrollieren. Anwohnerinnen der Upper West Side erhielten einen Fragebogen und waren angehalten, die Arbeit des DSC zu protokollieren. Die Ergebnisse dieser Mikrostudie teilte die WML dem einflussreichen City Club of New York und der New York Academy of Medicine mit; zwei bürgerliche Institutionen, die sich seit Jahrzehnten für Fortschritte in der Stadthygiene einsetzten.[92]

Diese Form der zivilen Kontrolle war sogar Commissioner Fetherston willkommen. Dieser versuchte zwischen 1914 und 1918 die Leistungen des DSC, besonders aber dessen Außenwirkung zu verbessern. Um die Gunst der WML und anderer Aktivistinnen bemüht, folgte er regelmäßig Vortragseinladungen, um über aktuelle Entwicklungen im Bereich der Stadthygiene zu berichten.[93] Umgekehrt lud Fetherston führende Vereinsmitglieder wie Ida S. Cohen und die unabhängige Aktivistin Flora Spiegelberg zu einer Ausstellung über die Arbeit des DSC ein. Die sechstägige Veranstaltung im November 1914 lockte über 27.000 Besucherinnen und Besucher an und präsentierte neben Fachvorträgen auch eine Ausstellung technischer Neuerungen. Cohen und Spiegelberg referierten am dritten Tag – in einer eigens eingerichteten »Frauen-Sektion«. In seinen einleitenden Worten würdigte Fetherson die WML und hob deren Engagement wie auch ihre konstruktive Kritik hervor:

There is an association of women in this city which has always given the Department of Street Cleaning the fullest co-operation—the Woman's Municipal League. [...] The street cleaner likes to be encouraged. He likes to have people tell him he has done his work well. He likes to have them recognize that fact. He gets enough criticism—there is no difficulty about that—but the helping hand is the thing that counts. Destructive criticism does not amount to anything. The way to work improvement is by constructive criticism, by helpfulness, not fault finding.[94]

91 Ida S. Cohen, Annual Report of the Riverside Branch, in: WML, Year Book, S. 74–78, hier S. 78.
92 New York Public Library Archives and Manuscripts, [im Folgenden NYPL], City Club of New York Records, General Correspondence Box 1, Ordner 1.3.
93 N-YHS, F128 JS1221.W66 C65 1908, John T. Fetherston, Municipal Cleaning, at Home and Abroad, Vortrag im Hauptquartier der Woman's Municipal League, 19.2.1914, in: A Collection of Printed Material Pertaining to the Woman's Municipal League of New York City (1908–1927).
94 Department of Street-Cleaning, Clean Streets through Education and Cooperation. Report of Exhibition and Tests of Street-Cleaning Appliances, New York 1914, S. 25.

Fetherston erkannte in den Frauen wichtige Verbündete im Ringen um die *hearts and minds* von New Yorks Bevölkerung, ohne deren Mitwirkung die Stadt nicht sauber zu halten war. Dabei betonte er, dass sich das Selbstverständnis des DSC ändern müsste, wofür er gezielt den Begriff *municipal housekeeping* verwendete. Fetherston griff dabei die Parallele zwischen häuslicher und öffentlicher Ordnung gezielt auf:

Now, viewing each of the 2,724 regular street sweepers ('White Wings') as a servant of the 'Municipal Housekeeper,' or as one of the City's housekeepers, charged with keeping clean a defined area, how do his duties compare with the cleaning responsibilities of the mistress of the average domicile? Taking as a basis the figures in our table of physical statistics a simple calculation in short division gives us the answer. The 'White Wing' on the average must clean up after 1,805 persons, 37 horses and 23 automobiles, not once a week, nor once a day, but many times each day on the route for which he is responsible.[95]

Auch wenn Fetherston letztlich die Leistungen seiner Straßenreiniger gegen die der Haushälterinnen aufrechnete, stellte er klar, dass das DSC im Dienste der Stadtbewohner stand. Eine derartige Wertschätzung trug zum kooperativen Verhältnis zwischen WML und Stadtreinigung bei. Das Straßenkomitee verfasste unter der Leitung Ida S. Cohens einen Handzettel, den der Verein aus eigenen Mitteln drucken und verteilen ließ. Darauf appellierte die WML an die Stadtbewohner, dass die Verantwortung für ein saubereres New York nicht allein beim DSC, sondern bei ihnen selbst lag:

STOP throwing papers on the streets. / STOP throwing papers in the cars. / STOP spitting on the walks, in the cars, or on stations, stairs and platforms. / This is YOUR CITY. / Why not make it clean? / Don't blame the Department of Street Cleaning. / It is doing its duty. / Do you do yours?[96]

Die Reinhaltung des öffentlichen Raums geriet zu einem moralischen Imperativ, der eng an die bürgerliche Pflicht geknüpft war und vorschrieb, etwaige Missstände nicht in erster Linie dem Department anzulasten.

Allerdings sah sich das DSC weiterhin öffentlicher Kritik ausgesetzt. Besonders die unter Fetherston gestiegenen Ausgaben schürten Zweifel, ob sich die Lage bessern würde. Daher warb Fetherston zwischen 1914 und 1918 auch außerhalb wohlwollender Kreise intensiv um Interesse an der Arbeit des DSC und stellte es, gemäß dem Vorbild Warings, als eine für die Stadt essenzielle Dienstleistung dar. Hierfür erhoffte sich Fetherston wenn nicht göttlichen, so doch kirchlichen Beistand, als er im Vorfeld einer zweiten DSC-Ausstellung ein Rundschreiben an New Yorks christliche Gemeinden versandte und darin bat, das Thema »Sauber-

---

95 Fetherston, Annual Report, 1915, S. 17.
96 N-YHS, F128 JS1221.W66 C65 1908, Woman's Municipal League, A Cleaner City, New York 1914, in: A Collection of Printed Material Pertaining to the Woman's Municipal League of New York City (1908–1927), Großschreibung im Original.

keit« in die Sonntagspredigt aufzunehmen. Priester James Curry von der katholischen St. James Kirche an der Lower East Side belehrte den Commissioner in einem offenen Brief in der *New York Times*, dass dieser sich besser auf sein Kerngeschäft konzentriere: »[...][L]et me suggest that instead of the proposed exhibition and parade you clean our city streets – the uncleanest of any streets that I have ever seen either here or in Europe, notwithstanding the handsome yearly appropriation of nearly $8.000,000.«[97]

Fetherstons Sendungsbewusstsein drückte sich auch in den Jahresberichten der Stadtreinigung aus. Während die Berichte unter seinem Vorgänger, William H. Edwards, nüchtern und knapp ausfielen, lieferten die Reporte unter Fetherston tiefere Einblicke in die Aufgaben des Departments und die alltägliche Arbeit seiner Mitarbeiter. Von Fotografien, Statistiken und Infografiken untermauert, kontextualisierte er die kolossale Aufgabe, vor der das Department stand. Für Fetherston gestaltete sich das Sauberhalten der Stadt als »physikalisches Problem«, das sich in Größe, Bevölkerungszahl und -dichte sowie der vielseitigen sozialen und nationalen Herkunft der Bewohner ausdrückte. Die Vielsprachigkeit New Yorks erschwerte zudem die öffentlichkeitswirksame Aufklärung über Vorschriften und Pflichten: nach dem US-Zensus von 1910 sprachen 23 Prozent (rund 345.000 Personen) der eingewanderten Bevölkerung kein Englisch.[98] Vor dem Hintergrund dieser strukturellen Herausforderungen versuchte Fetherston die explodierenden Ausgaben des Departments zu rechtfertigen. Während die Kosten für das DSC zwischen 1910 und 1913 von 9,36 auf 7,61 Millionen Dollar gesunken waren, stiegen die verwendeten Mittel im ersten Jahr unter Fetherston auf über 10,1 Millionen Dollar an.[99]

V. Konstruktive Kritik: Flora Spiegelberg und das Versprechen technologischer Zentralisierung

Die Sorgen um die sinnvolle Verwendung von Steuergeldern seitens des Departments trieben auch Flora Spiegelberg in ihrem Bestreben nach städtischer Sauberkeit an. Die Tochter deutsch-jüdischer Einwanderer zählte über zwanzig Jahre zu den prominentesten Vertreterinnen der Reformbewegung. Spiegelberg

---

97 Anon., Father Curry Says Streets Are Dirty, in: New York Times, 27.9.1915, S. 18.
98 Fetherston, Annual Report, 1914, S. 9. Dabei bemühte sich die Verwaltung schon früh, der Vielsprachigkeit der Stadt Rechnung zu tragen. Auf Englisch, Deutsch, Italienisch und Hebräisch klärte der Stadtrat bereits 1902 mit einem Handzettel über die hygienischen Verordnungen und die damit verbundenen Pflichten der Bevölkerung auf. Vgl. N-YHS, SY1902, no. 26, Department of Street Cleaning, »Householders, Tenants and Others are Warned that the Following Ordinance of the Board of Aldermen and Requirement of the Sanitary Code of the Board of Health Will Be Strictly Enforced ...«, 1902.
99 Fetherston, Annual Report, 1914, S. 20. Den dramatischen Anstieg schrieb er jedoch den Mehrausgaben für Schneebeseitigung zu.

unterstützte die Forderungen nach *municipal housekeeping* und analysierte das Reinigungssystem New Yorks systematisch. Ihr Einsatz für eine Umstrukturierung von Sammlung und Entsorgung, eine in Zonen arrangierte Verteilung städtischer Verbrennungsanlagen sowie die Verbesserung des Staubschutzes bei Müllwagen und Abfalltonnen trug ihr dabei den wenig schmeichelhaften Spitznamen »Old Garbage Woman of New York« ein.[100]

Von derlei Anfeindungen unbeeindruckt rief sie Frauen im ganzen Land auf, ihrem Beispiel zu folgen:

The city clean – sanitary, dustless, odorless, and flyless – that should be the slogan of every woman in this broad land. […] [L]et it be our part to make sure that the waste of daily living in every city, large or small, be disposed of according to the best scientific methods, so that it will not be a menace to the public health, and let it become a source of revenue instead of a loss that burdens the citizens with higher taxes. The present insanitary methods of collecting and disposing of garbage, street sweepings, ashes, and waste in nearly all American cities cause the illness and death, directly or indirectly, of thousands of men, women, and children and the loss of millions of dollars of the people's money. It is, therefore, the duty of the women of these cities to investigate the conditions which now exist and the better methods which are possible and, then to agitate the matter until public opinion will compel municipalities to adopt an economic and sanitary system. This is essentially work for women, a new field of labor, especially for those who have studied the better methods that obtain in Europe, particularly in Germany, where the principles of honesty, efficiency and economy are factors of the utmost importance in municipal housekeeping.[101]

Für Spiegelberg ging die Frage städtischer Sauberkeit weit über reine Ästhetik hinaus. *Municipal housekeeping* sah sie geprägt von der Chance auf politische Partizipation für und berufliche Betätigung von Frauen, der Gestaltung der städtischen Umwelt, die maßvolle Verwendung von Steuergeldern und letztlich die Kontrolle und Verbesserung von Reinigungspraktiken. Diese Zusammenhänge lassen sich als moralische Ökonomie verstehen, die neben maximalen Gewinnen und/oder Ersparnissen die gesellschaftliche Verantwortung wirtschaftlichen und planerischen Handelns in den Mittelpunkt stellt.

Wie viele ihrer Zeitgenossinnen leitete Spiegelberg ihre zahlreichen Vorschläge von der Praxis in europäischen und insbesondere deutschen Städten ab. Konkret schlug sie, wie schon die LHPA in den 1880er Jahren, die Unterteilung New Yorks in autonome Reinigungsbezirke nach dem Beispiel Berlins vor. Dabei ging es Spiegelberg weniger um die soziale Kontrolle von Straßenfegern, sondern mehr darum, erhöhte Transport- und Personalkosten an die städtische Peripherie zu vermeiden. Anders als Ida S. Cohen und die Leitung des DSC sprach

100 Sheri Goldstein Gleicher, Flora Spiegelberg. Grand Lady of the Southwest Frontier, in: Southwest Jewish History 1. 1992, http://swja.arizona.edu/content/flora-spiegelberg-grand-lady-southwest-frontier; vgl. auch Corey, King Garbage, S. 132 ff.
101 Flora N. Spiegelberg, The City Clean Should Be the Slogan of Women, in: New York Times, 8.12.1912, S. SM16.

sich Spiegelberg dabei für eine gemischte Sammlung der Abfälle und gegen eine Trennung nach Asche, Küchenabfällen und sonstigen Materialien aus, da sich so üble Gerüche und Brutstätten von Fliegen vermeiden ließen.[102] Mit Unterstützung Thomas Edisons drehte Spiegelberg 1914 einen Film, der durch seine »realitätsnahen«, »ekelerregenden« und »grafischen« Bilder die Krankheitsgefahr von Maden und Fliegen belegen und die gemischte Müllsammlung bewerben sollte.[103]

Trotz seiner potenziellen Gesundheitsgefährdung verstand Spiegelberg Müll als Ressource, die dem Stoff- und Produktionskreislauf wieder zugeführt werden musste.[104] Gesammelte Abfälle sollten hierfür in Bezirksstationen zentral nach verwertbaren und nicht verwertbaren Materialien getrennt werden. Für das Jahr 1913 schätzte Spiegelberg beispielsweise, dass New Yorks Müll zwischen zehn und fünfzehn Prozent nicht verfeuerter Kohle beinhaltete. Diese sollte zusammen mit den nicht nutzbaren Restmaterialien verbrannt und als Energiequelle zur Stromerzeugung für die Sortieranstalten und die umliegenden Gebäude verwendet werden. Selbst verbleibende Schlacke, so Spiegelberg, könnte als Beimischung in Zement als Baumaterial eine Verwendung finden. Spiegelberg war von den ungenutzten finanziellen Vorteilen für die Stadt überzeugt. Bis zu acht Millionen Dollar ließen sich ihren Berechnungen nach insgesamt jährlich einsparen, was rund achtzig Prozent des Budgets des DSC entsprach.[105]

Eine Umsetzung von Spiegelbergs Plan, Müllverbrennungsanlagen nicht nur in jedem der *five boroughs*, sondern in jedem Reinigungsbezirk zu errichten, hätte zwar die Anlagen nachhaltig operieren lassen und die Dienste des DSC durchaus sinnvoll gebündelt. Doch auch wenn die Konstruktion der Anlagen auf dem Papier geordnet und logisch wirkte, vollzogen sich konkrete Bauvorhaben in der Realität nur mühselig und oft gegen den Widerstand der Anwohnerschaft. Die Pläne der Stadtverwaltung, eine entsprechende Anlage in der südlichen Bronx zu errichten, erregten lebhafte und durch alle Bevölkerungsschichten reichende Proteste, die zu einer Flut von Petitionen und Briefen an das Büro des Bürgermeisters führte. Das grundlegende Argument war hierbei, dass Rauch und Gestank der Verbrennungsanlagen zu einer Abwertung von Immobilien und Grund-

102 NYPL, 3-VDK+, Flora N. Spiegelberg, A Dustless and Sanitary Collection of Ashes and Garbage, Vortrag vor der Woman's Health Protective Association, New York Academy of Medicine, 2.1.1912, in: Flora Spiegelberg, Garbage Collection and Disposal, New York City 1912–1930.

103 Department of Street-Cleaning, Clean Streets through Education and Cooperation, S. 23. Zum Einsatz von Filmen zu Erziehungs- und Bildungszwecken sowie zu deren emotionalen Effekten vgl. Anja Laukötter, How Films Entered the Classroom. The Sciences and the Emotional Education of Youth through Health Education Films in the United States and Germany, 1910–30, in: Osiris 31. 2016, S. 181–200.

104 Heike Weber, Den Stoffkreislauf am Laufen halten. Restearbeit und Resteökonomien des 20. Jahrhunderts, in: Kijan Espahangizi u. Barbara Orland (Hg.), Stoffe in Bewegung. Beiträge zu einer Wissensgeschichte der materiellen Welt, Zürich 2014, S. 145–171.

105 Anon., $8,000,000 Saving in City Incenerator. Mrs. Spiegelberg Advocates a Municipal Plant for Ash and Garbage Disposal, in: New York Times, 13.2.1914, S. 2.

besitz führten.[106] Derart massive Mobilisierungen lokalen Widerstands stellten auch eine Schwierigkeit für die Umsetzung von Spiegelbergs weitreichenden Zentralisierungsvorschlägen dar. Folglich passte sie ihre Entwürfe stetig an und versuchte Einwände gegen die Anlagen durch eine zumindest ästhetisch ansprechende Architektur abzumildern.[107]

Besorgt um die betriebliche Wirtschaftlichkeit des DSC monierte Spiegelberg, dass die Durchführung des gesamten Stadtreinigungsprozesses – einschließlich Müllabholung und Transport, über Zwischenlagerung und Sortierung bis hin zur endgültigen Entsorgung – nicht aus einer Hand erfolgte. Trotz der Bündelung von Straßenreinigung und Müllabfuhr durch das DSC vergab die Stadtverwaltung weiterhin Verträge an Subunternehmer, um etwa den Müll nach verwertbaren Materialien zu durchsuchen, auf Schiffe zu laden und vor der Küste im Meer versenken zu lassen. Diese Vertragspraxis ging noch auf die Amtszeit von George E. Waring zurück. Auch die Entsorgung der städtischen Abwässer fiel nicht in den Aufgabenbereich des DSC. Außerdem wurde – und wird bis heute – die Abholung und Entsorgung gewerblicher Abfälle ausschließlich durch private Unternehmen übernommen. Spiegelberg kritisierte, dass die Stadtverwaltung Entsorgungsunternehmen somit bezuschusste, während Reingewinne für recycelte Materialien nicht sämtlich in den städtischen Haushalt einflossen und wie im Fall der Entsorgungsanstalt auf Barren Island lediglich Konzessionen gezahlt wurden.[108]

Spiegelbergs Vorschläge wurden nur teilweise übernommen.[109] Drei Hindernisse standen ihren Strukturreformen im Weg. Erstens pflegte das DSC seit 1881 das (wachsende) Stadtgebiet in unterschiedliche Abschnitte zu unterteilen. Dabei war aber die Straßenreinigung und nicht, wie von Spiegelberg gefordert, die Müllabfuhr das ordnende Prinzip. Zweitens widersprachen die Pläne den wirtschaftlichen Eigeninteressen privater Entsorgungsunternehmen, die den Status quo über Kontakte zur städtischen Politik und Verwaltung erhalten wollten. Drittens bedeutete Spiegelbergs Forderung nach einer trennungslosen Sammlung und Abfuhr des Hausmülls eine 180-Grad-Wende gegenüber der seit den 1890er Jahren erprobten Praxis.[110]

106 New York Municipal Archives, Office of the Mayor, Low, Seth, Departmental Correspondence, Bronx Garbage Incinerator-Protests against 144th St. & Whitlock Ave, Box 1, Folder 2 1903.

107 Das Engagement und die Kreativität Spiegelbergs fanden über die Grenzen New Yorks und der USA hinaus Anerkennung. So wurden ihre Pläne etwa in der deutschen Fachpublikation *Die Städtereinigung* wohlwollend besprochen: »Frau Spiegelberg ist bekanntlich seit Jahren die Vorkämpferin eines gesunden, staubfreien Systems zur Beseitigung und Verwertung des Haus- und Strassenkehrichts in Amerika, speziell in ihrer Vaterstadt New York.« Städtehygiene in Amerika, in: Die Städtereinigung 8. 1916, S. 26 f., hier S. 26.

108 Corey, King Garbage, S. 101 f.

109 Die Entsorgung von festen und flüssigen Abfällen wurde erst mit der Umstrukturierung und Umbenennung des DSC in das Department of Sanitation zusammengefasst. Ebd., S. 117 f.

110 Ebd., S. 131 f.

Besonders dieser letzte Punkt trennte Flora Spiegelberg von anderen zeitgenössischen Initiativen. Die vereinten Bestrebungen des Departments, der New
York Academy of Medicine und der WML, die Bewohnerinnen und Bewohner
zu hilfreichen Elementen bei der Müllentsorgung zu erziehen, mussten stetig
wiederholt und jeder neuen Generation von Stadtbewohnerinnen und Stadtbewohnern beigebracht werden. Auch wenn die Wirtschaftlichkeit häuslicher
Abfalltrennung in Zweifel gezogen werden konnte, sprach für das Beibehalten
des Trennverfahrens die Stärkung eines zivilgesellschaftlichen Verantwortungs-
bewusstseins, das sich in der Sorge um Ordnung und Sauberkeit der eigenen,
unmittelbaren, städtischen Umwelt ausdrückte.

VI. Frauenvereine und die Politik der Sauberkeit

Den Entstehungsprozess von New Yorks modernem Müllentsorgungsregime
im Allgemeinen und *municipal housekeeping* im Speziellen als moralische Ökonomien zu erfassen, eröffnet die Perspektive auf die Verbindung von moralischen,
wirtschaftlichen und politischen Argumentationsmustern innerhalb der Debatte
um die idealtypische Stadt der Moderne. Damit verknüpfte konkrete Praktiken
des politischen Aktivismus verdeutlichen die Ausweitung des gesellschaftlichen
Aktionsrahmens vorrangig bürgerlicher Frauen sowie deren Einfluss auf die Veränderung wirtschaftlicher, sozialer und politischer Strukturen an der Wende vom
19. zum 20. Jahrhundert. Die dabei angewandten, moralisch fundierten Argu-
mente der Aktivistinnen waren Teil einer kalkulierten politischen Strategie. Erstens richtete sich diese sowohl auf die Öffentlichkeit als auch auf ausgewählte
städtische Institutionen und Entscheidungsträger. Zweitens bedienten sich die
Aktivistinnen eines rationalistischen Diskurses, der auf die technologiebasierte
Lösung des Müllproblems setzte. Zwischen 1880 und 1917 durchliefen ihre politischen Methoden einen Wandel von einer kommentierenden hin zu einer kon-
frontativeren Ausrichtung, ohne den Rahmen eines fürsorglichen Maternalismus
ganz zu verlassen.[111]
    Basierend auf geschlechterspezifisch konnotierten Vorstellungen von städti-
scher Schönheit gestalteten Vorreiterorganisationen, wie die LHPA, ihren sozialpolitischen Aktivismus als an die Verwaltung adressierte Beschwerde über un-
hygienische Zustände. Die Aktivistinnen betonten ihre alltagsgebundene Expertise,
eigneten sich zeitgenössisches Expertenwissen an und legitimierten ihr Handeln
über wissenschaftliche Kooperationen. Durch dieses Vorgehen strebte der Verein die Ausweitung häuslicher Ordnungsmodelle auf den Stadtraum an. Dieses
argumentative Vorgehen diente dem Sichtbarmachen der geleisteten Hausarbeit,
ohne dabei direkt die Trennung zwischen privater und öffentlicher Sphäre zu
hinterfragen.

111 Vgl. Koven u. Michel, Womanly Duties.

Die geschlechterspezifische Auffassung des Haushaltsbegriffs betraf für die Reformerinnen sowohl die hygienische als auch die ökonomische Ebene. Die sparsame und zielgerichtete Verwendung städtischer Finanzmittel stand im Mittelpunkt der zu Beginn des 20. Jahrhunderts deutlich vertretenen Forderungen einer als *municipal housekeeping* beschriebenen Reformpolitik. Der verantwortliche und effektive Umgang mit öffentlichen Geldern avancierte zu einer moralischen Prämisse für gutes Regieren. *Municipal-housekeeping*-Befürworterinnen wie Caroline Bartlett Crane unterstützten eine präsente und gestaltende Rolle der Frauen in diesen lokalpolitischen Angelegenheiten. Das Selbstvertrauen zur Beteiligung schöpften sie aus einer autodidaktischen Aneignung wissenschaftlicher und technischer Prozesse.

Die Anerkennung weiblicher Fähigkeiten von offizieller Seite, wie durch George E. Waring Jr. und John T. Fetherston, unterstützte diese Position. Warings radikale und öffentlichkeitswirksame Reform des DSC richtete sich gegen eine korrupte Klientelpolitik der Tammany Hall und setzte zudem auf die partizipative Mobilisierung der Stadtbewohnerinnen und Stadtbewohner. Nach Waring stand die Erziehung der Bevölkerung, insbesondere der Jugend, im Vordergrund der Bemühungen eine saubere Stadt zu gewährleisten, was nur unter Einbezug bürgerlicher Frauen gelingen konnte.

Diese kooperative Haltung spiegelte sich in den Aktionen der WML wider. Durch gezielte Information der breiten Bevölkerung und Anleitungen zum hygienischen und somit moralisch-verantwortlichen Verhalten trug der Verein zur Internalisierung bürgerlicher Ordnungsmuster bei.[112] Zu dieser Form von Gouvernementalität gehörte auch eine doppelte Überwachung von Sauberkeitsstandards. Zum einen kontrollierte die WML die Einhaltung vorgeschriebener Entsorgungspraktiken in lokalen Nachbarschaften, worin der klassenbezogene Führungsanspruch bürgerlicher Frauen im Bereich der Hygiene widerspiegelte. Zum anderen überwachte der Verein auch die Arbeit der Stadtreinigung. Dabei warben seine Vertreterinnen zugleich für eine Anerkennung und Verbesserung der Arbeitsbedingungen innerhalb des DSC und machten die WML zu einer wichtigen Verbündeten für die Administration.

Dass eine solche Kooperation durchaus kritisch und bisweilen konfrontativ verlaufen konnte, zeigt das Beispiel Flora Spiegelbergs. Nahezu desinteressiert an ästhetischen Aspekten verstand sie – ähnlich wie Bartlett Crane – *municipal housekeeping* als ideales Betätigungsfeld für Frauen. Spiegelberg überprüfte die Organisation der Arbeitsabläufe und forderte eine stärkere Zentralisierung von Entsorgungspraktiken, um die Wirtschaftlichkeit des DSC zu gewährleisten. Frauen, so Spiegelberg, waren zur Kontrolle und Gewährleistung einer sauberen Stadt verpflichtet und konnten hierin ein eigenes Arbeits- und Berufsfeld finden.

---

112 Hier weist das Konzept der moralischen Ökonomie eine Anschlussfähigkeit zu Michel Foucaults Überlegungen zur Gouvernementalität auf. Vgl. Michel Foucault, Geschichte der Gouvernementalität I: Sicherheit, Territorium, Bevölkerung. Vorlesungen am Collège de France 1977/1978, Frankfurt 2006, S. 18 f.

Die Untersuchung des sozialpolitischen Engagements der Frauenverbände und Reformerinnen verdeutlicht, dass die Entstehung moderner Müllentsorgungs-regime nicht an eine vertikale Durchsetzung von Ordnungssystemen gekoppelt, sondern auf verschiedenen Ebenen an die Beteiligung und den Austausch mit der Bevölkerung gebunden war.[113] In der Zusammenschau moralischer Setzungen, politischer Strategien, wirtschaftlicher Prognosen, sozialer Praktiken und wissen-schaftlich-technischer Modelle gaben die Aktivistinnen entscheidende Impulse für New Yorks beschwerliche Entwicklung zur modernen Metropole.

113 David Huyssen, Progressive Inequality. Rich and Poor in New York, 1890–1920, Cambridge, MA 2014.

Thomas Rohringer

Arbeitsfreude und Selbstvertrauen

Die moralische Ökonomie der Re-Integration Kriegsbeschädigter in Cisleithanien (1914–1918)

Abstract: This article argues that the social re-integration of disabled veterans can be analyzed as a "moral economy" distinct from the conflicts associated with programs for disabled veterans' welfare during the interwar years. Firstly, it examines how economic, sociological, and moral discourses became intertwined in defining disabled veterans as a social "problem" in 1914/15. Secondly, it analyzes the (often contradictory) conceptions of work used to rationalize and moralize the re-integration measures. Finally, it highlights how the confrontation between medical and vocational experts on the one hand and disabled veterans on the other shaped the role of work in re-integration efforts, demonstrating that this tension gave rise to concerns about disabled veterans' joy in their work and their self-confidence.

Am 27. Juli 1914 gab Kaiser Franz Joseph I. der Bevölkerung der Habsburgermonarchie mit der in elf Sprachen veröffentlichten Proklamation »An meine Völker« die Kriegserklärung an Serbien bekannt. Bereits wenige Monate später hatten sich die Hoffnungen auf einen kurzen und aufgrund des technischen Fortschritts »humaneren« Krieg zerschlagen. Überkommene militärische Vorgehensweisen versagten angesichts neuer Taktiken und Waffensysteme, die österreichisch-ungarische Armee hatte Ende Dezember 1914 bereits mehr als eine Million Tote, Verwundete und Kriegsverletzte zu beklagen.[1] Hinter der Front rückten Flüchtlinge aus Galizien und verletzte und erkrankte Soldaten die körperlichen und sozialen Folgen des Krieges in das Blickfeld der Öffentlichkeit.[2]

---

1 Holger H. Herwig, The First World War. Germany and Austria-Hungary 1914–1918, London 2014, S. 7–43; Manfried Rauchensteiner, Der Erste Weltkrieg und das Ende der Habsburgermonarchie 1914–1918, Wien 2013, S. 163–225; Helmut Kuzmics u. Sabine A. Haring, Emotion, Habitus und Erster Weltkrieg. Soziologische Studien zum militärischen Untergang der Habsburger Monarchie, Göttingen 2013, S. 224–228; die Zahlen sind entnommen aus Edmund Glaise-Horstenau (Hg.), Österreich-Ungarns letzter Krieg 1914–1918, Bd. 4: Das Kriegsjahr 1916, Beilage 4, Wien 1933; zu den Hoffnungen auf einen »humaneren« Krieg siehe John M. Kinder, Paying with Their Bodies. American War and the Problem of the Disabled Veteran, Chicago 2015, S. 34–45.

2 David Rechter, Galicia in Vienna. Jewish Refugees in the First World War, in: Austrian History Yearbook 28. 1997, S. 113–130; Alfred Pfoser u. Andreas Weigl (Hg.), Im Epizentrum des Zusammenbruchs. Wien im Ersten Weltkrieg, Wien 2013.

Wollte die Monarchie nicht ihre Legitimität einbüßen, musste sie diese Herausforderungen bewältigen. Dass Soldaten, die der Krieg in ihrer Gesundheit geschädigt hatte, nicht in der Armenfürsorge versorgt werden sollten, war jedoch
keineswegs selbstverständlich. Nach dem 1914 gültigen Militärversorgungsgesetz
existierten für Kriegsinvalide nur zwei grundlegende Formen staatlicher Versorgung: die nach militärischem Rang gestaffelte Invalidenpension oder die Unter-
bringung in einem Militärinvalidenhaus.[3] Wie zeitgenössische Politiker und
Wissenschaftler verletzte und erkrankte Soldaten als gesellschaftliches »Problem«
definierten, das durch Re-Integration gelöst werden konnte, und welche Maßnahmen sie setzten, um dieses Ziel zu erreichen, konstituierte eine spezifische
moralische Ökonomie. In ihr war der wirtschaftliche Nutzen für die Gemeinschaft eng verflochten mit individueller Erwerbsfähigkeit, charakterlicher Erziehung und gesellschaftlicher Anerkennung.

Der Schwerpunkt der Forschung zu den staatlichen Fürsorgemaßnahmen für
verletzte und erkrankte Soldaten lag bisher vornehmlich auf Großbritannien,
Frankreich, Deutschland und den USA.[4] Demgegenüber erhielt die Habsburgermonarchie erst in den letzten Jahren verstärkt wissenschaftliche Aufmerksamkeit.
Die Kriegszeit wurde hier jedoch vor allem auf die Genese der republikanischen
Sozialpolitik nach 1918 und ihrer zentralen Konflikte um die Rentengesetzgebung
hin befragt.[5] Dadurch geriet aus dem Blick, dass während des Krieges die Wiederherstellung der Erwerbsfähigkeit der verletzten und erkrankten Soldaten und
ihre moralisch-charakterliche Erziehung einander wechselseitig beeinflussten,

---

3 Laurence Cole, Military Culture and Popular Patriotism in Late Imperial Austria, Oxford 2014,
   S. 121–126.
4 Antoine Prost, Les anciens combattants et la société française 1914–1939, Paris 1977; Robert
   Weldon Whalen, Bitter Wounds. German Victims of the Great War 1914–1939, Ithaka 1984;
   Michael Geyer, Ein Vorbote des Wohlfahrtsstaates. Die Kriegsopferversorgung in Frankreich,
   Deutschland und Großbritannien nach dem Ersten Weltkrieg, in: GG 9. 1983, S. 230–277; Sa-
   bine Kienitz, Beschädigte Helden. Kriegsinvalidität und Körperbilder 1914–1923, Paderborn
   2008; Jessica Meyer, Men of War. Masculinity and the First World War in Britain, Basingstoke
   2009; Jay Winter u. Antoine Prost, René Cassin and Human Rights. From the Great War to the
   Universal Declaration of Human Rights, Cambridge 2013; Kinder, Paying with Their Bodies;
   Joanna Bourke, Dismembering the Male. Men's Bodies, Britain and the Great War, Chicago 1996;
   Maren Möhring, Kriegsversehrte Körper. Zur Bedeutung der Sichtbarkeit von Behinderung,
   in: Anne Waldschmidt u. Werner Schneider (Hg.), Disability Studies, Kultursoziologie und
   Soziologie der Behinderung. Erkundungen in einem neuen Forschungsfeld, Bielefeld 2007,
   S. 175–197; Julie Anderson, War, Disability and Rehabilitation in Britain. »Soul of a nation«,
   Manchester 2011; Heather R. Perry, Recycling the Disabled. Army, Medicine, and Modernity in
   WWI Germany, Manchester 2014.
5 Natali Stegmann, Kriegsdeutungen – Staatsgründungen – Sozialpolitik. Der Helden- und Opfer-
   diskurs in der Tschechoslowakei 1918–1948, München 2010; Marek Růžička, Péče o válečné in-
   validy v Československu v letech 1918–1938, Diss. Univerzita Karlova Praha 2011; Ke-chin Hsia,
   War, Welfare and Social Citizenship. The Politics of War Victim Welfare in Austria, 1914–1925,
   Diss. University of Chicago 2013; Verena Pawlowsky u. Harald Wendelin, Die Wunden des
   Staates. Kriegsopfer und Sozialstaat in Österreich 1914–1938, Wien 2015.

was konstitutiv für diese moralische Ökonomie der Re-Integration war.[6] Zuletzt arbeitete Karin Harrasser den Zusammenhang zwischen Prothetik und Prozessen der Subjektivierung heraus und lieferte damit wichtige Ansatzpunkte dafür, die Re-Integrationsmaßnahmen als moralische Ökonomie zu erfassen.[7]

Die wissenschaftliche Definition der Kriegsbeschädigten als »Problem«, das durch Re-Integrationsmaßnahmen gelöst werden konnte, knüpfte an ein umfassenderes Verständnis von Ökonomie und an verschiedene Felder sozialer Fürsorge an, wie im ersten Abschnitt dieses Beitrags erläutert wird.[8] Die Konflikthaftigkeit des Arbeitsbegriffes der Re-Integrationsmaßnahmen bildet den Gegenstand des zweiten Abschnitts. Zwischen Beamten, medizinischen und beruflichen Fachleuten musste einerseits ein Konsens über die Art der Erwerbstätigkeit, die Kriegsbeschädigte ausüben sollten, gefunden werden. Andererseits trafen die Vorstellungen von Experten und »kriegsbeschädigten« Soldaten über die »richtige« Form von Arbeit aufeinander. Diese Auseinandersetzungen führten zu einer entscheidenden Verschiebung. Bezweckte man mit den Re-Integrationsmaßnahmen zunächst, einem befürchteten moralischen Verfall der Soldaten vorzubeugen, richteten Mediziner und Gewerbefachleute infolge dieser Konflikte ihre Aufmerksamkeit auf die Selbsteinschätzung Kriegsbeschädigter als arbeitsunfähig. Der vierte Abschnitt analysiert, wie Mediziner in Reaktion darauf therapeutische Praktiken entwickelten, in denen Arbeitstätigkeit positive Emotionen hervorrufen sollte, um so die Wiederherstellung körperlicher Arbeitsfähigkeit mit charakterlich-moralischer Erziehung zu verbinden.

I. Re-Integration »als volkswirtschaftliches Problem«

»[D]er Arme weinte und sagte, dann bin ich ja nachher ein Krüppel, er möchte doch lieber sterben, als ein Krüppel sein […].«[9] Mit diesen Worten, so berichtete die böhmische Lokalzeitung *Teplitz-Schönauer Anzeiger*, soll ein verletzter Soldat aus der Stadt Teplitz-Schönau/Teplice-Šanov eine Amputation seines Fußes abgelehnt haben. Die ersten Zeitungsartikel, die im Herbst 1914 begannen, über Kriegsverletzte zu berichten, sprachen nicht von Re-Integration oder Wiederherstellung der Erwerbsfähigkeit kriegsverletzter Soldaten. Stattdessen glorifi-

---

6 Für Großbritannien siehe Jeffrey S. Reznick, Work-Therapy and the Disabled British Soldier in Great Britain in the First World War. The Case of Shepherd's Bush Military Hospital, London, in: David A. Gerber (Hg.), Disabled Veterans in History, Ann Arbor 2012[2], S. 185–228; die charakterliche Erziehung beleuchten kurz Pawlowsky u. Wendelin, Wunden, S. 139–146.
7 Karin Harrasser, Prothesen. Figuren einer lädierten Moderne, Berlin 2016.
8 Siehe zur Verflechtung von wissenschaftlicher Wissensproduktion und ihrem soziokulturellen Umfeld Steven Shapin, A Social History of Truth. Civility and Science in Seventeenth-Century England, Chicago 1994.
9 Anon., Ein Teplitzer im serbischen Spital verstorben, in: Teplitz-Schönauer Anzeiger, 21.10.1914, S. 4f., hier S. 4.

zierten diese Artikel die erlittenen Verletzungen oder lieferten Erzählungen von Hilflosigkeit und Abhängigkeit von privater Wohltätigkeit.[10] Zeitgenössische Akteure mussten die Auffassung, dass verletzte und erkrankte Soldaten nicht Aufgabe der Armenfürsorge oder privater Wohltätigkeit waren, sondern wieder erwerbsfähig gemacht werden sollten, erst durchsetzen.

Als Karl Stürgkh, Ministerpräsident Cisleithaniens, im Dezember 1914 Innenminister Karl Heinold von Udyński mit der Organisation einer umfassenden staatlichen Fürsorgeaktion für verletzte und erkrankte Soldaten beauftragte, war ein solcher Paradigmenwechsel bereits in vollem Gang. In den Ministerien Cisleithaniens beobachtete man die Maßnahmen im Deutschen Kaiserreich, öffentlichkeitswirksam hielt der Mediziner Anton Bum in Wien Vorträge über die Therapierbarkeit von Kriegsverletzungen und der ungarische Sozialwissenschaftler Emerich/Imre Ferenczi definierte es »als volkswirtschaftliches Problem«, Kriegsbeschädigte erneut erwerbsfähig zu machen.[11] Stürgkh selbst sprach in seinem Schreiben an den Innenminister nicht nur von einer Verpflichtung der Monarchie gegenüber ihren Soldaten, sondern auch vom Interesse des Staates daran, sie wieder in die Gesellschaft zu integrieren. Für den Ministerpräsidenten war es mit einer »modernen Staatsauffassung« unvereinbar, in ihrer Gesundheit geschädigte Soldaten und Angehörige Gefallener der Armenfürsorge zu überlassen.[12] Das Militärversorgungsgesetz von 1875 musste, so Stürgkh, den Anforderungen eines »Volksheeres« angepasst werden, indem der Anspruch auf Invalidenpension nach deutschem Vorbild statt auf Dienstrang und Dienstzeit auf einer Schädigung der Erwerbsfähigkeit im Beruf gründete.[13] Aber diese Ausweitung finanzieller Versorgung reichte in Stürgkhs Augen nicht aus, die umfassendere Aufgabe der Fürsorge für verletzte und erkrankte Soldaten liege in der medizinischen Rehabilitation, beruflichen Ausbildung und Arbeitsvermittlung.[14]

---

10 Siehe beispielhaft: Max Schächter, Amputationen an Verwundeten, in: Pester Lloyd, 22.10.1914, S. 2; Anon., Wunden, die heilig sind, in: Neues Wiener Journal, 26.10.1914, S. 3.

11 Zu Deutschland jüngst Perry, Recycling the Disabled; zu Bums Vorträgen Anon., Kriegsinvalide und die Verhütung der Krüppelhaftigkeit, in: Reichspost, 27.11.1914, S. 11; Anon., Die Verhütung der Krüppelhaftigkeit bei den Kriegsinvaliden, in: Arbeiterzeitung, 26.11.1914, S. 6; Emerich Ferenczi, Die Zukunft der Kriegsverletzten als volkswirtschaftliches Problem, in: Pester Lloyd, 8.12.1914, S. 12.

12 Österreichisches Staatsarchiv [im Folgenden ÖStA], Allgemeines Verwaltungsarchiv [im Folgenden AVA], Ministerium des Inneren [im Folgenden MdI], Präsidium [im Folgenden Praes.], 19, Kt. 1862, 19093/1914, Bekämpfung der Kriegsschäden für die Angehörigen der Wehrmacht und ihre Familien, Militärversorgungsgesetze und Anregung einer präventiven Hilfsaktion, Stürgkh an den Minister für Landesverteidigung, S. 1–4, Zitat Stürgkh S. 3.

13 ÖStA, AVA, MdI Praes., 19, Kt. 1862, 19093/1914, Bekämpfung der Kriegsschäden für die Angehörigen der Wehrmacht und ihre Familien, Militärversorgungsgesetze und Anregung einer präventiven Hilfsaktion, S. 1–8, hier S. 1 (Zitat Stürgkh). Zum Militärversorgungsgesetz und dessen Reform Pawlowsky u. Wendelin, Wunden, S. 52–71; Hsia, War, S. 23–45.

14 ÖStA, AVA, MdI, Praes., 19, Kt. 1862, 19093/1914, Bekämpfung der Kriegsschäden für die Angehörigen der Wehrmacht und ihre Familien, Militärversorgungsgesetze und Anregung einer präventiven Hilfsaktion, S. 1–8, hier S. 1.

Verletzte und erkrankte Soldaten führten der Bevölkerung die Schrecken des Krieges vor Augen. Eine erfolgreiche staatliche Fürsorge war daher für Stürgkh und Heinold notwendig, um das Ansehen der Monarchie in der Bevölkerung zu wahren.

Stürgkh machte den Innenminister in seinem Schreiben auf den Artikel des ungarischen Sozialwissenschaftlers Emerich/Imre Ferenczi im *Pester Lloyd* vom 8. Dezember 1914 aufmerksam.[15] Ferenczi fungierte als sozialpolitischer Referent der Stadt Budapest und war vor dem Krieg eine zentrale Figur der städtischen Sozialreform gewesen.[16] In dem Artikel, der mit »Die Zukunft der Kriegsverletzten als volkswirtschaftliches Problem« überschrieben war, empfahl er die betroffenen Soldaten durch berufliche Ausbildung und Arbeitsvermittlung wieder erwerbsfähig zu machen. Es galt, der Monarchie »die möglich größte Summe an Arbeitskraft [zu] erhalten«.[17] Die männliche Bevölkerung im erwerbsfähigen Alter zwischen dem 15. und dem 60. Lebensjahr wurde zeitgenössisch als der bestimmende Faktor für die »Produktionsfähigkeit eines Volkes« betrachtet, trotz der hohen Erwerbstätigkeit von Frauen in der Habsburgermonarchie.[18] Die schweren Verluste der ersten Kriegsmonate schienen die wirtschaftliche Leistungsfähigkeit der Monarchie ernsthaft zu bedrohen. Zahlreiche Zeitgenossen teilten diese Sorge und befürworteten Maßnahmen zur Re-Integration Kriegsbeschädigter als Teil einer »Ökonomie mit dem menschlichen Staatsgut«.[19] In diesem Sinne war die Bevölkerung selbst Gegenstand ökonomischer Überlegungen und die »volkswirtschaftliche« Aufgabe erkannten zeitgenössische Autoren eben nicht nur darin, der Monarchie die männliche Bevölkerung als Produktionsfaktor zu erhalten. Es ging ihnen gleichermaßen darum, wie es Ferenczi ausdrückte, »drohende soziale Gefahren«[20] abzuwenden, die von einem wirtschaftlichen und gesellschaftlichen Abstieg der betroffenen Soldaten und ihrer Familien ausgehen würden.

Ein solches Verständnis von Ökonomie, in der wirtschaftliche und moralische Faktoren zusammenwirkten, lehrten deutsch-, tschechisch- und ungarischsprachige Wissenschaftler, wie Eugen Philippovich (1858–1917), Albín Bráf (1851–1912) oder Julius/Gyula Kautz (1829–1909), an den rechts- und staatswissenschaft-

---

15 Ebd., S. 4.
16 Susan Zimmermann, Divide, Provide, and Rule. An Integrative History of Poverty Policy, Social Policy, and Social Reform in Hungary under the Habsburg Monarchy, Budapest 2011, S. 47.
17 Ferenczi, Zukunft, S. 12.
18 Zitat entnommen aus Eugen Philippovich, Grundriß der politischen Ökonomie, Bd. 1: Allgemeine Volkswirtschaftslehre, Wien 1904⁵, S. 53; zur weiblichen Erwerbstätigkeit Josef Ehmer, »Innen macht alles die Frau, draußen die grobe Arbeit macht der Mann«. Frauenerwerbsarbeit in der industriellen Gesellschaft, in: Birgit Bolognese-Leuchtenmüller u. Michael Mitterauer (Hg.), Frauen-Arbeitswelten. Zur historischen Genese gegenwärtiger Probleme, S. 81–103; Susan Zimmermann, Frauenarbeit, soziale Politiken und die Umgestaltung von Geschlechterverhältnissen im Wien der Habsburgermonarchie, in: Lisa Fischer u. Emil Brix (Hg.), Die Frauen der Wiener Moderne, Wien 1997, S. 34–52.
19 Rudolf Peerz, Unsere Sorge um die Kriegsinvaliden. Eine sozialpolitische Studie, Wien 1915, S. 9.
20 Ferenczi, Zukunft, S. 12.

lichen Fakultäten der Habsburgermonarchie. Philippovich, Bráf und Kautz unterrichteten aber nicht nur zukünftige Beamte, sie waren auch selbst als Politiker aktiv und in sozialreformerischen Kreisen bestens vernetzt. Sie vertraten eine empirisch und historisch fundierte Wirtschaftswissenschaft, wie sie als Historische Politische Ökonomie auch an deutschen, französischen und italienischen Universitäten einflussreich war. Sie untersuchten ökonomische Entwicklungen im Zusammenhang mit ihren historischen Bedingungen, wollten deren ethische, psychologische und soziale Implikationen erforschen und staatliche Sozialreformen informieren.[21] Im zeitgenössischen Konzept von Volkswirtschaft war es daher »sinnvoll«, die Re-Integration verletzter und erkrankter Soldaten als Schnittpunkt sozialer, ökonomischer und moralischer Aspekte zu begreifen.[22]

In seiner Argumentation, Kriegsverletzte »als volkswirtschaftliches Problem« zu begreifen, stützte sich Ferenczi auf seine eigenen Forschungen zu Arbeitslosen und besonders auf eine Studie, die Siegfried Kraus am Frankfurter Institut für Gemeinwohl zum »Berufsschicksal Unfallverletzter« durchgeführt hatte.[23] Die Ergebnisse seiner Untersuchung popularisierte Kraus selbst seit Oktober 1914 in Zeitungsartikeln und Vorträgen, verknüpfte sie explizit mit der Re-Integration verletzter und erkrankter Soldaten und brachte sich in die Diskussion um die Ausgestaltung von Fürsorgemaßnahmen im Deutschen Kaiserreich ein.[24] Kraus warnte davor, die Rehabilitation Unfallverletzter und Kriegsinvalider weiterhin nur als medizinische Aufgabe zu betrachten, und forderte, die medizinische Therapie um berufliche Ausbildung und Arbeitsvermittlung zu erweitern, da sich die bisherige Fürsorge für Unfallverletzte in seiner Studie als unzureichend erwiesen habe.

Um die Jahrhundertwende hatten Unfallversicherungsanstalten gemeinsam mit Medizinern begonnen, Anstalten einzurichten, an denen Chirurgen oder Orthopäden Unfallverletzte rehabilitativen Therapien unterzogen, etwa Übungen an sogenannten mediko-mechanischen Apparaten.[25] Ein großer Teil der von Kraus

---

21 Erik Grimmer-Solem u. Roberto Romani, In Search of Full Empirical Reality. Historical Political Economy, 1870–1900, in: European Journal of the History of Economic Thought 6. 1999, S. 333–364; Balázs Trencsényi u. a., A History of Modern Political Thought in East Central Europe, Bd. 1: Negotiating Modernity in the »Long Nineteenth Century«, Oxford 2016, S. 353–355; Antonie Doležalová, Welfare State or Social Reconciliation? The Social Question from the Perspective of an Economist (Albín Bráf), in: Zlatica Zudová-Lešková u. a., Theory and Practice of the Welfare State in Europe in 20th Century, Prag 2014, S. 177–198; Josef Weidenholzer, Der sorgende Staat. Zur Entwicklung der Sozialpolitik von Joseph II. bis Ferdinand Hanusch, Wien 1985.

22 Für diese Perspektive auf moralische Ökonomien siehe Didier Fassin, Das Leben. Eine kritische Gebrauchsanweisung, Berlin 2017, S. 19.

23 Die Studie erschien erst 1915 als Buch: Siegfried Kraus, Über das Berufsschicksal Unfallverletzter. Mit einem Zusatz über die Lage der Kriegsinvaliden, Stuttgart 1915.

24 Anon., Fürsorge für die Kriegsinvaliden, in: Soziale Praxis und Archiv für Volkswohlfahrt 24. 1914/15, H. 13, S. 301–303; Siegfried Kraus, Unfallverletzte und Kriegsverletzte, in: Frankfurter Zeitung und Handelsblatt, 31.10.1914, Zweites Morgenblatt, S. 3–4.

25 Greg Eghigian, Making Security Social. Disability, Insurance, and the Birth of the Social Entitlement State in Germany, Ann Arbor 2000, S. 117–157.

untersuchten Arbeiter habe jedoch auch nach der medizinischen Behandlung Schwierigkeiten, wieder Arbeit zu finden, und habe schließlich nur weniger angesehene und geringer qualifizierte Anstellungsverhältnisse erreicht, die ihrer Arbeitsfähigkeit nicht entsprächen. Dies bezeichnete Kraus als »wirtschaftlich-sozialen Verfall« bzw. als »Deklassierung«, die er nicht am Sinken des Einkommens festmachte, sondern am »soziale[n] Ansehen bzw. de[m] wirtschaftliche[n] Wert« der Arbeitstätigkeiten, die sie nach ihrem Unfall ausübten.[26] Kraus nutzte damit einen Begriff von »sozialer Deklassierung«, der gesellschaftliche Anerkennung und ökonomische Produktivität verband.

Kraus forderte nicht Arbeitsbeschaffung in Form simpler Tätigkeiten, wie es in der Armenfürsorge üblich war, sondern Beschäftigungsverhältnisse, die den Qualifikationen der Arbeiter entsprachen und ihnen gesellschaftliche Anerkennung verschafften.[27] Er knüpfte an zeitgenössische sozialfürsorgerische, sozialwissenschaftliche und kriminologische Debatten über Arbeitssuchende an, in denen hinterfragt wurde, dass moralische Defizite Arbeitslosigkeit verursachten.[28] Allerdings stellte Kraus einen anderen Konnex zwischen Arbeitslosigkeit und moralischem Charakter her. Mit sozialer Deklassierung gehe eine »moralische Deklassierung« einher, worunter er Verbitterung über die Verletzung und die Schwierigkeiten der Arbeitssuche, »seelische Entkräftung« und die Gewöhnung an den Erhalt einer Rente verstand.[29] Arbeitslosigkeit selbst führe also zur Ausbildung schlechter Angewohnheiten und langfristig zu deren Verfestigung in negativen Charaktereigenschaften, weshalb Kraus der sozialen Vernachlässigung der Kriegsbeschädigten bereits in einem kurzen Artikel aus dem Oktober 1914 »schwere seelisch-sittliche Gefahren« zuschrieb.[30] Daran knüpfte Ferenczi mit seinem Begriff der »sozialen Gefahren« an und hielt fest, dass selbst eine Invalidenpension, welche die Lebenskosten decken würde, »kein Glück«[31] für die Kriegsbeschädigten wäre. »Die größte Wohltat für sie und die Nation wird es sein, ihnen, beziehungsweise auch ihren Familien geeignete Erwerbsarbeit zu bieten.«[32] Somit war eine Verbindung zwischen ökonomischem Nutzen für den Staat, individueller Erwerbsfähigkeit, gesellschaftlicher Anerkennung und individueller Moralität hergestellt.

---

26 Kraus, Berufsschicksal, S. 12 f.
27 Zu den zeitgenössischen Debatten über Arbeitsbeschaffung innerhalb der Armenfürsorge in Berlin siehe Bettina Hitzer, Arbeiter- und Frauenkolonien für die Reichshauptstadt Berlin? Protestantische Obdachlosenfürsorge im Kontext urbaner Sozialpolitik um 1900, in: Beate Althammer (Hg.), Bettler in der europäischen Stadt der Moderne. Zwischen Barmherzigkeit, Repression und Sozialreform, Frankfurt 2007, S. 193–225.
28 Sigrid Wadauer, Establishing Distinctions. Unemployment Versus Vagrancy in Austria from the Late Nineteenth Century to 1938, in: International Review of Social History 56. 2011, S. 31–70.
29 Kraus, Berufsschicksal, S. 29, S. 33, S. 94 u. 101.
30 Kraus, Unfallverletzte, S. 4.
31 Ferenczi, Zukunft, S. 12.
32 Ebd.

Mediziner waren durch Vereinigungen und Publikationen ebenfalls eng mit Politischen Ökonomen und Gesellschaftswissenschaftlern vernetzt und hatten am selben biopolitischen Diskurs teil.[33] Als einer von vielen Medizinern ordnete Adolf Deutsch die Re-Integrationsmaßnahmen für Kriegsbeschädigte in dieses Projekt ein. Vor dem Krieg hatte er als Krankenkassenarzt gearbeitet, jenem neuen Betätigungsfeld, das entscheidend zur Entstehung einer sozialmedizinischen Disziplin in Wien beigetragen hatte.[34] Während des Krieges war Deutsch am Wiener Reservespital Nr. 11, der führenden Einrichtung der Kriegsbeschädigtenfürsorge in Cisleithanien, und als ärztlicher Berufsberater an der Wiener Amtsstelle für Arbeitsvermittlung an Kriegsbeschädigte tätig.[35] Bereits 1915 publizierte er einen kurzen Aufsatz zur »Psychologie der Invalidenfürsorge«, in dem er ausführte:

Es ist eine soziologische Tatsache, daß das ethische Niveau solcher Menschen im Laufe der Jahre unaufhaltsam sinkt, deren Existenzmöglichkeit von privaten und staatlichen Unterstützungen allein abhängt. Die Kinder solcher Almosenempfänger [...] wachsen dann selten zu arbeitsfähigen, arbeitswilligen und vollwertigen Menschen heran.[36]

Kriegsbeschädigten nicht irgendeine Arbeitstätigkeit, sondern eine Anstellung zu vermitteln, die ihren Qualifikationen entsprach, hatte in dieser Perspektive eine individuelle und kollektive, eine ökonomische und moralische Dimension. Die moralische Ökonomie der Re-Integration verletzter und erkrankter Soldaten erwuchs daher aus einem spezifischen wissenschaftlichen Blick auf Wirtschaft, Gesellschaft und Individuum.

II. Herausforderungen der Praxis

Innenminister Heinold machte in seinem Antwortschreiben an Ministerpräsident Stürgkh im Januar 1915 unmissverständlich klar, dass die Monarchie nicht über ausreichende institutionelle und personelle Kapazitäten verfügte, um die notwendigen Einrichtungen für Therapie, Ausbildung und Arbeitsvermittlung neu aufzubauen. Der Innenminister erklärte die Re-Integrationsmaßnahmen daher zu einer gesamtgesellschaftlichen Aufgabe; die Zivilgesellschaft sollte der Monarchie

33 Michael Hubenstorf, Die Genese der Sozialen Medizin als universitäres Lehrfach in Österreich bis 1914. Ein Beitrag zum Problem der Disziplinbildung und wissenschaftlichen Innovation, Diss. FU Berlin 1992, S. 157–194; Gerhard Baader, Eugenische Programme in der sozialistischen Parteienlandschaft in Deutschland und Österreich im Vergleich, in: ders. u. a. (Hg.), Eugenik in Österreich. Biopolitische Strukturen 1900–1945, Wien 2007, S. 66–139, hier S. 70–76.

34 Hubenstorf, Genese, S. 230–262.

35 Zur Geschichte des Reservespitals Nr. 11 siehe Pawlowsky u. Wendelin, Wunden, S. 117–123.

36 Adolf Deutsch, Die Psychologie der Invalidenfürsorge, in: Hans Spitzy (Hg.), Unsere Kriegsinvaliden. Einrichtungen zur Heilung und Fürsorge. Bilder aus dem k.u.k. Reservespital XI, Wien, Wien 1915, S. 97–104, hier S. 102–103.

jene personellen, institutionellen und finanziellen Handlungsmöglichkeiten verschaffen, die sie alleine nicht aufbringen konnte.[37] Am 16. Februar 1915 ordnete er die Einrichtung von »Landeskommissionen zur Fürsorge für heimkehrende Krieger« in den Kronländern der cisleithanischen Reichshälfte an.[38] Diese Kommissionen stellten den institutionellen Rahmen für die Kooperation von Militär- und zivilstaatlicher Verwaltung mit der Zivilgesellschaft dar.[39] Zusammen mit diesem Erlass wurde auch eine zentralstaatliche Vereinbarung zwischen den Ministerien verlautbart, nach der dem Militär die Verantwortung für medizinische Behandlung, Therapie und Ausstattung mit Prothesen zukam, während die Arbeitsvermittlung Aufgabe der Zivilstaatsverwaltung war, und die berufliche Ausbildung gemeinsam organisiert wurde.[40] Da der Staat den Landeskommissionen kein festes Budget zur Verfügung stellte, waren sie auf ehrenamtliche Tätigkeiten und Spenden angewiesen.[41] In jenen Kronländern, wo die staatliche Unfallversicherung Zentralen hatte, übernahm deren administratives Personal auch die Verwaltungsaufgaben der Landeskommissionen. Für die beruflichen Ausbildungslehrgänge für verletzte und erkrankte Soldaten kooperierten die Ministerien, die für landwirtschaftliche, kaufmännische und gewerblich-industrielle Ausbildung zuständig waren, und die ihnen unterstellten staatlichen Fachschulen mit Landeskulturräten, Gewerbeförderungsinstituten, Handelskammern und privaten Betrieben.[42] Diese Faktoren machten die Landeskommissionen zu wichtigen Foren des Austausches zwischen staatlicher Verwaltung und Zivilgesellschaft in einer Zeit, in der andere Räume, wie Parlament und Landtage, verschlossen waren.[43]

37 ÖStA, AVA, MdI Praes., 19, Kt. 1862, 19093/1914, Bekämpfung der Kriegsschäden für die Angehörigen der Wehrmacht und ihre Familien, Militärversorgungsgesetze und Anregung einer präventiven Hilfsaktion, S. 1–8, hier S. 1 f. u. S. 5; ebd., Antwort an den Ministerpräsidenten, 2.–6. Bogen; ÖStA, AVA, MdI Allg., Abt. 19, Kt. 2030, 5388/1917, Gewerblicher Invalidenunterricht, interministerielle Besprechung vom 4.12.1916, über prinzipielle Fragen, Protokoll aufgenommen über die am 4.12.1916 im Sitzungssaale des Ministeriums für öffentliche Arbeiten abgehaltene interministerielle Beratung über prinzipielle Fragen des gewerblichen Invalidenunterrichtes, S. 1–12, hier S. 2 u. S. 4; Ke-chin Hsia, Who Provided Care for Wounded and Disabled Soldiers? Conceptualizing State-Civil Society Relationship in First World War Austria, in: Joachim Bürgschwentner u. a. (Hg.), Other Fronts, Other Wars? First World War Studies on the Eve of the Centennial, Leiden 2014, S. 303–328.

38 In Böhmen trug die Landeskommission den Titel: Staatliche Landeszentrale für das Königreich Böhmen zur Fürsorge für heimkehrende Krieger/Státní zemská ústředna pro království České pro péči o vrátivší se vojíny. Im weiteren Verlauf wird von Landeskommissionen bzw. der Landeszentrale gesprochen werden.

39 Pawlowsky u. Wendelin, Wunden, S. 102–107; Hsia, Care.

40 Pawlowsky u. Wendelin, Wunden, S. 107–111.

41 Ebd., S. 105.

42 Anon., Invalidenunterricht, in: Mitteilungen des k.k. Ministeriums des Innern über Fürsorge für Kriegsbeschädigte, Nr. 2, August 1915, S. 23–25.

43 Die Landtage wurden mit Kriegsbeginn sistiert, der böhmische Landtag war seit 1913 aufgelöst, das Parlament seit März 1914 sistiert und zur Kriegserklärung nicht wiedereinberufen worden. Diese Perspektive auf das Verhältnis zwischen Staat und Gesellschaft während des Ersten Weltkrieges eröffnete Hsia, Care, S. 303–318.

Diese Kooperation von staatlicher Verwaltung und Zivilgesellschaft führte aber ebenso dazu, dass sich in den Re-Integrationsmaßnahmen verschiedene Wissens- und Tätigkeitsfelder sozialer Fürsorge verflochten, was zur Ausbildung der spezifischen moralischen Ökonomie der Re-Integration beitrug.

Die Durchsetzung der moralischen Ökonomie der Re-Integration gegenüber der militärischen »Ökonomie« der Mobilisierung der Bevölkerung für Militärdienst und Kriegswirtschaft war eine der zentralen Herausforderungen der Landeskommissionen. Der »Abnützungskrieg« der Isonzo-Schlachten und die schweren Verluste der Brussilow-Offensive im Sommer 1916 führten dazu, dass die Armeeführung ab Oktober 1916 ihre Bemühungen intensivierte, verletzte und erkrankte Soldaten möglichst schnell erneut zu mobilisieren.[44] Von den sieben Millionen Männern zwischen 18 und 55 Jahren, die bis zu diesem Zeitpunkt zur österreichisch-ungarischen Armee einberufen worden waren, waren eine Million zweihunderttausend in Kriegsgefangenschaft und eine Million tot oder invalid.[45] Kriegsbeschädigte mussten nicht unbedingt wieder frontdiensttauglich werden, schon ihr Einsatz zu »militärischen Hilfsdiensten« im Hinterland oder als Facharbeiter ermöglichte es, Männer für den Fronteinsatz freizustellen. Zwischen der Militärverwaltung und den Landeskommissionen häuften sich die Auseinandersetzungen über Wiedereinberufungen verletzter und erkrankter Soldaten, bevor deren Therapien oder Ausbildungskurse offiziell beendet waren oder nachdem sie eine Anstellung angetreten hatten.[46]

Mit fortschreitender Dauer des Krieges bedienten sich jedoch auch führende Kreise des Militärs des Vokabulars der Re-Integration. Nicht nur erkannte das Armeeoberkommando den Wert von Sozialpolitik zur Umgestaltung der Monarchie in seinem Sinne, wie Ke-chin Hsia betont.[47] Auch das Kriegsministerium versuchte der kriegswirtschaftlichen Mobilisierung Kriegsbeschädigter als Arbeitsbeschaffung Legitimität zu verleihen und kritisierte zivile Ministerien für ihr Versagen, Kriegsinvalide in staatlichen Betrieben zu beschäftigen. Das an der Jahreswende 1917/18 eingerichtete Ministerium für soziale Fürsorge wiederum lehnte es ab, Kriegsbeschädigten in Militärbetrieben Arbeit zu geben, weil ihnen dies keine dauerhafte Anstellung biete.[48] Diese Auseinandersetzung demonstriert die Wirkmächtigkeit, aber auch Konflikthaftigkeit der moralischen Ökonomie der Re-

---

44 Rauchensteiner, Weltkrieg, S. 419–428 und S. 541–551.
45 Vojenský ústřední archiv [im Folgenden VÚA], Vojenský historický archiv [im Folgenden VHA], Korpskommando 9 [im Folgenden KK9], Praes., 9850/1916, Protokoll über die vom 16.–20.10.1916 im Kriegsministerium abgehaltene Armeekonferenz (1. und 2. Verhandlungstag), S. 48–49.
46 Pawlowsky u. Wendelin, Wunden, S. 107–111 u. S. 136–138.
47 Hsia, War, S. 72–99.
48 ÖStA, Kriegsarchiv [im Folgenden KA], Kriegsministerium [im Folgenden KM], Abt. 9/IF, Kt. 1415, 1609/1917, Anstellung von KI bei militärischen Anstalten und Betrieben; ÖStA, Archiv der Republik [im Folgenden AdR], Bundesministerium für soziale Verwaltung [im Folgenden BMfsV], Sek. 2/Kb, Kt. 1356, 385/1918, Anstellung von Kriegsinvaliden in staatlichen Betrieben; eine andere Interpretation liefert Hsia, War, S. 218–221.

Integration, da sowohl Militär- als auch Zivilstaatsverwaltung für sich beanspruchten, die erneute Beschäftigung verletzter und erkrankter Soldaten zu verfolgen. Diese interministeriellen Debatten werfen ein Schlaglicht auf eine der zentralen Fragen der Re-Integration: Welche Beschäftigungsverhältnisse kombinierten individuelle Erwerbsfähigkeit mit gesellschaftlichem Nutzen? Die Beamten des Innenministeriums und der für die berufliche Ausbildung zuständigen Ministerien erklärten es im Juni 1915 zum Ziel der Re-Integrationsmaßnahmen, Kriegsbeschädigte in ihre Vorkriegs-Berufe zurückzuführen.[49] Nur in jenen Fällen, wo Verletzungen oder Erkrankungen diese Rückkehr unmöglich machten, sollten die Betroffenen zu neuen Berufen umgeschult werden. Das Ministerium für öffentliche Arbeiten betonte weiter, es gehe keinesfalls darum, ihnen »tunlichst rasch irgendeine Erwerbsmöglichkeit« zu verschaffen, sondern es sei das erklärte Ziel, verletzte und erkrankte Soldaten als »vollwertige, qualifizierte Arbeiter« ins Erwerbsleben zurückzuführen.[50]

Die Rückkehr in einen spezifischen Beruf war allerdings ein durchaus dehnbares Konzept; auch die Höherqualifizierung Kriegsbeschädigter zu Werkmeistern oder administrativen Tätigkeiten sowie die Spezialisierung in Detailarbeiten konnten darunter subsumiert werden, solange sie in derselben Branche erfolgten.[51] Bei bestimmten Berufsgruppen betrieb man die Rückkehr in den früheren Beruf prononcierter als bei anderen. Bauern und andere landwirtschaftliche Arbeitskräfte etwa sollten dem agrarischen Berufsfeld unbedingt erhalten bleiben. Bereits vor dem Krieg war die Migration der ländlichen Bevölkerung in die Städte als gesellschaftliches Problem gesehen worden, nach Kriegsausbruch machte die sich stetig verschärfende Versorgungskrise die Stärkung der Landwirtschaft zu einer brennenden politischen Frage.[52] Während des Krieges gab es zudem für private Unternehmen zahlreiche Motive, Kriegsbeschädigte zu beschäftigen. Dazu zählte zwar auch Verantwortungsbewusstsein gegenüber langjährigen Angestellten, der Mangel an Fachkräften aufgrund der Mobilisierung sowie die Hoffnung auf Staatsaufträge und bevorzugte Belieferung mit Rohstoffen stellten jedoch andere gewichtige Anreize dar. Unternehmer warben deswegen immer wieder bei staatlichen Stellen um die Vermittlung Kriegsbeschädigter.[53]

49 Mitteilungen des k. k. Ministeriums des Innern über Fürsorge für Kriegsbeschädigte, Nr. 1, Juli 1915, S. 12–14, hier S. 13.
50 Ebd., Nr. 2, August 1915, S. 23–25, hier S. 23.
51 Pawlowsky u. Wendelin, Wunden, S. 132–136.
52 Siehe zu den Bemühungen, sogenannte »Kriegerheimstätten« zu errichten: Hsia, War, S. 74–99; Anon., Bericht über die Tätigkeit der Staatlichen Landeszentrale für das Königreich Böhmen zur Fürsorge für heimkehrende Krieger im Jahre 1915, Prag 1916, S. 22; Anon., Jahresbericht der tirolischen Landeskommission zur Fürsorge für heimkehrende Krieger in Innsbruck für das Jahr 1916, in: Oswald Überegger (Hg.), Heimatfronten. Dokumente zur Erfahrungsgeschichte der Tiroler Kriegsgesellschaft im Ersten Weltkrieg, Innsbruck 2006, S. 408–420, hier S. 409.
53 Für derartige Fälle siehe ÖStA, KA, KM, Abt. 9/IF, Kt. 1230, 151/1916, Wimmer Johann, Gefr. – Urlaub; Národní archiv [im Folgenden NAP], Ministerstvo veřejných prací – Rakousko [im Folgenden MVP-R], Kt. 1043, 30977/1916, Lieferungsgenossenschaft der Schneidermeister in Prag III und IV, Werkstätte für Kriegsinvalide.

Zentralstaatliche und lokale Akteure waren daher wiederholt gezwungen zu verhandeln, was unter Rückkehr in den früheren Beruf zu verstehen sei und welche Kriterien für die Re-Integration angelegt werden sollten. Es waren nicht nur Orthopäden, Chirurgen, Internisten und berufliche Fachleute gefragt, um die individuelle Arbeitsfähigkeit einzuschätzen, sondern auch die Vertreter der landwirtschaftlichen Verbände oder der Handels- und Gewerbekammern, die ihr Wissen über lokale und regionale ökonomische Bedingungen und Erfordernisse einbringen sollten.[54]

Ein Beispiel für ein solches Abwägen bietet die Musikinstrumentenfabrik V. F. Červený und Söhne in Königgrätz/Hradec Králové in Böhmen. Im April 1916 bot sie der böhmischen Landeszentrale an, einen Metallpolierkurs für Angehörige der metallverarbeitenden Branche zu veranstalten, die aufgrund ihrer Kriegsverletzung nicht mehr in ihrem früheren Beruf arbeiten konnten. Derartige Lehrgänge in Privatunternehmen mussten zunächst vom Ministerium für öffentliche Arbeiten genehmigt werden, dessen Beamte jedoch beanstandeten, dass »die Anlernung von Invaliden zu einer ganz bestimmten mechanischen Detailarbeit für ein bestimmtes, privates Fabrikunternehmen« nicht den Absichten der Re-Integrationsmaßnahmen entspreche.[55] Diese Stellungnahme spiegelt die zeitgenössische Kritik an der zunehmenden Spezialisierung der Industriearbeit als monotone, abstumpfende Tätigkeit, die handwerkliche Kompetenzen verloren gehen lässt, wider, aber auch Bedenken, ob die Firma Červený tatsächlich an der Beschäftigung Kriegsbeschädigter oder nur an billigen Arbeitskräften interessiert war.[56] Hier eröffnet sich einerseits ein Spannungsfeld zwischen individueller Erwerbsfähigkeit und gesellschaftlichem Nutzen. Andererseits ging es darum, wie die Industrialisierung und industrielle Arbeit interpretiert wurden.

Kleingewerbliches Handwerk und Landwirtschaft hatten auch im relativ stark industrialisierten Böhmen nach 1900 noch einen bedeutenden Anteil an der Wirtschaft.[57] Der ärztliche Berufsberater Josef Pokorny hielt 1916 fest, dass man bei der Re-Integration Kriegsbeschädigter »nicht den Großbetrieb, sondern das

54 Hsia, War, S. 113; etwa: NAP, MVP-R, Kt. 1044, 34631/1917, Inspizierung der Invalidenschule an der schlesischen Landeserziehungsanstalt in Teschen; ebd., 4251/1917, Genehmigung von Unterrichtsveranstaltungen für Invalide.

55 NAP, MVP-R, Karton 1043, 36446/1916, Städtisches Gewerbemuseum in Königgrätz; Invalidenkurs für Metallpolierer.

56 Zur zeitgenössischen Problematisierung der Industriearbeit siehe Anson Rabinbach, The Human Motor. Energy, Fatigue, and the Origins of Modernity, Berkeley 1990; Sabine Donauer, Emotions at Work – Working on Emotions. The Production of Economic Selves in Twentieth-Century Germany, Diss. FU Berlin 2013, S. 42–95.

57 György Kövér, The Economic Achievements of the Austro-Hungarian Monarchy. Scale and Speed, in: András Gerő (Hg.), The Austro-Hungarian Monarchy Revisited, New York 2009, S. 51–83; Gerhard Meißl, Die gewerblich-industrielle Arbeitswelt in Cisleithanien mit besonderer Berücksichtigung der Berufszählungen 1890 und 1910, in: Helmut Rumpler u. Peter Urbanitsch (Hg.), Die Habsburgermonarchie 1848–1918, Bd. 9/1/1: Soziale Strukturen. Von der feudal-agrarischen zur bürgerlich-industriellen Gesellschaft, Lebens- und Arbeitswelten in der industriellen Revolution, Wien 2010, S. 323–377.

Kleingewerbe vor Augen haben« solle.[58] Weder würde, nach Ansicht der Beamten, durch einen solchen Kurs die individuelle Erwerbsfähigkeit der Betroffenen gesteigert, noch wäre den Zielen gesellschaftlicher Re-Integration gedient. Demgegenüber befürworteten Jan Šedivý, Referent der böhmischen Landeszentrale für Invalidenschulungskurse, und Josef Svatoš, Vertrauensmann des Ministeriums für öffentliche Arbeiten für die tschechischsprachigen Invalidenschulen in Böhmen, den Kurs. Sie sahen, gemäß einer tayloristischen Auffassung des Körpers, in Arbeitsteilung und Spezialisierung Chancen für Kriegsbeschädigte. Sie böten die Möglichkeit, Kriegsbeschädigte bei Arbeitsschritten zu beschäftigen, für die das Fehlen von Gliedmaßen oder der Einsatz von Prothesen keine Einschränkung darstellten. Diese Ansicht kam in zeitgenössischen Publikationen, wie Felix Krais' »Die Verwendungsmöglichkeiten der Kriegsbeschädigten in der Industrie, in Gewerbe, Handel, Handwerk, Landwirtschaft und Staatsbetrieben« oder Carl Kostkas »Erwerbsmöglichkeit in Industrie und Gewerbe für Kriegsbeschädigte«, zum Ausdruck. In tabellarischer Form wurden darin Professionen, Arbeitsschritte und körperliche Einschränkungen zueinander in Korrelation gebracht, um einen Überblick über jene Berufe zu liefern, die Kriegsbeschädigte noch ausüben konnten.[59] Šedivý und Svatoš schlossen damit an das physiologische und ökonomische Konzept einer objektiv messbaren und vergleichbaren (Arbeits-)Leistung an, die Kriegsbeschädigte erreichen mussten.

Dieses Paradigma vergleichbarer Leistung zog allerdings die Frage nach sich: Wie viel sollten Kriegsbeschädigte, die offiziell über die Verminderung ihrer Erwerbsfähigkeit als soziale Gruppe definiert wurden, als Arbeitskräfte verdienen? Die finanziellen Leistungen, die Kriegsbeschädigte von der Armee bezogen, solange sie noch im Militärdienst standen, dienten nicht nur Unternehmerkreisen als Argument dafür, ihnen geringere Löhne auszuzahlen. Selbst Einrichtungen der Re-Integration, wie die 1916 in Salzburg gegründete Kriegsinvaliden-Erwerbsgenossenschaft, vergüteten die Arbeitsleistung ihrer Mitglieder nur in geringem Ausmaß.[60] Finanzielle Prämien waren darüber hinaus das Bindeglied zwischen den ökonomischen und moralisch-erzieherischen Aspekten der sogenannten Arbeitstherapie, auf die im nächsten Abschnitt näher eingegangen wird. In diesem Spannungsverhältnis zwischen dem moralisch-erzieherischen und sozioökonomischen Wert, den man der erneuten Erwerbstätigkeit Kriegsbeschädigter beimaß, und der niedrigen Entlohnung ihrer Arbeitsleistung in der Praxis manifestiert sich die Widersprüchlichkeit der moralischen Ökonomie der Re-Integration.

---

58 Josef Pokorny, Über Berufsberatung von Kriegsbeschädigten, in: Wiener Medizinische Wochenschrift 66. 1916, Sp. 687–692, hier Sp. 688.

59 Felix Krais (Hg.), Die Verwendungsmöglichkeiten der Kriegsbeschädigten in der Industrie, in Gewerbe, Handel, Handwerk, Landwirtschaft und Staatsbetrieben, Stuttgart 1916; Carl Kostka, Erwerbsmöglichkeiten in Industrie und Gewerbe für Kriegsbeschädigte, Reichenberg 1916.

60 ÖStA, KA, KM, Abt. 9/IF, Kt. 1705, 695/1918, Inspizierung der KI Erwerbsgenossenschaft Salzburg.

Trotz dieser Konflikte waren sich Mediziner, Gewerbefachleute und Arbeits-
vermittler darin einig, dass sie dazu berufen waren, zu beurteilen, welche Arbeitsformen die in der moralischen Ökonomie der Re-Integration erwünschte
Verflechtung von ökonomischem Nutzen für die Gemeinschaft, individueller wirtschaftlicher Erwerbsfähigkeit und gesellschaftlicher Anerkennung mit sich brachten. Dass verletzte und erkrankte Soldaten die Werte und Ziele der Re-Integration
wiederum nutzten, um ihre eigene Vorstellungen von staatlicher Unterstützung
zu legitimieren, ist konstitutiv für das Konzept der moralischen Ökonomie. Sie
wandten sich brieflich an die Ministerien oder richteten Majestätsgesuche an den
Kaiser, brachten ihr Ansinnen bei Lazarettbesuchen von Mitgliedern der Habs-
burgerfamilie persönlich vor oder äußerten es in den Geschäftsräumen der neuen
Einrichtungen der Kriegsbeschädigtenfürsorge.[61] Wie zeitgenössische Experten
mit diesen Widersprüchen umgingen, sie zum Gegenstand wissenschaftlicher
Wissensproduktion machten und mit neuen Therapiearrangements darauf re-
agierten, ist ein zentrales Element der moralischen Ökonomie der Re-Integration.
    Der stellvertretende Leiter der Wiener Amtsstelle für Arbeitsvermittlung an
Kriegsinvalide, Richard Sudek, berichtete bereits 1915, dass Kriegsinvalide sich
gegen die Rückkehr in ihren früheren Beruf »sehr energisch« wehren würden
und beschrieb damit ein Problem, dem zahlreiche andere Protagonisten der
Re-Integrationsmaßnahmen ebenfalls begegneten.[62] Mit ihren Gesuchen um
Anstellung auf zumeist subalterne Positionen im Staatsdienst, als Amtsdiener,
Kanzleihilfskraft oder Postbote, brachten Kriegsinvalide alternative Vorstellungen
von Arbeit und ihren individuellen, gesellschaftlichen und moralischen Wert
zum Ausdruck. Für Kriegsinvalide des Mannschaftsstandes, die sich außerstande
sahen, ihren früheren Beruf weiter auszuüben, verhieß der öffentliche Dienst
ökonomische Sicherheit. Er verschaffte ihnen eine unbefristete Anstellung, regelmäßige Gehaltserhöhungen und eine Altersrente.[63] Aber ihre Gesuche sprechen
auch von dem Vertrauen, das sie in den Staat setzten, und von ihrem Interesse,
aktiv an ihm teilzuhaben.
    Die Auseinandersetzungen zwischen Soldaten und medizinischen und gewerb-
lichen Fachleuten tangierten zentral die Frage, wem die Deutungshoheit über die
Kriegsbeschädigung zukam. Die Experten beanspruchten sie für sich, mussten sie
sich aber selbst erst in einem Lernprozess erarbeiten. Moralische Zuschreibungen
wie etwa Arbeitsunwilligkeit lieferten etablierte Deutungsschemata für Situatio-

---

61 Zu Bittgesuchen während des Ersten Weltkrieges siehe Maureen Healy, Vienna and the Fall of
    the Habsburg Empire. Total War and Everyday Life in World War I, Cambridge 2004, S. 279–
    299; Christa Hämmerle, Bitten – Klagen – Fordern. Erste Überlegungen zu Bittbriefen öster-
    reichischer Unterschichtfrauen (1865–1918), in: BIOS 16. 2003, S. 87–110.
62 Richard Sudek, Arbeitsvermittlung an Kriegsinvalide, in: Österreichische Rundschau 45. 1915,
    Okt.–Dez., S. 49–55, hier S. 52.
63 Reichsgesetzblatt [im Folgenden RGBl.] 15/1914, Gesetz vom 25. Jänner 1914 »betreffend das
    Dienstverhältnis der Staatsbeamten und der Staatsdienerschaft (Dienstpragmatik)«, §§ 168–176;
    Waltraud Heindl, Josephinische Mandarine. Bürokratie und Beamte in Österreich, Bd. 2: 1848
    bis 1914, S. 140 u. S. 143–146.

nen »epistemischer Unsicherheit«,[64] wie aus einem Bericht der Schuldirektion der staatlichen Gewerbeschule in Asch/Aš in Böhmen hervorgeht:

Die meisten der kriegsbeschädigten Weber und Wirker zeigen wenig Lust, zu ihrem Beruf zurückzukehren; [...] sie erklären durch die Beschädigung einer Hand oder eines Armes, [...], die Fähigkeit zur Wiederausübung desselben verloren zu haben. Diesen Erklärungen mußte Glauben geschenkt werden, da das Gegenteil nicht bewiesen werden konnte. Nun hat aber die gefertigte Direktion in Erfahrung gebracht, daß bei einer hiesigen Firma ein 35-jähriger mechanischer Weber namens Ulrich Drosta in Diensten steht, der in seinem 16. Lebensjahr [...] die rechte Hand samt Unterarm verloren hat, und der trotzdem nicht nur als Weber Tüchtiges leistet, sondern auch alle in seine kleine Ökonomie einschlagenden Arbeiten selbst verrichtet.[65]

Die »Entdeckung« des einarmigen Webers ermöglichte es den Gewerbefachleuten der Schule, eine »objektive« Einschätzung von »Berufsunfähigkeit« vorzunehmen und die subjektive Wahrnehmung der Kriegsbeschädigten damit zu konfrontieren. Deren Selbsteinschätzung wurde sodann als Ausdruck subjektiver Gefühlslagen umgedeutet, sie »zeigen wenig Lust, zu ihrem früheren Berufe zurückzukehren«. Dadurch rückte die Schuldirektion die Aussagen der Kriegsbeschädigten in die Nähe der Arbeitsunwilligkeit und entzog ihren Wünschen nach Berufswechsel die Legitimation. In dieser Interpretation manifestieren sich drei eng miteinander verflochtene Vorgänge. Erstens verortete die Direktion die Selbsteinschätzung der Kriegsbeschädigten als arbeitsunfähig im Bereich individueller Emotionen. Damit eng verbunden war zweitens, dass sie die Wünsche der Kriegsbeschädigten als Arbeitsunlust moralisch abwertete. Beide Prozesse dienten dazu, den Expertenstatus von Medizinern und Gewerbefachleuten abzusichern, die ein objektives Urteil über Arbeitsfähigkeit und -unfähigkeit fällen könnten. Mit dieser negativen war jedoch drittens eine positive Moralisierung eng verwoben.[66] Die Direktion schrieb nicht nur Arbeit generell besonderen moralischen Wert zu, sondern einer bestimmten Einstellung zur Arbeit, die sich in der Bereitschaft manifestierte, in den früheren Beruf zurückzukehren. Darin unterschied sich die moralische Ökonomie der Re-Integration auch von der Moralisierung der Arbeit in der Arbeitslosen- und Armenfürsorge, in der Männer und Frauen irgendwelche, oft einfache Arbeiten ausführen mussten, um ihre Arbeitswilligkeit zu beweisen.[67]

Nur wenige Monate nach Beginn der Re-Integrationsmaßnahmen erlebten deren Vertreter also eine Art »produktives Scheitern«. Mediziner und berufliche Fachleute erlebten das Beharren der Kriegsinvaliden auf ihren eigenen Vorstel-

64 Ann Laura Stoler, Along the Archival Grain. Epistemic Anxieties and Colonial Common Sense, Princeton 2009, S. 14–51.

65 NAP, MVP-R, Kt. 1043, 27059/1916, Invalidenschulung für Weber; k. k. Lehranstalt für Textilindustrie in Asch an das k. k. Ministerium für öffentliche Arbeiten, 12.4.1916, unpaginiert.

66 Evelyn S. Ruppert, The Moral Economy of Cities. Shaping Good Citizens, Toronto 2006, S. 10 f.

67 Wadauer, Distinctions, S. 44.

lungen staatlicher Unterstützung als »Scheitern«, weil dadurch ihr beanspruchter Expertenstatus angefochten wurde. Produktiv waren diese Konflikte insofern, als sie zu einer Verschiebung innerhalb der moralischen Ökonomie der Re-Integration führten. Die Fachleute begannen, diese Auseinandersetzungen mit den Gefühlen und persönlichen Einstellungen der Kriegsbeschädigten zu erklären, und wollten durch ein spezifisches therapeutisches Instrumentarium die Emotionen der Soldaten beeinflussen.

III. Arbeit an der Person

Prothesen, Therapien und berufliche Ausbildung hatten, nach Ansicht der Mediziner, das Potenzial, die Arbeitsfähigkeit der Kriegsbeschädigten objektiv wiederherzustellen, daher suchten sie in den persönlichen Einstellungen der Betroffenen die Ursachen für die Konflikte mit den Kriegsbeschädigten.[68] An der Jahreswende 1914/15 betrachteten Politiker, Mediziner und Sozialwissenschaftler die Re-Integration verletzter und erkrankter Soldaten als Königsweg, um moralischen Gefahren vorzubeugen, die sie in Alkoholismus, Vagabundismus, Rentenpsychose und Abhängigkeit von der Armenfürsorge sahen. Diese Deutungsschemata spiegelten sich in den frühen Interpretationen der Konflikte zwischen Kriegsbeschädigten und Experten wider. Im Jahre 1915 erklärten Protagonisten der Landeszentrale Böhmen diese Auseinandersetzungen noch mit »persönliche[n] Eigenschaften der Kriegsinvaliden, [die] in die sogenannte Rentenpsychose ausarten«.[69] Im Verlauf der Jahre 1915 und 1916 veränderte sich jedoch das Erklärungsmuster dafür, warum verletzte und erkrankte Soldaten sich dagegen sträubten, in ihren früheren Beruf zurückzukehren. Als Josef Pokorny, ärztlicher Leiter der Invalidenschulen im Wiener Reservespital Nr. 11, in der Wiener Medizinischen Wochenschrift die Aufgaben des ärztlichen Berufsberaters für Kriegsbeschädigte beschrieb, stellte er es ins Zentrum, »dem Invaliden sein Selbstvertrauen wiederzugeben«.[70] Auch andere Mediziner, wie Adolf Deutsch oder Jiří V. Klíma, betonten nun die Bedeutung der »seelischen Einstellung«[71] und insbesondere des mangelnden »Selbstvertrauens«.[72] Zwar finden sich auch

---

68 Zur Überhöhung der Prothetik siehe Kienitz, Helden, S. 152–192; Harrasser, Prothesen, S. 110–117.

69 Anon., Bericht über die Tätigkeit der Staatlichen Landeszentrale für das Königreich Böhmen, S. 29.

70 Pokorny, Berufsberatung, S. 687 f.

71 Adolf Deutsch, Ärztliche Berufsberatung Kriegsbeschädigter im Rahmen der Arbeitsvermittlung, Wien 1917, S. 31; Adolf Deutsch schreibt Emotionen eine entscheidende Rolle in der Berufsberatung Kriegsbeschädigter zu, siehe ebd., S. 13–21.

72 Jiří V. Klíma, Výchova mrzáků, zvláště vojínů-invalidů ku práci výdělečné [Erziehung der Krüppel, insbesondere der Kriegsinvaliden zur gewerblichen Arbeit], in: Naše Doba. Revue pro vědu, umění a život sociální 23. 1916, S. 422–430 u. S. 524–532, hier S. 429 u. S. 525.

vereinzelt nationalistisch-rassistische Interpretationen, wenn etwa slowenisch-sprachigen Kriegsbeschädigten pauschal »eine Neigung, von der Landwirtschaft mit Hilfe der Invalidität in Kanzlei-, Staats- und andere öffentliche Dienste zu treten« attestiert wurde.[73] Die meisten Experten deuteten diese Neigung jedoch nicht als ererbten Charakterfehler, sondern begannen, sich mit Charakter und Emotionen der Kriegsbeschädigten zu befassen.[74]

Bereits vor dem Krieg hatte der deutsche Pädagoge und Begründer der sogenannten »Krüppelpsychologie«, Hans Würtz, den Standpunkt vertreten, dass körperbehinderte Kinder an einem Gefühl der Minderwertigkeit gegenüber ihren Mitmenschen litten.[75] Gemeinsam mit dem Orthopäden Konrad Biesalski war er einer der im deutschsprachigen Raum führenden Vertreter einer neuen überkonfessionellen Fürsorge für körperbehinderte Kinder, die Orthopädie und Pädagogik verband.[76] In Prag errichteten der Orthopäde Rudolf Jedlička und der Pädagoge František Bakule ein Heim für körperbehinderte Kinder nach ähnlichen Grundsätzen. Würtz und Bakule strichen bereits vor dem Krieg die Rolle von (handwerklicher) Arbeit für das Selbstwertgefühl körperbehinderter Kinder heraus. Die Erziehung zur Arbeitsfähigkeit war das ökonomische und soziale Ziel dieser Fürsorge für körperbehinderte Kinder, Würtz, Bakule und der eng mit dem Prager Heim verbundene Sozialhygieniker Jan Dvořák betrachteten jedoch die emotionale Dimension als ebenso wichtigen Bestandteil der Therapie. Nach Kriegsausbruch brachten sie sich und ihre therapeutischen Konzepte erfolgreich in die Re-Integration Kriegsbeschädigter ein.[77]

Für Würtz und Biesalski spielte dabei das Konzept des »Willens« eine entscheidende Rolle, cisleithanische Mediziner sprachen jedoch eher vom (fehlenden) Selbstvertrauen der verletzten Soldaten. Die Gründe für diesen Mangel an Selbstvertrauen verorteten sie in der Umwelt, einesteils in den gesellschaftlichen

73 Karl Polheim, Vorwort Arbeitsvermittlung, in: Anon., Die Kriegsbeschädigtenfürsorge in Steiermark. Tätigkeitsbericht der steiermärkischen Landeskommission zur Fürsorge für Heimkehrende Krieger über die Jahre 1915, 1916 und 1917, Graz 1918, S. 93–96, hier S. 95.

74 Otto Burkard, Über die Schulung Kriegsinvalider, in: Mitteilungen des k. k. Ministeriums des Innern über Fürsorge für Kriegsbeschädigte, Nr. 9, März 1916, S. 99–105.

75 Philipp Osten, Die Modellanstalt. Über den Aufbau einer »modernen Krüppelfürsorge« 1905–1933, Frankfurt 2004, S. 159.

76 Zu Hans Würtz siehe Oliver Musenberg, Der Körperbehindertenpädagoge Hans Würtz (1875–1958). Eine kritische Würdigung des psychologischen und pädagogischen Konzeptes vor dem Hintergrund seiner Biografie, Hamburg 2002; Petra Fuchs, »Körperbehinderte« zwischen Selbstaufgabe und Emanzipation. Selbsthilfe – Integration – Aussonderung, Berlin 2001, S. 20–39 u. S. 52–65; zu den europäischen Verflechtungen siehe Klaus-Dieter Thomann, Der »Krüppel«. Entstehen und Verschwinden eines Kampfbegriffs, in: Medizinhistorisches Journal 27. 1992, S. 221–271.

77 Zu Bakule siehe Yves Jeanne, Frantisek Bakule. Que la joie demeure, in: Reliance 23. 2007, S. 114–120; Jan Dvořák, Úprava péče o mrzáky. Sociologická studie [Die Ausgestaltung der Krüppelfürsorge. Eine soziologische Studie], in: Naše Doba. Revue pro vědu, umění a život sociální 14. 1907, S. 273–284; ders., První škola pro vojíny invalidy v Praze [Die erste Schule für invalide Soldaten in Prag], in: Národní listy, 22.11.1914, S. 9.

Vorstellungen von Behinderung als Arbeitsunfähigkeit und andernteils in den Bedingungen während der medizinischen Behandlung. Zeitgleich befassten sich Chirurgen, Ingenieure und Psychologen im Rahmen der Prothetik mit der Beziehung des Körpers zur Umwelt, mit Prozessen der taktilen Informationsübertragung und der motorischen Steuerung und entwickelten dabei, wie Karin Harrasser herausarbeitete, Konzepte der Rückkoppelung zwischen sensorischer Empfindung und Steuerung des Körpers.[78] 1917 vertrat Wilhelm Neutra, Chefarzt der Nervenabteilung des Garnisonsspitals im niederösterreichischen Baden, den Standpunkt, dass die Prothetik den individuellen, erworbenen Verhaltensweisen und Bewegungsmustern Rechnung tragen musste, wenn man erreichen wollte, dass Kriegsbeschädigte ihre künstlichen Gliedmaßen akzeptieren und verwenden.[79] Die Wechselwirkung zwischen Umwelt und Individuum sowie die Ausbildung erlernter, habitualisierter Verhaltensweisen entwickelte sich zu einem interdisziplinären Fragenkonnex der Re-Integration.[80] Das Ziel der Therapiemaßnahmen war damit nicht nur, die körperliche Arbeitsfähigkeit der Kriegsbeschädigten wiederherzustellen, sondern auch, dass sie ein spezifisches Selbstverhältnis einübten, um wieder zu erwerbsfähigen Bürgern zu werden.

Die Umwelt verletzter und erkrankter Soldaten umzugestalten war daher ein wichtiges therapeutisches Mittel, um ein solches Selbstverhältnis herzustellen. In den Lazaretten und Invalidenschulen appellierten Flugschriften im Stile der damals sehr erfolgreichen und beliebten Ratgeberliteratur an das Selbstvertrauen der verletzten und erkrankten Soldaten und versuchten, sie zur selbsttätigen Verbesserung ihrer Situation anzuleiten.[81] Schulleiter strebten danach, Menschen mit Behinderung, die einem Beruf nachgingen, als Lehrer oder Werkmeister in den Schulwerkstätten zu engagieren, damit sie als Vorbilder dienten.[82]

Das besondere Interesse der Experten richtete sich jedoch darauf, während der Behandlung den negativen Auswirkungen der Untätigkeit auf das Selbstvertrauen

---

78 Harrasser, Prothesen, S. 118–142.

79 Ebd., S. 133–138, hier S. 134.

80 Zur Genese wissenschaftlicher Diskurse über Gewohnheiten siehe Bernhard Kleeberg, Schlechte Angewohnheiten. Einleitung, in: ders. (Hg.), Schlechte Angewohnheiten. Eine Anthologie 1750–1900, Berlin 2012, S. 9–63, hier S. 25–63.

81 Anon., An unsere verwundeten und kranken Krieger, in: Österreichischer Arbeitsnachweis für Kriegsinvalide 1. 1915, S. 1; K. u. k. Militärkommando in Leitmeritz (Kriegsbeschädigtenfürsorge), An unsere verwundeten und kranken Krieger!, Leitmeritz 1916, in: Státní Okresní Archiv Liberec, Archiv města Liberce-W, Kt. 113, 106; zur Ratgeberliteratur des frühen 20. Jahrhunderts siehe Stephanie Kleiner u. Robert Suter, Konzepte von Glück und Erfolg in der Ratgeberliteratur (1900–1940). Eine Einleitung, in: dies. (Hg.), Guter Rat. Glück und Erfolg in der Ratgeberliteratur 1900–1940, Berlin 2015, S. 9–40; Stefanie Duttweiler, Glück durch dich Selbst. Subjektivierungsformen in der Ratgeberliteratur der 1920er–1940er Jahre, in: ebd., S. 41–59, hier S. 44–50.

82 NAP, MVP-R, Kt. 1043, 22017/1916, Invalidenschule; ebd., 27059/1916, Invalidenschulung für Weber; k. k. Lehranstalt für Textilindustrie in Asch an das k. k. Ministerium für öffentliche Arbeiten; zur Rolle der »Vorzeigeinvaliden« siehe Kienitz, Helden, S. 192–205.

der verletzten und erkrankten Soldaten entgegenzuwirken.[83] Diese Untätigkeit betrachtete man vor allem deswegen als Problem, weil sie den Kriegsbeschädigten Gelegenheit gäbe, sich über ihre Berufsunfähigkeit Sorgen zu machen und diese so langsam zu verinnerlichen.[84] Das wichtigste therapeutische Mittel wurde demnach die Gestaltung des Krankenhaus- und Schulungsalltags selbst, wie ein Erlass des Kriegsministeriums für die militärischen Rekonvaleszentenabteilungen demonstriert:

> [Es] erscheint aber als grundlegende Voraussetzung, daß bei jeder Gelegenheit auf die Gemütsbildung günstig eingewirkt werde. Nur dadurch werden die Invaliden von dem drückenden Gefühl der Hilflosigkeit befreit und verfallen nicht in Mutlosigkeit und Verbitterung wegen der Einbusse an Kraft und Lebensfreude. […] In diesem Zusammenhange muß mit entsprechendem Nachdruck auf die großen sittlichen Gefahren Bedacht genommen werden, die ihre Ursachen meist in der Beschäftigungslosigkeit haben.[85]

Diese Untätigkeit hinterließ in den Augen zeitgenössischer Experten also nicht nur Spuren in den Körpern, indem sie etwa zu Muskelabbau führte, sondern sie hatte auch einen negativen Einfluss auf die Beziehung der verletzten und erkrankten Soldaten zu sich selbst und ihren Fähigkeiten. Das Aufrechterhalten militärischer Disziplin durch militärisches Aufsichtspersonal in den Schulen und Werkstätten allein erachteten sie nicht als ausreichend, es galt, diese durch subtilere Formen der Erziehung zu ergänzen.[86]

Mediziner wie Hans Spitzy, Leiter des Wiener Reservespitals Nr. 11, sahen in der Arbeitstherapie das beste Mittel zu diesem Zweck.[87] Der Übergang von medizinischer Behandlung zu beruflicher Ausbildung war dabei oft fließend. Die Beschäftigung in den Werkstätten wurde als »Vorschulung«[88] betrachtet, die parallel zur orthopädischen Therapie schon eine fachliche Ausbildung vorbereiten sollte. Die Arbeitstherapie ergänzte ältere Therapieformen, wie sogenannte mediko-mechanische Apparate, hatte für Spitzy jedoch spezifische Vorteile.[89] Sie sollte Kriegsbeschädigte aus dem »verweichlichenden Spitalsleben«, wie er es

83 ÖStA, KA, KM, Abt. 9/IF, Kt. 1229, 705/1916, Bericht des Vertrauensmannes des M.f.ö.A. in Angelegenheit der Invalidenschulen, unpaginiert; Bericht der Landesstelle der k.k. Arbeitsvermittlung an Kriegsinvalide in Troppau über ihre Tätigkeit bis 30.6.1917, unpaginiert, in: NAP, MVP-R, Kt. 1044, 126036/1917, k.k. Arbeitsvermittlung an Kriegsinvalide, Landesstelle Troppau, Bericht.

84 Deutsch, Berufsberatung, S. 14 f.

85 KM Erlass Abt. 10, 152.810/1917, in: VÚA, VHA, KK9, Praes., 8248/1917, Entlassung der Invaliden in die Heimat. Beschäftigung der Invaliden in den Rekonvaleszenten-Abteilungen für Invalide.

86 Pawlowsky u. Wendelin, Wunden, S. 139–146.

87 ÖStA, KA, KM, Abt. 9/IF, Kt. 1229, 705/1916, Bericht des Vertrauensmannes des M.f.ö.A. in Angelegenheit der Invalidenschulen.

88 NAP, MVP-R, Kt. 1043, 3665/1916, Bericht des Gewerbeförderungsinstitutes in Eger.

89 Eghigian, Security, S. 117–157.

bezeichnete, herausholen.[90] Hier wird die Erziehung zur Arbeit auch als Prozess
der Wiederherstellung der Männlichkeit der Kriegsbeschädigten sichtbar, die
Zeitgenossen durch Arbeitslosigkeit, Abhängigkeit von Fürsorge und Untätigkeit
bedroht sahen.[91] Spitzy legte darüber hinaus großen Wert darauf, dass die Arbeit
mit individuell angepassten Werkzeugen den verletzten Soldaten »Freude machen« solle, da sie dadurch motivierter seien, an der Behandlung teilzunehmen.[92]
Arbeitstherapie war für ihn also explizit eine Möglichkeit, Kriegsbeschädigten
schon früh einen positiven Bezug zu ihrer eigenen Arbeitsfähigkeit zu vermitteln
und dadurch der Selbsteinschätzung als »berufsunfähig« entgegenzuwirken. Sie
bot medizinischen und gewerblichen Fachleuten zudem Gelegenheit, verletzte
und erkrankte Soldaten bei der Arbeit zu beobachten und das dabei gesammelte
Wissen für die Entscheidung über eine mögliche weitere Ausbildung zu nutzen.[93]
In der Arbeitstherapie kommt jene Verflechtung von ökonomischer Bewertung
der Arbeitsfähigkeit Kriegsbeschädigter mit ihrer moralischen Erziehung am
deutlichsten zum Ausdruck, die die moralische Ökonomie der Re-Integration
kennzeichnete.

Bereits 1915 führte das Wiener Reservespital Nr. 11 Arbeitstherapie ein und
bald folgten, oft in enger Kooperation mit den gewerblichen Fachschulen, weitere Krankenanstalten.[94] Hatte Spitzy bereits die Anpassung der Werkzeuge an
die körperlichen Defekte der Kriegsbeschädigten angeregt, so gestalteten andere Invalidenschulen die Arbeitstätigkeiten selbst entsprechend aus, um eine
positive emotionale Haltung zur Arbeitstätigkeit zu erreichen. Ferdinand Breinl,
Vertrauensmann des Ministeriums für öffentliche Arbeiten für die deutschsprachigen Invalidenschulen in Böhmen, berichtete über die Arbeitstherapie
in Reichenberg/Liberec, dass die Holzbearbeitung für Soldaten mit Arm- und
Handverletzungen besonders geeignet sei. Denn die Arbeitsschritte ließen die
Kriegsbeschädigten »das Fortschreiten ihrer einfachen Arbeiten und damit auch
ihre wachsende Leistungsfähigkeit leichter erkennen« und übten dadurch eine
»günstige psychische Wirkung auf die Invaliden« aus.[95] Die moralische Erziehung in der cisleithanischen Invalidenschulung fand somit auch über und mit
dem Körper statt. Indem Arbeitstätigkeit so gestaltet wurde, dass sie Therapie-
fortschritte und Erfolgserlebnisse vermittelte, sollte sie den Soldaten wieder zur

90 Hans Spitzy, Arbeitstherapie und Invalidenschulen, in: Gunnar Frostell, Kriegsmechanothera-
    pie. Indikation und Methodik der Massage, Heilgymnastik und Apparatbehandlung samt deren
    Beziehungen zur Kriegsorthopädie für Ärzte, ärztliches Hilfspersonal und Selbstbehandlung,
    Wien 1917, S. 157–170, hier S. 170.
91 Kienitz, Helden, S. 253–259.
92 Hans Spitzy, Invalidenfürsorge und Invalidenschulen, in: Neue Freie Presse, 8.1.1915, S. 9; ders.,
    Arbeitstherapie, S. 160.
93 ÖStA, KA, KM, Abt. 9/IF, Kt. 1226, 192/1916, Gewerberechtliche Ausnahmsbestimmungen für
    Kriegsinvalide.
94 NAP, MVP-R, Kt. 1043, 17089/1916, Bericht in Angelegenheit der Invalidenschulen.
95 Ebd.

Gewohnheit werden. Vertrauen in die eigene Arbeitskraft galt als Grundlage für Arbeitsfreude und Gegenmittel zur Arbeitsscheu. Hatten Arbeitspsychologen vor dem Krieg gute Arbeitsbedingungen insbesondere über das Fehlen negativer Emotionen definiert, entwickelten Mediziner und Pädagogen in der moralischen Ökonomie der Re-Integration therapeutische Maßnahmen, die darauf abzielten, Arbeitstätigkeit emotional positiv zu konnotieren.[96]

Diesen Zweck verfolgte man auch mit der Einführung sogenannter »Arbeitsprämien«, die die »Arbeitsfreude« verletzter und erkrankter Soldaten während der Therapie wecken sollten.[97] Während sie in militärischen Krankenanstalten eingeführt wurden, warf die konkrete Ausgestaltung solcher finanziellen Vergütungen für die Vertreter der Landeskommissionen eine Reihe von Fragen auf, die für manche so schwerwiegend waren, dass sie die Einführung von Arbeitsprämien ablehnten. Wie die Landeskommission Kärnten berichtete, stand sie vor der grundlegenden Herausforderung, woher die Invalidenschulen die finanziellen Mittel für Löhne nehmen sollten, die der enormen Teuerung der Kriegsjahre gerecht würden. Sie hinterfragte jedoch auch, ob Prämien überhaupt ihren Zweck erfüllten. Die Kommissionsmitglieder sahen sich vor ein Dilemma gestellt: Einen Pauschalbetrag hielten sie für »ungerecht«, da er Unterschiede im »Fleiss, der Geschicklichkeit, der Pünktlichkeit und der Art der Arbeit« nicht abbilden und der sozialen Praxis in Industrie und Gewerbe nicht entsprechen würde. Ein differenziertes Prämienschema hingegen würde nicht die Arbeitsfreude, sondern die »Unzufriedenheit« der Invalidenschüler schüren, da niedrige Prämien denjenigen, die gerade erst Therapie oder Ausbildung begannen, ihre geringere Arbeitsfähigkeit vor Augen führten.[98] Die Vertreter der Landeskommissionen blendeten in diesen Überlegungen aus, dass die Arbeitsfähigkeit verletzter und erkrankter Soldaten auch nach dem Ende der Behandlung und der Kurse den Anforderungen privater Unternehmer und Unternehmerinnen nicht entsprechen könnte. Ihre Einschätzung gleicher Bezahlung bei ungleicher Arbeitsleistung als »ungerecht« verweist allerdings auf eine alternative Moralisierung des Konzeptes objektiver Leistung. Die betriebswirtschaftliche Verwertbarkeit individueller Arbeit erhielt darin größere Bedeutung als ein individuell wie gesellschaftlich bestimmter Nutzen der Erwerbstätigkeit Kriegsbeschädigter. Darin war die Problematik der Zwischenkriegszeit, in der Kriegsinvalide als vermeintlich minderwertige Arbeitskräfte stigmatisiert wurden, bereits angelegt.[99]

Die moralische Ökonomie der Re-Integration war somit kein homogenes Gebilde, tragende Werte konnten auch geleugnet und ignoriert werden.[100] Be-

---

96 Donauer, Emotions at Work, S. 26.

97 ÖStA, KA, KM, Abt. 9/IF, Karton 944, 14/1915 Invalidenschulen des k. u. k. Reservespitals Nr. 11 in Wien, Bericht Prof. Grau.

98 ÖStA, AdR, BMfsV, Kt. 1362, 20713/1918, Landeskommission zur Fürsorge für heimkehrende Krieger in Kärnten, Klagenfurt, am 8.8.1918.

99 Siehe dazu die Analyse zum österreichischen »Invalidenbeschäftigungsgesetz« in: Pawlowsky u. Wendelin, Wunden, S. 414–430.

100 Fassin, Leben, S. 19.

sonders gut und medienwirksam ließ sich die Rückkehr zur Arbeit bei Kriegsinvaliden mit künstlichen Gliedmaßen inszenieren und in der offiziellen Bild-
propaganda einsetzen, um zu zeigen, wie man die sozialen Folgen des Krieges
bewältigten konnte. Im Gegensatz dazu wurden Soldaten, deren Verletzungen
oder Erkrankungen nicht in das Re-Integrationsparadigma passten, etwa weil
sie ihr Gesicht bis zur Unkenntlichkeit entstellten, in Heimen untergebracht und
dem öffentlichen Blick entzogen.[101] Psychisch erkrankte Soldaten sahen sich mit
dem Vorwurf der Simulation konfrontiert und wurden auf erbliche oder soziale Dispositionen untersucht.[102] Auch sie unterzog man, anknüpfend an psy-
chiatrische Praktiken der Vorkriegszeit, einer Arbeitstherapie, wobei Mediziner
bei ihrer Behandlung militärische Disziplin und Strenge als heilsam empfahlen,
während »falsch angebrachte[s] Mitleid und eine milde Rücksichtnahme« die
Männer nur in ihrer Krankheit bestärken würden.[103] Dieselben therapeutischen
Praktiken der moralischen Ökonomie der Re-Integration konnten also mit unterschiedlichen Werten verknüpft werden.

IV. Fazit: Ambivalenzen der moralischen Ökonomie

Im Juni und Juli 1917 veranstaltete das Wiener Museum für Kunst und Industrie eine Ausstellung mit Werkstücken aus den Invalidenschulen Cisleithaniens.[104]
Schon das Plakatmotiv veranschaulicht das Programm dieser Werkschau. Zwei
Figuren nehmen die Mitte des Plakats ein, rechts ein muskulöser, bärtiger Handwerker mit Arbeitsschürze und mannsgroßem Hammer, links ein Ritter in vol-
ler Rüstung und mit Schwert. Beide unversehrt und in betont maskulinisierter
Darstellung vereinen die Figuren Krieg und Arbeit in jener harmonischen Weise,

101 Werner Berthold, »Herrlicher noch als das Schwert schmückt Euch die Krone des Leids!«
   Kriegsbeschädigtenfürsorge im Ersten Weltkrieg in Niederösterreich, in: Achim Doppler
   u. a. (Hg.), Fern der Front – mitten im Krieg. Niederösterreich 1914–1918, St. Pölten 2014,
   S. 49–67; Melanie Ruff, Gesichter des Ersten Weltkrieges. Alltag, Biografien und Selbstdar-
   stellungen von gesichtsverletzten Soldaten, Stuttgart 2015.
102 Hans-Georg Hofer, Nervenschwäche und Krieg. Modernitätskritik und Krisenbewältigung in
   der österreichischen Psychiatrie (1880–1920), Wien 2004; Julia Barbara Köhne, Kriegshyste-
   riker. Strategische Bilder und mediale Techniken militärpsychiatrischen Wissens (1914–1920),
   Husum 2009.
103 VÚA, VHA, KK9, Militärarchiv [im Folgenden MA], Kt. 234, 55-23/1-2, Kriegsneurosen,
   Wahrnehmungen bei der Superarbitrierung, Bericht des Militärspitals Nr. 2 in Pardubitz,
   19.3.1917, unpaginiert. Zur Bedeutung der Arbeitstherapie siehe Paul Lerner, Hysterical Men.
   War, Psychiatry, and the Politics of Trauma in Germany, 1890–1930, Ithaca 2003, S. 142 f.
104 VÚA, VHA, KK9, MA, Kt. 221, 55–42/2-7, Invalidenschule für metallverarbeitende Gewerbe,
   II. Kurs, Aussig, 29.6.1916; Hartvig Fischel, Výstava průmyslových škol invalidních v c. k.
   Rakouském museu [Ausstellung der Invalidengewerbeschulen im k.k. österreichischen Mu-
   seum], in: Péče o vojýny válkou poškozené 2. 1918, S. 89–94.

die gesellschaftlich auch für die Kriegsbeschädigten vorgesehen, aber kaum ein-
gelöst war.[105]

Die Analyse der Re-Integrationsmaßnahmen für verletzte und erkrankte Soldaten in der cisleithanischen Reichshälfte der Habsburgermonarchie mithilfe des
Konzeptes der moralischen Ökonomie machte deutlich, dass die Re-Integrationsmaßnahmen nicht bloß als rationalisierende, ökonomische Nutzbarmachung
verletzter und erkrankter Soldaten zu betrachten sind. An ein umfassenderes
Verständnis von Ökonomie anknüpfend, erfassten cisleithanische Akteure verletzte und erkrankte Soldaten als ein »Problem«, das soziale, moralische und ökonomische Dimensionen umfasste und das durch Re-Integration gelöst werden
konnte. Indem sie die Rückkehr in den früheren Beruf als Ziel der gesellschaftlichen Re-Integration ausgaben, konstituierte sich die moralische Ökonomie der
Re-Integrationsmaßnahmen während des Krieges um spezifische Konfliktfelder,
Institutionen und Praktiken. Dies war jedoch kein *top-down*-Prozess. Die Kon-
frontation medizinischer und beruflicher Fachleute mit den Ansprüchen und
Forderungen verletzter und erkrankter Soldaten lieferte entscheidende Impulse,
sich mit deren Emotionen zu befassen und neue therapeutische Arrangements zu
entwickeln. Das Selbstvertrauen der Betroffenen wurde, neben den Verletzungen
und Krankheiten, zum Gegenstand der Therapie in den Werkstätten und Invalidenschulen. Die Analyse der therapeutischen Praktiken, die zusätzlich zur
Heilung des Körpers eine charakterliche Erziehung bezweckten, hat gezeigt, wie
die Re-Integrationsmaßnahmen auf die Herstellung spezifischer politischer und
ökonomischer Subjekte abzielten, indem bestimmte Arbeits- und Anstellungsverhältnisse moralisiert wurden. Gleichzeitig waren dieser moralischen Ökonomie
Widersprüche und Spannungsverhältnisse eingelagert. Dies betraf insbesondere
den Wert, der der Arbeit auf individueller, moralischer Ebene beigemessen
wurde, und dem Konzept einer objektiv mess- und vergleichbaren (Arbeits-)
Leistung, die sich in der konkreten, geringen Entlohnung Kriegsbeschädigter
widerspiegelte.

Bereits gegen Ende des Krieges zeichnete sich allerdings eine Transformation
dieser moralischen Ökonomie ab, als die Beamten des 1917 neu gegründeten
Ministeriums für soziale Fürsorge eine umfassende Reform der Sozialpolitik anstrebten. Sie erwogen dabei auch eine gesetzliche Regelung der Beschäftigung
Kriegsbeschädigter und rückten damit die staatliche Gestaltung struktureller
Dimensionen des Arbeitsmarktes anstatt die Therapierung individueller Charaktereigenschaften in den Vordergrund.[106] Mit der Verabschiedung neuer Ren-
tengesetze für Kriegsbeschädigte in den Nachfolgestaaten nach 1918, die ein
differenziert gestaffeltes System finanzieller Entschädigung für den Verlust an Erwerbsfähigkeit einführten, avancierte die Rente zum neuen zentralen Konfliktfeld

---

105 Wilhelm Wodnansky, Ausstellung der gewerbl. Kriegsinvaliden-Schulen im k.k. österreich.
    Museum für Kunst und Industrie Juni–Juli 1917, Wien 1917; einsehbar in der Wienbibliothek
    im Rathaus: https://www.digital.wienbibliothek.at/wbrobv/content/pageview/488203.
106 Pawlowsky u. Wendelin, Wunden, S. 416–419.

der Kriegsbeschädigtenfürsorge. Die Invalidenschulen als Orte beruflicher Ausbildung verloren ebenfalls an gesellschaftlicher Anerkennung und verschwanden wenige Jahre nach Kriegsende. Zudem veränderten sich die ökonomischen Rahmenbedingungen. Hatten während des Krieges noch Militär und Unternehmerschaft um Kriegsbeschädigte als Arbeitskräfte gewetteifert, herrschte nach der Demobilisierung in den Nachfolgestaaten hohe Arbeitslosigkeit. Damit verschwanden zentrale Institutionen, in denen die Wiederherstellung körperlicher Arbeitsfähigkeit mit moralischer Erziehung verknüpft war. In medizinischen und administrativen Diskursen über die Emotionen und Charaktereigenschaften der Kriegsversehrten gewann das Thema der Rentenpsychose gegenüber dem Selbstvertrauen an Bedeutung. Einzelne Aspekte, etwa die Ablehnung von Almosen und Mitleid und die Forderung nach Arbeitsbeschaffung, griffen zwar die Kriegsopferbewegungen der Nachfolgestaaten auf, die moralische Ökonomie der Re-Integration transformierte sich mit Kriegsende jedoch drastisch in eine moralische Ökonomie des Opfers, in der finanzielle Kompensation, symbolische Bedeutung und gesellschaftliche Anerkennung von Kriegsbeschädigungen und verlorenen Familienmitgliedern als Opfer für die Gesellschaft im Zentrum standen.[107]

107 Pawlowsky u. Wendelin, Wunden; Stegmann, Kriegsdeutungen; Sabine Kienitz, Der Krieg der Invaliden. Helden-Bilder und Männlichkeitskonstruktionen nach dem Ersten Weltkrieg, in: Militärgeschichtliche Zeitschrift 60. 2001, S. 367–402; Greg A. Eghigian, The Politics of Victimization. Social Pensioners and the German Social State in the Inflation of 1914–1924, in: Central European History 26. 1993, S. 375–403; Catherine Edgecombe u. Maureen Healy, Competing Interpretations of Sacrifice in the Postwar Austrian Republic, in: Mark Cornwall u. John Paul Newman (Hg.), Sacrifice and Rebirth. The Legacy of the Last Habsburg War, New York 2016, S. 15–34.

Reinhild Kreis

Make or Buy?*

Modes of Provision and the Moral Economy
of Households in Postwar Germany

Abstract: Make or buy? The question as to whether households should produce or purchase goods has been debated ever since industrialization diminished the significance of subsistence economies. The article interprets different modes of provision as moral economies that shaped markets and societies. The use of resources such as time, money, and materials reflected both moral and economic considerations, all of which were related to ideas about how skills, knowledge, and competences should be divided between genders, generations, and classes. The article draws on the example of West Germany during the postwar decades, a period in which economics and societal norms underwent profound transformations.

As good Catholics, many churchgoers of Cologne would have had to seriously reconsider their lifestyles after listening to the pastoral letter that was read out to them in early 1955. In this letter, cardinal Josef Frings recalled the dramatic changes in family life since the nineteenth century, many of which he attributed to industrialization, mass production, and mass consumption. "Industry," he declared, "has taken away many functions from the family by producing cheaper and in large quantities what families previously used to have to produce themselves painstakingly."[1] Even the education of children and youths was no longer a family matter, but increasingly delegated to the state, municipal institutions, and the church, the cardinal stated. While for many the easier access to goods and services sounded like a welcome multiplication of options and an easing of the workload, especially after years of deprivation during the Second World War and the postwar years, Frings feared these developments were dangerous. The decreasing importance of household production, he claimed, loosened ties among family members and put the family at risk of disintegration.[2] Since he considered

---

* I would like to thank Jan Logemann, Jürgen Finger and Gabriella Szalay for their helpful comments and suggestions.
1 Quotation from Lukas Rölli-Alkemper, Familie im Wiederaufbau. Katholizismus und bürgerliches Familienideal in der Bundesrepublik Deutschland 1945–1965, Paderborn 2000, p. 89 (all translations, if not otherwise stated, are by the author).
2 Ibid.

families to be the cornerstone of society, such a threat to family life posed a threat to the social fabric at large.

Frings was neither the first nor the only one to be concerned about changes in how households allocated tasks and responsibilities, time and money with regard to the production and use of goods and services. Before him, private individuals as well as politicians, social scientists, pedagogues, economists, and many others had voiced similar opinions on the nature and scope of household tasks and on consumer choices since the mid-nineteenth century. Like Frings, many of these observers focused less on the standard of living and predominantly on modes of provision and thus the ways in which households obtained goods and organized services. Theirs was a specifically modern concern. While the sumptuary laws of pre-modern times regulated which items people could possess and show publicly, mainly in order to preserve social hierarchies, attention in industrialized societies shifted towards the different forms of acquisition and provision, and thus to questions of production and consumption.[3]

To cardinal Frings and many others, it was not economic rationality, cost-efficiency, the functionality of goods, or the quality of services that mattered most. When comparing goods and services purchased on the market with the ones provided by household members, moral concerns, norms, and values were just as much part of the equation as were time and money. How resources were employed was both a moral and an economic question, with far-reaching ramifications: Comparative views on modes of provision entailed ideas about the distribution of skills and knowledge, responsibilities and obligations, and thus about the social order as well as the interrelation between humans and things. As such, they affected views on fundamental questions such as the education of children, the social relations between genders, generations, and classes. They inspired legislation, protest movements and, not least, shaped markets.

Modern households usually obtained goods and services through various channels.[4] Like pieces of cloth assembled in a patchwork quilt, households flexibly combined what they had purchased on the market with household production, public transfer payments and communal provisions, and with what they had inherited, found, stolen, borrowed or received as presents.[5] This article

---

3 On sumptuary laws in pre-modern times see e.g. Frank Trentmann, Empire of Things. How We Became a World of Consumers, from the Fifteenth Century to the Twenty-First, London 2016, pp. 37–43 and p. 63.

4 See as an example Susan Porter Benson, Household Accounts. Working-Class Family Economies in the Interwar United States, Ithaca, NY 2007.

5 For different ways of categorizing modes of provision see Alan Warde, Consumption, Food, and Taste. Culinary Antinomies and Commodity Culture, London 1997, p. 192; Thomas Welskopp, Konsum, in: Christof Dejung et al. (eds.), Auf der Suche nach der Ökonomie. Historische Annäherungen, Tübingen 2014, pp. 125–152, here p. 138; Frank Trentmann, Materiality in the Future of History. Things, Practices, and Politics, in: Journal of British Studies 48. 2009, pp. 283–307, here p. 295.

discusses political, entrepreneurial, and social attempts to influence and direct
household decisions on modes of provision through moralizing them. Its focus
is on household production, from do-it-yourself to home cooking. In an age of
mass markets, the distinction between purchases on the market and household
production as the primary ways of obtaining goods and services in private households was a complex and morally charged affair. Household decisions in this
context, however, not only refer to choices between different modes of provision
since households sometimes did not have a choice due to a lack of money, skills,
or available goods and services. Yet even under conditions of scarcity, household
members had some leeway in deciding how exactly, to which standard, and by
whom a task was to be completed.[6]

From the vast number of groups, institutions, organizations, and individuals that took part in the contested re-negotiating of household production and
consumption, three will be discussed in further detail, preceded by some brief
reflections on private households and their modes of provision as moral economies: first, government institutions and administrative bodies that attempted to
influence household behavior; second, advertisers and market researchers who
sought to sell their products and services; and third, protest movements that
aimed at changing modes of provision in private households from below. Their
suggestions, demands, and actions, as different as they were, each rested upon
the idea that modes of provision interlinked individuals and households with
both society and economy, and therefore with beliefs of what both spheres should
ideally look like, how they should be interrelated, and how household members
should contribute in order to reach that ideal state. Their efforts not only remind
us that households were a central locus of economic activity throughout the
twentieth century. They also remained a crucial focus of moral economies whose
actors frequently defied the logic of rational economic behavior posited by modern economists.

I. Private Households as Moral Economies

How households employed resources had been exposed to normative judgments
well before the postwar years.[7] With industrialization and urbanization, options
for combining different modes of provision had changed fundamentally. Work
outside the home, wages and the purchase of mass-produced items replaced

6 With a plethora of examples on how differently household chores can be conducted, see Jean-
  Claude Kaufmann, Mit Leib und Seele. Theorie der Haushaltstätigkeit, Constance 1999.
7 See Christa Müller, Von der lokalen Ökonomie zum globalisierten Dorf. Bäuerliche Überle-
  bensstrategien zwischen Weltmarktintegration und Regionalisierung, Frankfurt 1998, p. 131;
  Rebekka Habermas, Frauen und Männer des Bürgertums. Eine Familiengeschichte (1750–1850),
  Göttingen 2000, p. 63.

payment in kind and reduced the significance of subsistence economies.[8] As modes of production and consumption changed and an ever-growing variety of ready-made goods touted for customers in a nascent consumer society, temporal structures and forms of time use between paid work outside the home, reproductive labor and leisure changed too. In the face of rapidly changing circumstances, household members and outside observers had to scrutinize hitherto unquestioned routines: How should individual household members use their time? Which products and services should households purchase on the market, which services could they provide themselves? Within the household, how should tasks be divided between generations and genders? And who got to choose modes of provision, and to assign tasks and responsibilities?

Despite these profound transformations, households and their modes of provision have long been a "black box" of mainstream economic theory. The at least partial turn towards the household is linked to the name of Nobel Prize winner Gary Becker. In his 1965 article on the allocation of time he drew attention to household production and thus the productive function of households, rejecting the common view on households as mere consumers of goods and services.[9] A few years later, Becker again gained full attention when applying rational choice theory to spheres of life such as marriage, divorce, racial discrimination, child rearing, and, not least, the division of labor within households, claiming that they were markets dominated by cost-benefit calculation just as much as markets with monetary transactions such as investments in the stock market or the purchase of a new car.[10] Unlike previous economic theories, Becker interpreted moral considerations as part of the calculation, and not as a driving force detached from the quest for utility maximization. To him, norms and values were calculable in a way similar to incomes, skills, or time.[11]

---

8 On the complexity and diversity of economies and wage systems see e. g. Reinhold Reith, Lohn und Leistung. Lohnformen im Gewerbe 1450–1900, Stuttgart 1999; City Archive of Leipzig, Deutscher Verein für Werkunterricht/Lehrerseminar, no. 217, J. Elsenheimer, Der Handfertigkeitsunterricht und die Berufswahl. Referat des Lehrers an der Schülerwerkstätte des Vereins für Verbreitung von Volksbildung im Kursus der Zentrale für private Fürsorge, 4.5.1907, p. 8.

9 Gary S. Becker, A Theory of the Allocation of Time, in: The Economic Journal 75. 1965, pp. 493–517. Becker was by far not the first one to highlight the productive, value-creating work accomplished in the private household and without pay, but gained far more attention than his predecessors. See Maria Silberkuhl-Schulte, Welchen Wert hat die hauswirtschaftliche Arbeit? [1928], in: Hauswirtschaftliche Jahrbücher. Zeitschrift für Hauswirtschaftswissenschaft. Jubiläumsausgabe 50 Jahre, Munich 1978, pp. 57–64; Margaret G. Reid, Economics of Household Production, New York 1934.

10 Gary S. Becker, A Treatise on the Family [1981]. Enlarged Edition, Cambridge, MA 1983.

11 Ibid. On the discussion of Gary Becker's theories see for example June Carbone, Gary Becker. Neoliberalism's Economic Imperialist, in: Damien Cahill et al. (eds.), The SAGE Handbook of Neoliberalism, London 2018, pp. 154–166, here pp. 162–164; Florian Schulz and Hans-Peter Blossfeld, Wie verändert sich die häusliche Arbeitsteilung im Eheverlauf? Eine Längsschnittstudie der ersten 14 Ehejahre in Westdeutschland, in: Kölner Zeitschrift für Soziologie und Sozialpsychologie 58. 2006, pp. 23–49, here p. 43.

Households, I would argue by contrast, present a particularly interesting field of study because they reveal hierarchies and imbalances in power with regard to modes of provision and economic practices as linked to markets. Investigating modes of provision thus depict households very much as moral economies in the sense that moral considerations, norms, and values influenced both decisions on how to use, combine, and exchange resources, and their normative evaluation by household members and society. Moral economies are per se a matter of comparison in which economic and moral standards, expectations, and assumptions about outcomes are constantly compared, prioritized, and negotiated.[12] In fact, the study of modes of household provisioning confirms the extremely close interrelation between resource use and moral valuation, which has been described as the very core of morality.[13] As far as household provisioning is concerned, those whose habits did not fit into the norms of appropriateness faced reactions from ridicule to moral condemnation. Depending on time and context, choices such as buying new clothes instead of darning the old ones, using formula milk instead of breastfeeding a baby, or buying a car on credit instead of saving up for it counted as appropriate or inappropriate behavior and use of resources.[14] Those who violated accepted norms might have saved time or money, but ran the risk of being publicly scolded for neglecting dependents, wasting valuable resources, taking advantage of other household members, or denying them the love, care, and attention they deserved, in short: for getting their priorities wrong.

Here, two aspects deserve special attention. First, household production in (nascent) consumer societies is only very rarely completely detached from the market, but is rather a combination of "episodes" of consumption and production, as sociologist Alan Warde describes it.[15] Preparing a meal from scratch, painting the living room or knitting a sweater usually involves store-bought and industrially manufactured items such as pasta, sausages, salt, paint, a brush, knitting

---

12 On practices of comparison see Johannes Grave, Vergleichen als Praxis. Vorüberlegungen zu einer praxistheoretisch orientierten Untersuchung von Vergleichen, in: Angelika Epple and Walter Erhart (eds.), Die Welt beobachten. Praktiken des Vergleichens, Frankfurt 2015, pp. 135–159.

13 With respect to resources and the economy of social relations see Gabriele Jancke and Daniel Schläppi, Einleitung. Ressourcen und eine Ökonomie sozialer Beziehungen, in: id. (eds.), Die Ökonomie sozialer Beziehungen. Ressourcenbewirtschaftung als Geben, Nehmen, Investieren, Verschwenden, Haushalten, Horten, Vererben, Schulden, Stuttgart 2015, pp. 7–33, here pp. 15 f.

14 See for example Rudolf Wilke, Die Amerikanerin. Betrachtungen eines deutsch-amerikanischen Junggesellen, in: Allgemeine Deutsche Lehrerzeitung 60. 1908, no. 21, pp. 241–243; Flick-Werk. Reparieren und Umnutzen in der Alltagskultur, Stuttgart 1983; Jan Logemann, Americanization through Credit? Consumer Credit in Germany, 1860s–1960s, in: Business History Review 85. 2011, pp. 529–550; Timo Heimerdinger, Brust oder Flasche? Säuglingsernährung und die Rolle von Beratungsmedien, in: Michael Simon et al. (eds.), Bilder. Bücher. Bytes. Zur Medialität des Alltags, Münster 2009, pp. 100–110.

15 Alan Warde, Notes on the Relationship between Production and Consumption, in: id. (ed.), Consumption, vol. 2: Acquisition, London 2010, pp. 163–177, here p. 166.

wool and needles, as well as one's own "labor contribution,"[16] possibly combined with items such as herbs from one's own garden. It is important to note that household production is usually "prosumption"—a mixture of production and consumption—rather than a complete avoidance of market-based consumption.[17] Second, episodes of production and consumption are, at least to a certain extent, interchangeable. A family can eat dinner in a restaurant, have it delivered, heat up a frozen meal or cook from scratch. If they choose the latter, they can decide whether they want to buy the pesto they need in order to prepare a pasta dish, or buy the ingredients necessary to make their own pesto. Likewise, raising children or tending to other household members dependent on care can be left to professional institutions, or nannies and nurses can help with the task within the household, or the household members take care of each other without any outside help. To a certain degree, households can substitute purchased goods and services with their own unpaid labor and vice versa. This characteristic of private households is of particular importance since the combination of "episodes" of production and consumption had implications for the resource allocation in households and, through this, shaped their social structures and relations. It is exactly at this point where normative judgments typically came in.

Controversies regarding modes of provision were all about legitimization, predominantly about the legitimization of practices, norms, and values. Therefore, they can be described as controversies about the "emergence of normative orders."[18] Such orders pervade everyday life. They are "embedded in cultural, economic, political, communicative, and psychological contexts," and manifest themselves in institutions, habitualized practices, social conventions and rituals.[19] With regard to modes of provision, the results of former controversies about normative orders are omnipresent in daily life, from the opening hours of kindergartens and stores to the ritual of home-baked birthday cakes, from thematic priorities in school curricula to state funding for do-it-yourself home renovation. Although such orders often appear to be undisputable facts and not the result

---

16 Kai-Uwe Hellmann, Prosumismus und Protest. Eine Polemik, in: Forschungsjournal Soziale Bewegungen 29. 2016, no. 3, pp. 153–161, here p. 154.

17 The concept of "prosumption" is usually ascribed to futurist Alvin Toffler who predicted that it would become the dominant economic principle of the future. See Alvin Toffler, The Third Wave. The Classic Study of Tomorrow, New York 1980. While Toffler focused primarily on the future, economists, too—most prominently Gary Becker—have explained how households combined goods they had purchased on the market with the labor of household members and with other resources to obtain the commodities they wanted. See Becker, Theory of the Allocation of Time.

18 See Rainer Forst and Klaus Günther, Die Herausbildung normativer Ordnungen. Zur Idee eines interdisziplinären Forschungsprogramms, in: id. (eds.), Die Herausbildung normativer Ordnungen. Interdisziplinäre Perspektiven, Frankfurt 2011, pp. 11–30.

19 Ibid., p. 16 and p. 20. With a focus on the concept of moral economy, see Jaime Palomera and Theodora Vetta, Moral Economy. Rethinking a Radical Concept, in: Anthropological Theory 16. 2016, pp. 413–432, here p. 428.

of controversies and renegotiation based on norms, they could be, and were, frequently challenged.[20]

The postwar decades in West Germany are marked by transformation and intensified renegotiation of previous normative orders. Although recent historiography has emphasized that Germany had turned into a modern consumer society not as late as in the 1950s, but already by the late nineteenth century, the postwar decades nevertheless signal a qualitative change.[21] Household incomes increased rapidly, unemployment rates reached an all-time low, the economy prospered, and an ever-growing range of goods became available in shops.[22] At the same time, employment patterns started to change as well. Slowly, but steadily, married women and even mothers entered the work force.[23] Although considered to be only "surplus income" in addition to the "real" income of male wage earners, the revenues of married women increased the total household income, thus triggering further changes in the distribution of time and money in private households.[24] The example of West Germany during the second half of the twentieth century therefore allows for closer examining a period of transition from war and pre-war scarcity to an "affluent society" (John K. Galbraith).[25]

Yet why were variances with regard to modes of provision objects of morally charged debates, and often perceived as challenges, or even threats, as in the case in cardinal Frings' sermon? Why did anybody care whether someone's child ate lunch at school or at home, or whether others repaired broken objects or bought new ones?[26] To be sure, not all modes of provision have attracted this kind of attention at any given time, and some sectors have hardly been discussed as particularly moral economies. Whether women got their hair colored at the hair salon or used a product from the drugstore, or whether the neighbors booked

20 See Forst and Günther, Herausbildung normativer Ordnungen, pp. 17 f.

21 See Claudius Torp and Heinz-Gerhard Haupt, Einleitung. Die vielen Wege der deutschen Konsumgesellschaft, in: id. (eds.), Die Konsumgesellschaft in Deutschland 1890–1990. Ein Handbuch, Frankfurt 2009, pp. 9–24.

22 See Ulrich Herbert, Geschichte Deutschlands im 20. Jahrhundert, Munich 2014, pp. 619–623, pp. 627 f. and pp. 679–681; Michael Wildt, Am Beginn der "Konsumgesellschaft." Mangelerfahrung, Lebenshaltung, Wohlstandshoffnung in Westdeutschland in den fünfziger Jahren, Hamburg 1994.

23 See Christiane Kuller, Familienpolitik im föderativen Sozialstaat. Die Formierung eines Politikfeldes in der Bundesrepublik 1949–1975, Munich 2004, pp. 60–68.

24 On women's incomes as "additional incomes" (Zuverdienst) and the establishment of part-time jobs as the predominant form of employment for married women in West Germany see Christine von Oertzen, Teilzeitarbeit und die Lust am Zuverdienen. Geschlechterpolitik und gesellschaftlicher Wandel in Westdeutschland 1948–1969, Göttingen 1999.

25 John Kenneth Galbraith, The Affluent Society, Cambridge, MA 1958. On the challenges of affluence in Britain and the U. S. see Avner Offer, The Challenge of Affluence. Self-Control and Well-Being in the United States and Britain since 1950, Oxford 2007.

26 On these examples see Otto Speck, Kinder erwerbstätiger Mütter. Ein soziologisch-pädagogisches Gegenwartsproblem, Stuttgart 1956, p. 45 and pp. 54–57; Alice Weinreb, Hot Lunches in the Cold War. The Politics of School Lunches in Postwar Divided Germany, in: Karen Hagemann and Sonya Michel (eds.), Gender and the Long Postwar. The United States and the Two Germanys, 1945–1989, Baltimore 2014, pp. 227–252.

their holidays through a local travel agency, a catalogue, or online, never caused as much debate as the aforementioned examples. Despite the cyclical swings and unevenness of such debates, however, the general question remains why, and how, different modes of provision were frequently subject to moral evaluation.

Given the growing number of theoretically available options in an affluent society like West Germany, household provisioning was all about choice. Of course choices were structurally restricted in many ways, for example by financial means, access to information, infrastructures, and social pressure. But consumers nonetheless retained a degree of choice and this is where governments, the corporate sector, and social groups tried to intervene through regulations, incentives, or subtle nudging.[27] Opting for a particular mode of provision, however, always meant to forgo alternative options on the market and alternative lifestyle choices. The more options were available, the more important it was to find arguments that legitimized one's choice vis-à-vis others and oneself. The decision which option to pick and how to realize it, however, was only the first step, followed by practices, or, more precisely, by bodily performed practices of consumption and production. As such, practices of consumption and production played a significant role in the creation of identities as images both of the self and the other.[28] Household production interlinked producers, practices, and products in a particular way. Episodes of production and consumption as combined in household production therefore were always also episodes of identity creation, for example as "the breadwinner," "the home improver," "the housewife" or "the environmentalist." From this perspective consumption practices can be described as "technologies of the self," and therefore as a form of managing one's own body with regard to skills and techniques. They can be read as an expression of individual and/or social values and of the role models imposed on them.[29] Morals,

27 See Richard H. Thaler and Cass R. Sunstein, Nudge. Improving Decisions about Health, Wealth and Happiness, London 2009. As an example for a critical assessment of Thaler's and Sunstein's approach and with a broader concept of "choice architecture" see Karen Yeung, The Forms and Limits of Choice Architecture as a Tool of Government, in: Law & Policy 38. 2016, pp. 186–210.

28 How practices of consumption shaped identities between conformity and distinction has long been a topic of scholarly research. See for example Pierre Bourdieu, Distinction. A Social Critique of the Judgement of Taste [French original 1979], Cambridge, MA 1984; Andreas Wirsching, Konsum statt Arbeit? Zum Wandel von Individualität in der modernen Massengesellschaft, in: VfZ 57. 2009, pp. 171–199; Frank Trentmann, Consumer Society RIP. A Comment, in: Contemporary European History 20. 2011, pp. 27–31; Peter-Paul Bänziger, Von der Arbeits- zur Konsumgesellschaft? Kritik eines Leitmotivs der deutschsprachigen Zeitgeschichtsschreibung, in: ZF 12. 2015, pp. 11–38.

29 On the concept of "technologies of the self" see Michel Foucault, Technologies of the Self, in: Luther H. Martin et al. (eds.), Technologies of the Self. A Seminar with Michel Foucault, Amherst 1988, pp. 16–49. See also Maren Möhring, Die Regierung der Körper. "Gouvernementalität" und "Techniken des Selbst," in: ZF 3. 2006, pp. 284–290; Mary Rizzo, Revolution in a Can. Food, Class, and Radicalism in the Minnesota Co-op Wars of the 1970s, in: Etta M. Madden and Martha L. Finch (eds.), Eating in Eden. Food and American Utopias, Lincoln 2006, pp. 220–238, here p. 227.

norms and values entered the debates about modes of provision not only with an eye to individual decisions, but also because of their larger implications for social order and the place of household members within it. If household provisioning appeared to challenge social norms, these modes of production and consumption were no longer just a private affair.

II. Between Coercion and Incentives:
Modes of Provision and the State

Older generations still remember state-imposed restrictions in war and postwar times such as ration cards, the forced quartering of evacuees and refugees, or the prohibition of home-slaughtering and domestic production of butter. Although the administration was eager to present these restrictions as moral obligations on which victory and the survival of the nation depended, such measures were highly unpopular. And although severely sanctioned, violations of these regulations were commonplace.[30] Most citizens felt they were entitled to freely dispose of their possessions such as milk, pigs, and houses as they saw fit, and that the state had no right to interfere as far as the immediate needs of the household were concerned.[31] To this day senior citizens proudly tell stories about how they fooled the local policeman or other authorities, where they hid the sausages made from illegally slaughtered pigs and the butter churn, or how they had "organized" goods beyond their allocated ration.[32] Within a few years after the end of the war, things had gone back to "normal," they usually claimed, thus conveying the impression that state interference in private modes of provision was a thing of the past.

Radical and abrupt interventions of this kind remained indeed an exception in "normal" times. That does not mean, however, that West German authorities did not attempt to suggest lifestyles including modes of provision in private households on the basis of norms and values. On the contrary, they can be seen as

---

30 See for example Erich Langthaler, Schlachtfelder. Alltägliches Wirtschaften in der national-sozialistischen Agrargesellschaft 1938–1945, Vienna 2016, pp. 585–620; Beatrix Herlemann, Der Bauer klebt am Hergebrachten. Bäuerliche Verhaltensweisen unterm Nationalsozialismus auf dem Gebiet des heutigen Landes Niedersachsen, Hannover 1993, pp. 308–321; Jill Stephenson, Hitler's Home Front. Württemberg under the Nazis, London 2006, pp. 207–209.

31 See for example Rudolf Pörtner, Das Haus in der Kronprinzenstraße, in: id. (ed.), Mein Eltern-haus. Ein deutsches Familienalbum, Munich1988⁶, pp. 148–160, here pp. 157 f.

32 Daniela Münkel, Nationalsozialistische Agrarpolitik und Bauernalltag, Frankfurt 1996, p. 379 and p. 383; Elisabeth Domansky and Jutta de Jong, Der lange Schatten des Krieges. Deutsche Lebens-Geschichten nach 1945, Münster 2000, p. 304; Hans Friebertshäuser, Landleben und dörfliche Arbeitswelt in Hessen. Regionalkultur im Umbruch des 20. Jahrhunderts, Husum 2004, pp. 63 f.; Erich Draschba, Kühehüten und Kartoffelfeuer—Eine Kindheit auf dem Dorf, n. p. 2003, p. 224.

institutions and organizations that "produced and popularized [...] and mediated moral knowledge."[33]

Notions of gender relations provide a case in point. Incentives in the welfare system were based on the assumption that mothers, not childcare institutions, should take care of children, as in paragraph 1356 of the German Civil Code according to which, until 1958, wives were both "entitled and obliged to run the household" of the family.[34] Franz-Josef Wuermeling, Christian democrat, father of five and first Minister for Family Affairs in West Germany, declared it to be his duty to "make it easier for women to give up paid work outside the household." Like many others he found that leaving childcare and homemaking to others was not simply a decision between equally legitimate options, but that families with working mothers "suffered" from their being away during the day. Anyone else was just a "replacement."[35] Women who preferred to work outside the home instead of taking care of their children faced being accused of ranking material wishes and their own needs higher than the well-being of their families.[36] It was only in the 1960s that authorities and politicians began to recognize childcare institutions as an important site of childhood education and socialization.[37]

The West German policy towards the feeding of school children was closely interrelated with the question of who should raise children and is yet another striking example of how politics strongly suggested a specific form of provisioning to households. In 1950, the Federal Republic cancelled the school lunch program that had been installed during the occupation years to lessen the tense nutritional situation, making West Germany "virtually the world's only industrialized nation without school lunches."[38] While economic theories usually assumed "that the value of a good is the same whether provided through the market or in some other way," many West German authorities, political parties, scientists, and families thought otherwise.[39] To them, the nature of a meal changed with its commercialization, in this case for worse.[40] Nutrition was not everything that

33 Habbo Knoch and Benjamin Möckel, Moral History. Überlegungen zu einer Geschichte des Moralischen im "langen" 20. Jahrhundert, in: ZF 14. 2017, pp. 93–111, here p. 103.

34 On welfare policies see Dagmar Hilpert, Wohlfahrtsstaat der Mittelschichten? Sozialpolitik und gesellschaftlicher Wandel in der Bundesrepublik Deutschland (1949–1975), Göttingen 2012, pp. 210–270.

35 Franz-Josef Wuermeling, Die Mutter darf kein Aschenbrödel sein. Zur Frage der Berufstätigkeit von Ehefrauen, in: Bulletin des Presse- und Informationsamtes der Bundesregierung, no. 229, 7.12.1956, p. 2175.

36 See Kuller, Familienpolitik, pp. 291–293.

37 Ibid., pp. 294–298.

38 Alice Weinreb, Matters of Taste. The Politics of Food in Divided Germany, 1945–1971, in: Bulletin of the German Historical Institute 48. 2011, pp. 59–82, here p. 74. For more details, see ead., Hot Lunches.

39 Michael J. Sandel, What Money Can't Buy. The Moral Limits of Markets, New York 2012, p. 120.

40 Other forms and contexts of commercialization did not necessarily mean the devaluation of certain goods, for example family lunches at a restaurant. As an economic phenomenon, the "commercialization effect" has been discussed since the mid-1970s. According to political

mattered in a meal, and therefore school lunch was considered inferior to the home cooked meal prepared by a loving mother who ideally was a housewife or worked only part-time.[41] While other states in both the Eastern and the Western bloc promoted school lunches, the West German policy attempted to encourage families to stick to household production.

Likewise, school curricula initially recurred to equip children with skills along gender lines. While girls learned how to sew, knit, mend clothes, cook, and bake, boys were taught how to use tools necessary for woodwork and metalwork. But there was more to such subjects than acquiring manual skills. The 1950 curriculum for *Volksschulen* (primary and lower secondary education) in Bavaria, for example, additionally defined virtues such as frugality and inventiveness as major goals, and declared that children were also to learn how to distinguish between valuable and "genuine" items on the one hand, and artificial "kitsch" on the other.[42] By defining artifacts as either genuine or artificial, children learned that they should rank items according to morally charged standards of good and bad, right and wrong. The paragraphs on needlework and home economics reveal in even greater detail how social norms pervaded school curricula with regard to modes of provision. Again, the teaching of skills and working techniques was combined with the imparting of norms and values. Girls were expected to develop a motherly attitude and learn how their provisioning of the family affected their health, and even the national economy.[43] They shared some of the responsibility for the well-being of the family and the state. By teaching girls gardening techniques, the economic use of resources, and how to cook and bake from scratch, the state of Bavaria sought to ensure that girls knew how to live up to these responsibilities: not by going to the restaurant or heating up canned food, but by preparing home cooked meals according to the standards of healthiness as defined by the state.

Compared to the nineteenth and early twentieth centuries, such efforts to instill preferences for particular modes of provision in children through school education appeared modest with only a few hours of needlework, manual work,

philosopher Michael J. Sandel the concept was first mentioned in Fred Hirsch, Social Limits to Growth, Cambridge, MA 1976. See Sandel, What Money Can't Buy, pp. 120 f.

41 See Speck, Kinder erwerbstätiger Mütter; Erich Reisch, Familie und Zuhause—Die freie Zeit der Familie, in: Julius Dorneich (ed.), Ehe und Familie. Die Familie im Recht. Familienpädagogik. Die Familie in der Gemeinschaft, Freiburg 1959, col. 589–618, here col. 601. See also Weinreb, Hot Lunches.

42 Bayerisches Staatsministerium für Unterricht und Kultus (ed.), Bildungsplan für die bayerischen Volksschulen, Munich 1950, p. 33. Around 1950, roughly 80 percent of West German school children attended the *Volksschule*. The focus on virtues and on the distinction between true and false with respect to artifacts has a tradition that goes back to the origins of what later became manual training for boys *(Werkunterricht)*. See Reinhild Kreis, Mechanisierung als pädagogisches Argument. Schule, Arbeit und Konsum um 1900, in: Jahrbuch für historische Bildungsforschung 20. 2014, pp. 199–217.

43 Bayerisches Staatsministerium für Unterricht und Kultus, Bildungsplan für die bayerischen Volksschulen, pp. 34 f. Here, too, the curriculum continued older traditions. See Kreis, Mechanisierung.

and home economics per week.[44] It was only during the 1970s and 1980s, however, that the unequal treatment of genders vanished (at least in written curricula.) Subjects such as manual work, cooking, and needlework, either disappeared or became mandatory for all children. At the same time, curricula started to pay more attention to consumer education. To be sure, raising awareness for the different qualities of ready-made goods had been, although only occasionally, a topic of debate since the turn of the century.[45] From the 1960s to the 1980s, curricula contained both traditional references to textile work as a preferred and "useful" pastime, and a more progressive perspective which stressed how working with textiles helped children as future consumers to make informed decisions.[46] The focus, however, shifted to consumer education. The guidelines for *Hauptschulen* (successor of the *Volksschulen*, secondary modern schools) in Lower Saxony, for example, declared that students of all genders should "learn about the pros and cons of accomplishing a task through their own or through external labor, and to make decisions according to the needs of the household" by discussing topics such as domestic aid, dry cleaners, or frozen food.[47] By addressing children as consumers and not (only) producers, and by stressing gender equality, the boards of education in the German *Länder* adjusted to changing realities and de-moralized choices between household production and market-based purchases, at least to some degree.[48]

In other cases, it was rather the interpretative framework that changed. Thriftiness and the economical use of resources, long considered one of the most important virtues of a housewife, the prerequisite of successful family life, and therefore an educational goal, made a comeback in the 1970s, now with a focus on the conservation of resources and the preservation of the environment.[49] Publications such as the Club of Rome's 1972 seminal study on the "Limits to Growth" created awareness of the fact that the natural resources were limited, criticized

44 See for example Bärbel Ehrmann-Köpke, "Demonstrativer Müßiggang" oder "rastlose Tätig-keit"? Handarbeitende Frauen im hansestädtischen Bürgertum des 19. Jahrhunderts, Münster 2010, pp. 87–166; on debates on practical school subjects in periodicals for teachers see for example Kreis, Mechanisierung.
45 See ibid.
46 Niedersächsischer Kultusminister (ed.), Richtlinien für die Volksschulen des Landes Nieder-sachsen, Hannover 1963, p. 102; Niedersächsischer Kultusminister (ed.), Rahmenrichtlinien für die Realschule. Textiles Gestalten, Hannover 1984, p. 4 and p. 6.
47 Niedersächsisches Kultusministerium (ed.), Rahmenrichtlinien für die Hauptschule. Arbeit. Wirtschaft. Technik, Hannover 1988, p. 54.
48 As example for the joint education of boys and girls and for the shift towards consumer edu-cation, see Kultusminister des Landes Nordrhein-Westfalen (ed.), Richtlinien und Lehrpläne für die Realschule in Nordrhein-Westfalen. Hauswirtschaft, Cologne 1979, p. 10 and p. 25; Niedersächsischer Kultusminister, Rahmenrichtlinien Realschule, p. 4, p. 6 and p. 16; Nieder-sächsischer Kultusminister, Rahmenrichtlinien Hauptschule, pp. 39–41.
49 On the importance of thriftiness see for example Nancy R. Reagin, Sweeping the German Nation. Domesticity and National Identity in Germany, 1870–1945, Cambridge 2007, p. 18, pp. 36–38, p. 44, p. 48, p. 73, p. 103, p. 113, p. 143 and pp. 156 f.

the obsession with economic growth, and advocated a more responsible use of resources.[50] Among other organizations and institutions, school curricula slowly took up the cause of environment protection, and defined resource-efficiency and awareness of the consequences of one's own consumer behavior as an educational goal.[51] In Lower Saxony, students at *Hauptschulen* were to be prepared for their roles as future consumers by raising "awareness for the necessity to plan and act eco-consciously." Their "consumption behavior," a 1988 document explained, should be "guided by a feeling of responsibility towards nature."[52] Ninth grade students discussed "waste of resources" and learned about managing household supplies from an ecological perspective, and about alternatives to commercially available consumer goods with regard to cleaning products and foodstuffs.[53]

Apart from such future-oriented measures, state authorities began to implement programs that rewarded energy-saving measures of private households in the present. A 1978 law, for example, offered financial support for the refurbishment of apartment buildings and family homes if such measures led to considerable energy savings.[54] The law explicitly stated that do-it-yourself measures were eligible for funding as well. While no financial compensation for working hours was given, owners of family homes and owner-occupied apartments could receive state funding for expenses for supplies and materials related to energy-saving measures. The do-it-yourself industry was delighted, anticipating increased sales of insulating materials. As a consequence of rising energy prices, energy saving materials and measures became a popular topic in the do-it-yourself publications of the late 1970s and 1980s.[55]

These political initiatives to promote certain forms of household supply, resource, and labor allocation, are but a few of many examples of state incentives to change consumption behaviors based on moral considerations. Referring to

50 On the debates on "The Limits to Growth" see Elke Seefried, Zukünfte. Aufstieg und Krise der Zukunftsforschung 1945–1980, Munich 2015, pp. 267–292.
51 See Gerhard de Haan et al., Umweltbildung als Innovation. Bilanzierungen und Empfehlungen zu Modellversuchen und Forschungsvorhaben, Berlin 1997, pp. 5–9 and pp. 14–21; UNESCO-Verbindungsstelle für Umwelterziehung im Umweltbundesamt (ed.), Bericht über die Aktivitäten der Umwelterziehung in Bund, Ländern und überregionalen Institutionen, Berlin 1984.
52 Niedersächsischer Kultusminister (ed.), Rahmenrichtlinien Hauptschule, p. 8 and p. 15.
53 Ibid., pp. 58 f.
54 Bekanntmachung der Neufassung des Gesetzes zur Förderung der Modernisierung von Wohnungen und von Maßnahmen zur Einsparung von Heizenergie (Modernisierungs- und Energieeinsparungsgesetz—ModEnG) vom 12. Juli 1978, in: Bundesgesetzblatt 38. 1978, 18.7.1978, pp. 993–1001; Michael Krautzberger et al., Neue Staatszuschüsse und Steuervergünstigungen für Modernisierungs- und Energieeinsparungsmaßnahmen bei Wohnungen und gewerblichen Gebäuden. Das neue Modernisierungs- und Energieeinsparungsgesetz (ModEnG), Kissing 1978², on the funding of do-it-yourself contributions see ibid., p. 29 and pp. 100–106.
55 Energiesparen wird Gesetz, in: Heimwerkermarkt 1977, no. 7, p. 8. As an example for the various publications on energy saving materials and measures, see a series of articles in the magazine "Selbst ist der Mann" between January and August 1981.

the individual responsibility for the protection and preservation of the family, nature or living standards for the society as a whole, school curricula and legislative measures aimed at making resource efficiency an internalized routine. In a prosperous society in which life-threatening scarcity had diminished since the 1950s and where Minister for Economics Ludwig Erhard had famously promised "prosperity for all," enforcing normative modes of provision by means of compulsion and control became a thing of the past.[56] The more West Germans perceived themselves as "sovereign" consumers, and the higher values such as plurality and individualism ranked, the less likely it was that state authorities would resort to such means, even as new challenges such as the protection of the environment came to the fore. Despite the unease and skepticism with which many political and social observers watched the manifestations of mass consumption, politics limited itself mainly to incentives that awarded benefits as well and offered consumers a sense of "doing the right thing." It is these characteristics that set political attempts to impose moral standards on household provisioning apart from earlier periods characterized by scarcity, and from the East German dictatorship.[57]

III. Morality Sells: Market Research and Advertising

Politicians, parties, and the state were not the only ones who relied on morality in order to popularize particular modes of provision. With an ever-growing range of industrially produced goods entering stores during the postwar decades, advertising became all the more important in order to sell a particular product in an increasingly confusing array of choices. With regard to modes of provision, three types of goods changed established routines: first, products that substituted household production or reduced the domestic labor input to a minimum, such as baby food in glass jars, ravioli with sauce in cans, or ready-to-wear clothes. A second group of goods simplified household production to a considerable degree. Products such as non-dripping paint made redecorating much easier and cake mixes lowered the threshold for those who had little time or were inexperienced bakers. The third group consisted of products that opened up new fields of household production for the masses that previously had been reserved to professionals, like self-adhesive wallpaper, electric drills or seasoning mixes for foreign cuisines. Many of these products had been invented well before 1945,

---

56 Ludwig Erhard, Wohlstand für alle, Düsseldorf 1957.

57 While the West German state usually limited itself to incentives, on the other side of the inner-German border, authorities in the German Democratic Republic expressed their preferences more forcefully. Here, state organs and the Socialist Unity Party SED tried to coerce the East German population to resort to modes of provision that served the interests of the state by referring to moral standards. See Reinhild Kreis, A "Call to Tools": DIY Between State Building and Consumption Practices in the GDR, in: International Journal for History, Culture and Modernity 6. 2018, pp. 49–75.

but achieved commercial success or entered the market for private consumers only during the 1960s.[58] Likewise, advertising and market research were not new phenomena, but had a tradition that reached back to the late nineteenth century and the interwar period.[59] Postwar prosperity, the rise of mass media, and intensified transatlantic exchanges between West German and leading U.S. experts in the field (many of them émigrés from Europe) raised both awareness and budgets for the art of selling.[60]

The newly emerging forms of marketing "engaged in systematic attempts to understand and shape consumer behavior" beyond stimulus-response models.[61] The "consumer engineers" who first revolutionized market research in the Unites States during the 1930s and 1940s and then in Western Europe viewed the prevailing model of the rational *homo oeconomicus* as insufficient for understanding consumer decisions.[62] Drawing on psychological theories and experiments, these experts instead perceived consumers to be diverse, socially contextualized, and influenced by both emotions and values. They tried to identify the motivations behind consumer decisions, which were not necessarily consistent with contemporary notions of accepted and reasonable consumer behavior, and of which consumers themselves were frequently not even aware.[63] The psychology based search for motivations dominated market research in West Germany from the mid-1950s onwards.[64]

---

58 After electric drills were invented in 1895, it took around 60 years before they were sold to private citizens and not only to professional handymen. On the invention of the electric drill see Friedrich Trautmann, Bosch-Elektrowerkzeuge, in: Bosch Zünder 14. 1932, no. 4, pp. 77–80; Robert Bosch AG (ed.), Fünfzig Jahre Bosch 1886–1936, Stuttgart 1936, pp. 184–190. Cake mixes appeared first in stores in the early 20th century, but did not initially take off. See Uwe Spiekermann, Künstliche Kost. Ernährung in Deutschland, 1840 bis heute, Göttingen 2018, pp. 434 f.

59 For a brief overview see Stefan Schwarzkopf, In Search of the Consumer. The History of Market Research from 1890 to 1960, in: D. G. Brian Jones and Mark Tadajewski (eds.), The Routledge Companion to Marketing History, Abingdon 2016, pp. 61–83.

60 See Jan Logemann, Consumer Modernity as Cultural Translation. European Émigrés and Knowledge Transfers in Mid-Twentieth-Century Design and Marketing, in: GG 43. 2017, pp. 413–437.

61 See id., From Wartime Research to Postwar Affluence: European Émigrés and the Engineering of American Wartime Consumption, in: Hartmut Berghoff et al. (eds.), The Consumer on the Home Front. Second World War Civilian Consumption in Comparative Perspective, Oxford 2017, pp. 279–299, here p. 281.

62 On the term "consumer engineer" see Jan Logemann, Transnational "Consumer Engineers." European Immigrants and the Transformation of American Consumer Goods Marketing from the 1920s to the 1960s, Habilitation, University of Göttingen 2018, pp. 16 f. On the prevalence of concepts of "rational consumers" in West German marketing and market research, see Nepomuk Gasteiger, Der Konsument. Verbraucherbilder in Werbung, Konsumkritik und Verbraucherschutz 1945–1989, Frankfurt 2010, pp. 35–37 and pp. 53–67.

63 Logemann, Transnational "Consumer Engineers," pp. 145–148 and pp. 170–175.

64 See Gasteiger, Der Konsument, pp. 68–91.

While the market researchers of the second half of the twentieth century only very rarely used terms such as "moral" or "morality," their studies still revealed consumers to be influenced by and potentially open to moral considerations. As early as in the 1930s, market studies and even a few economists had suspected emotional and social motives behind consumer decisions.[65] The first German market research institute, the Gesellschaft für Konsumforschung (GfK), urged its correspondents to report such motives and unwritten norms with regard to modes of provision.[66] A study on domestic preserving in 1942 concluded that modes of provision between home canning and purchasing cans were motivated economically as well as socially. Some respondents feared they would be considered old-fashioned, the study declared, while others replied that home preserving was an essential feature of an "orderly household." Thus, "rational arguments," as the study called them, could easily be pushed aside by arguments "from another sphere," that is the sphere of values and norms.[67]

By the postwar years, studies began to take the "emotional component" into account more systematically.[68] They contained specific information about the moral economy of customers as a study on cake mixes from the early 1970s illustrates. Asked about their preferences, several women (men were not included in the study) stated they felt "almost like a fraud" or like they were only "pretending to bake although one does not really do a lot" when using a prepared mix.[69] A "guilty conscience," the study concluded, was the main obstacle preventing women from buying cake mixes since women felt they did not "live up to the role of a good housewife" when doing so, but instead considered themselves "wasteful" or "lazy."[70] Baking a cake from scratch, by contrast, was associated with fulfilling the expectations of a "good housewife."[71] At the same time, the study suggested that others indeed sometimes looked down on those who used cake mixes. Women who baked a lot from scratch declared they found people who used mixes "indolent [and] a little lazy." Those who used cake mixes on a regular basis, however, considered others who shared their preference to be modern and open to new experiences.[72] Designed as "psychological concept analysis," such market research studies took emotional and value-related motives into account

---

65 See Anne Schmidt, From Thrifty Housewives to Shoppers with Needs: On a Capitalist Program of Education, in: ead. and Christoph Conrad (eds.), Bodies and Affects in Market Societies, Tübingen 2016, pp. 167–187.

66 Gasteiger, Der Konsument, pp. 41–46.

67 GfK, Ergebnisse einer Untersuchung über die häusliche Vorratshaltung, in: Markt und Verbrauch 14. 1942, no. 3/4, pp. 49–87, here pp. 55 f. and pp. 59 f.

68 As an example see Archive of the Gesellschaft für Konsumforschung [hereafter Archive GfK, S 1972 042], Psychologische Konzeptionsanalyse "Dr. Oetker Sonntagskuchen," November 1972, p. 37. See also Gasteiger, Der Konsument, pp. 68–131.

69 GfK Psychologische Konzeptionsanalyse "Dr. Oetker Sonntagskuchen," p. 40.

70 Ibid., p. 38. The study also identified other reasons that prevented women from buying cake mixes, for example price and taste.

71 Ibid., p. 42.

72 Ibid., pp. 46 f.

when recommending how to best market a product. They revealed a broad spectrum of normative attitudes towards different modes of provision, all of which the company had to keep in mind when marketing their products.

Advertisements are a particularly rich source for moral references with regard to modes of provision. Unlike politicians, state authorities, and social activists, the manufacturers of consumer goods were usually not interested in shaping the social order per se, but in the creation and preservation of markets. Sales figures depended on the predominance of particular modes of provision. Articles such as baking powder, knitting wool, wallpaper or paint only sold well if people baked, knitted, and decorated at home on a regular basis. In order to preserve existing markets and to create new ones, manufacturers and advertising agencies frequently appealed to common moral attitudes prevalent in society that seemed compatible with the products they wanted to sell.

Some strategies lasted for decades. Dr. Oetker, a food giant who first became successful with the popularization of baking powder and pudding mixes around 1900, continuously portrayed women in their adverts as loving mothers and wives who fulfilled their obligations by baking cakes and preparing desserts for their families. The company adjusted their campaigns only very cautiously to the changing realities of the postwar decades. While an advertisement from 1930 portrayed a housewife who "did not shy away from the little trouble" of baking a cake for her loved ones, thus urging onlookers to do the same, the main character of the advertising campaigns in the 1950s, was married and had a job.[73] It was still her responsibility, though, to make her marriage work by hurrying home before her husband returned and preparing desserts for him every night. "A man wants to be won over every day anew," a 1954 TV spot claimed, and recommended that preparing cakes or puddings was the best way to do so.[74] "Men with a sweet tooth have a good character," the narrator continued, but warned at the same time: "Of course only if it [the dessert, R. K.] is a success." The spot left open what kind of male behavior women would be obliged to tolerate if the dessert was a failure, but emphasized once again: "Cake makes men gentle and amicable." Although using a humorous tone, the advertisement suggested that women were to blame if they failed to keep their marriages happy as it was their responsibility and duty.

In order to reassure female consumers of convenience products that they still could be considered good wives and mothers, other advertisement campaigns focused on suggesting reasons why it was legitimate to buy a certain product. Advertisements should offer customers a "moral permit" to indulge in purchasing the items offered to them, West German marketing theorist Hanns Kropff stated in the early 1950s. This verdict still held true during the following decades.[75] In this respect, advertising and marketing were supposed not only to affirm the values and norms customers already held, but to "modify values, norms,

73 Advertisement Dr. Oetker, in: Die kluge Hausfrau 6. 1930, no. 14.
74 The spot is available under: https://www.youtube.com/watch?v=072LrlGvSq8.
75 Quoted after Gasteiger, Der Konsument, p. 52.

preferences, and attitudes," thus getting customers to try out new products and modes of provision.[76]

The broad range of food products proves a good example. When pre-cooked or ready-to-eat meals started to fill supermarket shelves advertisements not only promised that the food tasted as good as a homemade meal, but stressed why it was good to always have a supply at home: when the proverbial "unexpected guests" dropped in, or on holidays, for bachelors, and, finally, for working women who still had to feed a family.[77] All of these suggestions signaled that those who bought prepared meals were neither lazy nor incapable of cooking (with the legitimate exception of single men), but had good reasons to avoid the labor of cooking. Even for those who still worried about falling into disrepute if caught using convenience products some advertisements had a ready answer: "Only you and we know your little secret," Dr. Oetker promised in a 1969 advertisement for a product that made baking a cheesecake easier.[78] Leading others to believe that she had baked a cake completely from scratch—usually considered dishonest and thus not in compliance with moral standards—was excusable if it allowed a woman to keep face.

A similar approach, although more subtle, characterized early advertising campaigns for electric tools such as drills, grinders, and saws that came on the market when home improvement became a popular hobby in the 1950s and 1960s. Here, it was not so much the fact that machines replaced physical work, but the high prices that required legitimization. After all, electric tools still were a costly affair. In 1958, the all-purpose-tool "Combi" by Bosch cost 172 Deutsche Mark.[79] For many households such a sum meant a considerable investment.[80] Advertisements therefore stressed longevity, multiple functions, and the multitude of tasks that could be completed, which made electric tools a good investment.[81] Spending money on do-it-yourself equipment was all the more justifiable since it allegedly benefited family life as well. Advertisements of the 1950s and 1960s in particular depicted men as fathers of a family who were in charge of any home improvement endeavor and did the main work, surrounded by family members who either watched admiringly, or who assisted their fathers and

---

76 Schmidt, From Thrifty Housewives, p. 187.

77 See for example Duke University, Hartmann Center, J. Walter Thompson, Frankfurt Office, Adv. Coll, Box 88, several advertisement campaigns for Maggi, 1958–1964; Advertisement Deutsche Konserven werden immer beliebter, in: Die kluge Hausfrau 1970, no. 38, p. 10; Advertisement Jensen's, in: Die kluge Hausfrau 1970, no. 50, pp. 12f.

78 Advertisement Dr. Oetker, in: Die kluge Hausfrau 1969, no. 16, p. 11. For a similar promise see advertisement Knorr, in: Constanze 1966, no. 34, p. 94.

79 Bosch Archive, EW 005/002, Catalogue "Bosch Combi Elektrowerkzeug MHD," 1958.

80 On incomes and spending patterns during the 1950s see Wildt, Am Beginn der "Konsumgesellschaft," pp. 59–75, particularly p. 66.

81 Bosch Archive, EW 005/002, Catalogue "Bosch Combi Elektrowerkzeug MHD," 1958. See also advertisement Metabo, in: Selbst ist der Mann 1959, no. 1, p. 6; advertisement Emil Lux, in: Selbst ist der Mann 1959, no. 6, p. 427.

husbands.[82] Do-it-yourself was not just about fixing and improving one's place of living, the images suggested, but as importantly an opportunity for men to bond with their children and wives. This way, advertisements for do-it-yourself products fit perfectly into contemporary discourses on fatherhood. From the late 1950s onwards, the patriarchic father of the previous decades gave way to a more democratic and less authoritarian ideal of "gentle fatherhood."[83] Catalogs and advertisements presented do-it-yourself as a way to be one of these new democratic fathers and husbands who had left behind the authoritarian style that had characterized the era of the two world wars: family men, respectable yet approachable, and men whose authority rested within their competence.

These advertisements shared the assumption that a majority of people ascribed particular qualities to handmade and homemade products, all of which rested upon the "ingredient" of personal effort and labor. Such preferences, however, did not mean that manufacturers of ready-made products could not commercially exploit norms and values. Baby food in glasses presents a striking instance to the contrary. The introduction of ready-to-eat meals for babies in the late 1950s was accompanied by large-scale advertising efforts. Infant nutrition had always been a highly controversial subject of debates stigmatizing mothers who did not breastfeed their babies. Only by the 1950s did opinions on artificial food slowly begin to change, but feeding babies industrially produced meals was still not very common.[84]

How did manufacturers attempt to convince mothers to give up feeding their children home-cooked purees? The answer was simple: by playing to fears the baby could be mal- or undernourished. Advertisements made it very clear that mothers still were the ones responsible for their baby's diet and wellbeing. The best way to meet these requirements was to purchase a product that was better than what a mother could offer. Purees in glasses, the advertisements of several brands stressed, were developed and constantly supervised by trained experts who, in contrast to mothers, had devoted their entire professional life to baby foods. Manufacturers claimed they produced vegetables and other foodstuffs according to the latest scientific evidence and without any chemical residues; processed the harvest immediately (whereas "vegetables that you prepare in your kitchen lose so many vitamins"); and the result contained everything a baby

82 See Wolfcraft, Heimwerker-Brevier, Weibern, n. d. [1960s]; Bosch Archive, EW 005/003, Catalogue "Bosch Combi. Das große Heimwerkerprogramm im Baukastensystem," 1965; of the many covers of the magazine *Selbst ist der Mann,* see the first number from November 1957.

83 Till van Rahden, Sanfte Vaterschaft und Demokratie in der frühen Bundesrepublik, in: Bernhard Gotto and Elke Seefried (eds.), Männer mit "Makel." Männlichkeiten und gesellschaftlicher Wandel in der frühen Bundesrepublik, Berlin 2017, pp. 142–156.

84 See for example Spiekermann, Künstliche Kost, pp. 86–106; Verena Limper, Die Säuglings-flasche. Dinghistorische Perspektiven auf Familienbeziehungen in der Bundesrepublik Deutschland und in Schweden (1950–1980), in: ZF 13. 2016, pp. 442–465; Heimerdinger, Brust oder Flasche. On sales numbers in the baby food market see Anon., Markt geräumt, in: Der Spiegel, 20.10.1965, no. 43, p. 98.

needed to be happy and healthy.[85] "No mother can do better than that," one advertisement stated very plainly,[86] and another one asked rather harshly: "Maybe you think that homemade is best? You get 'fresh' spinach, wash it, cook it, and add a little butter. And what is it then that you feed your baby? Vitamin-rich spinach? Spinach free from chemicals? Is the vegetable field right at your doorstep?"[87] If mothers really cared about their babies as society expected them to do, they should not let tradition, personal preferences, or social norms interfere with the food of their children. Being a good mother meant to step back and leave the nutrition to the experts.

In the West German consumers' republic, marketing and market research systematically identified and employed moral norms and values for commercial purposes. This approach was not invented, but fully established and professionalized in the postwar decades. While norms and values with regard to modes of provision remained contested and changed over time, they provided arguments to legitimize consumer choices as part of a morally informed mindset. This, certainly, has very little to say about the effectiveness of such appeals. Measuring the impact of marketing strategies was, and still is, a difficult issue. Nevertheless, by addressing norms and values as a pivotal element of everyday life, marketing and advertising contributed to placing consumers within imagined and performed normative and social orders increasingly shaped by consumption.

IV. Re-adjusting the Moral Compass:
Protest Movements and Household Production

When in the 1970s women in Italy, Great Britain, West Germany, and other countries demanded "wages for housework," their protest might have been the most explicit, concerted revolt against predominant modes of provision in private households ever. The women who initiated the campaign were active members of the women's movement. They categorically rejected the division of labor along gender lines, and, most importantly, the definition of housework as a "labor of love" that did not need to be paid or even acknowledged as productive work. Some feminist historians supported the claims for treating housework the same way as wage work by revealing the historical roots of the allegedly innate differences between genders that had led to notions of biologically determined "sexual stereotypes" and of a "natural" division between wage labor and "labor of love."[88]

85 Advertisement Herbana, in: Brigitte 1962, no. 3, p. 60; advertisement Alete, in: Brigitte 1962, no. 10, p. 32; advertisement Glücksklee, in: Die kluge Hausfrau 1967, no. 8, p. 9.
86 Advertisement Herbana, in: Brigitte 1962, no. 3, p. 60.
87 Advertisement Alete, in: Brigitte 1964, no. 23, p. 149.
88 See the groundbreaking articles by Gisela Bock and Barbara Duden, Arbeit aus Liebe – Liebe als Arbeit. Zur Entstehung der Hausarbeit im Kapitalismus, in: Frauen und Wissenschaft. Beiträge zur Berliner Sommeruniversität für Frauen Juli 1976, Berlin 1977, pp. 118–199; Karin

"Wages for housework" questioned views according to which household production such as cooking, baking, care work, sewing, cleaning, mending, deco-
rating, and so on was labor women did out of love for their families. Household
production, the protesters argued, paid off only as long as women were denied a
wage that corresponded to the labor they actually performed. If women were
paid according to their performances as "teachers and nurses and secretaries
and prostitutes and actresses and kindergarten teachers and hostesses and wait-
resses and maids-of-all-work," the basis on which household decisions on modes
of provision were made would disappear.[89] By juxtaposing fairness and justice
with current normative orders, the campaign attempted to replace one set of
moral values with another. While demands for "wages for housework" were
highly controversial within the women's movement, there was no doubt about
the injustice of a society that took female unpaid labor for granted and severely
limited women, not least in their chances to decide for themselves on modes
of provision.[90] Notwithstanding the internal differences and political reluctance
to implement laws that made domestic labor paid work, the campaign caused
"fundamental debates about what labor was and how labor, love, and gender were
interrelated" in politics, media, and society.[91]

It was not so much the idea of household production per se that caused protest,
but the unequal distribution of chances, opportunities, and expectations along
gender lines. In many ways, household production actually boomed during the
1970s and 1980s within the alternative milieu, which also included the women's
movement. The alternative milieu was eco-sensitive and strived for gender equality, criticized capitalism, traditional institutions from the state to the churches
to the family, and searched for a life in harmony with nature, with one another,
and, not least, with oneself.[92] Household production emerged as an inherent

Hausen, Family and Role-division. The Polarisation of Sexual Stereotypes in the Nineteenth
Century. An Aspect of Dissociation of Work and Family Life [German original 1976], in:
Richard J. Evans and W.R. Lee (eds.), The German Family. Essays on the Social History of
the Family in Nineteenth- and Twentieth-Centuries Germany, London 1981, pp. 51-83. For
international campaigns see Silvia Federici and Arlen Austin (eds.), Wages for Housework. The
New York Committee 1972-1977. History, Theory, Documents, New York 2017.

89 Pieke Biermann and Gisela Bock, Lohn für Hausarbeit vom Staat für alle Frauen, in: Courage
2. 1977, no. 3, pp. 16-21.

90 The most prominent feminist opponent of such demands was Alice Schwarzer who argued that
wages for housework would tie women to the household only stronger. She rather recommended
housework should be divided equally between partners. See Alice Schwarzer, Hausfrauenlohn?,
in: Emma 1977, no. 5, p. 3.

91 Ilse Lenz, Die Neue Frauenbewegung macht sich an die Arbeit, in: ead. (ed.), Die Neue
Frauenbewegung in Deutschland. Abschied vom kleinen Unterschied. Eine Quellensammlung,
Wiesbaden 2009, pp. 145-150, here p. 148.

92 See Sven Reichardt, Authentizität und Gemeinschaft. Linksalternatives Leben in den siebziger
und frühen achtziger Jahren, Berlin 2014. According to contemporary opinion surveys, roughly
10 to 15 percent of the younger generations described themselves either as being a part of
the alternative milieu, or as sympathizing with their attitudes and lifestyles. Since methods

part of such lifestyles, together with other alternative modes of provision such as purchases in second-hand stores, at flea markets, and in third-world stores. In alternative circles, knitting and weaving burgeoned, people built their own furniture from pallets and orange crates, and tie-dyed clothes. Some moved to communes in the countryside and tried, more or less successfully, to live off the land they cultivated.[93] Alternative lifestyles of this kind originated in the desire to distance oneself from prevalent consumption patterns, family structures, and commercial pressures, and to reconcile work and life, which were thought to be disintegrating in modern capitalist societies.[94]

The squatters of the early 1980s took such claims to a new level. In many West European and West German cities, adherents of the alternative milieu resorted to occupying empty and dilapidated buildings as an act of self-help, and in order to protest against what they perceived as a failed and misguided housing policy.[95] A small group within the West German squatter scene did not stop at illegally occupying houses in order to fight the housing shortage, but started to publicly renovate the buildings they had secretly moved into. None of these buildings, they claimed, needed to be torn down, rebuilt and rented out for sums only the better-off could afford as they suspected was the plan of many of the house owners who let their houses stay empty and rot.[96] By publicly occupying and repairing "their" buildings, the so-called *Instandbesetzer* aimed at raising awareness of goals such as affordable housing, the preservation of neighborhoods, open community spaces, the integration of life and work, equally distributed responsibilities, and ecological thinking. From this perspective, do-it-yourself not only referred to a mode of provision, but also to a mode of shaping the social environment, thus creating close ties between the household members, the neighborhood, and the house itself. While many politicians and citizens as well as parts of the media denounced the squatters as criminals, the occupiers also received considerable moral and financial support. It was not least the do-it-yourself approach that raised sympathies and made ordinary citizens across generational, professional and gender lines question housing policy and demand increased participation of citizens in urban development projects.

Living in accordance with such self-imposed standards, however, proved to be quite difficult. Not least with regard to modes of provision, many critics of

---

and definitions differed substantially, it is hard to extract exact numbers. The surveys show, however, that the alternative milieu consisted of "substantial parts of society and was popular among the younger generations." Ibid., pp. 41–43.

93 Ibid., pp. 351–497 and pp. 636–641.

94 Ibid., pp. 319–360.

95 See ibid., pp. 498–571.

96 On squatters who renovated houses (the so-called *Instandbesetzer*) see here and in the following Reinhild Kreis, Heimwerken als Protest. Instandbesetzer und Wohnungsbaupolitik in West-Berlin während der 1980er-Jahre, in: ZF 14. 2017, pp. 41–67. For an overview of the squatter movement since the 1970s in (West) Berlin, where most of the squatters lived, see the interactive map on: http://berlin-besetzt.de/

mainstream norms and values found it hard to change their routines. In popular how-to-guides everything sounded quite easy. In his two-volume "Handbook for better days," architect Rudolf Doernach promoted household subsistence as a way of achieving self-determination. He provided his readers with instructions on how to make everything themselves, from building a house to producing one's food, from solar energy to candles.[97] "Good foodstuffs," he claimed, "can never come from some loveless, alienated fodder-production for humans from god-knows-where. One can only make them oneself." He even went as far as to state "You only love what you can make yourself: candles, foodstuffs, society ..."[98] Although the author of a handbook himself, Doernach remained skeptical towards instructions. With regard to baking bread he wrote that the "self-invented and self-tested [is] always the best," thus inviting his readers to devise their own recipes.[99] The same, he wrote, held true for houses: "No one can make a better [plan] than you, for it is your house."[100]

In real life, things were not as easy. Bernd Leineweber, a sociologist, philosopher, and member of a commune in the Bavarian countryside, frequently struggled with how to live "properly." In his diary he noted: "We have difficulties to set [...] priorities. There are no reliable criteria with regard to decisions on economic behavior between consumption and saving, new purchases and re-use, spontaneity and organization of work, and so on."[101] He felt that "it is unclear whether work, better organization, saving, etc. are legitimate elements of planning," and wondered "whether a gentle use of resources really should demand our attention."[102] The principles of self-sufficiency with regard to foodstuffs and the renovation of the buildings, however, were never questioned. Working together, Leineweber felt, strengthened the group as a community.[103] Likewise, *Instandbesetzer* struggled with questions of morality such as how to deal with slackers, or with thefts of tools and materials, all of which led to endless and exhausting debates about working hours, responsibilities and levels of privacy.[104] Again it is evident that moral considerations with regard to the allocation of resources not only took into account the quality of goods and services, but also their impact on interpersonal relationships, social order, and the interrelation between humans and things.

97 Rudolf Doernach, Handbuch für bessere Zeiten, vol. 1: Bauen + Wohnen, Kleidung, Heimwerk, Wasser; vol. 2: Nahrung, Tiere, Energie, Bio-Mobile, both Stuttgart 1983.
98 Doernach, Handbuch, vol. 2, p. 32.
99 Ibid.
100 Doernach, Handbuch, vol. 1, p. 19.
101 Bernd Leineweber, Pflugschrift. Über Politik und Alltag in Landkommunen und anderen Alternativen, Frankfurt 1981, p. 59.
102 Ibid., p. 60.
103 Ibid., p. 59 and p. 61.
104 See for example Bernd Laurisch, Kein Abriß unter dieser Nummer. 2 Jahre Instandbesetzung in der Cuvrystraße in Berlin-Kreuzberg, Gießen 1981, pp. 108–116; Annette, Was hält mich hier bloß?, in: Häuserkampf, vol. 2: Wir wollen alles, Hamburg 2013, pp. 185–188.

Whereas the visions of protest groups and the alternative milieu in general often clashed with reality, their lifestyle choices did not remain without consequences. "Wages for housework" revitalized and pushed discourses about gender inequalities.[105] Later, feminist groups went even further and questioned predominant economic theories in general, arguing that allegedly objective studies such as Gary Becker's theory of New Home Economics were in fact highly normative and ignored hierarchies, desires, and individual interests within the household. They demanded nothing more than economic theories which took into account gender as a category as well as female perspectives, and which acknowledged that current concepts of national economics were highly gendered.[106] State authorities and political parties, too, had to acknowledge that they could not simply ignore the demands, concerns, and preferences of those who called for a re-adjustment of norms and values. The resulting programs, laws, and initiatives, however, did not go far enough in the eyes of the protesters, whereas state authorities and political parties felt they could not concede more.

The policy of the West Berlin Senate towards the squatter scene illustrates this dilemma. While fighting squatters as criminals who illegally occupied empty houses, the Senate also came to the conclusion that the city benefited from people who did not wait for others, but took matters in their own hands, and who had come up with an idea of how to improve the housing situation that was well worth considering. As a result, the city initiated a program that was the first to fund do-it-yourself renovations in turn-of-the-century apartment buildings.[107] By signing the subsidy agreement, however, the groups had to agree to the rules made by the city regarding use of spaces, quality, and organization of work.[108] Turning self-help into a state-sponsored program at the same time acknowledged and domesticated alternative modes of provisions. Put differently, examples like this show the opportunities and limitations in the process of "public re-negotiation between established norms on the one hand side and reflexive morality on the other."[109]

105 On the establishment and structures of West German "wages for housework" groups see Denise Lehner, "A New Ground for Struggle." Kulturelle Deutungsmuster und soziale Praktiken in der Debatte um einen "Lohn für Hausarbeit" in der autonomen Frauenbewegung der BRD in den 1970er Jahren, Master Thesis, University of Göttingen 2015.

106 See Edith Kuiper, Ökonomie. Feministische Kritik mikro- und makroökonomischer Theorien und Entwurf alternativer Ansätze, in: Ruth Becker and Beate Kortendieck (eds.), Handbuch Frauen- und Geschlechterforschung. Theorie, Methoden, Empirie, Wiesbaden, 2010³, pp. 591–600.

107 Kreis, Heimwerken als Protest, pp. 54–56.

108 Ibid., pp. 62–67.

109 Knoch and Möckel, Moral History, p. 96.

V. Conclusion

Histories of the Federal Republic of Germany often stress liberalization, pluralization, diversification, and individualization as defining developments of the postwar decades.[110] Norms and values that had long determined lifestyles and social status loosened their grip and lost their exclusiveness, and options multiplied with regard to lifestyles as well as consumer products and modes of provision. Why, then, did morals still matter when it came to the question how households provided themselves with goods and services? Why was the household still a moral economy?

Multiple options altered the role of moral considerations with regard to modes of provision fundamentally. In an affluent society, older frameworks of orientation proved to be insufficient. With regard to the allocation of time, money, and other resources, and to the shaping of social relations, what was considered legitimate and appropriate behavior? What could one legitimately claim and expect to have and to be? What could others legitimately expect to receive in terms of material goods, attention, and commitment? With growing options, norms and values did not only mark the (widening) boundaries of which behavior was considered appropriate, but offered guidance, orientation, and legitimization. References to norms and values served to support one's choices and, at times, to delegitimize others; they helped set priorities and shape both group and individual identities.

This was, however, a two-way street. Not only did people get to choose between different options, but mediators such as the state, schools, and advertisers frequently attempted to influence choices and practices as the examples have shown. As more options were available and competed with one another, moralizing options was one strategy to channel decision making processes. Modes of provision gained importance, because they had the power to strongly affect markets. The rise of the do-it-yourself industry between the 1950s and 1980s is a case in point. The multi-million Deutsche Mark market produced an ever-increasing range of materials, tools, and publications available for amateurs, and developed a new infrastructure of big box home improvement stores. For traditional craftspeople and small businesses this development proved to be a major challenge. In a desperate (and unsuccessful) move, craft organizations resorted to denigrating home improvement as black labor that jeopardized jobs, thus attempting to morally discredit a common hobby and a new mode of provision.[111]

Politicians, state authorities, protest groups, church officials like cardinal Frings, and others cared less about sales figures and infrastructures and more

---

110 See for example Andreas Rödder, Deutschland einig Vaterland. Die Geschichte der Wiedervereinigung, Munich 2009, p. 32; Herbert, Geschichte Deutschlands, p. 946, Edgar Wolfrum, Die geglückte Demokratie. Geschichte der Bundesrepublik Deutschland von ihren Anfängen bis zur Gegenwart, Stuttgart 2006, pp. 187–326.

111 See Jonathan Voges, "Selbst ist der Mann." Do-it-yourself und Heimwerken in der Bundesrepublik Deutschland, Göttingen 2017, pp. 126–150.

about the social and cultural consequences of changing habits and values. As daily routines, modes of provision were inscribed into bodies and minds, they represented and structured social orders, and affected how humans defined their interrelationship with things and the material environment in general. It was precisely because of such far-reaching consequences that modes of provision continued to be of interest to actors beyond the economic sphere.

Normative sources such as school curricula, advertisements, and political programs highlight intentions, not results. They do not reveal whether incentives had the desired effect, whether arguments convinced those they were targeted at, and whether attempts to moralize household decisions in general turned out to be successful. The overwhelming presence of values and norms in debates about modes of provision and household decisions, however, clearly indicates that they not only reflected existing preferences, but also helped to shape consumer choices and the social order.

Till Großmann

Moral Economies of Love and Labor in the GDR*

Family Values and Work Ethics in Advice Correspondence, circa 1960

Abstract: The article discusses the emergence of an East German middle-class habitus through public debates on marriage, gender roles, and work along with campaigns on the formation of the "socialist man." Hence, the realms of "family" and "economy" became closely linked sites of intensified moral disputes from the late 1950s to the mid-1960s. Focusing on readers' letters to the physician and author Rudolf Neubert, the article analyses ensembles of debates and practices as moral economies: they shaped values, emotions, and knowledge at workplaces and within families that both helped to establish and subvert values that were perceived as socialist.

In May 1967, Edith Wartburgk, a married woman with a job and a mother of two children, sought out professional advice about her marital issues. The 33-year-old turned to Rudolf Neubert, a well-known author and a professor of public health in Jena. She had read his "Fragen und Antworten" (Questions and Answers), an advice book on marriage, family, and sexuality, and felt inspired to write a letter of her own.[1] In it, she described her monotone everyday life:

I married in 1955. It was true love. But I can feel none of that any longer. My husband has become so indifferent and only thinks about himself and his own comfort. When he gets home from his shift the television starts barking.[2]

Wartburgk dreamt of going hiking, taking walks through the city, eating out, and going to the theater. She complained of being overburdened with her household chores and of being chronically nervous. She yearned for her and her husband to be a romantic couple. She made vague references to the promises of the socialist lifestyle, but only in order to criticize her breadwinner husband's ignorance of the strain she had to bear. Rudolf Neubert showed understanding for her outrage. His answer assured her that she was only demanding her "normal rights" as a

---

* Translated from the German by Adam Bresnahan.
1 Rudolf Neubert, Fragen und Antworten zum Neuen Ehebuch und zur Geschlechterfrage, Rudolstadt 1960.
2 Sächsisches Hauptstaatsarchiv Dresden [hereafter HStA], Personennachlass Rudolf Neubert 12741, no. 92, letter to Rudolf Neubert, Schwerin 26.5.1967, p. 1. All names of the letters' authors have been changed.

wife.[3] Up through the 1980s, most East Germans had similar desires: like Edith Wartburgk, they sought happiness in family life and occupational fulfillment.[4]

East German debates on morality, happiness, and self-realization were fused together in social discussions about marriage and family.[5] For the leadership of the governing Socialist Unity Party, the SED, these issues posed concerns about social demographics that had to be reconciled with economic interests and ideological positions like the ideal of the working woman. The party's "political economy" of building socialism weaved together morality and economics. Drawing on the young Marx, it set as one of its aims the liberation of the emotions, including love.[6] In 1884, Friedrich Engels bolstered Marx' critique of bourgeois marriage and family by situating the latter in the history of relations of ownership and production; August Bebel gave force to this claim in the service of the political project of women's emancipation.[7] The Leninist canon of Marxism prioritized the implementation of a socialist economy as a necessary condition for achieving equality of the sexes.[8] But how exactly socialist morals should be transported on the conveyor belt that ran from the factory floor to the living room was a matter of public debate.[9] In the 1950s, Rudolf Neubert became a prominent participant in discussions on what the "new marriage" was to look like. Up through the 1970s, Neubert engaged in thousands of written correspondences in which readers— men and women alike—related their marital problems.[10] In the following, I will demonstrate how these debates and exchanges of letters, which were grappling with how to make workplace and family into sites of self-realization for both

---

3 Ibid., no. 92, carbon copy, letter by Rudolf Neubert, [Dresden] 26.6.1967.

4 As claimed by GDR sociology, see Uta Starke and Kurt Starke, Einleitung. Liebe und Sexualität im Leben junger Menschen, in: Kurt Starke and Walter Friedrich (eds.), Liebe und Sexualität bis 30, Berlin (GDR) 1984, pp. 14–26.

5 Donna Harsch, Revenge of the Domestic. Women, the Family and Communism in the German Democratic Republic, Princeton 2007, pp. 2–11. On the power of the SED to enforce norms, see Andrew I. Port, Love, Lust, and Lies under Communism. Family Values and Adulterous Liaisons in Early East Germany, in: Central European History 44. 2011, pp. 478–505.

6 In the 1950s, GDR authors would quote Marx from an edition of the complete collection the so-called "Marx-Engels-Gesamtausgabe" (MEGA), edited in the USSR 1932. See the translation Karl Marx, Economic and Philosophic Manuscripts of 1844, in: id. and Friedrich Engels, Collected Works, vol. 3: "March 1843–August 1844," London 2010, pp. 229–346, here pp. 299–302 and p. 326.

7 First postwar editions of Engel's and Bebel's work were published in 1946. See their translations August Bebel, Woman under Socialism [1879], New York 1904; Friedrich Engels, The Origin of the Family, Private Property, and the State [1884], Chicago 1909.

8 A popular Soviet advice guide in the GDR was Anton S. Makarenko, Ein Buch für die Eltern [1937/50], Berlin (GDR) 1952. In the GDR, Lenin's take on marriage was discussed via referencing Clara Zetkin, Erinnerungen an Lenin [1929], Berlin (GDR) 1958², pp. 66–74.

9 See John Griffith Urang, Legal Tender. Love and Legitimacy in the East German Cultural Imagination, Ithaca, NY 2010, pp. 63–79.

10 The collection of epistolary exchanges between 1955 and 1976 can be found in HStA, 12741, nos. 59–100.

sexes, drew on traded middle-class ideals, and this despite their rhetorical commitment to the formation of a proletarian culture.[11]

This article describes the debates on the relation between workplace and family life as moral economies and analyzes one concrete site where these debates were carried out, namely in Rudolf Neubert's written correspondence with his readers. The concept of moral economies enables a heuristic perspective. It lays bare how vocabularies used to describe actions as both moral and economic mutually reinforced one another and opened space for agency.[12] The article details how letter writers developed specific forms of communication to address issues of family and work, morality and economy. The epistolary exchanges drew on knowledge about and techniques of self-representation that had been deployed in the first half of the twentieth century to prop up middle-class mores of family and working life.

Considering the aggressively anti-bourgeois public rhetoric in the GDR, to describe its hegemonic norms as "bourgeois" would not resonate with the historic self-understanding of East Germans. The self-descriptions contained in the letters to Neubert can neither be reduced to the notion of a self-defined bourgeoisie that sought refuge in private life, nor can they be simply described as a "yearning for bourgeois forms of living" driven by knowledge of the capitalist alternative embodied by West Germany.[13] Rather, the article shows how the letters' authors revived a middle-class habitus by making it fit with the ideal of the socialist personality and the conditions of postwar East German society.

Dagmar Herzog has compared the socialist state to the rapid transformation of values that took place in West Germany around 1968 in order to demonstrate that in the GDR, the dividing lines separating gender roles began to blur earlier.[14] One should be careful to note, though, that the history of state socialism cannot be told as a story of liberalization. The model state, the Soviet Union, had, since the 1930s, been enforcing pro-birth policies that criminalized abortion, made divorce more difficult, and retracted the reforms made on these issues in the 1920s.[15] In her research on postwar Czechoslovakia, Kateřina Lišková tells of

---

11 "Middle class" is used in this paper as an analytical concept to identify continuities. In the GDR, "bourgeois" and "bourgeoisie" were politicized concepts that had lost their sociological precision.

12 Didier Fassin, Compassion and Repression. The Moral Economy of Immigration Policies in France, in: Cultural Anthropology 20. 2005, pp. 362–387, here pp. 365 f.

13 See Karl-Siegbert Rehberg, Metamorphosen des Bürgertums. Reflexionen angesichts der Dresdner Entwicklung vom Residenzbürgertum zum Refugiumsbürgertum, in: Dresdner Hefte 26. 2008, no. 93, pp. 90–97; Peter Hübner, Das Jahr 1961 und die Kontinuität der Arbeitergeschichte in der DDR, in: id. and Klaus Tenfelde (eds.), Arbeiter in der SBZ—DDR, Essen 1999, pp. 15–38, here p. 34.

14 Dagmar Herzog, Sex after Fascism. Memory and Morality in Twentieth-Century Germany, Princeton 2007², pp. 184–219.

15 On the marginalization of non-heterosexual lifestyles in socialist states, see ead., Sexuality in Europe. A Twentieth-Century History, Cambridge 2011, p. 60, p. 75, pp. 100–106 and p. 130.

how, under the auspices of equality, gender relations were publicly debated and individual rights expanded, while after 1968 gender hierarchies came to be seen as a remedy for sinking birthrates and rising rates of divorce.[16] An analysis of East German readers' letters around 1960, the social background of their authors, their writing techniques and vocabulary, and Neubert's interpretation of them, can help refine some of our extant knowledge on advice literature in the GDR.[17] These epistolary exchanges offer insight into the genesis of new ideas about how life could or should be lived without leading us into the trap of tired dichotomies like collectivism and individualism, regime and individual.[18]

The conflicts expressed in the letters shine some light on how decisions, ideas, and interpretations gained force in gender relations and in occupational, familial, and political hierarchies.[19] Drawing on a similar corpus of readers' letters from Switzerland, scholars like Annika Wellmann and Peter-Paul Bänziger have traced out the productivity of introspective writing about the body and feelings as a form of "work on the self."[20] Similar processes can be seen outside capitalist consumer societies. In his study of Soviet diaries from the 1930s, Jochen Hellbeck identified an ethics of revolutionary individualism that informed practices of diaristic self-transformation.[21] I will show that in their correspondence with Neubert, East German seekers of advice learned how to grapple with frictions between family and occupation in the GDR and how to work on themselves. Investigating letters that dealt with love, I suggest that emotions help to configure moral economies. The bodily and linguistic dimensions of emotions never capture each other fully. People continuously negotiate and alter this uncertainty as emotions are solidified

---

16 Kateřina Lišková, Sex under Socialism. From Emancipation of Women to Normalized Families in Czechoslovakia, in: Sexualities 19. 2016, pp. 211–235.

17 On the thesis that SED and the public give in on matters of sexual morality due to pressure "from below," see Josie McLellan, Love in the Times of Communism. Intimacy and Sexuality in the GDR, Cambridge 2011, pp. 9 f. On advice literature see ibid., pp. 84–106. See also Eric Hunecke, Sex, Sentiment, and Socialism. Relationship Counseling in the GDR in the Wake of the 1965 Family Law Code, in: Scott Spector et al. (eds.), After the History of Sexuality. German Genealogies with and beyond Foucault, New York 2013, pp. 231–247.

18 For a plea for an analysis of everyday practices, see Wolfgang Engler, Die Ostdeutschen. Kunde von einem verlorenen Land, Berlin 1999, pp. 7 f. On marital and sexual morality see ibid., pp. 233–273. However, Engler's emphasis on everyday life points out the problematic identification of "individuality" and dissent.

19 Paul Betts, Within Walls. Private Life in the German Democratic Republic, Oxford 2010, p. 18. See also Harsch, Revenge.

20 Annika Wellmann, Beziehungssex. Medien und Beratung im 20. Jahrhundert, Cologne 2012, p. 12 and pp. 20–22; Peter-Paul Bänziger, Sex als Problem. Körper und Intimbeziehungen in Briefen an die "Liebe Marta," Frankfurt 2010, pp. 41–47; id., Liebe tun. Arbeiten an einer Emotion am Ende des 20. Jahrhunderts, in: Historische Anthropologie 17. 2009, pp. 1–16.

21 Jochen Hellbeck, Revolution on My Mind. Writing a Diary under Stalin, Cambridge, MA 2006, pp. 6–9, pp. 48–50 and pp. 347–359; Igal Halfin, Intimacy in an Ideological Key. The Communist Case of the 1920s and 1930s, in: id. (ed.), Language and Revolution. Making Modern Political Identities, London 2002, pp. 185–213.

in "emotional lexicons" and stabilized in rules and expectations, just as they have to be expressed and confirmed in social practice.[22] Therefore, I argue, emotions are deeply intertwined with the formation of dearly held or contested values and norms as well as the reasoning that sustains them.

Alongside a cursory survey of the some 2,700 exchanges Neubert had with his readers between 1955 and 1968, the article conducts a qualitative analysis of select correspondences. In the first section, I will offer a brief sketch of some key concepts of work morality and emotion rules that the SED and popular organizations made use of up through the mid-1960s to project new ideas about the relation between work life and family life. The second section then details the basic elements of Rudolf Neubert's scientifically informed advice literature. The third section lays out the topics of the epistolary exchanges. The forth part then analyzes the praxis of introspective and dialogical writing.[23] By treating epistolary exchanges as parts of the moral economies operating between families and workplaces, the article shows how authors' attitudes, emotions, and actions gained contour through their writing as well as through their attempts to frame their emotions in relation to public debates. Thus, the article seeks to understand the continuity of middle-class work ethics and family morality in the GDR and the ways in which they were adapted anew, influenced by and in turn, influenced discussions on gender equality in the "workers' and peasants' state".

I. The Morality of Work and the Joys of Life— Emotional Rules of the SED around 1960

GDR historiography has shown how the image of the industrial worker was invested with emotion in order to spur people to adopt an optimistic outlook, be proud, and feel a sense of honor in high-performing work.[24] Up through the mid-1960s, the industrial worker was viewed as the ideal-typical embodiment of the freedom promised by socialist relations of production and stood at the center

22 Ute Frevert, Defining Emotions. Concepts and Debates over Three Centuries, in: ead. et al., Emotional Lexicons. Continuity and Change in the Vocabulary of Feeling 1700–2000, Oxford 2014, pp. 1–31; Peter N. Stearns and Carol Z. Stearns, Emotionology. Clarifying the History of Emotions and Emotional Standards, in: American Historical Review 90. 1985, pp. 813–836; Monique Scheer, Are Emotions a Kind of Practice (And Is That What Makes Them Have a History)? A Bourdieuian Approach to Understanding Emotion, in: History and Theory 51. 2012, pp. 193–220.

23 Philipp Sarasin, Reizbare Maschinen. Eine Geschichte des Körpers 1765–1914, Frankfurt 2001, pp. 19–28, pp. 57 f., pp. 124–136 and pp. 211–217.

24 Rainer Gries and Silke Satjukow, "Wir sind Helden." Utopie und Alltag im Sozialismus, Erfurt 2008, pp. 25–38; Sylka Scholz, Vom starken Helden zum zärtlichen Vater? Männlichkeit und Emotionalität in der DDR, in: Manuel Borutta and Nina Verheyen (eds.), Die Präsenz der Gefühle. Männlichkeit und Emotion in der Moderne, Bielefeld 2010, pp. 203–228.

Till Großmann

of the officially propagated emotionology.[25] In the face of a shortage of labor power, resources, and modern industrial infrastructure, party and economic functionaries sought to mobilize the mental energy of East Germans by altering their "attitude towards work."[26] After 1953 and again after 1958, public campaigns began increasingly targeting the family as a site of personality development. Following the 17 June 1953 uprising, the party's "New Course" included a revised understanding of the relationship between the workplace and other spheres of life.[27] The happiness of the family was no longer to be subordinated to economic primacy, but was granted its own autonomy. At the same time, this autonomy gave the party occasion to identify individual lifestyles as preserves of outmoded attitudes, making them a legitimate subject for state-socialist interventions.[28] In the wake of the Fifth Party Congress of the SED in 1958, the party and popular organizations claimed that it was their responsibility to educate people on how to lead their lives—both at home and in the factory—in accord with what was vaguely called "Socialist Morality and Ethics." Beginning in 1959, the brigade movement translated the new party line into their motto "Work, learn, and live socialism," which fused together personality development and increased productivity. It encouraged workers to show interest in their colleagues' private lives, feel for them, and help each other; but it also encouraged them to be on the lookout for and intervene in allegedly immoral behavior, such as heavy drinking, dawdling at work, or infidelity.[29]

The public depictions of activists and workers' brigades foregrounded the rationalization of and emotional identification with one's work. The brigade movement emphasized more than friendship and camaraderie as goals of the collegial emotional culture. It also valorized emotions from family life: In newspaper articles on exemplary brigades, the competent, empathetic leaders were always dependable husbands and fathers who were capable of applying the emotional

---

25 In 1950, 40% of working people in the GDR worked in construction and industry. Staatliche Zentralverwaltung für Statistik (ed.), Statistisches Jahrbuch der Deutschen Demokratischen Republik 1970, Berlin (GDR) 1971, pp. 52f.

26 Rüdiger Hachtmann, Rationalisierung, Automatisierung, Digitalisierung. Arbeit im Wandel, in: Frank Bösch (ed.), Geteilte Geschichte. Ost- und Westdeutschland 1970–2000, Göttingen 2015, pp. 195–238, here pp. 209f.; Christoph Kleßmann, Arbeiter im "Arbeiterstaat" DDR. Deutsche Traditionen, sowjetisches Modell, westdeutsches Magnetfeld (1945 bis 1971), Bonn 2007, pp. 138–145, p. 273 and pp. 557–563.

27 Ibid., pp. 313f. and pp. 377–383.

28 See the characterization of the GDR as an "educational dictatorship," Dorothee Wierling, Erzieher und Erzogene. Zu Generationsprofilen in der DDR der 60er Jahre, in: Axel Schildt et al. (eds.), Dynamische Zeiten. Die 60er Jahre in den beiden deutschen Gesellschaften, Hamburg 2000, pp. 624–641, here p. 631.

29 Harsch, Revenge, pp. 131f. See Thomas Reichel, "Sozialistisch arbeiten, lernen und leben." Die Brigadebewegung in der DDR (1959–1989), Cologne 2011, p. 59; Peter Hübner, "Sozialistischer Fordismus"? Oder: Unerwartete Ergebnisse eines Kopiervorganges. Zur Geschichte der Produktionsbrigaden in der DDR, in: Alf Lüdtke et al. (eds.), Amerikanisierung. Traum und Alptraum im Deutschland des 20. Jahrhunderts, Stuttgart 1996, pp. 96–115.

skills, the pride, trust, and care they had acquired in family life to social relations at the workplace. These male "heroes" had learned the virtues of having a feeling of duty and responsibility at the workplace, which in turn enabled them to become "helpers" at home.[30] The regulated use of technology and one's own body was formed in the mold of male emotions.[31]

Judged against the ideal of the optimistic, rational industrial worker, women had to take a detour on their path to socialism. In the mid-1950s, half of the women in the GDR were counted among the "working." In every decade thereafter, the proportion of working women increased by ten percent.[32] In public campaigns to get women to see themselves as equal participants in the project of constructing a socialist society, the image of the working mother came out on top by the end of the 1950s.[33] During the 1950s, about thirty percent of working women were employed in industry. In 1960, a fifth of employed women worked in health and education.[34] Narratives on female activists and women's brigades gave a new spin on the trope of the difference between the sexes as a bodily difference. From literary tales about working women to empirical studies by public health practitioners on working conditions, women's lesser strength and greater susceptibility to illness were framed as problems to be resolved through technology and the aid of fellow workers.[35] Advice literature, novels, and the documentation of brigades' activities itself identified female emotional economies that ran on motherly care and concern.[36] Teachers and nurses were cast as paradigmatic examples of how

30 An early contribution to the public debate since 1958 is Werner Goldstein, Brigaden der kommunistischen Zukunft, in: Neues Deutschland, 10.12.1958, p. 5. Authors also drew on novels. Exemplary are Günter Glante and Wolfgang Neuhaus, Tagebuch eines Brigadiers, Berlin (GDR) 1960, pp. 7–25; Heinrich Siegrist, Stürmische Jahre, Weimar 1960. As an example of a brigade party and a "socialist wedding" hosted by a brigade, Ursula Langspach, Das Brigadetagebuch, Halle 1961, pp. 133–140. See also Reichel, Sozialistisch, p. 24, pp. 30–49, p. 59 and pp. 108–112.

31 Gries and Satjukow, Helden, pp. 10–12; Scholz, Vater, pp. 203–228.

32 See Gunilla-Friederike Budde, Einleitung. Zwei Welten? Frauenerwerbsarbeit im deutschdeutschen Vergleich, in: ead. (ed.), Frauen arbeiten. Weibliche Erwerbstätigkeit in Ost- und Westdeutschland nach 1945, Göttingen 1997, pp. 7–18, here p. 10.

33 See Anna Kaminsky, Frauen in der DDR, Berlin 2017², pp. 68–82; Gunilla-Friederike Budde, Frauen der Intelligenz. Akademikerinnen in der DDR 1945 bis 1975, Göttingen 2003, pp. 311 f.; Harsch, Revenge, p. 131.

34 See Zentralverwaltung (ed.), Statistisches Jahrbuch, 1955, pp. 117 f.; ibid., 1960/61, p. 193; ibid., 1971, pp. 58 f. GDR labor law sought to mitigate multiple responsibilities, but its norm remained traditional familial divisions of labor. Budde, Intelligenz, pp. 309–311; Ute Schneider, Hausväteridylle oder sozialistische Utopie? Die Familie im Recht der DDR, Cologne 2004, pp. 180 f.

35 See e.g. the sub-section "Mädchenfrage" in Langspach, Brigadetagebuch, pp. 99–101; Elfriede Paul, Untersuchungen über Ursachen und Dauer der Arbeitsunfähigkeit bei der Frau. Analyse der gesundheitlichen Lage der werktätigen Frauen auf Grund von Erhebungen in sechs Berliner Betrieben, Berlin (GDR) 1956, p. 7, pp. 35 f. and pp. 50–64.

36 Kaminsky, Frauen, pp. 37 f., pp. 75–81 and pp. 95 f.; on the socialist ideals and its contradictions, see Harsch, Revenge, pp. 87–89, pp. 115 f. and pp. 119 f.

women's emotional constitutions could be optimally channeled in productive labor.

Male workers were called upon to employ their strong will and their professional and political education to transform the male affection caused by work's demands into the enduring social emotions of camaraderie. Conversely, their female counterparts were supposed to translate the allegedly natural feminine emotions of empathy and motherly care into sustained feelings of solidarity. The gender-specific division of labor, which continued to find justification in notions of bodily and emotional differences, was seen as an opportunity to integrate women into the labor market; at the same time, it increased the moral pressure on women to get a job.[37] Towards the end of the 1950s, the debates on the purpose of work, family happiness, and the good of society gained steam. In the rhetoric of the SED, positive feelings were both the goal of a fulfilling occupation and a means of production in and of themselves. Concomitantly, the workplace was portrayed as a testing ground for productive, uplifting emotions in the home, and vice-versa.

II. "The Secret of Happy People"—
The Vocabulary of Healthy Marriage and Work Life around 1960

After 1953, works of popular science underwent a boom.[38] Literature on how to have a happy marriage featured concrete instructions and tips. This advice was framed as both contributing to the health of society and increasing workplace performance. The authors who cast themselves as trustworthy experts were mostly male doctors and pedagogues.[39] Beginning in 1945, public health specialists played a key role in shaping the official vocabulary on health and work morale in the GDR, first in the German Central Administration of Health, and later in the East German ministries.[40] The advice authors—including a handful of women writers—legitimated their writing through their medical practices and joined

---

37 Kaminsky, Frauen, pp. 73 f.; Budde, Intelligenz, p. 311.

38 See McLellan, Love, pp. 86–89.

39 Writing as doctor and psychologist: Hans-Joachim Hoffmann and Peter G. Klemm, Ein offenes Wort. Ein Buch über die Liebe, Berlin (GDR) 1956, p. 7. A pedagogue advised by doctors: Wolfgang Bretschneider, Sexuell aufklären—rechtzeitig und richtig. Ein Ratgeber für sexuelle Erziehung, Leipzig 1957, p. 7. Only a few female authors wrote books on pregnancy, domestic life, and raising children. For one with a large print run see Sonja Walter, Zwischen vierzehn und achtzehn. Ein Buch für junge Mädchen, Berlin (GDR) 1958. Aiming at young women as its audience see Gerhard Weber and Danuta Weber, Du und ich, Berlin (GDR) 1958².

40 Jessica Reinisch, The Perils of Peace. The Public Health Crisis in Occupied Germany, Oxford 2013, pp. 118–141. For SED's personnel policies, see Ralph Jessen, Akademische Elite und kommunistische Diktatur. Die ostdeutsche Hochschullehrerschaft in der Ulbricht-Ära, Göttingen 1999, pp. 51 f., pp. 130 f. and pp. 261–285.

the need for advice with diagnoses of social ills.[41] They drew the conclusion that the "return to normalcy" desired by their patients could only be accomplished by healing postwar society of the damage done by the fascist and capitalist past.

Between 1955 and 1961, Rudolf Neubert published eight advice books and numerous articles on work life, sexuality, and marriage.[42] He designed an approach to health based on the control of one's own body, offering readers an introduction to the functions of organs and the nervous system that drew on Pavlov's theory of conditioned reflexes.[43] In 1950, East German medicine and psychology had made the work of Pavlov and his Soviet students into a key point of reference.[44] In politically opportunistic, scientifically contemporary language, Neubert described a problem that he had begun working on during his time as an assistant at the German Hygiene Museum in Dresden before 1933, namely, that modern life disturbs psychical equilibrium.[45] The way in which Neubert depicted metabolism in numbers and mathematical functions, in tables, line and bar charts suggested a mode of causality that would make it possible to control the process. His evidence and illustrations borrowed from works by mostly German authors composed in the 1920s and 1950s.[46] He prescribed that reaching the psyche—the condition of exerting self-control—be accomplished through breathing, concentration, and relaxation exercises. Learning, reading, going to concerts and plays, and being involved in society were other activities Neubert proposed to reduce the monotone stress of work.[47] He commented on the organization of students and white-collar workers, quoted literature on "mental labor" from the interwar

---

41 Rudolf Neubert, Das neue Ehebuch. Die Ehe als Aufgabe der Gegenwart und Zukunft, Rudolstadt 1957, pp. 7–9 and p. 283; id., Gesundheit und geistige Arbeit, Jena 1958², pp. 11 f.

42 Neubert, born in 1898, doctoral degree in 1923, until 1933 researcher at the German Hygiene Museum in Dresden, after 1933 member of the NSDAP, 1939–1945 military doctor, 1946/47 scientific director of the German Hygiene Museum, after that teacher at the Dresden Polytechnic, after 1952 professor of public health in Jena. See HStA, 12741, no. 115, Rudolf Neubert, Lebenslauf, [1947]; see id., Mein Arztleben. Erinnerungen, Rudolstadt 1974, pp. 85–116.

43 Id., Gesundheit und Arbeit, Jena 1955, pp. 10 f.; ibid. 1958², pp. 24–26; id., Das Geheimnis froher Menschen, Jena 1961, p. 11, pp. 14 f. and pp. 20–24; id., Leben und Gesundheit, Leipzig 1966, p. 12.

44 Stefan Busse, Psychologie in der DDR. Die Verteidigung der Wissenschaft und die Formung der Subjekte, Basel 2004, pp. 57–67 and pp. 77–80.

45 Works on addiction prevention and healthy living alongside work on exhibitions: Martin Vogel and Rudolf Neubert, Grundzüge der Alkoholfrage, Dresden 1926; id., Der Mensch und die Wohnung, Dresden 1926; id., Freizeit, Dresden 1927. Older works were key for Neubert: Leopold Loewenfeld, Über die geistige Arbeitskraft und ihre Hygiene, Wiesbaden 1905; Otto Dornblüth, Hygiene der geistigen Arbeit, Berlin 1908.

46 Neubert, Gesundheit und Arbeit 1958², pp. 34–41 and pp. 54 f.; id., Geheimnis, p. 27, pp. 87 f. and p. 139. Neubert also sought to draw on debates from the psychology of work, see Edgar Atzler, Körper und Arbeit, Leipzig 1927.

47 Neubert, Gesundheit und Arbeit 1958², pp. 75–77. Plans repeated in: id., Leben und Gesundheit, pp. 183 f.

period, and even discussed West German debates on "manager's sickness."[48]
As early as 1947, Neubert published a booklet advising people to lead a frugal,
balanced life in order to sustain the "simple economy of the mind's equilibrium
of forces."[49] After 1955, the professor of public health made similar suggestions
when proposing the manipulability of conditioned reflexes as a way to adjust the
nervous system to the demands of industrial society.[50]

Neubert's conception of the "mental worker" latched on to widespread ideas
about the controlled masculinity of the socialist proletariat; but it also drew on
middle-class advice literature from the Weimar era. Running on the thesis that,
under socialist relations of production, mental work would supplant bodily labor,
Neubert's argument saw the demands of both office work and factory work converging.[51] Because Neubert was describing this convergence from the perspective
of a mental worker, the archetype of the industrial laborer gave way in his argument to the ideal of the mental worker. This shift could be taken advantage of in
the venture of making biologically different sexes equal. Following his dictum:
"Women are different than men down to their very metabolism,"[52] Neubert
sought to balance out bodily differences between the genders through the use of
technology, an efficient division of work and household organization.[53] There-
with, he quoted a basic Marxist claim. From Neubert's vantage point, working
mothers appeared as the ideal-typical "mental workers" par excellence.

Neubert also argued that in modern technological—that is to say, socialist—
society, living life the right way would enable the equality of marriage partners.
In "Das neue Ehebuch" (The new marriage book), published in 1957, Neubert
imagined that the mechanized work of the homemaker would be analogous to the
automatized workplace. A rational division of labor between husband and wife, he
thought, would make it possible for both to experience the consummation of their
love in parenthood and a decent career. Neubert again described the bodies of the
loving couple as biological stimulus-response machines whose nervous balance
needed to be looked after. Because women were more sensitive, Neubert claimed
"that, at least in the future, women will take on the leading role in love life."[54]

---

48 Neubert, Gesundheit und Arbeit 1958², p. 57, Neubert quotes Irene Hochrein-Schleicher and
   Max Hochrein, Unternehmerkrankheit. Entstehung und Verhütung, Stuttgart 1953.
49 Rudolf Neubert, Gesundheitspflege im täglichen Leben, Dresden 1947, p. 99.
50 Id., Geheimnis, pp. 15–18. Alfred Beyer and Kurt Winter, Geschichtliche Entwicklung, Inhalt
   und Definition der Sozialhygiene, in: id. (eds.), Lehrbuch der Sozialhygiene, Berlin (GDR)
   1953, pp. 3–22, here p. 17. See Alfred Beyer, Arbeit und Arbeitsbedingungen der Werktätigen,
   in: ibid., pp. 275–307, here pp. 305.
51 Neubert, Gesundheit und Arbeit 1958², pp. 10–21, especially pp. 20 f.; id., Geheimnis, pp. 100 f.
52 Id., Fragen, p. 122.
53 Id., Ehebuch 1957, pp. 154–156, pp. 222 f. and pp. 273 f. On public debates see id., Fragen,
   pp. 107–126.
54 Id., Ehebuch 1957, p. 154; Neubert's statement on sexual relations argued for an effect on
   the emotional education of spouses. He stressed this extension of the "leading role" beyond
   sexuality, id., Fragen, pp. 121 f.

The focus on women gave expression to anxieties that they could do particular damage to a marriage: frigid wives hindered themselves and their husbands from experiencing sexual fulfillment, while nymphomaniac seductresses threatened the maturation of young men.[55] The ideal scenario was that the marital division of labor and the wife's ability to make herself into the emotional bedrock of the relationship would give the young love the power to become a feeling that would last a lifetime.[56] Neubert summarized his advice in the form of a political message:

Because the bourgeois-capitalist order is breaking apart and no force in the world can stop this process, the happy chord of [bourgeois-capitalist] marriage mutates into dissonance. But no worries, a new harmony, a new sound of happiness made up of different chords will come into being.[57]

"Das neue Ehebuch" and other publications of the period repeated the mantra that men and women should turn their bodies into facilitators of a moderate lifestyle, which necessitated that they understand how to interpret the meaning of their own feelings, both for themselves and in the social contexts in which they arose.[58] Neubert underscored his theses with a series of anecdotes, most of which featured doctors, actors, or engineers who get burnt out in their claustrophobic postwar living conditions and work stress. In his discussions of infidelity as a key cause of divorce, Neubert took to task the hypocrisy of successful men in positions of responsibility who justified cheating on the grounds that their wives had not continued their education and would only hold their husbands back.[59] He countered that couples should see the husband's occupational success and the happiness of the family as a collaborative effort: "The activity of the wife of an artist or academic, of a minister or representative, of a doctor who provides her husband with the time, space, and atmosphere for his work is just as productive a labor as any other."[60]

The financial inequality within many marriages provided the impetus for the emphasis on acknowledging mutual responsibilities. On average, women were less well paid and less educated than their husbands, and their careers were often interrupted by phases when they had to care for young children. With reforms originally designed to adjust gendered legal privileges, the GDR's divorce law was altered in 1950 to abolish alimony, only guaranteeing that the husband pay child support.[61] Around 1960, experts tried to compensate for the consequences of this

---

55 See the thorough treatment of the disinhibition of men and women in id., Geschlechterfrage. Ein Buch für junge Menschen, Rudolstadt 1956[4], pp. 53–56.

56 Id., Ehebuch 1957, pp. 158 f., pp. 225 f. and pp. 275 f.

57 Ibid. 1957, p. 269.

58 Ibid. 1957, p. 10, p. 135 and p. 161; ibid. 1958[2], pp. 178 f. See e.g. Bretschneider, Sexuell, p. 23, p. 36 and pp. 144 f.

59 Neubert, Ehebuch, 1957, pp. 191–193.

60 Ibid. 1957, p. 225.

61 Budde, Intelligenz, pp. 400–404. On marriage law, Schneider, Hausväteridylle, pp. 247–252.

rule: In order to prevent single women from falling into poverty and to prevent unwanted demographic changes, they advised courts to require couples considering divorce to take part in couples' counseling and to only approve petitions for divorce—which were permitted on the grounds of irreconcilable differences without necessarily finding one partner culpable—after one or both parties had given detailed explanations of their desire for separation.[62] Neubert's ideal moral economy of marriage made a plea for women to go to work, all the while acknowledging the continued dominance of the husband in financial matters. He tried to compensate for this inequality through his moralizing appeal to the couple's sense of responsibility.

Reviewers read the "Ehebuch" as a controversial contribution to debates on gender equality. Neubert was criticized for his argument that the couple should constitute the motor of occupational advancement and personal development. The editors of Neues Deutschland, the SED's party newspaper, which had one of the highest print runs in the GDR, even gave half a page to a highly critical letter to the editor composed in the language of gender equality. The letter posed the concise question: "What is the difference between the book's suggestions and the bourgeois ideal: 'And indoors ruleth the housewife so modest'?" It charged that Neubert was stuck on the "model of the old patriarchal family" grounded in the principle that "the father, head of the house, and breadwinner be kept in a good mood."[63] The fact that Neubert burdened women with the lead role in a happy marriage received no sympathy from the critic, who thought it unjustified: "Doesn't the harmony of marriage depend on both partners?"[64]

Letters directly addressed to Neubert expressed irritation with the book, too. Some women accused him of lacking a sense for the economic and emotionally distraught situation of women living under the "surplus of women" brought about by the war.[65] Female letter writers composed their charges against both Neubert and his critics in the jargon of the SED. One reader of the weekly Wochenpost saw the "'ideal' of the 'working woman'" as the cause for the "fatigue and constant exhaustion of women, who are compelled to overtax their bodies and minds under the double burden of home and occupation."[66] More often than not, however, Neubert received letters of praise.[67] One woman defended his account of

---

62 Advice on marriage law in: Wolfhilde Dierl, Liebe Ehe—Scheidung?, Leipzig 1959², p. 35; McLellan, Love, pp. 80 f.; Harsch, Revenge, p. 284 and pp. 286–297.

63 Horst Krahn, Und drinnen waltet die züchtige Hausfrau?, in: Neues Deutschland, 4.1.1958, p. 10.

64 Ibid.

65 See e.g. HStA, 12741, no. 70, letter to Rudolf Neubert, Halle 1.1.1961; ibid., no. 70, letter to Rudolf Neubert, Halle 25.1.1961. On "Recht auf Liebe" see e.g. ibid., no. 74, letter to Rudolf Neubert, Bismarck 23.2.1962.

66 Ibid., no. 59, copy, letter to Wochenpost, Dresden 9.12.1957, one page typescript. Neubert was a guest contributor to the Wochenpost up through the 1970s.

67 For a positive review see Elfriede Brüning, Ehe auf neuen Wegen, in: Neues Deutschland, 16.11.1957, p. 10.

the difference of the sexes in a letter to *Neues Deutschland*: "In addition, the marriage book provides clear biological and psychological explanations for why it is desirable that the woman take a leading role in romantic relationships."[68] Many readers considered the professor an ally. They saw in his books strong arguments for the expansion of childcare services, for their demands that their husbands help out more around the house, and for their desire that the woman's side be heard in marital conflicts.

The imperative of constantly working on one's personality and emotions was at the foundation of the view of marriage as a lifestyle and an art to be mastered. By promising that equality might be achieved through an acknowledgment of gender differences, Neubert's advice literature helped give new life to the notion that raising children and keeping house was women's natural task and relativized the fact that women had to juggle multiple responsibilities.[69] Its language gave support to the idea that some jobs were "women's jobs," diminishing their prestige and providing justification for lower wages, thus reproducing old inequalities.[70] At the same time, the debate ignited by Neubert's work gave occasion for people to point out the deficits of "really existing" gender equality. Along with asking readers to reflect and act on the recommendations made in his books, he also encouraged couples to speak about what they had read with one another. He also held his own ear open: "I ask you to write me if it helped you or saddened you. In the next edition, I will gladly include all good suggestions..."[71]

III. Readers' Letters to Neubert around 1960

In 1960, Neubert published "Fragen und Antworten zum 'Neuen Ehebuch' und zur 'Geschlechterfrage'" (Questions and Answers to "The New Marriage Book" and "The Gender Question"), a small selection of his correspondence with readers. In the introduction, he stated that "written expression" could "open up further discussion" that might help couples put advice into practice.[72] Neubert compared

---

68 [Contribution by Irmtraud Dams] Um das eheliche Zusammenleben. Leserinnen schreiben ihre Meinung zum "Neuen Ehebuch" von Professor Neubert, in: Neues Deutschland, 8.2.1958, p. 12.

69 For such a relativization see Neubert, Fragen, pp. 120 f.

70 Budde, Intelligenz, pp. 291–306.

71 Neubert, Ehebuch 1957, p. 9. Neubert gave the address of his institute in Jena. Ibid., p. 283.

72 Neubert, Fragen, pp. 5 f. The first published correspondence was: Hanns Schwarz, Schriftliche Sexualberatung. Erfahrungen und Vorschläge mit 60 Briefen und Antworten, Rudolstadt 1959. A selection of readers' letters and responses to them was published by Hoffmann and Klemm, Wort 1960⁶, pp. 245–329. The letters to the editor column "Unter vier Augen gesagt" (Spoken one-on-one) of the FDJ newspaper *Junge Welt* started in 1963 and was edited by a doctor. A selection was published in: Klaus Trummer, Unter vier Augen gesagt. Fragen und Antworten über Freundschaft und Liebe, Berlin (GDR) 1966.

the correspondence with counseling sessions.[73] Between 1955 and 1960, Neubert received about 550 letters; by 1963, the number had more than doubled. After 1965, the stream of letters slowly tapered off. Early on, about twice as many men wrote to Neubert as women, but in the run of the 1960s, the ratio equaled out. More than a third of those who wrote indicated their occupation and about half gave their age. Two-thirds of them were between 18 and 30, about a fourth were older, and 13 percent were younger than 18.[74] The letters' authors were not only relatively young; they also represented an above-average level of education.[75] Forty percent of those who indicated their profession had attended a university or polytechnic school, and about twenty percent were employed in jobs that required training or a degree beyond a high school diploma. About a quarter of them worked in salaried positions or in the service sector. Just ten percent identified as industrial workers or communal farmers. Only a handful of those who sent Neubert letters exclusively identified as housewives. Many named the profession they had originally been trained for. The composition of correspondents did not reflect that of Neubert's readership as a whole. But those who Neubert called "mental workers" were more likely to state their occupation and link it to their personal development. Besides, the published selection gave insight into how Neubert read the letters, treating them as logs on how people lived their lives. The responses reveal the implicit assumption that readers needed an expert to help them properly grasp the significance of their experiences.

In a letter from September 1958 that was not published in the collection, 29-year-old Sabine Beyer took Neubert literally: "I would like to ask you to take me on as a counseling patient." In her clean, steady handwriting, she filled four standard pages with concerns that she "at least wanted to voice out in a letter."[76] Beyer, a reader of the "Ehebuch," had been married for five years and had two children: "In appearance, our marriage seems ideal, and for years it has fulfilled most of the criteria laid out in your 'Ehebuch.' But neither my husband nor I are really satisfied."[77] The couple had sexual issues. Beyer sought to forge a connection between the painfulness of her pregnancy, her chronic menstrual cramps, and her lack of desire towards her husband on the one hand and the demands of everyday life on the other. The mother of two had had to give up her job as a teacher: "For 3½ years now I have been out of work and just take care of my home and my family."[78] Her husband worked as an engineer with the state train service:

---

73 Karl Dietz and Rudolf Neubert, Vorbemerkung, in: Schwarz, Sexualberatung, pp. 3–5. Neubert, Fragen, pp. 5 f. and pp. 223 f.

74 The target audience of "Geschlechterfrage" and "Ehebuch" were between 16 and 30 years old. Id., Ehebuch 1957, p. 9.

75 In the GDR around 1960, 18- to 30-year-olds made up 29 % of people "working age" between 16 and 65. See Zentralverwaltung (ed.), Statistisches Jahrbuch, 1961/62, pp. 30–32.

76 HStA, 12741, no. 61, letter to Rudolf Neubert, [Dresden] 7.9.1958, 4 pages manuscript, here p. 1.

77 Ibid.

78 Ibid.

"At 5 in the morning he gets up, around 8 in the evening we start winding down. By then, we are usually so exhausted that we fall asleep in the middle of whatever we end up trying to do."[79] The shortcomings of other aspects of their relationship, she wrote, ultimately came to the surface in their sex life. Beyer wanted to see in sexual intimacy the expression and consummation of romantic love. She blamed her marital crisis on her weak will and on her body, worn down by the stress of the postwar years. Both, she believed, made happiness nearly impossible to achieve for her and her hard-working husband.[80] In his response, Neubert opined that Beyer's marriage was "not in itself in danger, but simply overstrained."[81] His suggestions said nothing about the intimate life of the couple, nor did he say anything about the need for the working husband to bring home some kind of new ethics or morals from his workplace. Instead, Neubert described Mr. Beyer as a vessel that was transferring the tensions and exhaustion of his workplace into the family. Thus, he shifted the responsibility to Ms. Beyer's husband: "In short, the whole problem should not be addressed through sex life, but through the regimen of your everyday life."[82]

Male and female readers alike saw themselves placed in the difficult position of having to understand the history of their own physical and psychological development, view it in the context of their relationship with their partner, and then abstract one level higher and situate it in the context of society as a whole. Those who sought advice framed their problems in biographical anecdotes and made references to social advancement, hard work, and pride, all key tropes of the official East German ideology of building a socialist society. More than any others, white-collar workers, businesspeople, and the so-called "intelligentsia" treated personal accomplishments as granting them a right to personal happiness. Only very few made references to Marxist theory beyond cursory remarks on socialism.[83] Their language was generally informed by popular science, psychology, and physiology, which they used to interpret their problems as effects of the hardships experienced during the war and the postwar years. This enabled them to articulate their calls for more childcare and access to housing, better organized workplaces, and more family-friendly working hours as concerns of GDR citizens actively interested in participating in the development of socialism. In a similar fashion, complaints sent to labor organizations and state institutions in the form of petitions could also be reframed as constructive criticism.

79 Ibid., p. 3.
80 Ibid., p. 4.
81 HStA 12741, no. 61, carbon copy, letter by Rudolf Neubert, [Jena] 10.9.1958, one page typescript.
82 Ibid.
83 Advice publications too limited positioning themselves within Marxism to forewords and afterwords. In Neubert's opus most prominently in: "Leit- und Streitsätze über die neue Ehe," in: Neubert, Ehebuch 1957, pp. 279 f. Reference in the foreword of a later edition, ibid. 1964[13], p. 10. See Bretschneider, Sexuell, p. 38 and p. 41. Explicit on the socialist way of life as a personal responsibility see Bernd Bittighöfer, Du und der andere neben Dir, Berlin (GDR) 1965, pp. 5–7; Autorenkollektiv, Lebensweise und Moral im Sozialismus, Berlin (GDR) 1973.

Petitions were relics of a formalized mode of correspondence much older than the GDR itself; they gave people the chance to tell higher-ups about their concerns regarding all sorts of issues.[84] In his request that readers "speak out in writing" or, in German, engage in "schriftliche Aussprache," Neubert promised readers the right to participate in the construction of advice and to object to things they disagreed with. After 1945, the ambiguous concept of "Aussprache" was ubiquitously used to denote discussions in all kind of contexts, from personal conflicts to public debates. The German term indicated the presence of a dispute that needed to be laid out on the table and cleared up. Eventually, "Aussprache" came to imply a definite outcome after matters were talked over. Besides its usage in common parlance around 1960, the term promised participation, yet masked over hierarchies in party and enterprise as it became part of official SED jargon.[85] Understanding marriage counseling as "Aussprache" thus surreptitiously gave the expert the last word. In the years after 1958, Neubert described his written correspondence with readers as part of a network of counseling institutions and discussion circles that could be found in all spheres of society. He supported this notion with the argument being made by the brigade movement that personal development was a process embedded in a plurality of social relations.[86] After the Fifth Party Congress of the SED, officials encouraged members of local party branches, unions, and enterprises to talk about domestic issues with their peers. In cases of infidelity, domestic violence, and alcoholism in particular, the way in which workers' brigade councils and conflict committees positioned themselves as authorities with the right and expertise to intervene drew on traded practices of appealing to superiors, priests, and doctors. Neubert's correspondence with his readers served as one further juncture in a broad moral economy that bridged family life and working life.

A few months after the Fifth Party Congress, Margarete Strauss turned to multiple instances of authority with the plea that they help save her marriage. In the fall of 1958, she also wrote two letters to Rudolf Neubert in deliberate, flawless handwriting. The mother of three had been abandoned by her husband, who was now living with a significantly younger woman, who he got to know during his work in one of the GDR's mass organizations. Of their time together, Ms. Strauss

---

84 See Ina Merkel and Felix Mühlberg, Eingaben und Öffentlichkeit, in: ead. (ed.), "Wir sind doch nicht die Meckerecke der Nation." Briefe an das Fernsehen der DDR, Berlin 2000², pp. 9–32.

85 For an assessment of the hierarchies in "Aussprachen" see e.g. Walter Ulbricht, Die gegenwärtige Lage und die neuen Aufgaben der Sozialistischen Einheitspartei Deutschlands. Referat und Schlußwort auf der II. Parteikonferenz der SED vom 9.–12. Juli 1952, Berlin (GDR) 1952, p. 54, p. 64, p. 75 and pp. 81 f. See Hyunseon Lee, Geständniszwang und "Wahrheit des Charakters" in der Literatur der DDR. Diskursanalytische Fallstudien, Stuttgart 2000, p. 21.

86 In the first edition, the "Ehebuch" little discussed the institutions of everyday life in socialism, Neubert, Ehebuch 1957, pp. 249 f. This was filled in in later editions, first in the supplement A. Chartschew, Familie und Kommunismus. Beilage zum "Neuen Ehebuch" von Rudolf Neubert, in: Neubert, Ehebuch 1961⁹, not continuously paginated, pp. 1–24. For revisions see Neubert, Ehebuch 1964¹³, p. 318.

wrote: "The first years of our marriage were filled up with economic concerns. Until in 1951 when my husband changed his career, getting qualified as a vocational school teacher."[87] She got a job to improve the family's financial situation and spoke of herself confidently: "Even during his retraining and afterwards I always endeavored to move forward."[88]

His departure from the everyday life of his family apparently gave the husband occasion to reconsider what Margarete Strauss described as a loving relationship: "Suddenly, after 11 years of marriage, he seems to have realized that our life together was never harmonious (that is his opinion now)."[89] She defended herself against the charge that she had been uninterested in the intellectual and professional development of her husband.[90] She followed this up with an ironic leading question: "And now I ask you, is that the kind of socialist morality in the family that our state asks of us?" She wrote that her husband had unilaterally fled from his obligations: "Now, I as mother have to bear the entire burden of raising my 3 children." She stated that this forced her to relinquish her claims to family life, love, and happiness: "Just because my husband all of a sudden found a woman who in his opinion 'better' suits him."[91] Instead of considering Mr. Strauss' accounts of his own emotions, his wife attributed authority only to emotions that spurred people to take responsibility for others. She placed her situation in a larger context: "Such cases as the one I have recounted are not able to bolster the foundation of our state, namely the family."[92]

Neubert agreed with his reader. Influenced by the recent Party Congress, he advised her to speak about her husband's behavior to his employer and local party leadership.[93] Ms. Strauss had, indeed, already taken this step and had gotten her husband's colleagues and fellow party comrades to demand that he "clear things up."[94] Mr. Strauss sought to do this by filing for divorce. But when his petition was rejected, two party representatives from the school showed up to Margarete Strauss' house, pushing her to accept their colleague's decision as the lesser of two evils. Strauss wrote:

They said I had almost caused my husband to lose his job because I had spoken to the party leadership. He himself stated that he would never return to his family and would even rather give up his party membership. But if he did that, he would not be able to continue working as a teacher at the school.[95]

87 HStA, 12741, no. 67, letter to Rudolf Neubert, Triptis 8.10.1958, 6 pages manuscript, here pp. 1 f.
88 Ibid., pp. 2 f.
89 Ibid., p. 3.
90 HStA, 12741, no. 67, letter to Rudolf Neubert, Triptis 24.10.1958, 4 pages manuscript, here pp. 3 f.
91 Ibid., no. 67, letter to Rudolf Neubert, Triptis 8.10.1958, pp. 4 f.
92 Ibid., p. 6.
93 HStA, 12741, no. 67, carbon copy, letter by Rudolf Neubert, [Jena] 13.10.1958.
94 Ibid., no. 67, letter to Rudolf Neubert, Triptis 24.10.1958, p. 4.
95 Ibid., pp. 1 f.

Conjoining the institutions and personnel of the committees and offices of both party and workplace was explicitly conceived of and deployed as a method of rule by the SED. But local decisions in particular were largely dependent on local strategic considerations. In the face of a shortage of skilled workers, the vocational school teacher Strauss was protected by party and employer from interventions that might harm his standing. The SED thus fell short of fulfilling his wife's hopes that it might wield its moral power to balance out her dependency on her husband.

The letters of lamentation about infidelity among colleagues gave expression to the difficulties people were having juggling the interrelations between feelings of collegiality, friendship, and romance in the years around 1960. The official line after 1958 was that knowledge, values, and emotions from work life were supposed to influence those in family life, and vice-versa; moreover, the capacity to love was seen as being dependent on the experience of other social emotions. This postulate, however, made acknowledging and understanding one's own feelings and those of others a necessity. In the first edition of his "Fragen und Antworten," printed in 1960, Neubert gave special consideration to the perspectives and problems described by women, reversing the ratio of letters written by men to those written by women: of the 53 letters printed, 38 had been composed by women.[96] His comment on the concerns of women was that: "Their thoughts primarily revolve around real equality, the possibility of the full development of man and woman, and, on the same footing: the happy upbringing of our children…"[97]

Despite this, happiness in the family and the realization of occupational ambitions stood at odds for some women, and not only in the sense that they had to bear a double workload, but also when it came to finding a partner in the first place. In December 1960, two female chemists got to the heart of the matter in telling Neubert about the difficulties they had both experienced finding a partner. After years of schooling and now working as supervisors, they related being confronted with the uncomfortable fact that most men older or the same age as them with similar qualifications were already married.[98] Although both were involved in their workers' brigades, they remained "lonely in the crowd."[99] In the 1960s, women too justified giving up on their marriages on the grounds that they posed a barrier to occupational advancement. At the same time, many women demanded the recognition of their everyday domestic chores as a form of labor. In 1966, for instance, a housewife headed off a series of letters with the statement: "To all appearances, things are going well between us." The qualified chemist had met her husband during their studies and had continued to work

96 See Neubert, Fragen, p. 223. The collection during this period contained in: HStA, 12741, nos. 59–63 and nos. 67–70.
97 Neubert, Fragen, pp. 109 f.
98 HStA, 12741, no. 69, letter to Rudolf Neubert, Leipzig 3.12.1960, 3 pages manuscript, here p. 2.
99 Ibid., pp. 1 f.

after marriage: "The job was good and offered perspectives for the future."[100] She had three children and quit her job, while her husband worked on his doctorate. She admitted to Neubert that she was tired of a marriage that failed to live up to her hopes that it would enable her to "develop as a person, posit new goals, tackle new problems, and be recognized."[101] Neubert's calls for reflection had an inverse, offering an occasion for readers to analyze the deficits of their marriage.

In 1957, marriage and divorce rates had served Neubert in his "Ehebuch" as tools for diagnosing the crisis of "bourgeois marriage." By the 1960s, however, they irritated him. From a low point in 1958, the annual number of divorces had risen by a quarter ten years later to about 29,000. By 1974, this number had doubled.[102] With the increase in divorces came an increase in the ratio of divorce proceedings initiated by women, from 53.4 percent in 1958 to about 64 percent ten years later.[103] The letters written to Neubert illustrate that these developments came in the wake of shifting views on personal development outside of marriage and that social reevaluations of the duties of husband and wife towards one another had made a real impact. In his replies, Neubert articulated his disappointments by voicing his perception that people gave in too quickly to strong emotions. He accused men of being easily excited, leading them to make irresponsible decisions, while women latched on to "fantastic ideas" and failed in their roles as emotional bulwarks in their marital relations. During the course of the 1960s, the advice author repeated his pleas that people live modestly, work hard, understand their body, and learn how to analyze their emotions before acting on them.[104] The appeal to know oneself and one's partner and to engage in truthful, open discussion brought Neubert to place renewed focus on the techniques of communication themselves.

IV. Written Expression as a "Means to Self-Transformation"

Neubert responded to most readers' letters with little more than a few sentences, comprising a brief assessment of the problem and a recommendation to seek out a marriage counselor. Letters that inspired Neubert to dictate a longer reac-

---

100 HStA, 12741, no. 90, letter to Rudolf Neubert, Freiberg 4.11.1966, 6 pages manuscript, here p. 2.

101 Ibid., p. 3. See HStA, 12741, no. 65, letter to Rudolf Neubert, Freiberg 3.12.1966, 4 pages manuscript; ibid., no. 65, letter to Rudolf Neubert, Freiberg 2.2.1967, 2 pages manuscript.

102 Statistisches Bundesamt (ed.), Statistisches Jahrbuch 1989 für die Bundesrepublik Deutschland, Stuttgart 1990, p. 60 and p. 69; Zentralverwaltung (ed.), Statistisches Jahrbuch, 1990, p. 365.

103 Harsch, Revenge, pp. 294 f.

104 For a later conclusion see Rudolf Neubert, Was nicht in der Statistik steht, in: Richard Halgasch (ed.), Wir bleiben zusammen. Eine Diskussion um Ursachen von Ehekrisen, Leipzig 1971, pp. 53–71.

tion were characterized by a variety of stylistic devices and expressions, unique handwriting, and clean typescripts, all of which contributed to the impression that their author was a heterosexual family woman or man genuinely interested in self-improvement. In these cases, Neubert showed empathy, wrote that he had read the letter with "great interest," and told the letter's writer they were a "valuable person." Occasionally, people sought to increase their chances of getting a response by referencing their membership in the SED. Neubert's readers tried to use well-known, practiced techniques to relate their issues and communicate their emotions in a believable fashion.[105]

After 1958, such techniques of written self-examination were thematized as being part of the GDR's national proletarian culture.[106] Union leaders noted economic breakthroughs and workers' personal achievements in collective diaries.[107] The prototypes for this cultural-political valorization of introspective writing could be traced back to Soviet cultural policies during the 1917 October Revolution.[108] Snippets from diaries published in union, factory, and municipal newspapers offered concrete insights into the thoughts and travails of everyday people.[109] Manuals for workers interested in writing offered surveys of the last two centuries of diaristic writing, beginning with Rousseau's "Confessions."[110] Neubert's concept of the economy of mental forces resonated with these updated older notions of the connection between thinking, feeling, and writing.[111] In the early 1950s, poet and GDR Minister of Culture Johannes R. Becher described the "diary as a life-form" and a "means to self-transformation": "The process of writing in a diary has effects on everyday life. Thus, the diary can go beyond the person and help shape personality."[112] Becher drew an analogy between the act

---

105 This treatment of emotional action and responses to it follows Scheer, Emotions, pp. 209–216.

106 See e.g. Willi Köhler, Alle Künste werden blühen, in: Neues Deutschland, 26.4.1959, p. 3.

107 Jörg Roesler, Das Brigadetagebuch—betriebliches Rapportbuch, Chronik des Brigadelebens oder Erziehungsfibel?, in: Evemarie Badstübner (ed.), Befremdlich anders. Leben in der DDR, Berlin 2000, pp. 151–166.

108 See Christa Wolf, Die Literatur der neuen Etappe. Gedanken zum III. Sowjetischen Schriftstellerkongreß, in: Neues Deutschland, 20.6.1959, p. 7; Hans Radbandt, Vorwort zur Deutschen Ausgabe, in: Maxim Gorky, A. M. Gorki und die Geschichte der Fabriken und Werke. Sammelband zur Unterstützung der Arbeit an der Betriebsgeschichte, Berlin (GDR) 1964, pp. 6–14. See Hellbeck, Revolution, pp. 37–42 and pp. 55–65.

109 Reichel, Sozialistisch, pp. 108–112. Merve Lühr, Tagebuch schreiben im Kollektiv. Brigadetagebücher in der DDR zwischen Ideologie und Alltagspraxis, in: Janosch Steuwer and Rüdiger Graf (eds.), Selbstreflexionen und Weltdeutungen. Tagebücher in der Geschichte und der Geschichtsschreibung des 20. Jahrhunderts, Göttingen 2015, pp. 163–185.

110 Langspach, Brigadetagebuch, pp. 11–36, especially pp. 20–28. See ead., Wie schreiben wir unser Brigadetagebuch?, Berlin (GDR) 1964; Autorenkollektiv, Briefe an schreibende Arbeiter, Halle 1961.

111 See Albrecht Koschorke, Körperströme und Schriftverkehr. Mediologie des 18. Jahrhunderts, Munich 2003², pp. 163–165 and pp. 170–177.

112 Johannes R. Becher, Auf andere Art so große Hoffnung. Tagebuch 1950. Eintragungen 1951, Berlin (GDR) 1955, p. 20. The literary diary is extensively quoted in: Langspach, Brigadetagebuch, pp. 30–32.

of reading and rewriting and the act of giving an account of oneself. Speaking on GDR radio in 1964, the writer Christa Wolf counted diaries among her "most exciting reads" of the last few years.[113] She stated that the emotional impact that reading diaries had on her was informed by her conviction that personal journals were "unfalsified expressions of inner and outer experiences."[114] Wolf conceived of the diary as a "tool" that required editing and reflection in order to accurately capture reality.[115] These takes on the diary form did not simply treat writing as a way of better understanding one's own emotions in themselves, but went further in seeing the emotions fleshed out in the act of writing as instruments that could help writers gain insights into their psychological and social lives.[116]

Becher, Wolf, and others' accounts demonstrated that the established conception of autobiographical writing as a practice of private self-expression found continued resonance in the GDR.[117] The people who wrote to Neubert often drew on these techniques of introspection. For instance, in 1961, Mr. and Ms. Häussler from Berlin read the recently published "Fragen und Antworten," and in the hopes of working through a marital crisis caused by Mr. Häussler's infidelity, each wrote a letter to Neubert.[118] Paul Häussler, a man in his mid-thirties, had worked as a mechanic before studying history and going on to find employment at a research institute. The couple had met at the institute's library, fell in love, and married a year later.[119] Evi Häussler was four years younger than her husband and had a son from a previous relationship. Trained as a pharmacist's assistant, she later worked as a librarian and, after having two children with her new husband, became a stay-at-home mom. Of the two, it was Evi Häussler who emphasized her belief that happiness in marriage was the product of a division of labor, writing: "He was freed of having to deal with household tasks... He wrote his dissertation, I edited it for him, etc., and I thought he was happy."[120] Evi Häussler saw her husband's occupational success as a key part of a happy family. But her husband could not sympathize with her identification with domestic labor. He felt embarrassment and shame when his colleagues and fellow party members asked about his wife. In 1960, Paul Häussler fell in love with his secretary. Mr. Häussler's excitement about his new love was reflected in his account of the shortcomings

---

113 Christa Wolf, Tagebuch—Arbeitsmittel und Gedächtnis, in: ead., Die Dimension des Autors. Essays und Aufsätze, Reden und Gespräche, 1959–1985, Berlin (GDR) 1986², pp. 13–27, here p. 14. Written for radio in 1964, first printed in 1972. See ibid., p. 461.
114 Ibid., p. 20.
115 Ibid., p. 27.
116 See Langspach, Brigadetagebuch, pp. 207 f. and p. 215.
117 See Lühr, Tagebuch, pp. 183 f.
118 Both letters are dated 31.3.1961. In the following I distinguish between, first, the letter by Evi Häussler as letter I to Neubert, Berlin 31.3.1961, 3 numbered pages typescript (HStA, 12741, no. 71); second, the letter by Paul Häussler as letter II to Neubert, Berlin 31.3.1961, 4 numbered pages typescript (ibid.).
119 Ibid., p. 1.
120 Letter I to Neubert, p. 1.

of his marriage. He felt that he had found in his secretary a soulmate who could understand and support him in his work. In contrast, he wrote that he and his wife had originally thought of themselves as both romantic partners and collaborators in their work, but each had different conceptions of the role they themselves and the other were to play in the relationship.[121]

Evi and Paul Häussler wrote of misunderstandings, jealousy, rage, and nervousness. Both wanted to discuss things in a matter-of-fact way and both blamed the other for how they felt.[122] In the letters, both sought to portray themselves as reasonable persons and to give a convincing account of their own emotions. The couple underscored the significance they attributed to openly expressing themselves. Paul Häussler explained:

Our letters, my wife is also writing one to you, so that you can hear both sides, will be very long, which is why we are writing them on a typewriter, in order to make it easier for you to read. If you would prefer handwritten letters, we will happily compose handwritten copies and send them to you.[123]

Paul Häussler distinguished between handwritten and typed in the belief that the actual form and appearance of the manuscript might allow one to draw conclusions from the about the writer's personality, emotions, and degree of self-control. The typed pages, however, demonstrated that the couple had engaged in considerable thought and discussion about what they were writing. The act of reading, editing, and commenting on the other's letters evidenced that both had personal stakes in the experiment. Paul Häussler's introductory remark on the length of the letters suggests that they had gone through multiple versions, revealing that the couple had taken seriously Neubert's advice about the way in which writing could help one understand and govern one's feelings. Both quoted from Mr. Häussler's diary, who described writing in it: "It is for me—especially when I am dealing with difficult issues—a relief to put my thoughts down on paper, even if they are often not fully worked out."[124] Paul Häussler had already read his wife's letter before he typed out his own, referencing it multiple times, and Evi Häussler, too, read that of her husband, as she commented on it in two separate postscripts. Paul Häussler's claim that he wrote in a flow of "spontaneous thoughts and feelings" in order to change his emotions through rational reflection fit well with the couple's efforts to heed Neubert's advice by trying to understand their feelings, see them as keys to happiness, and use them as impulses for their own actions.[125] The husband remarked that: "Even while writing the letters, we got into discussions on a number of points that might help us get along better."[126]

121 Letter II to Neubert, p. 2.
122 Letter I to Neubert, p. 3.
123 Letter II to Neubert, p. 1.
124 Ibid., p. 4.
125 Ibid.
126 Ibid.

Neubert viewed his epistolary exchange with the Häusslers as an exemplary "Aussprache" and praised the way in which they dug deep in their communication with one another and with him. He told them that they were well "on their way to recovery" and that he, thanks to the clear letters written by both, could avoid making a "false diagnosis," even though he was far away.[127] Nevertheless, the complicated process, the series of accusations, and the disputes over the accuracy of the other's claims illustrated well the limits of speaking out and expressing one's own feelings. Those seeking advice from Neubert were often incapable of talking about their feelings and desires with others or believed that they were not being taken seriously. For instance, Edith Wartburgk, in her aforementioned letter from 1967, felt helpless and unable to articulate herself to her husband. Diverging expectations and life goals often posed an insurmountable barrier to communication.

Up through the end of the 1960s, male advice authors and the constantly growing number of women joining them in the field thought long and hard about the difficulties of expressing oneself correctly.[128] By now, a number of new books on marriage counseling had come into print. They based their claims on up-to-date, standardized surveys of sexual practices in the GDR, of the duration of relationships, and of people's happiness and emotional sensitivity.[129] Many of the surveys had been conducted by researchers involved in the development of the then still young field of social psychology in the GDR.[130] Around the same time, studies conducted by industrial-organizational psychologists identified conflicts and poor communication among colleagues as a cause of missed shifts, low productivity, and inhibited personal development.[131] The method they suggested for overcoming these issues included group discussions that had to be carried out in an empathetic, thoughtful manner. Influential in these new forms of workplace conflict resolution was the SED leadership's agenda of training "socialist planners and leaders" who, after the Sixth Party Congress in 1963, were tasked with increasing productivity in the framework of the "New Economic System."[132]

---

127 HStA, 12741, no. 71, carbon copy, letter by Rudolf Neubert, [Jena] 27.4.1961, 2 pages, here p. 1.

128 See Lykke Aresin, Sprechstunde des Vertrauens. Fragen der Sexual-, Ehe- und Familienberatung, Rudolstadt 1967, p. 93. Jutta Resch-Treuwerth took over the column "Unter vier Augen gesagt" of Junge Welt in 1971. Jutta Resch-Treuwerth (ed.), Unter vier Augen. Liebesbriefe aus zwei Jahrzehnten, Berlin 1996, pp. 8 f. and p. 15. The most successful book was Siegfried Schnabl, Mann und Frau intim, Rudolstadt 1969. In 1990 the book reached its 18th edition.

129 See e.g. Rolf Borrmann, Jugend und Liebe. Die Beziehungen der Jugendlichen zum anderen Geschlecht, Leipzig 1966.

130 Busse, Psychologie, p. 186 and p. 217.

131 See e.g. Hans Hiebsch and Manfred Vorweg, Über Gegenstand, Aufgaben und Methoden der marxistischen Sozialpsychologie, in: Deutsche Zeitschrift für Philosophie 11. 1963, pp. 577–594; id., Einführung in die marxistische Sozialpsychologie, Berlin (GDR) 1966, p. 80; Karl Hecht, Der Mensch neben Dir. Physio-psychologische Grundfragen der Menschenführung, Leipzig 1966.

132 Kleßmann, Arbeiterstaat, p. 586; Reichel, Sozialistisch, pp. 211 f. and pp. 340 f.

Marriage advice literature from the second half of the 1960s promoted good communication based on the principle that successful discussions that had a strong, healthy effect on both parties needed to be conducted with the right demeanor, a shared vocabulary, and the "art of listening."[133] Recommending sympathetic communication at the workplace and the home once again acknowledged and operationalized the intrinsic role of emotions in the moral economies of East Germans.

V. Conclusion

When, in 1967, Edith Wartburgk wrote to Neubert about her unhappy marriage, she did it with the mindset that she, an educated woman who agreed with the expert's opinions, had earned the right to be happy:

> Maybe I am too oversensitive a[nd] demanding but I am not demanding. A little bit of attention now and then can serve as a show of mutual love and respect. Please, dear Professor, give me advice, what should I do? I am so distraught and please excuse me if I have been difficult to understand sometimes. I am ʷᵃˢ very agitated as I wrote this letter.[134]

The letters bear traces of the authors' emotions. The conventionalized forms of writing were a medium for the reproduction of a once middle-class habitus informed by early twentieth-century public health and its concept of the "mental worker." The expressions of humility and meticulous handwriting in the epistolary exchanges between Neubert and his readers evidence the exertion many people took to adapt certain practices for themselves. More importantly, perhaps, the correspondences laid fertile ground for the creation of categories that privileged those who were able and willing to depict themselves as hardworking people focused on family while tailoring their writing to the requisite tropes.

    The moral economies expressed in readers' letters to Neubert exemplify two phases of intense change in the entangled history of work, morality, and the self. In the years around 1960, speaking one's mind was viewed as a means to leading a good, healthy life, which in turn was based on the notion that self-realization was part of the project of building a new society. However, Neubert's letters archive a set of social values that were reformed in the second half of the 1960s, as more weight was placed on the individual's right to self-realization. Statistical studies began loosening the old knot created by the perception that health, happiness, and normality were inextricably bound up with one another, and this trend found expression in advice literature, which began to thematize types of relationships and sexual practices that they had remained silent about in the past. Until the

---

133 Hecht, Mensch, pp. 110–112 and p. 118.
134 HStA, 12741, no. 92, letter to Neubert, 26.5.1967, p. 3. Deletion in manuscript.

end of the 1960s, the new emphasis on communication skills mirrored and accelerated a shift in advice literature. A new sensibility for individual growth took center stage in debates about self-transformation and in relationship advice. As moral economies continued to produce norms that spanned household and workplace, they vested more authority in emotions and increased credibility in personal demands for self-fulfillment, in contrast to old pleas to exert self-discipline and adhere to prescriptive and narrow norms of marital life. In the 1970s, the "leading party's" self-arrogated right to intervene in citizens' personal lives and social acceptance of non-conformist lifestyles drifted apart.

In his writings, Neubert ascribed a special role to women. The growing number of working women forced the public health expert to rethink gender roles in a way that would do justice to shifting socio-economic conditions and everyday habits. His affirmation of biological difference had two consequences: On the one hand, it provided justification for burdening women with responsibilities both at home and at work; on the other, it made it easier to address gender parity. But the limits of Neubert's opinions on women's strivings for self-determination are evidenced in his hand-wringing over threats to female health and emotional susceptibility. Nevertheless, at the end of the day, positions like Neubert's complex views on gender equality at least gave women instruments to help bolster their demands.

In the 1970s, leading an "authentic" life and realizing one's potential were elevated to the status of ideals in the GDR. Indeed, books like Christa Wolf's "The Quest for Christa T.," published in 1968, and "Patterns of Childhood," in 1976, were often read as advice literature.[135] Published posthumously in 1974, Brigitte Reimann's novel about the unsatisfying occupational life and unhappy love life of the young architect "Franziska Linkerhand" had a similar reception.[136] Readers, men and women alike, sought in these books insights into their own lives as citizens of the GDR. What they found were women who, in their rejection of masculine paternalism and the strictures of proletarian identity, explored and gave life to their own voice.

---

135 See Christa Wolf, Nachdenken über Christa T., Halle 1968, first translated as ead., The Quest for Christa T, New York 1971; ead., Kindheitsmuster, Berlin (GDR) 1976, first translated ead., A Model Childhood, New York 1980, since 1984 as "Patterns of Childhood." See also multiple interviews, e.g. ead., Projektionsraum Romantik. Ein Gespräch, in: ead. and Gerhard Wolf (eds.), Ins Ungebundene gehet eine Sehnsucht. Gesprächsraum Romantik. Prosa und Essays, Berlin (GDR) 1985, pp. 376–393, here pp. 388–393.

136 See Brigitte Reimann, Franziska Linkerhand, Berlin (GDR) 1974.

List of Authors

Björn Blaß, Max-Planck-Institut für Bildungsforschung, IMPRS Moral Economies of Modern Societies, Lentzeallee 94, 14195 Berlin, E-Mail: blass@mpib-berlin.mpg.de

Anna Danilina, Max-Planck-Institut für Bildungsforschung, IMPRS Moral Economies of Modern Societies, Lentzeallee 94, 14195 Berlin, E-Mail: danilina@mpib-berlin.mpg.de

Prof. Laurence Fontaine, Centre Maurice Halbwachs PSL, Université Paris Sciences et Lettres, 48 Boulevard Jourdan, 75014 Paris, Frankreich, E-Mail: laurence.fontaine@ehess.fr

Prof. Dr. Dr. h. c. Ute Frevert, Max-Planck-Institut für Bildungsforschung, Lentzeallee 94, 14195 Berlin, E-Mail: sekfrevert@mpib-berlin.mpg.de

Till Großmann, Max-Planck-Institut für Bildungsforschung, IMPRS Moral Economies of Modern Societies, Lentzeallee 94, 14195 Berlin, E-Mail: grossmann@mpib-berlin.mpg.de

PD Dr. Reinhild Kreis, Universität Mannheim, Historisches Institut, Schloss, 68131 Mannheim, E-Mail: rkreis@mail.uni-mannheim.de

Thomas Rohringer, IFK Internationales Forschungszentrum Kulturwissenschaften, Kunstuniversität Linz in Wien, Reichsratsstraße 17, 1010 Wien, Österreich, E-Mail: rohringer@ifk.ac.at

Dr. Mischa Suter, Universität Basel, Departement Geschichte, Hirschgässlein 21, 4051 Basel, Schweiz, E-Mail: mischa.suter@unibas.ch